THE LAW RELATING TO AGRICULTURE

Rog Wood
Auchentaggart
Sanquhar

The Law Relating to Agriculture

IAN S. STEPHENSON, M.A. LL.B. (Cantab.)
Clements Inn,
John Mackrell and Local Government
Prizeman

SAXON HOUSE | LEXINGTON BOOKS

Published by
SAXON HOUSE, D. C. Heath Ltd.
Westmead, Farnborough, Hants, England

Jointly with
LEXINGTON BOOKS, D. C. Heath & Co.
Lexington Mass. U.S.A.

ISBN 0 347 01029 6
Library of Congress Catalog Card Number 73-16547

Printed in Great Britain
by Unwin Brothers Limited
The Gresham Press, Old Woking, Surrey
A member of the Staples Printing Group

Contents

Foreword   ix

Preface   xi

1 THE LAND LAW

The fee simple absolute in possession   1
The fee tail   3
Life interest   4
Reversions   6
Remainders   6
Leaseholds   6
Settlements and trusts for sale   7
Co-ownership of land   14
Appointment, removal and retirement of trustees   14
Leaseholds further considered   15
Fixtures   18
Third party rights against the land of another   19
Natural rights   25
Public rights of way   25
Mortgages   26
Covenants affecting the fee simple   29
Licences   32
Adverse possession of land   32

2 AGRICULTURAL LEASES

Definition of 'agricultural land' and 'agricultural holding'   39
Creation of agricultural tenancies   40
The terms of the tenancy   43

3 TYPES OF BUSINESS ORGANISATION

Ordinary partnerships   80

Companies	84
Co-operative societies	94
Trusts	103
Mutual organisations	104
Agricultural associations and the Restrictive Trade Practices Act, 1956	106

4 WILLS AND INTESTACY

Wills	111
Intestacy	117
Administration	120
Restriction on the freedom of testamentary disposition	122

5 TAXATION

Taxation of self-employed persons: Schedule D	127
Taxation of employees: Schedule E	139
Income from land: Schedule A	143
Income from woodlands	147
General liability to income tax	148
Capital gains tax	151
Corporation tax	159
Estate duty	163
Value added tax	182

6 TOWN AND COUNTRY PLANNING AND COMPULSORY PURCHASE

Town and country planning	199
Compulsory purchase of land and compensation	219

7 CONTRACT, SALE OF GOODS AND HIRE-PURCHASE

Contract	261
The sale of goods	277
Hire-purchase	292

8 GENERAL PURPOSE OF THE LAW OF TORT

Negligence	310

Nuisance 312
Animals 314
The master's liability for his servant's torts 318

9 THE LEGAL POSITION OF THE OCCUPIER OF THE PREMISES

Occupier's liability 323
Entry on the land in pursuance of a contract 326
Trespassers 327
Landlord's duty of care 329
Rights against trespassers 330

10 SOME OBLIGATIONS OF THE EMPLOYER TOWARDS HIS EMPLOYEES

Claims by an injured employee against the State 337
Claims by an injured employee against his employer 337
Employer's obligation to insure against liability 342
Some further obligations of the employer 343
Unfair dismissal 347
Redundancy payments 349

11 INSURANCE

General principles 359
Life insurance 362
Fire insurance 364
Consequential loss insurance 366
Liability insurance 366
Livestock insurance 366
Motor vehicle insurance 367

12 THE INSTITUTIONS OF THE EUROPEAN ECONOMIC COMMUNITY

European Economic Community legislation 374
The provisions of the Treaty of Rome concerning agriculture 376
The Agriculture Guidance and Guarantee Fund of the European
    Economic Community 377

Appendix I   Agricultural Holdings Act, 1948 (as amended).
First Schedule: Matters for which provision is to be made in
written tenancy agreements   383
Appendix II   The Agriculture (Maintenance, Repair and Insurance
of Fixed Equipment) Regulations, 1948   385
Appendix III   Agricultural Holdings Act, 1948 (as amended).
Second, third, fourth and fifth Schedules: Improvements   389
Appendix IV   Rates of estate duty applicable to deaths on or after
31 March 1971   393
Appendix V   European Communities Regulation (EEC) No. 1105/68
of the Commission of the 27 July 1968 on the procedure for
granting aids for skimmed milk for animal feeding stuffs   394

Table of Statutes   399
European Community Legislation   415
Table of Statutory Instruments   416
Table of Cases   419
General Index   431

Foreword

The general purpose of the Agricultural Adjustment Unit of the University of Newcastle upon Tyne is to collect and disseminate information to enable the agricultural industry to adapt easily and efficiently to the changing conditions which it encounters.

The environment within which farmers operate is complex, involving economic pressures and institutional, political and social factors. In recent years we have received helpful comments and suggestions for further material from a number of people who have attended our conferences and courses or have read our publications. Among the many topics which have been mentioned one of the more persistent demands has been for a new book discussing law from the farmers' point of view. In consequence Mr Stephenson of the Department of Law in the University of Newcastle upon Tyne who has co-operated with the Unit in several of its activities was invited to undertake such a task. It was then arranged that the publication should appear in the Saxon House Studies series.

We believe that this book will occupy a valuable place in the library of contemporary agricultural literature since it sets out in clear and precise terms the most relevant sections of British Law for agriculture. Although obviously not in a position to offer detailed legal advice both the author and the Unit would welcome comments or criticisms from readers either on the detailed content of the book or on wider issues arising from it.

J. Ashton
Director,
Agricultural Adjustment Unit

Preface

This book is written for those who wish to obtain a working knowledge of the law relating to agriculture. It does not purport to do more than this; thus it is advisable to remember that, as regards virtually every chapter in the book, there are specialist works running in most cases to considerably more than the entire length of the book. Such works are admirable for the specialist, and a specialist practitioner should always be consulted by a person who realises that he has a problem of a legal nature, but in order to impel this person to do so it is first necessary that he should realise that a legal problem concerning himself has arisen which merits taking further specialist advice; this book is written in order to give him a basic grasp of the law sufficient to enable him to realise the basic legal problem which confronts him and which merits the taking of further advice. The reader should also bear in mind that the law changes from time to time; the details of the counter-inflation and tax legislation, for example, are ephemeral.

I meditated long on whether to include a chapter on the law of bankruptcy, since I have yet to meet a farmer who was not, according to his own ready admission, teetering on the verge of it; despite this state of affairs, subsequent observation led me to note that none of these despondent gentlemen in fact fell over the verge, and hence to conclude that the chapter could be omitted with some degree of safety.

I wish to express my thanks to the Agricultural Adjustment Unit of Newcastle University, since it was the comments of the Unit while I was giving a number of lectures for them which first brought home to me the probable need for a work of this type; I should also like to express my thanks in particular to Professor Ashton, Professor Rogers, Graham Ross and Paul Weightman of that Unit for their assistance and encouragement, and in particular to Alec Hayden without whose assistance with the mechanics of production it might never have been completed. I should also like to thank colleagues Professor Calvert, David Harte and John Mickleburgh who where kind enough to read individual chapters and to make many helpful comments, and to Ian Dawson who bore a particularly heavy burden in this respect.

I am responsible for the contents of the book other than the Index and Tables of Cases and Legislation, and should like to thank Richard S. Haig-Brown for his stalwart efforts in relation to the latter. The law in this book is, with tiny exceptions, that which was in force on 31 May 1973.

xi

1 The Land Law

All land in England and Wales is owned by the Crown, and consequently all land which is occupied by someone other than the Crown is held in tenure from the Crown either directly or indirectly. Nowadays, however, the occupier renders no return for his tenure (and hence the theory of tenure is of no practical significance) except in the one case of a lease. Since persons other than the Crown cannot own the land, what the law permits them to own is the right to enjoy the land for a period of time (known as their 'estate' in the land); the land law lays down in what manner and to what extent and to whom time may be sliced up and distributed for this purpose. A discussion of this now follows.

The fee simple absolute in possession

This is the nearest equivalent to absolute ownership which the law permits and, since nowadays the tenant in fee simple renders nothing in return for his interest, it in practice amounts to absolute ownership. Thus such a person may dispose of his interest in the land either by will or by gift, sale or exchange while he lives. It is said that he owns everything 'up to the sky and down to the centre of the earth' as far as the boundaries of his land, although despite this it has been ruled that an intrusion into only the air space at a considerable height above the land does not constitute a trespass,[1] but there is some doubt concerning the correctness of this decision. In general he may use his land as he thinks fit, including the ability to allow it to deteriorate, or indeed deliberately to damage it, with legal impunity. But he is subject to any rights which third parties may have against his land, such as the right to walk over it (*post*, pages 19–26). Moreover the physical condition of his land may possibly involve him in civil liability to pay damages to a third party who is injured in consequence, such as a visitor injured by the dangerous state of his land (*post*, pages 323–7), or if his land constitutes a nuisance (*post*, pages 312–14). Most importantly, he is in many ways hampered by Acts of Parliament in the enjoyment of the ownership of his land; such Acts include the town and country planning legislation, whereby he needs planning permission to develop his land (*post*, pages 201–7); Acts relating to compul-

1

sory purchase, whereby public authorities may take his land from him in return for compensation on a basis prescribed by legislation (*post*, pages 219–52); the public health and housing legislation, under which the owner is restricted as regards the construction, materials, size of rooms and the like of new buildings erected by him, and may be required to repair or even demolish houses considered to be defective; all his interest in petroleum existing in its natural condition and in coal has been taken away from him.

Although he does not own wild animals on his land he has the exclusive right to catch, kill and take the carcasses of them while they are on his land. If water flows through the subsoil of the land, he cannot take it except for the domestic purposes of his household or with a licence granted by a river authority.[2] As regards water flowing in a defined channel through the land, again he cannot as a rule take it without a licence from the river authority; the main exception is when the water is taken for use on a holding comprising the land through which the water flows and any other land held with it, and the use is for either the domestic purposes of the occupier's household or for agricultural purposes other than 'spray irrigation'.[3] If he owns the land on both banks of the stream, he has the sole right to fish unless either he bought the land expressly without the right to fish or he has granted that right to someone else; if he owns the land on one bank of the stream only, he is presumed to have the sole right to fish up to the middle of the stream nearest to his bank, subject again to his having bought the land expressly excluding the right to fish or his having granted the right away.

A disposition of land either by deed or by will passes the fee simple or other interest which the grantor had power to convey in the land, unless a contrary intention appears in the deed or will.[4]

The word 'absolute' in relation to a fee simple signifies that it is perpetual and not liable to end on the happening of some particular event; such an interest can be created at law without employing the device of a trust. Fee simples which are not 'absolute', such as a gift 'to A in fee simple until he marries' can only subsist through the medium of a trust (*post*, pages 103–4); however this is not true of some, and perhaps all, conditional fee simples.[5]

In general the owner of a fee simple which is less than 'absolute' has the same rights of dealing with the land as has the owner of a fee simple absolute (see *post*, pages 7–12), save that he cannot personally benefit to any greater extent than the interest in the land which he himself owns and he may be restrained from committing acts of wanton destruction.

2

The fee tail

A fee tail is created by granting land to a person and the heirs of his body; under such a grant when that person dies the right to inherit is, unless the entail has been barred (see *post*, pages 3–4), restricted to his descendants, which is to be contrasted with the grant of a fee simple which can pass to his other relatives. The word 'tail' signifies that the heirs who can inherit are a restricted category.

A fee tail may be further restricted such as by granting the land in tail male, so that only male descendants claiming continuously through males can inherit, or by a grant to a person and the heirs of his body by a named spouse, so that any descendants which he might procreate through union with another spouse would have no claim to inherit the land.

To create an entail by deed nowadays the words of the deed must either state that the land is conveyed to the grantee 'in tail', or that the land is conveyed to the grantee 'and the heirs of his body' although as regards the last three words only any expression amounting to 'of his body' will suffice.[6] The same words must be used in a will in order to create an entail.[7]

An entail nowadays can only exist through the medium of a trust (*post*, pages 7–15). If the descendants who alone can inherit under an entail die out, the entail is at an end. Apart from this danger of the interest ceasing altogether, the tenant in tail in possession, cannot (save under the express powers conferred by the Setled Land Act, 1925; (see *post*, pages 7–12), while the entail subsists convey the land to anyone else beyond the duration of the life of the tenant in tail, since if he were able to do so this would defeat the claim of his heirs and so cannot be permitted; in other respects the rights of the tenant in tail are akin to those of a fee simple owner, thus he may for example damage the land. By Act of Parliament a tenant in tail in possession may bar the entail and acquire the fee simple absolute by means of a disentailing assurance, i.e. a deed of conveyance transferring the land to someone to hold it on trust for, usually, the benefit of the former tenant in tail.[8] The tenant in tail in possession may also do this by will, provided he is of full age, the will is made or confirmed after 1925, and the will refers specifically either to the entailed property, or the instrument under which it was acquired, or the testator's entailed property generally; the purpose of this last requirement is in order to ensure that it is made absolutely clear on the face of the will that the testator intended to bar the entail, so as to avoid the possibility of doubt on the matter.[9]

If the tenant in tail is out of possession (which for this purpose includes receipt of rent and profits or the right to receive them), he cannot bar the entail by will at all. If he seeks to bar the entail by a disentailing assurance (as previously explained) during his lifetime, the effect of this will vary, depending on whether or not he has obtained the consent of a functionary known as the protector of the settlement, who is usually the person in possession of the land but excluding a mere lessee. If the consent of the protector is obtained, the effect of the disentailment is to produce a fee simple absolute; without such consent, the effect is to produce a base fee, which is an interest which will only last so long as issue of the former tenant in tail who are entitled to inherit are in existence, and is thus a rather unsatisfactory interest of somewhat uncertain duration.

Although entails were once popular, at any rate among large landowners, they are nowadays relatively infrequent, largely because of estate duty (*post*, pages 163–82).

Life interest

Such an interest ends on the death of the person whose life is to be the measure of its duration; this person is of course normally the grantee himself, though it is possible to make a grant 'to A during the life of B' in which event A or his successors in title are entitled to enjoy the land until B dies. Life interests of the former kind are frequently created.

In order to create a life interest words showing an intention to create no larger interest than this must normally be used, since a disposition whether by deed or will *prima facie* passes the fee simple or other the whole estate which the grantor had power to convey (*ante*, page 2).

Nowadays a life interest can only exist through the medium of a trust; the owner of the life interest has wide powers of dealing with the land conferred on him by the Setled Land Act, 1925 (*post*, pages 7–12).

A tenant for life may find himself liable for committing waste, which technically is committed by any act altering the state of the land. First there is ameliorating waste, which consists of improving the land; a claim for damages made by other persons interested in the land will not succeed because they suffer none, and an injunction (*post*, pages 273–4) will be granted only if the court thinks fit.[10] Secondly there is permissive waste, which is committed by mere inertia and usually consists of allowing buildings to fall into disrepair. The life tenant is not liable for permissive waste unless the document granting the land to him imposes an obligation to repair upon him.[11] Thirdly there is voluntary waste such as opening a mine in the land, though not working a mine already open,[12] or cutting

4

timber. [13] Timber comprises oak, ash and elm if the tree is at least twenty years old and has not deteriorated until it lacks a reasonable quantity of useable wood, and other trees which by local custom are considered timber. A tenant for life is liable for voluntary waste unless the document creating his interest stated that he should not be thus liable. However a tenant for life nowadays enjoys considerable statutory powers to open mines and cut timber (*post*, pages 8–10). Finally there is equitable waste, which consists in acts of wanton destruction, such as deliberately stripping the fabric of a house, [14] or cutting ornamental timber. Even if the life tenant has been exempted from liability for voluntary waste, this will not protect him if he commits equitable waste unless the document clearly showed an intention that he should be legally free to commit this also.

The remedies if actionable waste is committed are to seek an injunction to restrain this, either with or without an action for damages or for an account of the proceeds of the waste.

Even if the tenant for life is impeachable for waste he may take wood and timber for repairing his house on the land or for use as firewood in the house, or for making and repairing agricultural implements or repairing fences. Moreover if the land is cultivated mainly for the purpose of producing timber which is cut and sold regularly the tenant can do this in the course of proper management of the timber.

The tenant for life may also cut trees which are not classified as timber, and dead trees unfit for use as timber.

Beyond this, a life tenant who is expressly exempted from liability for voluntary waste may cut and sell all timber and pocket the proceeds, [15] provided he does not commit equitable waste. But if the tenant for life is liable for voluntary waste, and *prima facie* he is so liable, he can only cut timber with the consent of his trustees or a court order, and three-quarters of the proceeds of the sale must be added to the capital of the trust. [16] He will thus be entitled to the income of three-quarters of the proceeds of sale until his death, and the remaining quarter is paid wholly into his personal pocket.

As to mines, a life tenant who is exempted from liability for waste may work old mines, or open and work new ones and pocket all the proceeds. If liable for voluntary waste, he can continue to work a mine which was already open when his interest commenced, but cannot open and work new mines. Any life tenant may grant a mining lease for up to 100 years and pocket three-quarters of the rent, save that if he is liable for voluntary waste and the mine was unopened when his interest commenced he is only entitled to one-quarter of the rent. [17] The balance of the rent is added to the capital of the trust.

Since the life tenant cannot know exactly when he will die, the law confers upon his representatives the right to enter the land after his death and reap cultivated crops which the dead life tenant had sown and which were still growing when he died.

Reversions

A reversion arises when a person entitled to an interest in land gives the possession and enjoyment of it to someone else for a shorter time than the whole of his own interest, so that when the interest so granted expires by the passage of time the land will revert to the original owner or his transferee. Thus if A owns land in fee simple, and creates a life interest in his land in favour of B, the land will revert to A or A's transferee on the death of B.

Remainders

A remainder arises if a land owner grants the right to enjoy the land for a time to someone else, and then by the same document grants to a third person a right to enjoy the land which is to commence after the first grant has run its course. Thus if A owns the fee simple in the land and grants the enjoyment of the land firstly to A for life, secondly to B for life to take effect after the death of A, and thirdly to C in fee simple to take effect on the deaths of A and B, B and C have remainders in the land until they respectively become entitled to possession. Nowadays remainders can only be created through the medium of a trust, and the same is true of reversions unless the reversion is to take effect upon the expiry of a leasehold.

Leaseholds

Leasehold interests are distinguished from the interests in land already mentioned in that the maximum duration of the leasehold is fixed in time. That duration will of course vary with the individual lease, and might thus be, for example, either a lease for a week or a lease for 10,000 years. The fact that the lease may not last for the full time originally specified, because for example the landlord and tenant might agree to put an end to it earlier, is not considered as an infringement of the notion of a fixed

6

maximum duration, because that is to be interpreted in the sense of the maximum duration being known subject to any steps which the parties may take either to curtail or extend it. Thus a periodic tenancy, such as a lease from year to year, falls within this since the duration is known, though subject to the possibility of extension if neither party gives notice to quit. A leasehold is nowadays the only interest in land where the tenant in practice renders something to the person from whom he holds the land in return for his interest. A leasehold interest can exist without employing the device of a trust, and so can the landlord's fee simple in reversion expectant upon determination of the lease because, although to be capable of subsisting without a trust the fee simple absolute must be in possession, possession is defined as including receipt of the rents and profits or the right to receive them.[18] Leaseholds are discussed further at pages 15–18.

Settlements and trusts for sale

Settlements and trusts for sale are mutually exclusive; the latter, which will be dealt with in more detail later, usually arise either because the grantor stated when he conveyed the land that it was to be held on trust for sale or where the land is held in co-ownership.

Settlements are here considered in detail first. The primary meaning of the word 'settlement' is to connote that there are successive interests existing in the plot of land, such as on a grant of land to A for life, remainder to B in fee simple, but there is also a settlement if the land is held for the benefit of an infant and in a few other minor cases. If the land is settled, wide powers of dealing with it have been conferred by Act of Parliament on 'the tenant for life'; the term 'tenant for life' is defined to include others beyond the holder of a life interest in the property, and in fact comprises any adult who is for the time being beneficially entitled in possession to the whole of the net income produced by the property; if there is no person so entitled, as for example because part of the income is to be accumulated for a while, or if the person who would otherwise be tenant for life is an infant, then the powers which would normally be exercisable by the tenant for life in relation to the land will instead be exercised by the trustees of the settlement, unless the person creating the settlement appoints someone else to exercise the powers in the absence of the tenant for life. In addition to the exercise of this function, there must be trustees of the settlement in order to receive and manage capital money relating to the settlement which may arise, for example, on the sale of part of the settled land, and to keep an eye, at any rate to some extent,

7

upon the exercise of his statutory powers by the tenant for life.

The tenant for life can of course do as he wishes with his own beneficial interest in the land, such as sell it, mortgage it or give it away. In addition, in order to simplify the machinery for selling the land should it become desirable to do so, the tenant for life of freehold land will normally have the whole legal fee simple absolute vested in him, even though beneficially he does not own it and he is only capable of dealing with the land in a manner affecting interests in it other than his own so far as he is permitted to do so by the Settled Land Act, 1925. The principal powers which the Act confers upon the tenant for life are:

1   He may sell the settled land or any part of it. [19] In almost all cases he must obtain the best monetary consideration that can reasonably be found, but a purchaser who deals in good faith with the tenant for life is conclusively presumed to have given the best price reasonably obtainable. The purchaser from the tenant for life will take free from the successive beneficial interests which arose under the trusts, but will in general take the land subject to easements (*post*, pages 19—24), mortgages (*post*, pages 26—9), restrictive covenants (*post*, pages 29—32) and certain other third-party rights.

2   He may exchange the settled land for other land situated in England or Wales, and capital money belonging to the trust may be used in order to adjust any differences in value between the respective plots. [20]

3   He may lease the land for up to 999 years for the purpose of building or forestry, up to 100 years for mining and up to 50 years for any other purpose. The lease must be at the best rent reasonably obtainable, having regard to any premium taken, but in a building lease a nominal or reduced rent may be accepted for the first 5 years of the lease and in a forestry lease for the first 10 years; various other restrictions and formalities must be complied with.

4   He may carry out certain improvements to the settled land which are specified in the Third Schedule to the Settled Land Act. The list is extensive, and the improvements fall into three categories; the cost of all categories is initially payable out of the capital money belonging to the trust, but as regards some improvements the trustees cannot require the outlay to be gradually recouped out of the income produced by the land, as to others the trustees must so require, and as to the remainder the trustees have a discretion whether to so require. Before the trustees can pay for the cost of the improvement from money in their hands, there must either be an order of the court directing such payment, or the certificate of a competent engineer or able practical surveyor who has been employed independently of the tenant for life and stating that the work has been

properly done and what sum is properly payable in respect of it. If the cost of the improvement is ultimately to be recouped from the income of the trust, the trustees may order that this be done by anything up to a maximum of fifty half-yearly instalments. [21] The general policy of the Act in this matter is that only improvements of a permanent nature are to be permanently paid for out of capital, whereas improvements of a temporary nature may initially be financed from capital but will be required to be repaid by instalments out of income. By a strange anomaly, however, the Agricultural Holdings Act, 1948, permits the cost of current repairs to fixed equipment (including buildings) on agricultural land to be paid from capital without requiring any replacement out of income, thus enabling the tenant for life to impose the cost of such repairs upon the remainderman. Where the tenant for life carried out such improvements from his own money and then called on the trustees to refund this sum from the capital of the settled fund, it was held that the tenant for life was, notwithstanding this recoupment, entitled to keep for himself the benefit of income tax allowances given in respect of the improvements. [22]

5   He may mortgage the fee simple to raise money for certain specified purposes set out in the Act, such as paying for the improvements just mentioned or raising equality money which may be necessitated on the exchange of the settled land for other land.

6   He may, subject to certain conditions, grant a written option to purchase or take a lease of all or any part of the settled land, but the time which may elapse after the grant of the option and before it is exercised cannot exceed 10 years.

7   He may take a lease of other land, including mines and the like, which can conveniently be held or worked with the settled land, and when the life tenant dies the unexpired portion of the lease will devolve with the settled land.

Consent to exercise of powers

In some instances, of which the following are the most important, the tenant for life can only exercise his powers with the consent of the trustees or with an order of the court. This applies if he wishes:

(a)   to dispose by way of sale, lease, mortgage or exchange of the principal mansion house, the pleasure grounds and park and land usually occupied therewith (if the house is usually occupied as a farmhouse, or if its site and the pleasure grounds, park and land usually occupied with it do not exceed 25 acres, the house will not be considered to be a principal mansion house. But consent to the disposition is only required if either the settlement was made before 1926 and does not expressly dispense with consent, or it was made after 1925 and expressly requires consent);[23]

(b) to cut and sell the timber if the tenant for life is liable for voluntary waste (*ante*, pages 4–5);

(c) to compromise and settle disputes relating to the settled land; here the written consent of the trustees is required.

Safeguards for the remaindermen

The other beneficiaries under the settlement could obviously be adversely affected by transactions carried out by the tenant for life in relation to the settled land. To some extent they are safeguarded by the following rules:

1   The tenant for life is trustee both of the land and of his powers, and in exercising his powers must have regard to the interests of all parties entitled under the settlement. [24]. Thus the court could intervene if he seeks to sell the land at a price well below its value,[25] or to make an undesirable investment;[26] moreover a teetotal tenant for life has been restrained from leasing a public house, which was part of the settled land, on the terms that no intoxicating liquor should be sold in it. [27] It is not, however, thought that a tenant for life who sells the settled land in order to obtain a higher income, thereby robbing the remaindermen of the enhanced capital value which might in many instances reasonably be expected to have resulted in a few years time had the land been retained, would incur any liability towards the remaindermen on this ground.

2   In certain cases the tenant for life needs consent from another quarter before he can exercise his powers, as above explained (*ante*, pages 9–10).

3   All receipts of capital in relation to the settled land are capital money and must be paid, not to the tenant for life, but to the trustees of the settlement, who must either be not less than two in number or a trust corporation such as the Executor and Trustee Department of a Bank, or into court. The capital money represents the land from which it had its origin, and must be held in trust for the same persons and for the same interests as the land itself was held. The capital money will be invested in 'trustee investments'; these are specified in the Trustee Investments Act, 1961 or the trust instrument, and usually include government stock and, subject to certain restrictions, shares in United Kingdom public companies and mortgages of land. The tenant for life is entitled to decide which investment shall be chosen from amongst the permitted range, but if he does not do so the trustees decide.

Although the tenant for life is empowered to buy or take a lease of the settled land for himself in his private capacity, his statutory powers to dispose of the land pass to the trustees of the settlement for the purpose of this transaction.[28]

The tenant for life must give at least one month's notice by registered post to the trustees and their solicitors if known before exercising any of the powers, and there must be at least two trustees or a trust corporation to receive the notice (although a lease granted for not more than 21 years without taking a premium and without exempting the lessee from liability for waste may be made without notice to the trustees). The object presumably is to enable the trustees to prevent any improper dealing by seeking an injunction from the court. However this safeguard is weakened in that it seems that the tenant for life need not go into detail about what he proposes to do unless he is mortgaging the land, although if the trustees ask him he must give details of his intention; further, the trustees are apparently under no liability for failure to bring an action which they might have brought,[29] and indeed may waive the notice altogether,[30] and in any event a person dealing in good faith with the tenant for life is not concerned to inquire whether due notice was given.[31]

His powers cannot be restricted

Almost any power which the settlement purports to confer on anyone other than the tenant for life is instead by statute given to the tenant for life himself.[32] Moreover any clause in any document which purports or tends to prevent or discourage the tenant for life from exercising his statutory powers is void.[33] Thus a clause that the tenant for life shall lose his beneficial interest if he ceases to reside on the settled land is void if the reason of his ceasing to do so is that he has sold or let the land,[34] but is valid if he ceases to reside irrespective of any intention to use his statutory powers since it cannot than be said that he has been either prevented or discouraged.[35]

Even if the tenant for life parts with his beneficial interest, he does not in general thereby lose his statutory powers. But if he transfers his beneficial interest, with intent to extinguish it, to the person next entitled under the settlement, his powers become exercisable as if the former tenant for life were dead.[36] Moreover if the tenant for life has ceased to have a substantial beneficial interest in the land and either consents to a court order being made or has unreasonably refused to exercise his statutory powers, any person interested in the land may apply to the court for an order authorising the trustees to exercise his powers on his behalf and in his name;[37] gross neglect of the land does not necessarily show an unreasonable refusal to exercise the powers.[38]

Trusts for sale

Land held on trust for sale falls clean outside the Settled Land Act, even though successive interests in the land may have been created by the trust for sale. The Law of Property Act, 1925, provides that only 'an immediate binding trust for sale' will count as a trust for sale for this purpose.[39] There have been some highly technical interpretations of these words, but the main points are that there must be a duty to sell as opposed to a mere power of sale, and that a trust to sell at a future date will not fall within the definition until that date is reached, since until then the trust to sell is not 'immediate'.

Creation of trusts for sale

The person creating the disposition of the land may expressly state in it that the land is to be held on trust for sale (known as an 'express trust for sale'). A trust for sale may also be imposed by statute in certain circumstances, thus when persons are entitled to the land as co-owners (*post*, page 14) the Law of Property Act, 1925, usually imposes a trust for sale, and so does the Administration of Estates Act, 1925, on the property of a person who dies without leaving a will (*post*, page 117); these are 'statutory trusts for sale'.

The trustees for sale, who must not be more than four in number, and must be least two in number or a trust corporation if they are to receive capital money, have all the powers conferred by the Settled Land Act, 1925, on the tenant for life of settled land and the trustees of it.[40] But it is lawful for the document creating the trust to provide that these powers can only be exercised if the consent of specified persons has first been obtained.[41] If the consent of more than two persons is stipulated, a *bona fide* purchaser for value will be protected if he gets the consent of any two of them,[42] but the trustees will commit a breach of trust if they do not obtain all consents which were stipulated. However the court has power, on application by any person interested, to dispense with the need for consent if consent cannot be obtained,[43] as where the person whose consent is necessary refused to give it.[44] Where land is held on trust for sale, the trustees have an implied power to postpone selling the land unless the document creating the trust states otherwise.[45] Thus if all the trustees agree the sale of the land may be postponed indefinitely, but if they cannot agree the land must be sold even if the majority of the trustees desire to retain it;[46] this is because all trustees must concur before they can exercise a power, such as the power to postpone sale, and if the power is not exercised the duty to sell prevails. But in the case of a statutory trust for sale the trustees must consult the adult beneficiaries entitled in possession to the rents and profits of the land until sale, and must give effect to the wishes of the majority in value so far as is consistent with the general interests of the trust.[47] A purchaser is not concerned to see that this requirement has been observed, and it should be noted that in the case of an express trust for sale there is no requirement that the trustees must consult the beneficiaries unless the document creating the trust for sale says that they must. If, however, the beneficiaries are all of full age and unanimous in their views the trustees must act in accordance with their directions.[48]

The trustees may revocably and in writing delegate their powers relating to leases and management to the person of full age who is beneficially entitled for the time being to the income of the property;[49] if they refuse to delegate, the court may if it thinks fit compel them to do so.[50]

A sale by the trustees of land held on trust for sale will pass the land to the buyer freed from the rights of the previous beneficiaries, provided the buyer pays the purchase money to the trustees, who must be at least two in number, or to a trust corporation or into court. The rights of the beneficiaries subsist in the capital money, and it will be invested in the same way as capital money arising from settled land (*ante*, page 10).

Settled land compared with land held on trust for sale

If the person making the disposition wishes to prevent the land from being dealt with, this can best be achieved, curiously enough, under the trust for sale in that the trustees can be required to obtain the consent of specified persons before making a disposition (although the court may if it thinks fit dispense with a refusal to give consent; *ante*, page 12).

Although the details of the documents which must be used to give effect to either settlements or trusts for sale are beyond the scope of this work, it is relevant and true to say that much greater complexity attaches in this respect to settled land, and thus the trust for sale is usually to be preferred on this score.

In a trust for sale it is normally the trustees who have the powers of dealing with the land, but in settled land the powers are in the tenant for life. Thus if the person who would be the tenant for life if the land was settled land is a bad manager, this would suggest the desirability of creating a trust for sale and choosing competent trustees to manage.

Co-ownership of land — joint tenancy and tenancy in common

The complexities of this topic are considerable and lie outside the scope of this work; it is sufficient to say here that those beneficially entitled to land in co-ownership may either be joint tenants or tenants in common of the beneficial interest. It is usually undesirable that they should remain beneficial joint tenants, because if they are so and one of them dies his beneficial interest will pass on his death to the remaining joint tenants, to the obvious detriment of his family; this 'right of survivorship', as it is called, does not apply to tenancy in common. A beneficial joint tenant can sever his beneficial interest, thus turning himself into a beneficial tenant in common, in a number of ways, including merely serving notice in writing upon the other joint tenants of his desire to do so. [51] It should here be mentioned, in order to mitigate confusion in those who peruse documents relating to their land, that where land is held in co-ownership, and hence under a trust, the law usually stipulates that the trustees' title to the land, as distinct from the rights of the beneficiaries to benefit under the trust, must be held in joint tenancy in order to simplify dealing with the land when it comes to be sold; this matter of the trustees' title is however quite separate from the mode in which the beneficiaries hold their rights to benefit under the trusts, thus it in no way precludes their rights to benefit (even if the trustees are also beneficiaries under the trust) from being held either in joint tenancy or as tenants in common according to the wishes of the parties as expressed in the documents.

Appointment, removal and retirement of trustees

Reference has frequently been made to the fact that certain interests in land can only be created through the use of a trust; it is thus desirable to consider briefly how trustees are appointed, removed or able to retire. The first trustees are usually appointed by the person creating the trust, but if he neither does this nor specifies the mode of appointing them at that time it may be necessary in incur the expense of going to court in order to secure the appointment of trustees. A person who has been appointed trustee need not accept the trust if he does not wish to do so, provided he disclaims the trusteeship before he has undertaken it either expressly or impliedly by acting in a manner appropriate to a trustee.

Nowadays not more than four trustees of land can be appointed unless the land is held on charitable trusts, [52] but there is no limit to the number of trustees of property other than land.

An appointment of new trustees is made by the person nominated by the trust instrument for that purpose, failing which by the surviving or continuing trustees, failing which by the personal representatives of the last remaining trustee; if all these fail, appointment may be made by the court. [53]

If a trustee is removed, this is usually either because he is unfit to act or incapable of acting, or the trust instrument contains an express power of removal which is now exercised, or the court exercises its inherent jurisdiction where removal is necessary for the safety of the trust property or the welfare of the beneficiaries, which includes friction between the trustees and the beneficiaries concerning the administration of the trust. [54]

A trustee may retire under an express power to do so contained in the trust instrument, or with leave of all the beneficiaries, who must also all be adults and not be mental patients, or with leave of court, which will only be granted if there is good cause. He may also retire by executing a deed with the consent of the continuing trustees and the person (if any) expressly empowered by the trust document to appoint new trustees, provided that after his retirement at least two trustees or a trust corporation still remain.[55]

Leaseholds further considered

The grant of a lease creates an interest for a fixed period of certain duration, usually in return for the payment of rent and performance of other obligations by the tenant. A leasehold interest can, and almost invariably does, subsist without the use of a trust to create it.

A lease by its nature confers on the tenant the right of exclusive possession of the property leased. Generally speaking a fully effective lease can only be created by deed, but a lease for not more than three years which takes effect in possession and is at the best rent reasonably obtainable without taking a premium can be in any form.[56] But if there is a written memorandum of the terms of the lease or agreement to lease, signed by the defendant, or an act of part performance (*post*, pages 265–6) the court will usually order the defendant to perfect the matter by making a grant by deed; until he obtains a lease perfect in form the intending lessee is in some respects regarded by the law as being in the same position as if this had been done, but meanwhile he is relatively insecure in certain respects and in particular his interest will not bind a third party who buys a legal interest in the land unless the intending lessee's interest has already been registered in the Registry of Land Charges kept for the purpose of al-

15

lowing this and other interests to be protected by registration.

If a tenant of land transfers the whole of the remainder of the unexpired portion of the tenancy to a third party, he is said to assign his interest; if he transfers an interest for a lesser period than the whole of what still remains to him, he is said to sublet the land. The importance of the distinction lies in the fact that on an assignment the current landlord and the assignee of the tenancy are entitled to sue each other for breach by either party of such of the covenants contained in the lease as touch and concern the land; in a sub-lease the sub-lessee cannot sue or be sued by the original landlord. Covenants which 'touch and concern the land' include covenants by the tenant to pay rent, to repair the property, to insure against fire, to use as a private dwelling house only and not to assign the lease without the consent of the landlord; they also include covenants by the landlord to supply water to the premises leased and not to build on part of the adjoining land.

The respective obligations of landlord and tenant towards each other will usually be expressly set out in the lease, but certain undertakings are implied into the lease as a matter of law unless it expressly states to the contrary. The landlord impliedly undertakes that the tenant shall have quiet enjoyment of the land; this means that there will be no act or omission after the commencement of the tenancy, done either by the landlord or those rightfully claiming under him, which causes physical interference with the tenant's enjoyment of the property. The landlord also impliedly undertakes that he will not derogate from his grant, meaning that he will not do an act rendering the premises substantially less fit for the purpose for which they were let. [57]

There are also implied undertakings by the landlord relating to certain dwellings. If a house is let at a rent not exceeding eighty pounds per year in London and fifty-two pounds elsewhere (or half these amounts if the contract of letting was made before 6 July 1957), it is an implied condition of the contract of tenancy that the house is fit for human habitation at the start of the tenancy, and the landlord also impliedly undertakes that he will keep the house in this condition throughout the tenancy; any agreement to the contrary is void. [58] The 'rent' here means the gross rent payable to the landlord, without deduction for any rates or other outgoings for which the landlord is liable in his turn. [59] This source of liability only extends to defects of which the landlord has notice; [60] moreover breach of this implied contractual obligation only makes the landlord liable under the contract to the tenant, and not to third parties who are strangers to the contract of tenancy and are injured by the landlord's failure to carry out the obligation, [61] although such a third party may have a cause of action under the law of tort. Furthermore, the implied contractual obligation does not extend to tenancies of houses entered into for at least three years and on the terms that the tenant is to put the house in a condition reasonably fit for human habitation. [62]

If a lease of a dwelling house is granted after 24 October 1961 for a period of less than seven years it is deemed to contain an implied covenant by the landlord:

(a)   to keep in repair the structure and exterior (including drains, gutters and external pipes) and
(b)   to keep in repair and proper working order the installations in the house (i) for the supply of water, gas and electricity and for sanitation (including basins, sinks, baths and sanitary conveniences but not other fixtures, fittings and appliances for making use of water, gas and electricity) and (ii) for space heating or heating water.

Any agreement to the contrary is only valid in so far as the County Court authorises this as reasonable. If the landlord has an option to terminate the lease within seven years it is treated as a lease for less than seven years, but if the tenant has an option under the lease to remain there for more than seven years this is regarded as a lease for more than seven years. [63] It will be noted that the rent and rateable value have no bearing upon the existence of this obligation.

In any lease of a dwelling house for less than seven years there is an implied covenant by the landlord to keep in repair the structure and exterior (including drains, gutters and external pipes), and to keep in repair and working order installations in the house for the supply of water, gas, electricity and for sanitation (including basins, baths, sinks and sanitary conveniences but not other fixtures and fittings for making use of water, gas and electricity) and for space heating or heating water.

There are implied undertakings by the tenant to pay rent, to pay tenant's rates and taxes, and to permit the landlord to enter and view the state of repair of the premises if the landlord is liable to repair them. A tenant for a fixed term of years is also liable for voluntary and permissive waste,[64] which means that the tenant must keep the property in the condition in which he got it. In a yearly tenancy the tenant must use the premises in a tenantlike manner, which includes such things as cleaning the chimneys when necessary, mending a fuse, unstopping a blocked sink and turning off the water before going away in winter time; he is probably also liable to keep the premises wind and water tight,[65] although in *Warren* v. *Keen*[65a] doubt was expressed concerning the meaning and even the existence of this implied obligation. A weekly tenant need only use the premises in a tenantlike manner, but need not keep them wind and water tight, and a monthly tenant is probably in the same position.

The tenant's right to assign or sublet

Unless otherwise agreed, a tenant is free to assign, sublet or part with the possession without the landlord's consent. Hence a covenant is frequently inserted in the lease prohibiting any of these things, and if the covenant is broken the tenant will be liable in damages to the landlord and the terms of the lease may entitle the landlord to forfeit the lease.

Fixtures

'Land' includes not only physical land and buildings but also certain rights over land such as mortgages, casements and profits (*post*, pages 19—29). Land also includes fixtures; the test for deciding whether an article has become a fixture depends upon the degree of its annexation to the soil and the purpose of the annexation. As regards the degree of annexation, an article which merely rests on the ground by its own weight, such as a dutch barn standing on sockets let into the ground, is *prima facie* not a fixture.[66] The annexation of the article to the soil, or the lack of it, constitutes a *prima facie* indication whether the article is a fixture or not, but it is still necessary to consider the purpose of the annexation; if the article was annexed merely to enable its owner to enjoy it as an article, such as a valuable tapestry fastened to strips of wood nailed on the wall, it is not a fixture. [67] But if the purpose of the annexation was to benefit the use and enjoyment of the land as such, such as statues and stone vases which were part of the general ornamental design of a house and its grounds, the article will become a fixture. [68] A stone wall marking the farm boundary or dividing fields will thus presumably be a fixture. (It is here convenient to mention that a boundary wall is, at any rate where there is evidence that both owners of the adjoining land have exercised dominion over the whole wall, rebuttably presumed to belong equally to those owners, and that where two plots of land are separated by a hedge and a ditch it is rebuttably presumed that the hedge and ditch belong to the owner of the land on the side of the ditch on which the hedge is.)

If an article is a fixture then *prima facie* it passes with the land and must be left for the benefit of the owner of the fee simple. But a lessee may remove his trade, ornamental or domestic fixtures at or before the end of the tenancy; agricultural fixtures are not regarded as trade fixtures and are governed by special rules. [69] On the death of a life tenant his representatives may remove his trade, ornamental and domestic fixtures as against the remainderman, but the statutory right of removal of agricultural fixtures does not apply.

Once a contract to sell land has been made, all fixtures at the time of its making pass by implication to the purchaser, unless otherwise stated in the contract. [70]

Third party rights against the land of another

Rentcharges

A rentcharge is a rent charged on land where there is no tenure between the parties; rent payable under a lease is a rent service. A rentcharge is itself land, and can therefore be held for any of the interests for which land can be held, such as for life or for a fixed period of years. If the rentcharge is not paid punctually, the remedies are either to sue the freehold tenant for the time being of the land on which the rent is charged, [71] or to distrain if the rentcharge is twenty-one days in arrears or, if the rentcharge is forty days in arrears, to enter into possession of the land and take the income until the arrears and costs have been paid, or to lease the land to trustees on trust to raise the arrears and costs by any reasonable means. [72]

A land owner may free his land from a rentcharge which is charged upon it by paying to the rentcharge owner a sum representing the capital value of the rentcharge as certified by the Minister of Agriculture, Fisheries and Food. [73]

Easements and profits

An easement is a right attached to a plot of land which confers the right on the occupier of that land (the dominant land) either to use the land of someone else in a particular way, such as by walking over a path on it, or to restrict the way in which the land is used by that other person, such as by preventing him building so as to infringe a right to light attached to windows on the dominant land. A profit is a right to enter and take something capable of ownership, such as wood or fish, from the land of another.

An easement must benefit the dominant land, and the two plots of land must not both be owned and occupied by the same person since a man cannot have a right against himself. The right must be sufficiently definite

19

to be capable of being granted by deed. There cannot be an easement for the general free flow of air over land, or conferring the right to a view, but an easement can exist for the flow of a definite amount of light to a particular window or the passage of air through a defined channel.[74]

Easements may be created by legislation, by express or implied grant or by prescription. An express grant should be made by deed, but if there is a written contract to create an easement or an act of part performance (*post*, pages 265–6) the court will usually order that a grant in proper form be made.

As regards implied grant, the general rule is that if a person conveys part of his land and wishes an easement to arise in his favour for the benefit of the land which he retains, he must reserve the easement expressly, and no easements will be implied in his favour except (a) a way of necessity if without this the land retained cannot be reached at all and (b) intended easements which form an extremely narrow category and comprise little beyond mutual rights of support from buildings leaning on each other. But the position is much more favourable as regards implication in favour of the grantee of part of the land, thus in addition to a way of necessity and intended easements over the land retained by his grantor there will be implied for his benefit such rights over the land retained by the grantor which would have been easements but for the common ownership and which were continuous and apparent and necessary to the reasonable enjoyment of the property granted, and which had been and were at the time of the grant used for the benefit of the part granted (*Wheeldon* v. *Burrows*).[75] The words 'continuous and apparent' appear to signify that there is some mark on the premises, such as a worn path or windows enjoying light, which would signify to a person who inspected the property and who was reasonably conversant with the law of easements that some such right might have existed but for the common ownership prior to the grant.

Gifts by will of part of the land are treated in the same way as grants by deed for the purpose of implying easements in favour of the grantee over the land retained,[76] and when the grantor makes simultaneous grants of parts of his land to two or more grantees, each grantee will obtain the same easements over the other's land as he would have obtained if the grantor had retained the land.[77] But if the grantor first sells part of his land and later conveys the rest of the land to a different grantee, the second grantee can acquire no more easements over the land which was first conveyed than the grantor himself retained after he had conveyed it.

By section 62 of the Law of Property Act, 1925, a conveyance of land also conveys 'all... liberties, privileges, easements, rights, and advantages

20

whatsoever, appertaining... to the land, or any part thereof, or, at the time of conveyance,... enjoyed with... the land or any part thereof', unless a contrary intention appears in the conveyance. 'Conveyance' includes a lease as well as a grant by deed, but does not include a mere contract to convey or lease. The effect of the section is not only to transfer easements which prior to the conveyance existed for the benefit of the land conveyed, but also to convert advantages over the land retained, which prior to the conveyance would have been easements or profits but for the common ownership, into easements and profits for the benefit of the land granted; this is so whether or not they were 'continuous and apparent', or reasonably necessary to the enjoyment of the property granted. But the section cannot turn into an easement or profit an 'advantage' previously enjoyed which is incapable of exhibiting the characteristics of an easement or profit.[78] The section only applies to the conveyance and not to the contract of sale, thus there seems nothing to prevent the grantor inserting words in the conveyance restricting its operation to such rights as he is obliged to pass to the grantee, and on a sale of land these rights comprise easements subsisting prior to the conveyance, ways of necessity, intended easements and such rights as pass by virtue of the rule in *Wheeldon* v. *Burrows* (*ante*, page 20); the grantor is therefore entitled to insert limiting words into the conveyance that no more shall pass than these.

Prescription

Prescription is founded on the view that if long enjoyment of use of someone else's land is proved, the enjoyment will usually be assumed to have had a lawful origin. There are three types of prescriptive claim, but in each case the plaintiff must show that he has used the right as if he was entitled to it (user 'as of right'), which means that his user must not have been contentious, secretive or by permission of the owner of the allegedly servient land. Generally speaking the user must have been by or on behalf of the fee simple in the dominant land (although the easement of light is an exception) against the fee simple in the servient land; thus in general a tenant cannot prescribe against his landlord or against another tenant of the same landlord, since if he could the result would be that the landlord would acquire an easement over his own land.[79] But a claim to a profit need not always be made on behalf of the fee simple in the dominant land.

There are three different foundations upon which a prescriptive claim may be based. Firstly, there is common law prescription which depends upon proof that enjoyment of the right has lasted since 1189, the time of the beginning of legal memory, although proof of twenty years user as of right is *prima facie* proof of user since 1189. But the claim fails if it is proved that user could not have existed since 1189, as for example a claim to light in respect of the windows of a building shown to have been erected after 1189. [80]

In order to overcome the failure of a claim based on prescription if it was shown that the user began after 1189, the courts invented a second type of prescriptive claim known as lost modern grant; this means that if long continued enjoyment of the alleged easement can be shown (twenty years is usually sufficient for this purpose) the court will presume that an actual grant has been made after 1189 of the right to enjoy the easement in fee simple and that the deed of grant has unfortunately been lost. [81] A claim based on lost modern grant must however fail if it is proved that throughout the period after user of the alleged easement began there was no one capable of making a grant of the easement in fee simple in the servient land, as would for example be the case where the land was held throughout by a series of life tenants; [82] this is probably so despite the Settled Land Act, 1925 (*ante*, pages 7–9) since the life tenant could only make a grant under the Act in return for full consideration.

The third type of claim is a claim based on the Prescription Act, 1832; although the interpretation of some of its details is a matter of controversy, the general effect of the Act is reasonably clear. It provides that an easement which has been enjoyed for twenty years, and a profit which has been enjoyed for thirty years, as of right and without interruption cannot be defeated merely by proof that user commenced after 1189; [83] this removes the weakness of common law prescription. The Act further provides that an easement enjoyed for forty years, and a profit enjoyed for sixty years, as of right and without interruption is to be deemed 'absolute and indefeasible' unless enjoyed by written consent. [84] All periods of enjoyment referred to in the Act must be those immediately before the lawsuit concerning the alleged right, thus, however long the user, there is no right to any easement or profit under the Act until the matter has been successfully litigated. [85] As regards interruption, the Act provides that nothing shall be deemed an interruption unless it has been acquiesced in by the owner of the allegedly dominant land for at least one year after he had notice of the interruption and of the person responsible for it. [86]

In all claims the user must be as of right; if the user is only enjoyed by consent given by the owner of the allegedly servient land, this consent if given during the prescriptive period defeats the claim whether the consent be oral or written, but in the case of a claim based upon the longer period it is probable that an oral consent given before the prescriptive period commenced and not renewed subsequently will not defeat the claim. Further, whereas in the case of a claim based on the shorter period any time during which the allegedly servient land has been in the hands of an infant, lunatic or tenant for life must be deducted from the period[87] and, quite apart from the statute, if the land was let to a tenant before the user began then no user as of right against the fee simple owner will commence until that tenancy expires, [88] yet if the claim is based on the longer period the only permissible deduction is that if the servient land has been held for a life tenancy or a lease exceeding three years during the user, the years during which the land was so held can be deducted provided the reversioner resists the claim within three years of the end of the life tenancy or lease;[89] the restricted right of deduction thus conferred does not apply to a claim to a profit. The advantages, therefore, of basing a claim upon the longer rather than the shorter period where the facts so warrant are that sometimes an oral consent will not defeat the claim and that the disabilities which can be pleaded in deduction of the duration of prescriptive user are much cut down.

Special rules are laid down by the Prescription Act regarding a claim to the easement of light. The Act provides that actual enjoyment of the access of light to a building for twenty years without interruption confers an absolute right to the light unless it was enjoyed by written consent. [90] Thus user as of right need not be shown and only written consent will defeat the claim; moreover no disabilities concerning the owner of the servient land can be pleaded in bar of a claim to light under the Act, and, exceptionally, a tenant can prescribe for light under the Act against his own landlord or against another tenant of the common landlord. [91]

By the Rights of Light Act, 1959, a servient owner who realises that his neighbour may be in process of gradually acquiring a prescriptive claim to light may prevent time from running any further in favour of his neighbour if the servient owner simply registers a notice as a local land charge, which will then be treated as a physical obstruction of the light. [92] The servient owner must send a notice in the prescribed form to the local authority for registration, and the notice must state that its registration is intended to represent an obstruction of the access of light. The notice usually remains effective for one year unless it is cancelled before then, and is renewable.[93]

Remedies for interference with easements and profits

The owner of the easement may himself abate the interference with it, provided he uses no more force and does no more damage than is reasonably necessary and there is no likelihood of a breach of the peace, but the exercise of this remedy is so hedged about with these and perhaps other restrictions that it is generally inadvisable to have recourse to it. He is usually better advised to bring an action for damages, or an injunction or a declaration, or any combination of these.

Extinguishment of easements and profits

This may be accomplished in any of three ways. Firstly, the right may be expressly released; in order to be formally perfect the release should be by deed, but if there is a written contract to release or part performance (*post*, pages 265–6) the court will order that a deed of release must be executed. Secondly, the right can be extinguished by abandonment; mere neglect to use the right is not in itself sufficient,[94] because an intention to abandon the right must be shown, but twenty years non user may raise a rebuttable presumption of abandonment. [95] Thirdly, the right is extinguished if both the ownership in fee simple absolute and the occupation of both plots of land come to be united in the same person. [96]

Extent of easement of way

Disputes often arise concerning the extent to which the right of way may be used, such as whether it can only be used on foot or whether it extends to wheeled traffic. The basic rules governing this matter are as follows: (a) if the right was created by express grant, its extent primarily depends on the words of the deed; (b) if created by implied grant, the extent primarily depends upon the surrounding circumstances existing at the time of the grant;[97] (c) if created by prescription, it depends upon the extent to which the right was enjoyed during the prescriptive period,[98] although this refers to the type of user rather than to numbers or frequency.

Extent of right to light

An easement of light can only exist in relation to a window or other defined aperture in a building, and the amount of light which can legally be acquired as a right is that which is sufficient for the ordinary user of the premises;[99] thus a diminution in the amount of light which has previously been enjoyed is not actionable provided sufficient light is left for ordinary user of the premises.

Natural rights

Natural rights differ from easements in that natural rights are conferred on the landowner by operation of law and, unlike easements, do not have to be acquired by grant or prescription. An example of a natural right is that every landowner has the right to have the surface of his land, unencumbered by buildings, supported by his neighbour's land; this natural right of support does not extend to buildings nor to the additional burden of support which is the result of their presence, but if support is withdrawn and in consequence the land of the plaintiff would have fallen even had there been no buildings, thus infringing his natural right, the damages recoverable in respect of this extend to the buildings also.[100] Another example of a natural right is that a landowner through whose land a stream flows on the surface through a defined channel has the right to object if the stream is dammed or diverted by another landowner higher up the stream.[101]

Public rights of way

These may be created by legislation; for example, a local authority can in general, and subject to Ministerial confirmation and payment of compensation, by order create a public footpath if thought expedient to do so, having regard to the extent to which the path would add to the convenience or enjoyment of a substantial section of the public or the convenience of persons resident in the area, and to the effect which creation of the path would have on the rights of persons interested in the land and to the needs of agriculture and forestry.[102] They may also be created by proof that the owner of the land dedicated the way to the public and that the public accepted, acceptance normally being demonstrated by user of the way. Long user by the public will often raise a presumption of dedication as well as acceptance. The Highways Act, 1959, states that twenty years uninterrupted enjoyment as of right by the public of a way over land establishes the right of way unless the landowner proves that there was no intention to dedicate it.[103] Lack of intention to dedicate can be shown either by closing the way for at least one day in each year, or by exhibiting a notice disproving the intention and visible to those using the way, or by depositing with the local authority a map and statement of what ways the owner admits to be highways and renewing the statement at intervals of not more than six years by statutory declaration.[104]

A fluctuating body of persons, such as the inhabitants of a parish, cannot acquire easements since all easements are presumed to have had their origin in a deed of grant and a fluctuating body cannot take such a grant. They may however acquire analogous rights by means of a claim based on a local custom, but in order to succeed the custom must be certain, reasonable, uninterrupted, and have been in existence as far back as the year 1189, though such an origin may be presumed if there has been long enjoyment and there is no proof to the contrary.

Mortgages

A mortgage of land is the transfer of an interest in land as security for and in return for a loan of money. The mortgage of an estate in fee simple absolute in possession is made by granting the lender (known as 'the mortgagee') a long lease, usually for a period of three thousand years, as security, or by a charge by deed expressed to be by way of legal mortgage, the effect of which is to create no actual lease but to give the mortgagee the same rights, powers, protection and remedies as if he had a lease. A mortgage of a leasehold interest is made by granting the mortgagee a sub-lease, or by a charge by deed expressed to be by way of legal mortgage. Alternatively the borrower (known as 'the mortgagor') may mortgage the land informally by mere written agreement to grant a mortgage or by depositing the title deeds of his land with the mortgagee by way of security.

If, however, the interest which is being mortgaged only arises under a trust, such as a life interest, the mortgage is usually made by transferring the mortgagor's beneficial interest to the mortgagee in return for the loan with an undertaking to transfer it back to him when the loan is paid off; mortgages made informally are also possible. In all mortgages there will be an arrangement for giving up the security when the loan is repaid.

Although the terms of the mortgage usually state that the loan is to be repaid within a short period, usually six months, after the mortgage was created, yet in practice neither party as a rule takes this seriously as regards actual repayment; since the courts regard a mortgage as essentially a device to provide security for repayment of the loan, the court will in general permit the mortgagor to pay off the loan long after the contractual date for repayment has expired. But it is convenient to the mortgagee to fix the contractual date of repayment at a date not far ahead, because most of his remedies for enforcing the security, if need be, only arise when the contractual date for repayment has expired. If the mortgagor wishes to redeem after the contractual date, he will have to give reasonable notice of his intention to do so or pay interest in lieu of notice; six months notice will often be required, though less will suffice for informal mortgages which are usually of a more temporary nature.

The court will be astute to set aside what it regards as unfair terms in the mortgage which are to the detriment of the mortgagor, thus for example an option conferred by the mortgage document on the mortgagee to purchase the mortgaged property is a void option. [105] Any clauses in the mortgage which are unconscionable or which, after the mortgagor has paid back the loan, seek to prevent him from regaining his property free from any stipulation restricting its use to the benefit of the mortgagee fall within this ban. [106]

Remedies of the mortgagee

A mortgagee has five remedies which he may use in order to get paid. Firstly, he may of course sue for the capital sum owing to him or for any interest which is owing, provided of course that in either case the contractual date on which these sums were to be paid has passed by without payment.

Secondly, once the contractual date for repayment of the capital has gone by, and provided the mortgage was made by deed, a statutory power to sell the mortgaged property arises, [107] unless the contrary has been agreed between the parties. But the mortgagee cannot exercise this power until, in addition, he has either served notice on the mortgagor requiring repayment of the capital and such repayment has not been made within three months thereafter, or payment of interest has been at least two months in arrears, or there has been a breach by the mortgagor of some other obligation resting upon him and imposed either by the mortgage deed or the Law of Property Act, 1925. [108] The effect of a valid sale is to extinguish the mortgagor's interest in the property and to transfer the whole of the interest which was mortgaged to the buyer, subject only to any mortgages on the property ranking in priority to that of the mortgagee who exercised the power of sale. The mortgagee must apply the proceeds of sale firstly in paying the costs of the sale, secondly in paying what is owing to himself and lastly in paying the surplus, if any, to the person who ranks next below him in entitlement to the mortgaged property, who if there were no mortgages subsequent to his own would be the mortgagor. Provided the mortgagee acts in good faith and with reasonable care, he need not delay selling if the market is depressed in order to wait for a better price. [109] But a mortgagee who is a building society must take reasonable steps to get the best price reasonably obtainable. [110]

Thirdly, once the contractual date for redemption has passed the mortgagee may apply to the court for an order that the mortgagor should henceforth be debarred from repaying the loan and retrieving his property; such an order is termed a 'foreclosure order'. In foreclosure proceedings any interested party can ask the court to order a sale of the mortgaged property instead. If the court proceeds to make a foreclosure decree, it will usually order that this shall not come into effect for a further six months, during which the mortgagor and any mortgagees ranking in priority below that of the person applying for the foreclosure decree are given a chance to raise the money and pay off the person seeking foreclosure. Even after that period has gone by without such payment having been made, the court can sometimes be induced to reopen the foreclosure on payment at a later date if there are special circumstances, such as the mortgaged property being an old family estate of particular sentimental value to the mortgagor.

Fourthly, a mortgagee whose security consists in the granting of a lease or sub-lease to him is clearly entitled, unless otherwise agreed, to take possession of the mortgaged property once the mortgage is made; if however the grant of his security did not take the above form, it is somewhat doubtful whether he may enter into possession in this way. The objectives of taking possession could be either as a prelude to selling the property with vacant possession, or to intercept the rents and profits and apply them to payment of interest on the mortgage. In practice, however, the mortgagee rarely enters into possession for the latter purpose, and if he does he will be required by law to give the mortgagor credit, not only for the sums which the mortgagee in fact received, but also for the amounts which he ought to have received by a diligent and prudent management of the property. [111]

Finally, the mortgagee may appoint a receiver of the rents and profits of the mortgaged property. This power arises and becomes exercisable in exactly the same circumstances as apply to the mortgagee's power of sale (ante, page 27). The appointment is made in writing by the mortgagee, but the receiver is deemed to be in law the agent of the mortgagor, thus responsibility for the acts and defaults of the receiver falls upon the mortgagor. [112] The receiver will apply the income in payment of outgoings relating to the property, then his own commission, and then in paying interest due under the mortgage; any surplus income must be applied in reduction of the capital sum outstanding under the mortgage if the mortgagee so directs in writing, otherwise it will be paid to the person who would have received it if no receiver had been appointed, who is usually the mortgagor. [113]

Priority of mortgages

A mortgagee of the fee simple absolute in possession or of a leasehold interest in land should, unless he takes possession of the title deeds of the land from the mortgagor, register his mortgage as a land charge in the Land Charges Registry in order to preserve his priority. If, however, he takes a mortgage of an interest arising under a trust, priority should be preserved by giving notice in writing of his interest to the trustees of that trust; [114] if there are no trustees of the trust at the moment, or if notice can only be served with unreasonable cost or delay, it is permissible to endorse the trust instrument instead with a memorandum of the mortgage, and this will have the same effect as regards priority. [115]

Covenants affecting the fee simple

A covenant is a promise contained in a deed. The covenant is obviously enforceable by the law of contract as between the original contracting parties, though if it was made for the benefit of land belonging to the person receiving the covenant, known as 'the covenantee', that person could generally only recover nominal damages if he had parted with his land before the breach of the covenant took place. The benefit of a covenant relating to the covenantee's land can also in general pass with the land to his successors in title, and this is so regardless of whether the covenant was positive, such as to supply cold water to the land, or negative, such as not to build on the land. The burden of a positive covenant will not however pass with the fee simple so as to be enforceable against the successors in title to the servient land of the person who gave the covenant (known as 'the covenantor'); the burden of a restrictive covenant can however pass with the servient land so as to affect the successors in title to that land provided certain conditions are satisfied. [116] If both the dominant and the servient land have changed hands since the covenant was originally given, in order to see whether the covenant is still enforceable it is necessary to trace whether the benefit of the covenant has passed to the successor in title of the dominant land and whether the burden of the covenant has passed to the successor in title of the servient land. As has been seen, the burden of a positive covenant will not run with the fee

29

simple so as to bind the successor in title to the servient land, but the burden of a negative covenant may do so. The conditions for this to occur are, firstly, the covenant must be negative in nature, although if it is so it is immaterial whether it is positive in form; thus a covenant to maintain Leicester Square Garden in an open state uncovered with any buildings has been held to be negative in nature.[117] Secondly, the covenant must benefit the land retained by the covenantee. Thirdly, the burden of the covenant must have been intended to run with the covenantor's land and not to be merely personal to him, but covenants relating to land made after 1925 are deemed to have been made by the covenantor on behalf of himself, his successors in title and the persons deriving title under him or them unless a contrary intention appears,[118] and will therefore *prima facie* run with the land. Finally, the covenant will not bind a person who takes a fee simple absolute in possession or a leasehold interest in the land for money or money's worth without notice of the covenant and who did not acquire his interest in the land by virtue of a trust. As to what constitutes notice of a restrictive covenant, if the covenant was created after 1925 then it must be registered as a land charge in the Land Charges Registry, and either registration, whether the person now claiming the servient land knew of the registration or not, or actual knowledge by him of the covenant's existence will constitute notice. As regards restrictive covenants created before 1925, notice will depend on what the buyer of the servient land ought to have discovered from inspection of the title deeds and the like when he purchased the land.

The benefit of a restrictive covenant will pass to and be enforceable by a successor in title to the dominant land, provided the covenant was of benefit to the land of the covenantee; moreover the benefit of the covenant must have been passed to the covenantee's successor in title who now seeks to enforce the covenant, and this can be done either by showing that the benefit of the covenant was expressly assigned to him together with the land, or that the wording of the covenant when first taken showed that it was for the benefit of the land or made with the covenantee in his capacity as owner of the land, or that there is a building or analogous scheme under which both plaintiff and defendant derive title to the land under a common vendor who had previously laid out his land in plots under a building scheme and imposed restrictions on all the plots for the benefit of the other plots, all parties purchasing the plots with the knowledge of the restrictions and on that basis.[119]

A covenantee who over-estimates the area of his land which is capable of being benefited by the restrictive covenant runs the risk of the covenant failing altogether;[120] this danger can be averted if the covenant is expressed to be for the benefit of 'the whole or any part or parts' of the covenantee's land, in which event the holder of any part of the land which is in fact benefited may be able to enforce the covenant.[121]

Anyone who is doubtful as to whether or not his land is affected by an enforceable restrictive covenant can apply to the court for a declaration as to whether the land is so affected and to what extent. [122]

Discharge or modification of restrictive covenants

A restrictive covenant can only be enforced, except as between the original contracting parties, if an injunction could be granted to restrain a breach of it, and thus as far as the plaintiff is concerned a result equivalent to discharge of the covenant will occur if the court refuses to grant an injunction. An injunction will be refused if the court thinks it would be unfair to grant it; this may apply if the plaintiff has been guilty of undue delay, such as where he knew of the breach and took no action to enforce the covenant until five years later, [123] or if the plaintiff has remained so long inactive in the face of such open breaches of similar covenants which he could have enforced against third parties as to justify a reasonable belief that he no longer intends to enforce the covenant against anyone, [124] or if the character of the neighbourhood has, since the covenant was taken, been so utterly changed as to empty the covenant of all value. [125]

Furthermore, a person may apply to the Lands Tribunal for the discharge or modification of a restrictive covenant affecting either a fee simple absolute or a leasehold made for more than forty years of which at least twenty-five years have expired. [126] If the tribunal do so, the tribunal may direct the applicant to pay to the person entitled to the benefit of the restrictive covenant such sum as it thinks just in order to make up for any loss or disadvantage suffered in consequence of its discharge, or to make up for any effect which the covenant had when it was first imposed in reducing the price paid for the land affected by it. Before discharging or modifying a covenant the tribunal must be satisfied that because of changes in the character of the property or the neighbourhood or other circumstances the covenant ought to be deemed obsolete, or that the persons of full age and capacity for the time being entitled to the benefit of the covenant have expressly or impliedly agreed to its modification or discharge, or that they will not be injured by this course. The tribunal may also make such an order if satisfied that the restriction does not secure any benefits of substantial value or advantage to those entitled to the benefit of the covenant or that the covenant is contrary to the public interest, and that money will adequately compensate for any loss or disadvantage which will be suffered in consequence of its discharge or modification. The Tribunal's powers are set out in section 84 of the Law of Property Act, 1925, as amended by the Landlord and Tenant Act, 1954, section 52, and the Law of Property Act, 1969, section 28(3).

Licences

A licence is a permission given by the occupier of land to another person (called the licensee) to enter on the land and do something which would otherwise be a trespass; a licence, unlike a lease, does not usually confer a right to the exclusive possession of the land. There are several types of licence. A mere permission, gratuitously conferred, to enter on the land for a specified purpose can be withdrawn at any time provided reasonable notice of revocation is given. [127] Alternatively, the licence to enter may be for the purpose of taking away something from the land, such as an entry to cut down and remove a tree. A licence of this type is irrevocable if properly created, [128] and this may require the use of a deed although a written contract to grant it will usually be upheld. Thirdly, there is a type of licence which is given in return for something of value but which confers no right to take anything from the land; an example would be a permission to enter a field to watch the local agricultural show in return for payment of the entrance fee, and here it seems that a well-behaved licensee is in general entitled to stay on the land during the period for which his licence was granted despite any purported revocation of it. [129]

It seems that a licensee will not be entitled to enforce either a gratuitous or contractual licence to be on the land against the successors in title of his licensor. [130]

Adverse possession of land

The right of an owner to his land is by statute extinguished if the land is held in adverse possession for a sufficiently long period; the adverse possessor takes a title based on his adverse possession from the moment of his entry, but he is at that time liable to be evicted by persons having a better legal claim to the possession; as the years go by the rights of those persons may be extinguished by lapse of time, with the result that eventually no one is legally entitled to evict the adverse possessor.

The usual time allowed for recovery of land is twelve years from the date when the cause of action accrued. [131] Time begins to run against an owner entitled to immediate possession of the land once a possession adverse to him commences, so that he is barred at the end of twelve years continuous adverse possession. A remainderman or reversioner whose interest does not follow an entail is usually allowed the longer alternative of twelve years from when the adverse possession commenced or six years after his interest fell into possession. [132] In the case of a lease for a fixed period time does not run against the landlord until the lease expires. [133] As regards a written periodic tenancy, time runs from the end of the tenancy; as to an oral periodic tenancy, time runs from the end of the first period or the last payment of rent, whichever is later.

In *Hayward* v. *Chaloner* [134] a piece of land was let on an oral tenancy to the rector of a parish at a rent of ten shillings a year. After a time no rent was offered or paid, nor was it demanded by the successive landlords as they were all staunch supporters of the church. After the rent had been unpaid for over twenty years the then rector sought to sell the piece of land, claiming a title based on the adverse possession of himself and previous rectors. The Court of Appeal held by a majority that the current rector and his predecessors as rector had been in adverse possession of the land since the last payment of rent, thus the title of the previous owners of the land was extinguished.

As regards mortgages, the mortgagor's right to repay the money and regain his property unencumbered is barred if the mortgagee has been in continuous possession of the land for twelve years without receiving any payment from the mortgagor during that period and without giving a written acknowledgement of the mortgagor's title. Conversely the mortgagee's rights are barred twelve years after the capital was due to be repaid or the last payment of capital or interest from the mortgagor was received or the mortgagor made a written acknowledgement of the mortgagee's title, whichever of these last happened. Not more than six years arrears of mortgage interest are recoverable by action, although a mortgagor who wishes to repay the mortgage must act fairly and pay off all arrears of interest.

Only six years arrears of rent are recoverable by action or distress, and in the case of an agricultural holding only one year's arrears is recoverable by distress,[135] although up to six years arrears can be claimed by action.

Time does not run in favour of a trustee when sued by a beneficiary for fraud or fraudulent breach of trust, or for recovery of the trust property or its proceeds in his possession or which he previously received and converted to his own use. [136] In other cases the period is usually six years from when the cause of action accrued.

These periods are extended if the owner of an interest in land was under disability when his right of action accrued, in which event he is allowed an alternative period of six years from the date when his disability ceases or he dies, whichever first occurs, subject to a maximum period in the case of land of thirty years. [137] However, if the action is based on the fraud of the defendant or someone through whom he claims or their agents, or the right of action is concealed by the fraud of such a person, time does not begin to run against the plaintiff until he discovers or could with reasonable diligence have discovered the fraud. [138] Similar rules apply concerning an action 'for relief from the consequences of a mistake', [139] although these words have a narrow meaning.

A written and signed acknowledgement of the plaintiff's title, made by or on behalf of the person in whose favour time is running and made to or for the account of the person whose title is being barred, will start time running afresh unless it is made after the title has already been extinguished. [140]

Notes

1   See *post*, pages 333–4; *Clifton* v. *Viscount Bury* (1887) 4 T.L.R. 8.
2   Water Resources Act, 1963, sections 23 and 24.
3   Water Resources Act, 1963, sections 23, 24 and 135.
4   Law of Property Act, 1925, section 60(1); Wills Act, 1837, sections 28 and 34.
5   Law of Property (Amendment) Act, 1926.
6   Law of Property Act 1925, sections 60(4) and 130(1).
7   Section 130(1).
8   Fines and Recoveries Act, 1833, and Law of Property Act, 1925.
9   Law of Property Act, 1925, section 176.
10   *Doherty* v. *Allman* (1878) 3 App. Cas. 709.
11   *Re Cartwright* (1889) 41 Ch.D. 532.
12   *Dashwood* v. *Magniac* [1891] 3 Ch. 306.
13   *Honywood* v. *Honywood* (1874) L.R. 18 Eq. 306.
14   *Vane* v. *Lord Barnard* (1716) 2 Vern. 738.
15   Lewis Bowles's Case (1615) 11 Co. Rep. 79b.
16   Settled Land Act, 1925, section 66.
17   Settled Land Act, 1925, sections 45–47.
18   Law of Property Act, 1925, section 205(1).
19   Settled Land Act, 1925, section 38.
20   Section 39.

[21] Section 84(2).
[22] *Re Pelly's Will Trusts* [1957] 1 Ch. 1.
[23] Section 65.
[24] Section 107(1).
[25] *Wheelwright* v. *Walker* (No. 1) (1883) 23 Ch. D. 752 at page 762.
[26] *Re Hunt's Settled Estates* [1906] 2 Ch. 11.
[27] *Re Earl Somers*, deceased (1895) 11 T.L.R. 567.
[28] Section 68.
[29] Section 97.
[30] Section 101(4).
[31] Section 101(5).
[32] Section 108(2).
[33] Section 106(1).
[34] *Re Orlebar* [1936] Ch. 147.
[35] *Re Haynes* (1887) 37 Ch.D. 306.
[36] Section 105(1).
[37] Section 24(1).
[38] *Re Thornhill's Settlement* [1940] 4 All E.R. 83.
[39] Law of Property Act, section 205(1).
[40] Law of Property Act, 1925, section 28(1); *ante*, pages 7–12.
[41] Section 28(1).
[42] Section 26(1).
[43] Law of Property Act, 1925, section 30.
[44] *Re Beale's Settlement Trusts* [1932] 2 Ch. 15.
[45] Section 25(1).
[46] *Re Mayo* [1943] Ch. 302.
[47] Section 26(3) as amended.
[48] *Saunders* v. *Vautier* (1841) 4 Beav. 115, affirmed Cr. and Ph. 240.
[49] Section 29(1).
[50] Section 30.
[51] Law of Property Act, section 36(2).
[52] Trustee Act, 1925, section 34.
[53] Trustee Act, 1925, sections 36(1) and 41.
[54] *Letterstedt* v. *Broers* (1884) 9 App. Cas. 371.
[55] Trustee Act, 1925, section 39(1).
[56] Law of Property Act, 1925, section 54(2).
[57] *Aldin* v. *Latimer Clark, Muirhead & Co.* [1894] 2 Ch. 437.
[58] Housing Act, 1957, section 6.
[59] *Rousou* v. *Photi* [1940] 2 K.B. 379.
[60] *McCarrick* v. *Liverpool Corporation* [1947] A.C. 219.
[61] *Ryall* v. *Kidwell* [1914] 3 K.B. 135.

62 Section 6(2).
63 Housing Act, 1961, sections 32 and 33.
64 *Ante*, pages 4–5; Statute of Marlbridge, 1267.
65 *Wedd* v. *Porter* [1916] 2 K.B. 91.
66 *Elwes* v. *Maw* (1802) 3 East, 38.
67 *Leigh* v. *Taylor* [1902] A.C. 157.
68 *D'Eyncourt* v. *Gregory* (1866) L.R. 3 Eq. 382.
69 Agricultural Holdings Act, 1948; *post*, pages 60–1.
70 *Phillips* v. *Lamdin* [1949] 2 K.B. 33.
71 *Thomas* v. *Sylvester* (1873) L.R. 8 Q.B. 368.
72 Law of Property Act, 1925, section 121.
73 Section 191.
74 *Cable* v. *Bryant* [1908] 1 Ch. 259.
75 *Wheeldon* v. *Burrows* (1879) 12 Ch. D. 31.
76 *Phillips* v. *Low* [1892] 1 Ch. 47.
77 *Swansborough* v. *Coventry* (1832) 2 Moo. and Sc. 362.
78 *International Tea Stores Co.* v. *Hobbs* [1903] 2 Ch. 165.
79 *Kilgour* v. *Gaddes* [1904] 1 K.B. 457.
80 *Duke of Norfolk* v. *Arbuthnot* (1880) 5 C.P.D. 390.
81 *Dalton* v. *Angus & Co.* (1881) 6 App.Cas. 740.
82 *Roberts* v. *James* (1903) 89 L.T. 282.
83 Prescription Act, 1832, sections 1 and 2.
84 Sections 1 and 2.
85 *Hyman* v. *Van den Bergh* [1908] 1 Ch. 167.
86 Section 4.
87 Section 7.
88 *Daniel* v. *North* (1809) 11 East 372.
89 Section 8.
90 Section 3.
91 *Morgan* v. *Fear* [1907] A.C. 425.
92 Section 2(1).
93 Section 3.
94 *Ward* v. *Ward* (1852) 7 Exch. 838.
95 *Moore* v. *Rawson* (1824) 3 B. and C. 32.
96 *Lord Dynevor* v. *Tennant* (1888) 13 App. Cas. 279.
97 *Corporation of London* v. *Riggs* (1880) 13 Ch.D. 798.
98 *Williams* v. *James* (1867) L.R. 2 C.P. 577.
99 *Colls* v. *Home and Colonial Stores Ltd.* [1904] A.C. 179.
100 *Stroyan* v. *Knowles* (1861) 6 H. & N. 454.
101 *Swindon Waterworks Co. Ltd.* v. *Wilts & Berks Canal Navigation Co.* (1875) L.R. 7 H.L. 697.

102 Highways Act, 1959, sections 28, 31, 32.
103 Section 34(1).
104 Section 34.
105 *Samuel* v. *Jarrah Timber and Wood Paving Corporation, Ltd.* [1904] A.C. 323.
106 *Biggs* v. *Hoddinott* [1898] 2 Ch. 307.
107 Law of Property Act, 1925, section 101(1).
108 Section 103.
109 *Davey* v. *Durrant* (1857) 1 De G. and J. 535.
110 Building Societies Act, 1962, section 36.
111 *White* v. *City of London Brewery Co.* (1889) 42. Ch.D. 237.
112 Law of Property Act, 1925, section 109.
113 Section 109(8).
114 Law of Property Act, 1925, sections 137 and 138.
115 Section 137(4).
116 *Tulk* v. *Moxhay* (1848) 2 Ph. 774.
117 *Tulk* v. *Moxhay, supra.*
118 Law of Property Act, 1925, section 79.
119 *Elliston* v. *Reacher* [1908] 2. Ch. 374.
120 *Re Ballard's Conveyance* [1937] Ch. 473.
121 *Marquess of Zetland* v. *Driver* [1939] Ch. 1.
122 Law of Property Act, 1925, section 84(2).
123 *Gaskin* v. *Balls* (1879) 13 Ch.D. 324.
124 *Chatsworth Estates Co.* v. *Fewell* [1931] 1 Ch. 224.
125 *Westripp* v. *Baldock* [1939] 1 All E.R. 279.
126 Law of Property Act, 1925, section 84, as amended by Landlord and Tenant Act, 1954, section 52.
127 *Aldin* v. *Latimer Clark, Muirhead and Co.* [1894] 2 Ch. 437.
128 *James Jones and Sons, Ltd.* v. *Earl of Tankerville* [1909] 2 Ch. 440.
129 *Hurst* v. *Picture Theatres, Ltd.* [1915] 1 K.B. 1.
130 *Clore* v. *Theatrical Properties, Ltd.* [1936] 3 All. E.R. 483; *National Provincial Bank, Ltd.* v. *Ainsworth* [1965] A.C. 1175.
131 Limitation Act, 1939, section 4(3).
132 Section 6(2).
133 Section 6(2).
134 [1968] 1 Q.B. 107.
135 Agricultural Holdings Act, 1948, section 18.
136 Limitation Act, 1939, section 19(1).
137 Section 22.
138 Section 26.
139 Section 26.
140 Sections 23 and 24.

2 Agricultural Leases

The law with regard to this matter is mainly, although by no means wholly, contained in the Agricultural Holdings Act, 1948.

Definition of 'agricultural land' and 'agricultural holding'

To be agricultural land within the meaning of the Act the land must be used for agriculture, and must either be so used for the purposes of a trade or business or be designated as agricultural land by the Minister.[1] 'Agriculture' is defined to include horticulture, fruit growing, seed growing, dairy farming and livestock breeding and keeping, the use of land as grazing land, meadow land, osier land, market gardens and nursery grounds, and the use of land for woodlands where that use is ancillary to the farming of land for other agricultural purposes.[2] An 'agricultural holding' means the whole of the agricultural land comprised in a contract of tenancy, (excluding land let to a tenant during his continuance in any office, appointment or employment held under the landlord).[3] In *Blackmore* v. *Butler*[4] the defendant when negotiating for the lease of a farm made it clear that he also wanted a tenancy of an adjacent cottage for occupation by one of his farm workers. Nevertheless the tenancy of the farm was granted without including the cottage because at that time the cottage was already occupied, but it was understood between the parties that as soon as alternative accommodation had been obtained for that occupant of the cottage a tenancy of the cottage would then be created in favour of the defendant; subsequently the cottage became vacant and this was in fact done, the cottage thereafter being occupied by a farm labourer employed by the defendant. The cottage had always in the past been used to house a farm labourer. The plaintiff purchased the landlord's interest in the cottage and then served notice to quit on the defendant, who served a counter-notice under section 24(1) of the Agricultural Holdings Act, 1948 (*post*, page 55), claiming the protection of the Act. The court held that although the cottage was held under a separate tenancy, the cottage itself was on the facts of this case 'land used for agriculture' and 'agricultural land' within the 1948 Act, and was an agricultural holding.

If the purposes for which the land is let are mixed, it seems that the whole of the land will be an agricultural holding if the predominant purpose of the letting was for agriculture. In *Howkins* v. *Jardine*[5] a landlord granted a yearly tenancy, containing provisions appropriate to a lease of an agricultural holding, of seven acres of land and three cottages on that land. The tenant, who farmed other land in addition, sublet the three cottages to persons not engaged in agriculture. The question was whether the whole subject-matter of the tenancy came within the protection of the 1948 Act. The court held that the lease was in substance a lease of an agricultural holding since the cottages were ancillary to the land and the terms of the agreement were appropriate to an agricultural holding, thus the whole of the subject-matter of the contract of tenancy came within the protection of the 1948 Act.

Furthermore, a letting for mixed purposes can be agricultural even where the tenant derives the bulk of his income from the non-agricultural use of the land. In *Dunn* v. *Fidoe*[6] land comprising an inn, outbuildings, and twelve acres of orchard and pasture were let to a tenant. The inn did a substantial trade, and the tenant also made substantial profits, mainly by the sale of fruit, from the land. The inn provided the larger and more constant part of the tenant's income. Although the buildings were designed as an inn they were also used to a small extent for the tenant's agricultural business. It was held that the whole of the premises including the inn constituted an agricultural holding and the tenant was protected as to the whole by the 1948 Act.

Creation of agricultural tenancies

Like other tenancies, an agricultural tenancy is usually created by deed; although a document not under seal containing written evidence of the terms and signed by the defendant or his agent, or an act of part performance (see *post*, pages 265–6) is effective for most legal purposes (see *ante*, page 15), it is better to have a deed since the deed has full legal efficacy. However a tenancy of agricultural land, like that of any other land, can be created orally and with full legal efficacy provided it takes effect in possession for a period not exceeding three years and is at the best rent reasonably obtainable without taking a lump sum capital payment; the fact that the tenant might occupy the premises for longer than three years, as could for example be the case with a tenant holding under a tenancy from year to year who in fact remains on the premises for a number of years, does not make it a tenancy for a period exceeding three years.

Grants made for less than a year

It is in general impossible to create a tenancy of an agricultural holding for less than a tenancy from year to year, and any agreement to let or licence (*ante*, page 32) land to be used.as agricultural land will take effect as a tenancy from year to year even if it purports to be for a shorter period; however this does not apply if (a) the Minister of Agriculture, Fisheries and Food gave his prior consent to the agreement, or (b) the agreement relates to the use of the land only for grazing or mowing during a specified period of the year. This is laid down in section 2(1) of the 1948 Act. An agreement concerning the use of the land for three hundred and sixty-four days for grazing or mowing only has been held to fall within the second exception, as three hundred and sixty-four days is a specified period of the year.[7] In *Lory* v. *London Borough of Brent*[8] a substantial area of grassland in poor condition was let to the plaintiff for a period of one year less one day, the plaintiff agreeing to 'keep the land as grassland only and not to plough it except in the interests of good husbandry on a crop rotation basis'; the plaintiff in fact ploughed the land and grew cereal crops on it over a period of three years, the council accepting rent during this period. It was held that the agreement took effect as a tenancy from year to year and was not within the second exception because ploughing and producing crops excluded the use of the land for grazing during the period specified in the agreement.

The rules in section 2(1) apply to an agreement under which a licence is granted to occupy land for use as agricultural land under such circumstances that if the interest granted were a tenancy from year to year the grantee would be a tenant of an agricultural holding, thus the grant of the licence must not be made to the licensee during his continuance in any office, appointment or employment held under the landlord.[9] Moreover the licensee must be a person who during the currency of the licence would have exclusive occupation of the premises against the licensor. In *Harrison-Broadley* v. *Smith*[10] a woman became entitled on the death of her husband to remain in occupation of an estate which included a large quantity of farm land; she then entered into a partnership with the defendant to farm the land, and it was agreed that the partnership could be ended by twelve months' notice on either side given at any time. Subsequently the woman served a valid notice on the defendant ending the partnership, but the defendant declined to quit the land and contended that under section 2(1) of the Agricultural Holdings Act, 1948, he had a right to stay on the land and continue to farm it. This tenancy, if it existed, would be vested in the partnership. It was held that the partnership could not be held to have a licence to occupy the land as agricultural land 'because I cannot give myself a licence, and I cannot give myself a licence jointly with somebody else, for I already have a right to go on the land, and it is tautologous to talk of myself as allowing myself to on my own property . . . the person to whom the licence is granted must be somebody other than the grantor of the licence . . . all that the defendant had was a licence to go on the land for the purpose of the partnership business. If that is so, the partnership has come to an end . . .'[11]

In *Goldsack* v. *Shore* [12] it was held that a gratuitous licence to occupy land cannot amount to an 'agreement' whereby a person is granted a licence to occupy land for use as agricultural land within the Agricultural Holdings Act, 1948.[13]

Grants for two years or more

Where a lease of an agricultural holding is granted for a period of two years or more, the tenancy will upon the expiration of that period *prima facie* continue as a tenancy from year to year and on the terms of the old tenancy so far as applicable unless, not less than one nor more than two years before the date fixed for the expiration of the original tenancy expires, either party has served upon the other a written notice of intention to terminate the tenancy. [14]

Grants between one and two years

A tenancy for a term certain exceeding one year but less than two years is a 'contract of tenancy', and agricultural land so held is an agricultural holding within the 1948 Act and subject to its general provisions, but the tenancy ceases when the period stated therein expires; it is not converted into a tenancy from year to year by any of the preceding rules. [15]

Extension of certain tenancies in lieu of claims to emblements

The word 'emblements' means a right given by law to the tenant of an estate (*ante*, page 1) which has unexpectedly come to an end without the fault of the tenant, as for example by the cessation of the landlord's interest; the right is a right of the tenant to take the crops which are growing on the land when his estate comes to an end. Emblements are restricted to such vegetable products of the soil as are annually produced by the labour of the cultivator. Section 4 of the Agricultural Holdings Act, 1948, in part removes the right of the tenant of such a holding to enter and take emblements, and confers instead a right of continued occupation subject to notice; where the tenancy of an agricultural holding held by a tenant at a rent at or near the full annual value determines by the death or cesser of the estate of any landlord entitled for his life or for any other uncertain interest, instead of claims to emblements the tenant shall continue to hold and occupy the holding until the occupation is determined by a twelve months' notice to quit expiring at the end of a year of the tenancy, and shall then quit upon the terms of his tenancy in the same manner as if the tenancy were then determined by effluxion of time or any other lawful means during the continuance of his landlord's estate.

General considerations

An agricultural tenancy is usually in effect a tenancy for the life of the tenant (unless the tenant himself wishes to quit) because the only ground on which the landlord can be certain of recovering possession of the land is by serving notice to quit on the death of the tenant (see *post*, pages 54–6). This being so, tenancies granted at the outset for long fixed periods are usually undesirable since they impose a degree of rigidity upon both landlord and tenant, the tenant usually being unable to quit the holding during that time and the landlord being unable to obtain a revision of the rent, despite the falling value of money, unless the lease expressly provides for a periodic rental revision.

The landlord is in general unwise to grant a farm tenancy to a farming company since the company, being a distinct and separate legal person from its members (see *post*, pages 84–5), will not die and thus the landlord is unlikely ever to succeed in regaining possession of the land. This difficulty does not apply to partnerships, since in law a partnership is merely regarded as consisting of the individuals who are in partnership and not as a distinct legal person (see also *post*, pages 84–5).

The terms of the tenancy

The terms of the tenancy are usually expressly agreed by the parties and set out in a written tenancy agreement. The express terms will be supplemented by the terms implied by the law into tenancy agreements (see *ante*, pages 16–18), except insofar as the implied terms are capable of exclusion by agreement to the contrary and are inconsistent with the express terms. A custom relating to agriculture which is prevalent throughout the district in which the holding lies will be implied into every agricultural tenancy within the district, unless the tenancy agreement itself or an Act of Parliament stipulates to the contrary. The custom must be a reasonable one otherwise it will be void, and the existence of the custom must be proved by the party seeking to take advantage of it. In *Wedd* v. *Porter* [16] the Court of Appeal held that a tenant from year to year of a farm and buildings at a rent, who has not entered into any other express agreement with his landlord save as to the amount of the rent, is under an obligation implied by law to use and cultivate the land in a husbandlike manner, according to the custom of the country (subject to any relevant statutory provision). This custom is incorporated into every agricultural tenancy agreement unless negatived by the express terms of the agreement.

Restriction of the landlord's claim for breach of the terms of the tenancy

If the tenant breaks a covenant or condition in the tenancy which should have been performed by him, the landlord cannot recover in respect of this any larger sum than the damage which he actually suffers, notwithstanding that the tenancy agreement may stipulate that the tenant shall pay a higher figure. [17]

Lack of written agreement; procedure for settling the terms of the tenancy by agreement or by arbitration

If there is no written agreement containing the terms of the tenancy, either landlord or tenant may request the other to agree the terms in writing, and in default of such agreement to refer the matter to arbitration whereupon the arbitrator will fix the terms so far as the parties cannot agree them. Moreover a written tenancy agreement which contains no guidance on the matters set out in the First Schedule to the 1948 Act can be amplified as regards those matters by using the same procedure.[18] The matters comprise in brief the names of the parties; particulars of the holding sufficient to identify its extent; the period for which the holding is to be let; the rent and when it is payable; who is liable to pay the rates; requiring one or other of the parties to enter into a covenant as regards the maintenance and repair of fixed equipment; a covenant by the landlord to reinstate buildings damaged by fire, if this is required to fulfil his responsibilities under the rules of good estate management, and a covenant by him to insure such buildings against damage by fire; a covenant by the tenant that if harvested crops grown on the holding to be consumed there should be destroyed by fire, he will return to the holding the full equivalent manurial value of the crops so far as required under the rules of

44

good husbandry, and that he will insure all such crops against fire; a power for the landlord to re-enter on the holding if the tenant fails to perform his obligations. These matters are set out in full in Appendix I of this book.

Maintenance, repair and insurance of fixed equipment

Except where inconsistent with the terms of a written agreement between landlord and tenant, the terms relating to the maintenance, repair and insurance of fixed equipment, including buildings, which have been pre-scribed by regulations [19] made under section 6 of the 1948 Act by the Minister of Agriculture, Fisheries and Food are deemed to be incorporated into every tenancy contract of an agricultural holding. Under the Regula-tions, which are set out in full in Appendix II of this book, the landlord is in general responsible for executing all repairs and replacements to the main and exterior walls, and to the roofs, floors, doors and windows of the farmhouse, cottages and farm buildings, and to the water supply and sewage disposal systems; he is also responsible for insuring the farmhouse, cottages and farm buildings against fire and making good fire damage, and for painting or creosoting exterior wood and iron work. The landlord is entitled to recover from the tenant half the reasonable cost of carrying out certain specified works for which he is made responsible.

Insofar as the landlord is not responsible under the Regulations, the tenant is obliged to repair and leave clean and in good tenantable repair and condition the farmhouse, cottages and farm buildings, together with all fixtures and fittings, drains, sewers, water supplies, fences, hedges, ditches, roads, yards and similar items, and to clean and keep in good order roof valleys, gutters and pipes; he must also report to the landlord damage to any items for whose repair and replacement the landlord is responsible. He must also replace or repair all works rendered necessary by the wilful act or negligence of himself, any member of his household or any of his employees. It is the tenant's obligation to paint, paper, colour or limewash, whichever is appropriate, the interior of the buildings, to execute minor roof repairs, and to maintain hedges and dig out and cleanse ponds, water courses and ditches.

If either landlord or tenant fails to carry out the work for which he is made responsible by the Regulations, the other party is entitled, after having made a written request for the work to be done and waited in vain for a specified period thereafter, to perform the work and recover the cost from the other party.

Where the provisions of a written agreement between the parties with

45

regard to the maintenance, repair and insurance of fixed equipment differ substantially from those laid down by the Regulations, either party may ask the other to vary the agreement so as to make it conform with the Regulations, and if they cannot agree about this may refer the matter to arbitration. The arbitrator must consider whether, disregarding the rent payable, the terms of the agreement relating to the maintenance, repair and insurance of the fixed equipment are justifiable having regard to the circumstances of the holding and of the landlord and tenant; if he concludes that the terms of the agreement relating to this matter are not justifiable, he may vary them in such manner as seems reasonable and just. [20] If liability is transferred from the tenant to the landlord in consequence of the arbitration, the landlord may require the arbitrator to fix, and the tenant to pay, compensation in respect of any previous failure by the tenant to discharge the liability which hitherto rested upon him; [21] if liability is transferred to the tenant, the tenant has similar rights. [22] The arbitrator is also empowered to vary the rent of the holding if he thinks it equitable to do so in consequence of any provision contained in his award. [23] The arbitrator's award operates from the date when it is made or such later date as may be specified in the award. [24]

Right to dispose of produce and vary system of cropping

Despite any agreement between the parties or custom to the contrary, though subject to certain exceptions relating to smallholdings and the like, [25] an agricultural tenant may dispose of the produce of his holding, other than manure, and practise any system of cropping the arable land. He may do this without incurring any liability provided he makes adequate provision, in the event of disposing of the produce, to return to the holding the full equivalent manurial value of the sale or removal of the crops in breach of agreement or custom, or, in the case of a system of cropping, to protect the holding from injury or deterioration. [26] In applying this provision regarding cropping, arable land does not include grass land which under the contract of tenancy is to be kept in the same condition throughout the tenancy. [27] In relation to a yearly tenancy, the above provisions do not apply as regards the year before the tenant quits the holding nor to any period after he has given or received notice to quit which results in his leaving, nor, with regard to any tenancy, concerning the year before it terminates. [28]

If the tenant exercises the above powers to crop and dispose of produce despite any custom or agreement to the contrary, the landlord may when the tenant quits the holding at the end of his tenancy recover damages from him for any injury or deterioration to the holding caused by the exercise of these powers. Alternatively he may seek to obtain an injunction during the continuance of the tenancy restraining the tenant from exercising the powers so as to injure or deteriorate the holding or be likely to do so, [29] but in any legal proceedings seeking an injunction there must first have been an arbitration as to whether the tenant has acted in this matter in such a way as to injure or deteriorate the holding or be likely to do so; the arbitrator's award will be conclusive proof of the facts stated in it concerning this matter, not only when he seeks the injunction but also if he claims damages at the end of the tenancy. [30]

Right to burn heather or grass

Where the lease contains a clause prohibiting or restricting the burning of heather or grass by the tenant, the Agricultural Land Tribunal (*post*, page 48) may remove or relax this provision if, after giving the landlord or other person concerned an opportunity of stating his views, the Tribunal is satisfied that the clause is preventing or impeding the proper use of the land for agriculture and that in the circumstances it is expedient to remove or relax it. [31]

The provision of fixed equipment by the landlord

Where, on the tenant's application, the Agricultural Land Tribunal are satisfied that it is reasonable, having regard to the tenant's responsibilities to farm the holding in accordance with the rules of good husbandry (*post*, page 49), that he should carry on an agricultural activity on the holding to the extent and in the manner specified in the application, and that:

(a)   unless fixed equipment is provided the tenant in so carrying on that activity will contravene requirements imposed by or under any Act, or
(b)   that, in using fixed equipment already on the holding which it is reasonable that he should use for purposes connected with that activity, requirements imposed by or under any Act will be contravened unless the equipment is altered or repaired,

the Tribunal may, under section 4 of the Agricultural Holdings Act, 1948, direct the landlord to carry out, within a period specified in the direction, such work for the provision or, as the case may be, alteration or repair of the fixed equipment as will enable the tenant to comply with those requirements. There is a proviso preventing such a direction being made in respect of an activity not carried on on the holding for at least three years prior to the application, unless the Tribunal are satisfied that the starting of the activity did not (or, where not yet started, will not) constitute or form part of a substantial alteration of the type of farming carried on on the holding. No direction can be made unless there has been a prior request in writing by the tenant to the landlord, and the landlord has either refused to do the work or has not agreed to carry it out within a reasonable time thereafter; the work must not be work covered by any contractual or statutory obligation, and regard must be had by the Tribunal to the landlord's responsibilities to manage the land in accordance with the rules of good estate management (*post*) and to the time the holding may be expected to remain a separate holding and to any other material considerations. Failure by the landlord to comply with a direction gives the tenant the same remedies as if the direction was an obligation of the contract of tenancy, and a right to do the work himself and recover the reasonable cost from the landlord. The rent may be increased for improvements carried out in compliance with a direction.[32]

An Agricultural Land Tribunal has been established for each of eight areas covering England and Wales, such areas being constituted for that purpose by order of the Lord Chancellor.[33] Their task is to hear and determine matters which by various Acts of Parliament are entrusted to them to decide. Each Tribunal consists of a chairman or deputy, who must be a barrister or solicitor of not less than seven years' standing, and two other members; the two other members are appointed from panels representing the interests of farmers and the owners of agricultural land respectively.[34]

Procedure before the Tribunals, such as the taking of evidence, the inspection of land and the service and forwarding of documents, is regulated by the Agricultural Land Tribunals and Notices to Quit Order, 1959,[35] as amended.

Good estate management

An owner (*prima facie* the person who holds the legal estate in fee simple; *ante*, pages 1–2) of agricultural land will fulfil his responsibilities to manage it in accordance with the rules of good estate management insofar as his management is reasonably adequate to enable an occupier of the land, who is reasonably skilled in husbandry, to maintain efficient production as regards the kind, quantity and quality of the produce. The character and situation of the land, and the extent to which the owner is providing, improving, maintaining and repairing the fixed equipment on the land are among the circumstances relevant to determining this; if the land is occupied by a person other than the owner, the owner's responsibilities do not include the duty to maintain and repair fixed equipment if it has been agreed that this responsibility shall fall upon the occupier. [36]

Good husbandry

The occupier of an agricultural holding fulfils his responsibilities to farm it in accordance with the rules of good husbandry so long as a reasonable standard of efficient production is being maintained with regard to both the kind of produce and the quantity and quality of the produce, at the same time keeping the holding in such condition as will enable similar standards to be maintained in the future; relevant circumstances include the character and situation of the land and the standard of management by the owner. [37] Without prejudice to the generality of the above, regard must be had to the extent to which:

(a)   permanent pasture is being properly mown or grazed and maintained in a good standard of cultivation and fertility and in good condition;

(b)   the manner in which arable land is being cropped is such as to maintain that land clean and in a good state of cultivation and fertility and in good condition;

(c)   the unit is properly stocked where the system of farming practised requires the keeping of livestock, and an efficient standard of management of livestock is maintained where livestock are kept and of breeding where the breeding of livestock is carried out;

(d)   the necessary steps are being taken to secure and maintain crops and livestock free from disease and from infestation by insects and other pests;

(e)   the necessary steps are being taken for the protection and preservation of crops harvested or lifted, or in course of being harvested or lifted;

(f)   the necessary work of maintenance and repair is being carried out. [38]

If the holding is occupied by a person other than the owner, that person is not obliged to carry out any work of maintenance or repair which it is the owner's duty to carry out in order to fulfil his responsibilities to manage in accordance with the rules of good estate management. [39]

Alteration of rent

Either landlord or tenant may by notice in writing served on the other party demand that an arbitration take place on the question of what rent shall be paid for the holding as from the next ensuing day on which the tenancy could have been determined by notice to quit given at the date of demanding the reference to arbitration;[40] the demand for arbitration must be worded in accordance with this provision. The reference of the rent to arbitration must actually take place within the year after the written demand for it has been served, and the date of the reference is the date on which the arbitrator is appointed to conduct it. [41]

The arbitrator may increase or reduce the rent or leave it unchanged. The rent properly payable is the rent at which, having regard to the terms of the tenancy (other than those relating to rent), the holding might reasonably be expected to be let in the open market by a willing landlord to a willing tenant, there being disregarded (in addition to the matters mentioned below) any effect on rent of the fact that the tenant who is a party to the arbitration is in occupation of the holding. [42] This not only places the rent on a market value basis but fixes it on a new tenant, as distinct from a sitting tenant, basis. The arbitrator must disregard any increase in rental value attributable to improvements carried out wholly or partly at the tenant's expense (whether or not the expense will be recouped from a government grant), unless the landlord gave an equivalent allowance or benefit in consideration of the improvements or the tenant was obliged to make the improvements by the terms of his contract of tenancy. [43] Moreover the continuous adoption by the tenant of a system of farming which is more beneficial to the holding than the system required by the contract of tenancy or, if no system is laid down by the contract, more beneficial than the system normally practised on comparable holdings, is deemed for this purpose to be an improvement executed at the tenant's expense. [44] The arbitrator must disregard any increase of rental value due to improvements carried out by the landlord insofar as these improvements are covered by a government grant. The rent must not be fixed at a lower amount because of dilapidations, deterioration or damage to buildings or land caused or permitted by the tenant. [45]

Reference of the rent to arbitration cannot be demanded if any resultant change of rent would take effect earlier than three years from the expiration of any of the following dates: the commencement of the tenancy, or the date when a previous alteration of rent (whether by agreement or arbitration) took effect or the date when an arbitrator's direction took effect that the rent should remain unchanged. [46] But this restriction on the right to demand arbitration does not apply to alterations of rent made by an arbitrator when drawing up the terms of a written tenancy agreement (*ante*, pages 44–5) or in recognition of a change in the burden of liability for the maintenance, repair or insurance of fixed equipment (*ante*, pages 45–6), nor to increases of rent consequent upon the landlord having carried out certain improvements (*post*, pages 51–2), nor reductions of rent due to his having resumed possession of part of the holding (*post*).

The Counter-Inflation (Agricultural Rents) (No.2) Order, 1973,[47] makes provision for restricting rent increases in relation to tenancies of agricultural holdings and other tenancies of agricultural land. The contents of the Order are not, however, likely to be durable.

Where the landlord resumes possession of part of the holding, either in consequence of a clause in the contract of tenancy entitling him to do so or of a valid notice to quit, the tenant is entitled to a reduction of rent proportionate to that part of the holding, and taking into account the depreciation in value to him of the part which he retains which is caused by the severance or the use to be made of the part severed; the amount of the reduction will be settled by arbitration. [48]

Increase of rental due to landlord's improvements

The landlord may charge an increased rent in respect of the following improvements carried out by him; an improvement carried out by agreement with, or at the request of, the tenant; a drainage improvement if landlord and tenant fail to agree the terms of compensation; a long-term new improvement (as set out in Part II of the Third Schedule to the Agricultural Holdings Act, 1948) carried out after the Agricultural Land Tribunal has consented; an improvement made in compliance with a direction given by the Minister under statutory powers; an improvement carried out in accordance with a provision included in an approved livestock rearing land improvement scheme at the request or with the consent of the tenant; the provision of sanitary or washing facilities for employees in compliance with a notice requiring this under the Agriculture (Safety, Health and Welfare) Provisions Act, 1956 (*post*, page 341); an improvement in the form of works for the supply of water to the holding executed in pursuance of directions or of an approved scheme; an improvement carried out in compliance with a direction given by the Agricultural Land Tribunal under section 4 of the Agriculture Act, 1958 (*ante*, pages 47–8). The landlord must serve notice of increase of rent on the tenant within six months after the improvement was completed. The rent can be increased by an amount equal to the increase in the rental value of the holding attributable to the making of the improvement, disregarding any part of the value of the improvement for which the landlord is reimbursed by a government grant. The rental increase can be charged from the date of completion of the improvement, and if the parties cannot agree concerning the increase the matter must be referred to arbitration. [49]

The ploughing of grassland

The ploughing of meadowland or of permanent pasture is *prima facie* an act of waste (*ante*, pages 4–5) and contrary to good husbandry, and thus will be restrained by injunction even though the tenancy does not expressly prohibit the ploughing; if however the ploughing is done to improve the meadow and does improve it, an injunction will not usually be granted. [50] The statutory right conferred by section 11 of the 1948 Act to practise any system of cropping which protects the holding from injury or deterioration (*ante*, pages 46–7) only applies to arable land.

But where the contract of tenancy of an agricultural holding provides for the maintenance of specified land or a specified proportion of the holding as permanent pasture, either party may by notice in writing demand a reference to arbitration under the Act as to whether it is expedient in order to secure the full and efficient farming of the holding that the amount of land required to be maintained as permanent pasture should be reduced. On such a reference the arbitrator may direct that the contract of tenancy shall have effect subject to such modifications of its provisions as to land which is to be maintained as permanent pasture or is to be treated as arable land, and as to cropping, as may be specified in the direction. If he directs a reduction in the area of land which under the contract of tenancy is to be maintained as permanent pasture, he may order that the contract of tenancy shall have effect as if it provided that on quitting the holding on the termination of the tenancy the tenant should leave as permanent pasture, or should leave as temporary pasture sown with seeds mixture of such kind as may be specified in the order, such area of land (in addition to the area of land required by the contract of tenancy, as modified by the direction, to be maintained as permanent pasture) as he may specify; the area of land required to be so left must not exceed the reduction in the area of permanent pasture ordered by the direction. [51]

There are complex statutory provisions under which the tenant may be entitled to statutory compensation for pasture laid down by him. [52] But no compensation is claimable by a tenant on any ground whatever for any pasture laid down in pursuance of an order made by an arbitrator consequent upon his direction reducing the area of land which under a contract of tenancy is to be maintained as permanent pasture. [53]

52

Right to require record of condition of holding to be made

Either party may, at any time during the tenancy, require a record to be made of the condition of the buildings, fences, gates, roads, drains and ditches on, and the cultivation of, the holding. The tenant may also require the making of a record of any improvements executed by him or in respect of which he, with the written consent of the landlord, paid compensation to an outgoing tenant; he may also require a record to be made of any fixtures which he is entitled to remove (*post*, pages 60–1). If the parties cannot agree on the person who is to make the record, the Minister will appoint that person; unless otherwise agreed the cost of making the record will be shared equally between the landlord and the tenant. [54]

Power to enter the holding

The landlord or any person authorised by him may at all reasonable times enter on the holding in order to view its state, or to fulfil the landlord's responsibilities to manage it in accordance with the rules of good estate management, or to provide or improve fixed equipment on the holding apart from those responsibilities. [55]

Any person authorised by the Minister may enter land at all reasonable times and inspect it for the purpose of deciding whether and how any powers conferred by the 1948 Act should be exercised in relation to the land or whether and how any direction given under the Act has been complied with; if so requested this person must produce documentary evidence of his authority in relation to the land. At least twenty-four hours notice of intention to enter as of right must first have been given. [56]

Damage to crops by game

If the tenant sustains damage to his crops from deer, pheasants, partridges, grouse or black game, and if the right to take and kill the game is vested neither in him nor in anyone claiming under him except the landlord, and if the tenant has not written permission to kill the game, he is entitled to be compensated by the landlord for this damage if it exceeds five pence per acre of the area over which the damage extends;[57] any agreement to the contrary is void. Written permission conferred on the tenant to kill any one of the specified kinds of game excludes compensation for damage caused by that kind. [58]

Unless the parties agree the amount of compensation after the damage was suffered, the amount must be determined by arbitration. No compensation is claimable unless notice in writing of the damage was given to the landlord within one month after the tenant became or ought reasonably to have become aware of the damage, and the landlord was given a reasonable opportunity to inspect it. Moreover written notice and particulars of the claim must have been given to the landlord within one month after the end of the calendar year, or such other twelve month period as is agreed between landlord and tenant, in respect of which the claim is made. [59]

Where the right to kill and take the game is vested in some person other than the landlord, the landlord is entitled to be indemnified by that person against all claims for compensation made as above. [60]

Security of tenure

As has already been seen (*ante*, pages 41–2), provision is made in the 1948 Act for the conversion of interests less than a tenancy from year to year into tenancies from year to year, and for the continuation of tenancies for terms of two years and upwards as tenancies from year to year, so that the tenant has the right to continue his tenancy until it is terminated in accordance with the notice to quit provisions of the Act.

Duration and service of notice to quit

Despite any agreement to the contrary, and whether given by landlord or tenant, a notice to quit the holding or part of the holding is invalid if it purports to end the tenancy before the expiration of twelve months from the end of the current year of the tenancy. This restriction does not however apply if a receiving order in bankruptcy is made against the tenant, or if the notice is given in pursuance of a clause in the contract of tenancy authorising the resumption of possession of the holding or some part of it for a specified purpose other than agriculture, or to a notice given by a tenant to a sub-tenant. [61]

A notice to quit the whole or part of the holding is duly given, as are other notices and requests under the Act, if delivered to the person to whom it is to be given, or left at his proper address or sent to him by registered post. [62] Service on the secretary or clerk of an incorporated company or body is service upon that company or body. [63] The proper address for the purpose of serving a notice is, in the case of the secretary or clerk of an incorporated company or body, its registered or principal office, and in any other case the last known address of the person in question. [64]

The effect of the notice to quit

Where notice to quit an agricultural holding or part of the holding is given to the tenant, and not later than one month from the giving of the notice to quit the tenant serves on the landlord a counter-notice in writing requiring that section 24(1) shall apply to the notice to quit, then, subject to the provisions of section 24(2) (*post*), the notice to quit shall not have effect unless the Agricultural Land Tribunal consents to its operation. [65] The above provision does not apply where:

(a)   the Agricultural Land Tribunal has consented to the operation of the notice to quit before it is given and that fact is stated in the notice; or

(b)   the notice to quit is given on the ground that the land is required for a non-agricultural use for which planning permission has either been granted or is not required, and that fact is stated in the notice; or

(c)   the Tribunal, on an application made not more than six months before the giving of the notice to quit, was satisfied that the tenant was not fulfilling his responsibilities to farm the holding in accordance with the rules of good husbandry and certified that it was so satisfied, and that fact is stated in the notice; or

(d)   at the date of the giving of the notice to quit the tenant has failed to comply with a notice in writing served on him by the landlord requiring him within two months from the service of the notice to pay any rent due in respect of the agricultural holding to which the notice to quit relates, or within such reasonable period as was specified in the notice to remedy any breach by the tenant that was capable of being remedied of any term or condition of his tenancy which was not inconsistent with the fulfilment of his responsibilities to farm in accordance with the rules of good husbandry, and it is stated in the notice to quit that it is given by reason of this; or

(e)   at the date of giving notice to quit the interest of the landlord in the holding to which the notice relates had been materially prejudiced by the commission by the tenant of a breach, which was not capable of being remedied, of any term or condition of the tenancy that was not inconsistent with the fulfilment by the tenant of his responsibilities to farm in accordance with the rules of good husbandry, and it is stated in the notice that it is given by reason of this; or

(f)   at the date of the giving of the notice to quit the tenant had become bankrupt or made a composition with his creditors, and it is stated in the notice that it is given by reason of this; or

(g)   the tenant with whom the contract of tenancy was made had died within three months before the date of the giving of the notice to quit, and it is stated in the notice that it is given by reason of this. [66]

The notice to quit given by the landlord must make it clear whether he is proceeding under section 24(1) or section 24(2). 'If a landlord desired to put himself in a position to take advantage of subsection (1) should he fail under subsection (2), the wise course would be to serve two notices to quit, one under subsection (1) and the other under subsection (2). What he could not do was to serve a notice which did not make it plain under which subsection he was intending to proceed'.[67]

'A landlord who means to give a notice to quit under section 24(1) of the Act of 1948 will, if he is wise, refrain from giving any reasons for doing so'. [68]

Where the notice is given under section 24(2) it is essential that the relevant ground should be identified in the notice without ambiguity.

As regards ground (c) above, the landlord may apply to the Agricultural Land Tribunal for a certificate that the tenant is not fulfilling his responsibilities to farm in accordance with the rules of good husbandry.[69] Procedure is governed by the Agricultural Land Tribunals and Notices to Quit Order. [70]

As regards paragraph (d) above, every notice served on the tenant requiring him to remedy a breach of the terms of the tenancy must be in a prescribed form and must specify the period within which the breach is to be remedied. If work of repair, maintenance or replacement is required by the notice the period must be a minimum of six months, and any further notice requiring the doing of any such work served on the tenant less than twelve months after the earlier notice is to be disregarded unless the earlier notice was withdrawn with the tenant's agreement in writing.[71] The appropriate forms are set out in the Agriculture (Forms of Notices to Remedy) Regulations, 1964.[72]

In *Stoneman* v. *Brown* [73] the tenant of a market garden was served with a notice under paragraph (d) above requiring him to pay an overdue instalment of rent; the tenant did not pay this rent until more than two months after receipt of the notice, but did so before notice to quit was served on him. It was held that once the tenant allowed the two months to expire without payment, his statutory security of tenure was lost even if he paid before the notice to quit was actually given.

A tenant who wishes to contest that

(a) the land is required for a use, other than for agriculture, for which planning permission has been granted or is not required; or

(b)   the tenant had failed to comply with a notice by the landlord requiring him to pay rent due or to remedy a breach of covenant; or

(c)   the landlord's interest has been materially prejudiced by a breach of covenant not capable of being remedied

must, within one month of the service of the notice to quit, serve on the landlord notice in writing requiring the question to be determined by arbitration;[74] the operation of the notice to quit is suspended until the termination of the arbitration. The Lord Chancellor may by order provide for any question arising under section 24(2) to be determined by arbitration;[75] the arbitration will take place in accordance with section 77 and the Sixth Schedule of the 1948 Act.

If a notice to remedy served under paragraph (d) above requires the doing of any work of repair, maintenance or replacement it is termed a 'Notice to do work'; if the notice specifies several breaches of the terms of the tenancy as requiring to be remedied, it is not enough for the tenant to remedy some of them.[76] If he wishes to contest liability under his tenancy for any work specified in the notice, he must within one month after receipt of the notice to do work serve on the landlord a notice in writing specifying the grounds on which and the items in respect of which he denies liability and requiring the question to be determined by arbitration under the 1948 Act.[77]

The tenant cannot wait until he receives notice to quit and then raise the issue of his liability to do the work as this matter is only capable of being decided by an arbitration required within one month after receipt of the notice to do work.

As regards paragraph (g) above (death of the tenant, with whom the contract of tenancy was made, within three months before the giving of notice to quit), if the contract of tenancy was made with two or more persons jointly the notice to quit can be served within three months of the death of the survivor or last survivor of them.[78] Where a tenancy of an agricultural holding has been assigned the landlord may serve a notice to quit on the assignee within three months of the original tenant's death and no counter-notice can be served by the assignee.[79]

In *Costagliola* v. *Bunting*[80] the tenant of the land died in 1932 and his widow continued in possession of the land as his personal representative (*post*, page 120) until her death in 1956. It was held that a notice to quit stated to be given by reason of her death within three months beforehand was invalid, since the widow had been in possession as personal representative and was not the tenant 'with whom the contract of tenancy was made' unless a new contract of tenancy had been made between herself and the landlord, and on the facts no new contract of tenancy had been made.

In *Jenkin R. Lewis and Son Ltd.* v. *Kerman*[81] assignments took place, after a lease of agricultural land had been created, of the tenant's interest on the one hand and the landlord's interest on the other, and various revisions of rent were agreed. The present landlord served notice to quit on the present assignee on the ground that the original tenant had died within three months before the giving of the notice. The present assignee of the land contested its validity on the ground that the original tenant was not the person with whom the contract of tenancy under which the current assignee held the land had been made, in that a new tenancy agreement with a later tenant had come into existence upon the making of the rental revisions. The court held that the new rental agreements did not on the facts show any intention to create a new tenancy but rather to continue the old tenancy, and that a mere agreement for a rental increase did not necessarily result in a new tenancy, hence the notice to quit served on the death of the original tenant was valid. It was further held that a revision of the rent of an agricultural holding such as is envisaged by section 8 of the 1948 Act (*ante*, pages 49—51) (whether the revision is settled by arbitration or by agreement) does not of itself involve the creation of a new contract of tenancy; as this was a letting subject to and within the framework of the Agricultural Holdings Acts, the possibility of a rental revision conferred by the statute was something inherent in the lease itself.

As regards the consent of the Agricultural Land Tribunal under section 24 (*ante*, page 55) to the notice to quit, the Tribunal must withhold consent to the notice unless satisfied as to one or more of the following matters specified by the landlord in his application for consent, *viz*:

(a) that the carrying out of the purpose for which the landlord proposes to terminate the tenancy is desirable in the interests of good husbandry as respects the land to which the notice relates, treated as a separate unit; or
(b) that to carry out that purpose is desirable in the interests of sound management of the estate of which the land to which the notice relates forms part or which that land constitutes; or
(c) that to carry it out is desirable for the purposes of agricultural research, education, experiment or demonstration, or for the purposes of enactments relating to smallholdings or allotments; or
(d) that greater hardship would be caused by withholding than by giving

consent to the operation of the notice; or

(e)   that the landlord proposes to terminate the tenancy for the purpose of the land being used for a use, other than for agriculture, not falling within paragraph (b) of section 24(2) (*ante*, page 55).

Even though satisfied concerning the above matters, the Tribunal must nevertheless withhold consent to the operation of the notice to quit if in all the circumstances it appears to them that a fair and reasonable landlord would not insist on possession. [82]

The procedure on applications for consent is governed by the Agricultural Land Tribunals and Notices to Quit Order, 1959. [83]

In *Davies* v. *Price* [84] an Agricultural Land Tribunal agreed to the operation of a notice to quit because 'the landlords have satisfied the tribunal that it is in the interests of efficient farming of the land in question to terminate the tenancy of the appellant'. Parker L. J. held that 'This provision [paragraphs (a) and (b) *ante*] in section 25. . . involves a comparison between what I may call the present régime under the existing tenant and the proposed régime which will appertain in future if the tenancy is terminated. . . The less efficiently the land is being farmed by the existing tenant, the easier it will be for the landlord to say that the proposed user, if the tenancy is terminated, will be more efficient. But it seems to me that a landlord must give some evidence of the proposed user and the tribunal can then and must proceed to make a comparison'.

Landlord contracting to sell the holding after giving notice to quit

If notice to quit land comprised in an agricultural holding is given to the tenant, and at any time during the currency of the notice a contract is made to sell the landlord's interest in the land or any part of it, then the notice to quit becomes void unless within three months before the making of the contract of sale the landlord and tenant agree in writing that the notice shall be valid or within one month after the contract of sale the tenant elects in writing to the landlord that the notice shall be valid. [85]

Notice to quit part of the holding

Although at common law notice to quit only part of the premises let is invalid, yet in the case of an agricultural holding let on a yearly tenancy such a notice is not invalid if given in order to adjust the boundaries between agricultural units or to amalgamate the whole or parts of such units, or in order that the land may be used for a variety of objects including the erection of farm labourers' cottages or other houses with or without gardens, the provision of gardens for farm labourers' cottages or other houses, the provision of allotments or smallholdings, and the planting of trees. The landlord's notice to quit part of the premises must state the permitted object in pursuance of which it is given. [86]

The tenant is entitled to receive compensation for quitting the part, and to a proportionate reduction of rent which takes into account any depreciation in the value to him of the rest of his holding caused by the severance or by the use to be made of the part severed; alternatively the tenant is entitled, within twenty-eight days after the giving of the notice to quit, to serve on the landlord a written counter-notice stating that the tenant accepts the notice as a notice to quit the entire holding, and if so the notice to quit will operate accordingly. [87]

If the landlord has severed his reversion (i.e. where he has parted with the whole of his reversionary interest in only part of the land comprised in the tenancy), a person entitled to a severed part of the reversion may serve notice on the tenant to quit the whole of that severed part; an agricultural tenant thus served with notice to quit may within twenty-eight days thereafter serve on the persons separately entitled to the severed parts of the reversion a written notice that he accepts the notice to quit as a notice to quit the entire holding. [88]

Prohibition of removal of manure and certain crops after notice to end the tenancy

Where notice to terminate the tenancy of an agricultural holding is given either by the landlord or the tenant, the tenant must not, unless there is written agreement to the contrary, thereafter sell or remove from the holding any manure or compost or any hay, straw or roots grown in the last year of the tenancy unless the landlord consents in writing to this being done;[89] (this will only operate if the tenant actually quits in consequence of the notice).

Tenant's right to remove fixtures

Judicial decision shows that a tenant is not, so far as case law is concerned, entitled to remove fixtures (see *ante*, pages 18–19) erected by him for agricultural purposes. [90] But, by section 13 of the 1948 Act, where the tenant affixes to his agricultural holding or acquires any engine, machinery, fencing or other fixture, or erects or acquires any building for which he is not entitled to compensation, and the fixture or building is not so affixed or erected pursuant to some obligation to do so or instead of some fixture or building belonging to the landlord, then the tenant is entitled to remove such a fixture or building either during the continuance of the tenancy or before the expiration of two months after the tenancy expires. However this right of removal is only exercisable on the following conditions. The tenant must first have paid all rent owing by him and satisfied all his other obligations to the landlord. He must not do any avoidable damage when removing the fixture or building, and must make good all damage which he does by the removal. At least one month before both the exercise of the right of removal and before the end of the tenancy, the tenant must have given written notice to the landlord of his intention to remove the fixture or building, and within that month the landlord may by written notice to the tenant elect to purchase any fixture or building comprised in the notice at its value to an incoming tenant. It is, however, permissible by agreement between landlord and tenant to exclude the above statutory rules relating to fixtures and buildings, and if any custom exists entitling the tenant to remove fixtures he may act in accordance with the custom and without regard to the statute.

Compensation for the departing tenant

The departing tenant may be entitled to compensation either by agreement with his landlord, by custom or by statute; in practice this matter is nowadays almost wholly regulated by statute.

If notice to quit is given or a written agreement to surrender possession is made on or after 1 March 1948, and the tenant leaves the holding on or after 30 July 1948, the rules as to compensation contained in the Agricultural Holdings Act, 1948, will apply. If only part of the holding is quitted, the statutory rules regarding compensation will in general apply to that part. No compensation is payable in respect of anything done in pursuance of an order made consequent upon an arbitrator's direction reducing the area of land in the holding which is required to be maintained as permanent pasture (*ante*, page 52; section 63(1)).

A landlord or tenant who is entitled to compensation under the 1948 Act cannot be debarred from it by contrary agreement. [91] In *Coates* v. *Diment* [92] a clause in the tenancy agreement purporting to give the landlord the right to re-enter without notice on such of the land as he might later require for specified purposes was held to be a void clause, as its effect would be to prevent the tenant from claiming compensation under certain heads, since it would prevent him giving notice, as required by the Act,[93] before the end of the tenancy of his intention to claim compensation.

Improvements made by the tenant are mostly divided for legal purposes into improvements begun before 1 March 1948 and those made after that date. As regards those begun before 1 March 1948, the measure of statutory compensation is the value of the improvement to an incoming tenant.[94] The improvements specified in Part I of the Second Schedule do not carry a right to compensation unless the landlord had given his prior written consent to the carrying out of the improvements; there are numerous other detailed rules[95] too lengthy for inclusion in the body of the text in a work of this nature; the relevant extracts from the Second, Third, Fourth and Fifth Schedules as amended are, however, printed as Appendix III.

As regards improvements begun on or after 1 March 1948, the tenant is usually entitled on quitting the holding to obtain compensation for these and for the tenant-right matters set out in Part II of the Fourth Schedule to the 1948 Act; it is immaterial whether the tenant himself entered into occupation of the holding before or after 1 March 1948, but if he did so beforehand he is not entitled to compensation in respect of the tenant-right matters in Part II of the Fourth Schedule unless before the end of the tenancy he gives written notice to the landlord stating his election that the Schedule is to apply to him as regards those matters.[96]

A tenant who remains on the holding during a succession of tenancies does not lose his right to statutory compensation for improvements begun by him on or after 1 March 1948 merely by reason of the fact that the improvements were made during a tenancy other than the one at the end of which he quits the holding.[97]

A tenant who on his entry paid to the outgoing tenant, with the written consent of the landlord, any compensation payable by the landlord in respect of the whole or part of an improvement begun since 1 March 1948, or who paid to the landlord himself the amount of compensation payable to an outgoing tenant, is entitled when he quits to claim compensation for this in the same way as the outgoing tenant would have been entitled had he remained tenant and quitted the holding at the same time as the tenant himself quits.[98] Further, a tenant who on entry paid to the landlord any sum in respect of the whole or part of such an improvement is entitled, unless otherwise agreed in writing with the landlord, to claim compensation on quitting the holding in the same way, if at all, as he would have been entitled if he had been tenant when the improvement was carried out and the improvement or part of it had been carried out by him.[99] Government grants received are to be taken into account in assessing the statutory compensation for such improvements.[100]

The amount of compensation pavable for improvements of a long-term character begun on or after 1 March 1948 is the increase attributable to the improvement in the value of the agricultural holding as a holding, having regard to its character and situation and the average requirements of tenants reasonably skilled in husbandry;[101] these improvements are set out in the Third Schedule of the 1948 Act. In general the tenant is not entitled to be compensated for such improvements unless the landlord gave his written consent to them either unconditionally or upon such terms as to compensation or otherwise as may be agreed in writing between them; if the written agreement deals with the compensation, the measure of compensation is regulated by the agreement. [102]

But as regards such long-term improvements as are begun on or after 1 March 1948, and are specified in Part II of the Third Schedule, a tenant aggrieved by the landlord's refusal to consent to the improvement or by the terms which the landlord wishes to impose may, after giving written notice of his intention to the landlord, apply to the Agricultural Land Tribunal for approval to his carrying out the improvement. After giving both parties the chance to make representations, the Agricultural Land Tribunal may approve the carrying out of the improvement either unconditionally or on such terms as seem just, or may withhold approval. If approval is granted the landlord may within one month thereafter serve written notice on the Tribunal and on the tenant that he himself proposes to carry out the improvement; unless the landlord does this, or if the landlord fails to carry out the improvement within a reasonable time despite notifying his intention to do so, the Tribunal's approval takes effect as if it were consent given in writing by the landlord on such terms as the Tribunal imposes. [103]

The measure of compensation under the Act for short-term improvements begun on or after 1 March 1948 is their value to an incoming tenant calculated in accordance with the method prescribed by regulations;[104] these improvements are specified in Part I of the Fourth Schedule to the 1948 Act. Compensation for the tenant-right matters specified in Part II of the Fourth Schedule is governed similarly, [105] but should a written contract of tenancy specify the measure of compensation for those tenant-right matters then that measure will prevail. [106]

Compensation for tenants of market gardens

The tenant of a market garden has all the rights of the tenant of an agricultural holding, because the definition of 'agriculture' in section 94 of the Agricultural Holdings Act, 1948, includes the use of land as market gardens, provided it is used for the purposes of a trade or business in accordance with section 1. It has been held that growing bulbs is not market gardening.[107] There are certain special and detailed rules in the Act relating to market gardens.[108]

Tenant's right to compensation for disturbance and reorganisation

Compensation for disturbance may be claimable by the tenant if he quits the holding in consequence of a notice to quit served on him by the landlord, or in consequence of a counter-notice given by the tenant under section 32 of the 1948 Act after receiving notice to quit part of the holding under section 31 (*ante*, pages 59–60). But this compensation cannot be claimed where the notice to quit was one in respect of which the right to serve a counter-notice was excluded under section 24(2) (*ante*, pages 55–6) by virtue of obtaining a certificate of bad husbandry, or failure to comply with a notice to pay rent due or to remedy a breach of a term or condition of the tenancy, or the bankruptcy of or compounding with the creditors of the tenant, or the death of the tenant with whom the contract of tenancy was made within three months prior to the notice to quit.[109]

The compensation for disturbance is the sum representing such loss or expense directly attributable to the quitting of the holding as the tenant unavoidably incurs upon or in connection with the sale or removal of his household goods, implements of husbandry, fixtures, farm produce or farm stock on or used in connection with the holding; it includes any expenses reasonably incurred by him in the preparation of his claim for compensation except the costs of an arbitration to determine the right to or amount of the compensation. Compensation is payable, without any proof by the tenant of such loss or expense, at an amount equal to one year's rent of the holding at the rate at which rent was payable immediately before the termination of the tenancy; the tenant may not claim more than this unless before the sale of the goods, implements, fixtures, produce or stock he gave the landlord a reasonable opportunity of making a valuation, and gave written notice at least one month before the termination of the tenancy of his intention to make such a claim, and in such case the compensation must not exceed two years' rent.[110]

Where the tenancy terminates because the tenant, having received a valid notice to quit part of the holding under Section 31, serves a counter-notice accepting the notice as notice to quit the whole (*ante*, pages 59–60), then if the part of the holding affected by the landlord's notice is less than one-quarter of the original holding, and the rest of the holding

64

is reasonably capable of being farmed as a separate holding, compensation for disturbance is restricted to that part of the holding to which the notice to quit relates.[111]

Where compensation for disturbance is payable, then notwithstanding any contrary agreement an additional sum equal to four times the annual rent of the holding (or in the case of part of the holding four times the appropriate part of the rent) is payable by the landlord to the tenant to assist in the reorganisation of the tenant's affairs except in the following circumstances. [112] This sum is not payable if:

(a) the Agricultural Land Tribunal has consented to the operation of the notice to quit and stated in its reasons that it is satisfied as to any of the statutory grounds of consent relating to good husbandry, sound estate management, use for research or smallholdings, or hardship, and a statement of the reasons is included in the notice to quit; or

(b) the notice to quit contains a statement that the carrying out of the purpose for which the landlord proposes to terminate the tenancy is desirable on any of those grounds other than hardship and, if an application for consent to the operation of the notice is made to the Agricultural Land Tribunal, the Tribunal does so consent and states in the reasons for its decision that it is satisfied as to any of those grounds; or

(c) the notice to quit states that the landlord will suffer hardship unless the notice has effect and, if such an application as aforesaid is made in respect of the notice, the Tribunal consents to its operation and states in the reasons for its decision that it is satisfied that greater hardship would be caused by withholding consent than by giving it; or

(d) the restrictions on the operation of notices to quit do not apply to the notice by virtue of special provisions contained in the Agriculture Act, 1967, regarding the amalgamation or reshaping of agricultural units. These exceptions do not apply, and therefore the additional reorganisation compensation is payable, where the reasons given by the Tribunal for its consent include its being satisfied that the landlord proposes to terminate the tenancy for the purpose of the land being used for a non-agricultural purpose of a kind which does not exclude the counter-notice procedure, or where the reasons given include its being satisfied that to carry out the purpose for which the landlord proposes to terminate the tenancy is desirable in the interests of sound estate management and its decision contains a statement that it would have been satisfied that the landlord proposed to terminate the tenancy for such a non-agricultural purpose had that matter been specified in the application for its consent. [113]

A sum paid as reorganisation compensation is not taxable in the hands of the recipient; it seems that the landlord will be unable to obtain tax relief on the amount paid unless the expenditure can be brought within the head of 'management' (*post*, page 146).

Where the tenancy of an agricultural holding or part of it terminates by reason of a notice to quit under a provision authorising the resumption of possession for some specified non-agricultural purpose and the tenant quits the holding or part in consequence, then compensation, additional to any other compensation, is payable by the landlord to the tenant of an amount equal to the value of the additional benefit, if any, which would have accrued to the tenant if the tenancy had been terminated by the notice to quit on the expiration of twelve months from the end of the year of the tenancy current when notice was given. [114]

Compensation for tenant having adopted an especially beneficial system of farming

If the tenant can show that by his having continuously adopted a system of farming more beneficial to the holding than was required by his contract of tenancy, or, if the contract of tenancy was silent on the point, than the system normally practised on comparable agricultural holdings, the value of the holding as such has been increased during his tenancy, he will be entitled to compensation from his landlord for this increase in value when he leaves the holding; in assessing the increase in value regard must be had to the character and situation of the holding and the average requirements of tenants reasonably skilled in husbandry. This compensation is only claimable if a record of the condition of the holding had been made under section 16 (*ante*, page 53), and if the tenant had given written notice to the landlord of his intention to claim compensation at least one month before the end of his tenancy; [115] presumably the value at the date when the record was made is the starting-point for the assessment of any increase.

Due allowance must be made for any compensation agreed or awarded to the tenant for the improvements specified in the Second and Third Schedules and Part I of the Fourth Schedule and for the matters specified in Part II of the Fourth Schedule, [116] and the section does not entitle the tenant to any compensation in respect of these matters to which he would not be entitled apart from the section. [117]

General points concerning the tenant's claim

Compensation is payable to a tenant under the Act only when his tenancy has terminated and when he has quitted the holding. The landlord, who is responsible under the Act for payment of the compensation, is defined as 'any person for the time being entitled to receive the rents and profits of [the] land'.[118] It is important to know who the landlord is because not only is he the person responsible for the payment of compensation but also because notices under the Act must be given to him. By section 92(5) the tenant may serve upon or deliver any notice to the person who has been hitherto entitled to the rents and profits of the holding until he is informed that such person is no longer entitled to the rents and profits and is given notice of the name and address of the new landlord.

Compensation of landlord for deterioration of the holding

When the tenant quits the holding at the end of his tenancy, the landlord is entitled to recover from him compensation for any dilapidation or deterioration of or damage to any part of the holding or anything on it which is caused by the tenant's failure to fulfil his responsibilities to farm in accordance with the rules of good husbandry.[119] The amount of the compensation is the cost, reckoned at the time of the tenant leaving the holding, of making good the dilapidation, deterioration or damage.[120] Alternatively the landlord can claim compensation under section 57(3) in respect of the above matters under the written contract of tenancy if its terms entitle him to do so, but can only do this when the tenant quits the holding at the end of his tenancy. But in *Kent* v. *Conniff*[121] it was held that section 57(3), correctly interpreted, does not prevent the landlord claiming damages from the tenant during the continuance of the tenancy for breach of covenant to repair; the amount claimable will be subject to the restriction imposed by section 15 (*ante*, page 44). In *Boyd* v. *Wilton*[122] the landlord served notice at the end of the tenancy containing claims for compensation both under the contract of tenancy and under section 57(1) of the 1948 Act; at the arbitration the landlord abandoned his claims except those arising under the tenancy agreement. It was held that claims to compensation can be made in the alternative, provided the landlord at some later stage elects which alternative he wishes to pursue.

Where a landlord can show, on the tenant's quitting the holding on the termination of the tenancy, that the value of the holding has been generally reduced whether by reason of dilapidation, deterioration or damage as set out in section 57(1) or otherwise by the tenant's non-fulfilment of his responsibilities to farm in accordance with the rules of good husbandry, he is under section 58 entitled to recover from the tenant compensation, insofar as he is not compensated under section 57(1) or, in accordance with section 57(3), under the contract of tenancy, of an amount equal to the decrease attributable thereto in the value of the holding as a holding, having regard to its character and situation, and to the average requirements of tenants reasonably skilled in husbandry. Under section 58 compensation can be recovered for general deterioration of the holding over and above compensation for making good the specific matters set out in section 57, but any compensation recovered under section 57 must be brought into account so that the landlord does not recover twice over. The landlord cannot recover compensation under section 58 unless he has, not less than one month before the termination of the tenancy, given a written notice to the tenant of his intention to claim such compensation; such a notice is not required for a claim for particular compensation under section 57.

Where the tenant has remained on the holding during two or more tenancies, the landlord does not lose his right to claim compensation under either section 57 or section 58 in respect of any dilapidation, deterioration or damage merely because this occurred during a tenancy of that tenant other than that at the end of which he quits the holding. [123]

In order to enable the landlord to prove that there has been a general deterioration in the holding, it is clearly advantageous that a record of the condition of the holding should have been made under section 16 (*ante*, page 53).

Procedure for settlement of claims

Unless a particular provision of the 1948 Act states to the contrary, any claim based on custom, agreement or the Act and made by either landlord or tenant against each other and arising on or out of the ending of the tenancy of the agricultural holding or part of it must be settled by arbitration under the Act. [124] Such a claim will be invalid unless before the expiration of two months from the end of the tenancy, or, if the tenant lawfully remains in occupation of part of the holding after the ending of the tenancy and the claim relates to that part, from the end of his occupation, the claimant has served written notice on the other party of his intention to make the claim. The notice must specify the nature of the claim, but it is sufficient if the notice refers to the statutory provision, custom or term of an agreement under which the claim is made. [125]

The parties may within four months after the end of the tenancy or, where the tenant remains in lawful occupation after the end of the tenancy of that part of the holding to which his claim relates, after the end of his occupation, settle the claim by agreement in writing. The Minister may extend this period by a maximum of two successive periods of two months, but if the claim has not been settled within that time it ceases to be enforceable unless within one month thereafter or such extended period as the Minister may allow the parties appoint an arbitrator or one of them applies for an arbitrator to be appointed. [126]

A single arbitrator will determine the matter, [127] and if the parties cannot agree concerning his appointment the arbitrator will be appointed by the Minister. Within fourteen days after his appointment the parties must deliver to him a statement with particulars of their cases; at the hearing before the arbitrator the parties will be confined to the matters set out in their statements and particulars unless the arbitrator allows amendments or additions. At the hearing the parties must submit to being examined by the arbitrator either on oath or affirmation [i.e. statement made by someone who does not wish to take the oath], and must produce all samples and documents within their power if so required; witnesses shall, if the arbitrator thinks fit, be examined on oath or affirmation. The arbitrator may, and must if the County Court so directs on the application of either party, state a case for the opinion of the County Court upon any point of law which arises during the arbitration; this opinion will bind the arbitrator. The arbitrator must make and sign his award within fifty-six days of his appointment or such longer period as the Minister directs. [128]

The costs of the arbitration are in the arbitrator's discretion, but the arbitrator must take into consideration the reasonableness or unreasonableness of the conduct of the parties, and may disallow such costs as he considers to have been unnecessarily incurred by either landlord or tenant. [129]

If any sum agreed to be paid by either landlord or tenant or awarded as compensation or costs is not paid within fourteen days after the payment becomes due (which in the case of an award must not be later than one month after delivery of the award), [130] payment can be enforced by obtaining a County Court order to that effect. [131]

Where an amount becomes due to a tenant of an agricultural holding in respect of compensation from the landlord, and the landlord fails to discharge this liability within one month thereafter, the tenant is entitled to obtain from the Minister an order charging the holding with payment of the amount due. [132]

Agricultural dwellings

A tenancy of a dwelling house is not a tenancy given statutory security of tenure under the Rent Act, 1968, provided the dwelling house is comprised in an agricultural holding within the meaning of the Agricultural Holdings Act, 1948, and is occupied by the person responsible for the control (whether as tenant or as servant or agent of the tenant) of the farming of the holding. [133]

Recovery of possession of dwelling occupied by an agricultural employee

The statutory security of tenure afforded by the Rent Acts, in consequence of which it is very difficult for the owner to regain possession of a dwelling house which he has let, is only applicable where a tenancy has been created, and does not protect a person who is only a licensee (*ante*, page 32). The fact that part of the remuneration of an employee takes the form of granting him a right to occupy a house in order that he may more conveniently carry out his work, and that a money value is placed upon this right, does not rule out the possibility that he is only a licensee.[134] An employee may be a service occupier, which means that he is a licensee holding under a particular type of licence whereby he is required to live in the house in order to facilitate the better performance of his duties; this can apply to a farm worker. [135] A service occupancy can however only arise if the employer expressly and with reason requires the employee to reside in the particular premises in order to secure the better performance of the employee's duties, or where the circumstances make it necessary [136] or perhaps overwhelmingly convenient [137] that he should do so.

A 'protected tenancy', carrying security of tenure, is a term covering most tenancies of dwelling houses, [138] but it does not include the interest held by a licensee or by a service occupier.

If a tenancy, as distinct from a mere licence, has been created in favour of an employee, the landlord may nevertheless succeed in regaining possession if (a) the court thinks it reasonable to award the landlord possession, and (b) the house is reasonably required by the landlord for occupation as a residence by some person who is either engaged in the wholetime employment of the landlord or of some tenant of the landlord, or is a person with whom, conditional on housing accommodation being provided, a contract for such employment has been made; moreover the existing tenant whom it is now sought to evict must have been in the employment of the landlord or of a former landlord, the house must have been let to him in consequence of that employment and the employment must now have ceased. [139] The landlord therefore cannot begin proceedings to recover possession on this ground until he has entered into a contract (which could be made conditional upon recovery of possession) with the new employee, although possession will not be obtained, at the earliest, until the court has given judgement in the litigation.

The court may, and sometimes must, suspend an order for possession of premises occupied by a person who is holding over after the end either of his tenancy (not being a tenancy with statutory security of tenure) or of a period during which, otherwise than as a tenant, he had exclusive possession of the premises under the terms of his employment, if in either case he occupied the premises under the terms of his employment as a person employed in agriculture. The protection also extends to a widow or widower residing with the tenant at the tenant's death or, if the tenant left no such widow or widower, any member of the tenant's family so residing. Without prejudice to any other power to postpone or suspend a possession order, if the court makes an order for possession it may suspend the execution of the order on such terms and conditions as it thinks reasonable. [140] Moreover if the order for possession is made within the period of six months after the date when the former tenancy or period of exclusive possession came to an end, then (without prejudice to any other power to postpone or suspend for any period) the court must suspend the execution of the order, on such terms as it thinks reasonable, for the remainder of the period of six months, unless the court considers that it would be reasonable not to do so and is satisfied either:

(a)   that other suitable accommodation is, or will within the period be made, available to the occupier or (b) that the efficient management of any agricultural land or the efficient carrying on of any agricultural operations would be seriously prejudiced unless the premises are available for occupation by a person employed or to be employed by the owner or (c)   that greater hardship would be caused by the suspension of the order until the end of the period than by its execution within the period; or (d)   that the occupier, or any person residing or lodging with him, has been causing damage to the premises or been guilty of nuisance or annoyance to persons occupying other premises. If in proceedings for recovery of possession the court makes an order for possession but suspends its execution under these provisions, the court must make no order for costs, unless it thinks, having regard to the conduct of the owner or the occupier, that there are special reasons for making such an order. [141] 'The occupier' means the tenant under the former tenancy, or the widow or widower of the tenant under the former tenancy residing with him at his death or, if the former tenant leaves no such widow or widower, any member of his family residing with him at his death. [142]

Recovery of possession of dwelling once occupied by an agricultural employee

Where a dwelling house which has at any time been occupied by a person under the terms of his employment as a person employed in agriculture is let on a 'regulated tenancy' (the definition[143] of this is complex, but includes most tenancies) and the landlord would, apart from the security of tenure conferred by the Rent Act on most occupiers of dwellings, be entitled to recover possession of it, the court must make an order for possession if:

(a)   the tenant neither is nor at any time was so employed by the landlord and is not the widow of the person so employed; and

(b)   not later than the 'relevant date' (in most instances the date of commencement of the regulated tenancy in question),[144] the tenant was given notice in writing that possession might be recovered under this provision; and

(c)   the court is satisfied that the dwelling house is required for occupation by a person employed or to be employed by the landlord in agriculture.

The court must also order possession of a dwelling house subject to a regulated tenancy of which, apart from the security of tenure conferred by the Rent Act on most occupiers of dwellings, the landlord would be entitled to recover possession, if:

(a)   the last occupier of the dwelling house before the relevant date (see above) was a person, or the widow of a person, who was at some time during his occupation responsible for the control of the farming of the land which formed, together with the dwelling house, an agricultural unit; and

(b)   the tenant is neither a person nor the widow of a person who is or has at any time been responsible for the control of the farming of any part of the land nor a person nor the widow of a person who is or at any time was employed by the landlord in agriculture; and

(c)   the creation of the tenancy was not preceded by the carrying out of an amalgamation approved for the purposes of a scheme; and

(d)   not later than the relevant date the tenant was given notice in writing that possession might be recovered under this provision; and

(e)   the court is satisfied that the dwelling house is required for occupation either by a person responsible or to be responsible for the control of the farming of any part of the land or by a person employed or to be employed by the landlord in agriculture. Where the relevant date was

72

before 9 August 1972, proceedings for possession must be commenced by the landlord within five years from the date on which the last occupier before the relevant date went out of possession. [145]

Notes

1   Agricultural Holdings Act, 1948, section 1(2).
2   Section 94(1).
3   Section 1(1).
4   [1954] 2 Q.B. 171.
5   [1951] 1 K.B. 614.
6   [1950] 2 All E.R. 685.
7   *Reid* v. *Dawson* [1955] 1 Q.B. 214.
8   [1971] 1 All E.R. 1042.
9   Section 1(1); *ante*, page 39.
10   [1964] 1 All E.R. 867.
11   *Per* Harman L.J.
12   [1950] 1 K.B. 708.
13   Section 2(1).
14   Section 3.
15   *Gladstone* v. *Bower* [1960] 2 Q.B. 384.
16   [1916] 2 K.B. 91.
17   Section 15.
18   Section 5.
19   Agriculture (Maintenance, Repair and Insurance of Fixed Equipment) Regulations, 1948, S.I. 1948 No. 184.
20   Section 6(2).
21   Section 7(1).
22   Section 7(2).
23   Section 7(3).
24   Section 7(5).
25   Agriculture Act, 1970, sections 37, 64, Schedule 4.
26   Agricultural Holdings Act, 1948, section 11(1).
27   Section 11(5).
28   Section 11(4).
29   Section 11(2).
30   Section 11(3); Agriculture Act, 1958, section 8(1) and First Schedule.
31   Hill Farming Act, 1946, section 21(1); Agriculture Act, 1958, section 8, Schedule 1.

[32] Agriculture Act, 1958, section 4, extending Agricultural Holdings Act, 1948, section 9; *post*, pages 51—2.

[33] Agriculture (Areas for Agricultural Land Tribunals) Order 1959, S.I. 1959 No. 83 as amended.

[34] Agriculture Act, 1947, section 73(2) and Schedule 9; Agriculture Act, 1958, section 8(1) and Schedule 1.

[35] S.I. 1959 No. 81.

[36] Agriculture Act, 1947, section 10.

[37] Agriculture Act, 1947, section 11(1).

[38] Section 11(2).

[39] Section 11(3).

[40] Section 8.

[41] *Sclater* v. *Horton* [1954] 2 Q.B. 1.

[42] Agricultural Holdings Act, 1948, section 8(1), as substituted by Agriculture Act, 1958, section 2.

[43] Section 8(2).

[44] Section 8(4).

[45] Section 8(2).

[46] Section 8(3).

[47] The Counter-Inflation Act, 1973, sections 11. 23(2) and Schedule 3; The Counter-Inflation (Agricultural Rents) (No. 2) Order 1973 S.I. 1973 No. 1717.

[48] Agricultural Holdings Act, 1948, section 33.

[49] Agricultural Holdings Act, 1948, section 9(1), as amended by Agriculture Act, 1958, section 4.

[50] *Simmons* v. *Norton* (1831) 7 Bing. 640.

[51] Agricultural Holdings Act, 1948, section 10, as substituted by Agriculture Act, 1958, Schedule 1.

[52] Agricultural Holdings Act, 1948, sections 35—37, 41—47, 51—55, Second and Fourth Schedules.

[53] Section 63 as amended by Agriculture Act, 1958, section 8(1) and First Schedule.

[54] Section 16.

[55] Section 17.

[56] Section 91.

[57] Section 14.

[58] *Ross* v. *Watson*, [1943] S.C. 406.

[59] Section 14.

[60] Section 14(3).

[61] Section 23(1).

[62] Section 92(1).

63 Section 92(2).

64 Section 92(4).

65 Section 24(1), as amended by Agriculture Act, 1958, section 8(1) and First Schedule.

66 Section 24(2), as amended by Agriculture Act, 1958, section 8(1) and First Schedule.

67 *Per* Salmon L.J. (citing *Cowan* v. *Wrayford* [1953] 1 W.L.R. 1340) in *Mills* v. *Edwards* [1971] 2 W.L.R. 418.

68 *Per* Cross L.J. in *Mills* v. *Edwards, ante.*

69 Section 27, as amended by Agriculture Act, 1958, section 8(1) and First Schedule.

70 1959, S.I. 1959 No. 81.

71 Agriculture (Miscellaneous Provisions) Act, 1963, section 19.

72 S.I. 1964 No. 707.

73 [1973] 1 W.L.R. 459.

74 Agriculture (Notices to Remedy and Notices to Quit) Order 1964 S.I. 1964 No. 706 as amended by S.I. 1972 No. 1207.

75 Agricultural Holdings Act, 1948, section 26, as substituted by the Agriculture Act, 1958, section 8(1) and First Schedule.

76 *Price* v. *Romilly* [1960] 3 All E.R. 429.

77 Agriculture (Notices to Remedy and Notices to Quit) Order, 1964 S.I. 1964 No. 706; S.I. 1972 No. 1207.

78 Agriculture (Miscellaneous Provisions) Act, 1954, section 7.

79 *Clarke* v. *Hall* [1961] 2 Q.B. 331.

80 [1958] 1 All E.R. 846.

81 [1971] Ch. 477.

82 Agricultural Holdings Act, 1948, section 25(1), as substituted by Agriculture Act, 1958, section 3(2).

83 S.I. 1959 No. 81.

84 [1958] 1 W.L.R. 434.

85 Section 30.

86 Section 31.

87 Sections 32 and 33.

88 Section 32.

89 Section 12(1).

90 *Elwes* v. *Maw* (1802) 3 East 38.

91 Section 65(1).

92 [1951] 1 All E.R. 890.

93 Sections 34(2) and 56; *post*, pages 64 and 66.

94 Section 37.

95 Sections 35–45 and Second Schedule.

[96] Section 47.

[97] Section 54.

[98] Section 55(1).

[99] Section 55(2).

[100] Section 53.

[101] Section 48.

[102] Section 49.

[103] Section 50; Agriculture Act, 1958, sections 8 and 10, First and Second Schedules.

[104] The Agriculture (Calculation of Value for Compensation) Regulations, 1969, S.I. 1969 No. 1704 as amended by S.I. 1972 No. 864.

[105] Section 51(1).

[106] Section 51(2).

[107] *Watters* v. *Hunter* 1927 S.C. 310.

[108] Sections 67–69 and Fifth Schedule.

[109] Section 34(1) of the 1948 Act.

[110] Section 34(2) of the 1948 Act.

[111] Section 34(4).

[112] Agriculture (Miscellaneous Provisions) Act, 1968, sections 9 and 10.

[113] Agriculture (Miscellaneous Provisions) Act, 1968, section 10.

[114] Agriculture (Miscellaneous Provisions) Act, 1968, section 15(2).

[115] Agricultural Holdings Act, 1948, section 56(1).

[116] Section 56(2).

[117] Section 56(3).

[118] Section 94(1).

[119] Section 57(1).

[120] Section 57(2).

[121] [1953] 1 All E.R. 155.

[122] [1957] 2 Q.B. 277.

[123] Section 59.

[124] Section 70(1).

[125] Section 70(2) and (5).

[126] Section 70(3) and (4).

[127] Section 77(1).

[128] Sixth Schedule; Agriculture (Miscellaneous Provisions) Act, 1963, section 20.

[129] Sixth Schedule.

[130] Sixth Schedule.

[131] Section 71.

[132] Section 72.

[133] Rent Act, 1968, section 2(1).

[134] *Torbett* v. *Faulkner* [1952] 2 T.L.R. 659.

[135] *Higgs* v. *Browne* [1946] L.J.N.C.C.R. 149.

[136] *Hirst* v. *Sargent* (1966) 65 L.G.R. 127.

[137] *Ford* v. *Langford* [1949] L.J.R. 586.

[138] See Rent Act, 1968, section 1.

[139] Rent Act, 1968, section 10 and Schedule 3.

[140] Rent Act, 1965, section 33.

[141] Rent Act, 1965, section 33; Agriculture Act, 1970 section 99.

[142] Rent Act, 1965, section 33(2).

[143] Rent Act, 1968, section 7(2).

[144] Rent Act, 1968, section 10; Schedule 3.

[145] Rent Act, 1968, section 10(2); Schedule 3; Agriculture Act, 1970, section 100; Agriculture (Miscellaneous Provisions) Act, 1972, section 24.

3 Types of Business Organisation

The purpose of this chapter is to consider the farmer, not merely as a separate individual, but as a person wishing to carry on business in conjunction with others. 'There is a growing awareness that marketing by individual farmers is totally inappropriate where very large numbers of such units face a small number of large buyers'.[1] The purpose of the combination need not, of course, be confined to marketing only.

Basically there are three types of vehicle which he may choose to be the carrier of his purpose; these are partnerships, companies and registered societies, but partnerships and companies contain further subdivisions into different kinds of partnership and different kinds of company; one chooses the particular kind which one thinks will best further one's primary purpose. A trust may also sometimes be found to be appropriate for use either alone or in conjunction with one of the above. The primary reasons for entering into business in combination with others are to achieve, by pooling the capital and labour resources of the participants, the economies of scale which can accrue to large enterprises with regard to such things as expensive buildings and machinery. Nevertheless the success of the enterprise must in the end primarily turn upon the efficiency with which it is conducted and not merely on the amount of capital which is poured into it. Thus it should always be borne in mind that to enter into combination with others will almost certainly involve at least a partial loss of control of one's own business destiny, hence one should always be careful to weigh up the extent to which this will be so and the efficiency and compatibility of those with whom control will henceforth be at best shared; it is also possible that control might effectively pass altogether to others, since one might find oneself regularly outvoted in the new organisation. Taxation (*post*, pages 127–82) is another factor which should constantly be borne in mind.

'The latest generation of co-operatives differs from its forerunners in, first, selectivity of membership and, second, internal discipline. The evidence of this discipline is the written contract, which now almost invariably supplements the rules or other constitutional document of the organisation concerned'.[2]

Ordinary partnerships

Definition and commencement

Partnership may be defined as the relationship which subsists between persons carrying on a business in common with a view to profit;[3] 'person' includes a company, hence two or more companies can be in partnership with one another. The maximum number of partners which is usually permissible by law is twenty.[4] This will be adequate except for very large organisations requiring substantial capital; the use of a company, as will be seen later, permits a larger number of persons to be associated in the business enterprise. Common reasons for entering into a farming partnership include a combination of two or more farmers desirous of sharing the use of expensive buildings and equipment, or the introduction of a son or other member of the family into the business to enhance his status and interest and as a step towards reducing taxation. It must always be borne in mind that the general trend of taxation in this country is to tax most heavily the person who has a large income, or a large capital. The rate at which tax is levied on his income, or on each pound of capital, rises steeply until it amounts virtually to statutory confiscation of very large estates upon the death of their owners. The broad solution is simple in principle, considering the tax aspect alone; the family cake must be carved into fairly even slices and distributed among the family. Thus if the income from the farm is high, a high rate of tax may be avoided by splitting the income within the family; one way to effect this is to make the members of the family partners in the farming, although of course there must be some factual evidence to support the alleged date of commencement of the partnership. In *Waddington* v. *O'Callaghan*[5] a deed of partnership was signed on 11 May 1929, and expressed to operate from 1 January 1929, but for tax purposes the partnership was held to have commenced on the later of these dates since there was no factual evidence to support its previous existence. Although the family, or such members of it as are of appropriate age and ability, can be partners in the farming business without the land itself necessarily becoming part of the partnership assets, a transfer by the parent of part or the whole of the ownership of the land to the younger members of the family will, provided the parent lives long enough thereafter, avoid some or all of the estate duty which would otherwise fall on it the death of the parent (*post*, pages 166—9). The land could be conveyed into the sole ownership of the child (or children) and then leased back to the partnership at a full rent, so that only the lease forms part of the partnership assets, or the ownership of the land could be made an asset of the partnership, in which event when each partner dies estate duty would be borne on his share of the assets. But to obtain relief against estate duty the parent must survive the gift for at least seven years (with some relief after four years; see *post*, page 166), so it is little use postponing action until after being notified by one's doctor that one has a serious disease! Capital gains tax (*post*, pages 151–9) may be incurred on the disposal.

In law a purely verbal agreement is sufficient to create a partnership, but in practice it would be most unwise to rely upon such an agreement, and a solicitor should be employed to draw up a partnership deed under carefully considered instructions.

The farm itself, if it is to become an asset of the partnership, can either be held by its original owner who in writing will then declare himself trustee of the land for the partnership, or the land can be conveyed to trustees (not more than four in number, who could be the partners themselves) to hold on trust for the partnership. If the partnership is merely to take a lease, the owner can lease the land to trustees (as above) for the partnership.

Agency of partners

Partnership law is founded on the implied authority of any partner to act as agent for and thus to bind his fellow partners. Thus by the Partnership Act, 1890, anyone known to be a partner is presumed to have the authority of his co-partners to bind them to transactions which are in the ordinary course of the type of business in question (e.g. purchase of livestock and farm machinery in a farming partnership).[6] Thus it is essential to choose one's partners with care, since one may find oneself in law committed to a purchase of which one disapproves and about which one was not consulted. Moreover any clause in the partnership deed forbidding one's partner to act thus will have no effect on third parties who are ignorant (as will usually be the case) of the restriction,[7] although breach of the contract of partnership will of course entitle the innocent partner to claim damages for breach of contract from the offending partner. All partners are liable for torts (see chapter 8, pages 309–20) committed by a partner in the ordinary course of the firm's business or with the authority of his fellow partners.[8]

Implied rules governing the partnership

The Partnership Act, 1890, lays down many rules applicable to partnerships. It is most important, however, to grasp that most of these rules can (and sometimes should) be excluded by contrary clauses in the deed setting up the partnership. A selection of the most important rules now follows.

Since the relationship between partners is founded upon mutual trust, partners are required by law to show the utmost good faith towards one another in every way. They must render true accounts and full information of all matters affecting the partnership.[9] A partner must *prima facie* account to the firm for any profit made by him from carrying on a business competing with that of the partnership,[10] or from his use of the partnership property, firm name or business connection.[11]

Partners share profits and bear losses equally[12] (although their capital contributions may have been unequal).

No interest is payable to partners on their capital before profits are ascertained, but 5 per cent interest is payable on any loan which, after the partnership has been created, a partner then makes to the partnership.[13]

Every partner may take part in managing the business and inspect the books of the partnership.[14]

Disputes concerning *ordinary* matters connected with the business are decided by a majority of the partners.[15] But all must consent before the partnership business can be changed, a new partner introduced or a partner expelled.[16]

Unless a fixed duration is agreed upon, a partnership can be brought to an end at any time by a partner giving notice of his desire to do so,[17] and the death or bankruptcy of a partner automatically ends the partnership.[18]

It may well, for example, be thought desirable to provide, contrary to the above rules, for interest to be paid on capital, where the capital contributions are unequal, before computing profit, and that there shall be no automatic dissolution on death and that a period of notice of intention to dissolve shall be given.

One may conclude that the partnership deed should deal with the following topics at least:

1   The nature of the business and the name under which the partnership chooses to trade. Any name may be chosen, but if the name does not consist of the true surnames of all partners it must be registered under the Registration of Business Names Act, 1916.[19]

2   How the capital is to be contributed, and whether interest on it is to be allowed before computing profits.

3   The banking account and who signs cheques.

4   In what proportion profits (and hence losses) are to be divided.

5   Who is to manage the business, and any restrictions on the authority of an individual partner (but see *ante*, page 81).

6   Accounts.

7   The duration of the partnership, including the effect of a partner's death and length of notice of dissolution.

It should be pointed out that each partner is personally liable to the full extent of his partnership or private assets for the whole of the firm's debts; he must look to his co-partners to compel them to bear their share and, should they prove insolvent, he will have to stand the loss himself insofar as he cannot get it from them.

Dissolution of partnership

Dissolution usually takes place either in accordance with a clause providing for it contained in the partnership deed, or by a court order that the partnership be dissolved; a court order can be granted on a number of grounds including the permanent incapacity of a partner, conduct by a partner which is prejudicial to the business, wilful or persistent breaches of the partnership agreement, the fact that the business can only be carried on at a loss, or the court thinking it just and equitable to dissolve.[20] In the case of a partnership entered into for an undefined time the partnership can be dissolved by one partner serving notice on the others of his intention to dissolve; dissolution will take effect from the date stated in the notice, or if no date is stated then as soon as the notice is received.[21]

Upon a dissolution any partner can insist that the firm's assets be realised, the firm's debts paid and any surplus distributed among the partners.[22] The assets must be applied in paying first the outside creditors of the firm; unless otherwise agreed the surplus must then be applied in repaying to partners any loans which they have made to the firm, then in repaying their capital contributions, and finally in dividing the remainder among the partners in the same proportion as that in which profits are divisible. If losses have been made by the firm, all debts to outside creditors must be borne by the partners from their business or private assets. As between the partners themselves, losses, including losses of partnership capital as well as the sums owed to outside creditors of the firm, must unless otherwise agreed be borne by the partners in the same proportion in which they shared profits.[23]

A limited partnership must have at least one general partner who is liable without limit for all the partnership debts, and have one or more limited partners whose own liability is limited to the amount of capital which the limited partner has agreed to contribute.[24] A limited partnership is created by filing with the Registrar of Companies a document stating, among other matters, the names of the partners, describing every limited partner as such and stating the amount of capital which the limited partners are liable to contribute,[25] 50p per £ 100 capital duty is payable to the government on the capital sum for which the *limited partner* is liable.[26] A limited partner cannot take part in the management (if he does he becomes liable for the firm's debts without any limit) and has no power to bind the firm; disputes relating to ordinary matters concerning the business are decided by a majority of the general partners. Subject to contrary agreement, a limited partner cannot withdraw from the firm except by transferring his share with the consent of the general partners, whereupon the transferee takes over the limited partner's position. The death or bankruptcy of a limited partner does not dissolve the partnership, nor can he dissolve the partnership by notice.[27]

Not many limited partnerships have been created in the past, mainly because a company could instead be formed under which all the members could (if so desired) take part in the management and yet all retain limited liability to contribute to the debts of the organisation. But by Act of Parliament almost all companies have been required to make their accounts available to the public,[28] whereas partnerships are not required to do so. Hence it may be that limited partnerships will become more frequent, particularly when some of those associated in the venture are willing to undertake unlimited liability for its debts whereas others wish to restrict their liability.

Companies

The first point to grasp is that a company when formed is a new and distinct legal person, entirely separate from its members, whereas a partnership is not a distinct legal entity but merely consists of the individuals who compose it. If follows that the company can own land and other property, make contracts and has an existence unaffected by the death of its members.

The distinct and separate legal personality of the company is vividly illustrated by the important case of *Salomon* v. *Salomon & Co. Ltd.*[29] Mr Salomon was the owner of a boot and shoe business. He subsequently incorporated a company to buy the business from him; he took as payment a large number of shares in the company, one share each being allotted to his wife and to his five children and the remainder to Mr Salomon and also a kind of mortgage upon the assets of the company to secure the rest of the purchase price which was left outstanding as a debt due to Mr Salomon from the company. Subsequently the company became insolvent and went into liquidation, and Mr Salomon claimed to be entitled as a secured creditor to priority of payment out of the company's assets before the claims of its unsecured creditors. The unsecured creditors asserted that the company was a sham and in essence the same person as Mr Salomon himself since he controlled the company by virtue of his ownership of nearly all the shares in it, but the court held that the company, having been formed in compliance with the requirements of the Act of Parliament governing the creation of companies, was an entirely distinct legal person from Mr Salomon; Mr Salomon's transaction with the company was consequently valid and entitled him to priority of claim on its assets.

If a company wishes to indulge in a possibly risky line of business it may find it convenient to take advantage of the separate legal personality of each company and thus create a subsidiary company, with the parent company as its principal shareholder, to undertake the new business so that liability in the event of unsuccessful trading would fall only on the assets of the subsidiary company and not on the parent company.

Classification of companies

Companies can be classified according to the extent of the liability of the *members* to contribute to the assets of the company. Thus we have:

1 *Companies in which liability is limited by shares.* The constitution of the company will state its maximum permissible capital, i.e. the number of shares and their nominal value, say 100,000 shares nominal value £1 each; there is almost complete freedom of choice as to the number of shares and their value. Each member states how many shares he will take up and pay for, and payment to the company of the nominal value of each share he takes frees him from further liability (unless he has agreed with the company to pay an additional sum, called a premium, on each of his shares in addition to their nominal value, in which event he must pay

the premium also), no matter what the debts of the company may be. Thus it behoves those trading with the company to ascertain what its capital is!

2   *Companies in which liability is limited by guarantee.* The constitution of the company will state how many members it will have, and each member will undertake to pay a specified sum (e.g. £100; any figure may be chosen) if needed to pay the debts of the company; having paid it he incurs no further liability. Such companies are usually formed for non-commercial purposes.

3   *Unlimited companies.* Here the members are liable without any limit to the full extent of the debts of the company. This is a great disadvantage if losses seem fairly likely to rank as a possibility, but of little significance if one is virtually assured of profitable trading. If assured of regular profits, unlimited companies are advantageous in that they do not bear the 50p per £100 duty on the company's capital which is exacted from companies limited by shares and limited partnerships, and provided they are independent of any limited company they do not have to file accounts [30] annually as other companies must with the Registrar of Companies, which they are open to inspection by any member of the public who cares to walk along to Companies House and pay a minute search fee. Hence some limited companies have recently converted themselves into unlimited companies.

Formation of the company

There are firms of lawyers who specialise in the manufacture of companies, and a company newly formed and ready to trade may be purchased from such a firm at a cost of around £60. However, it is often advisable to have a company with a constitution specially adapted to one's own particular requirements instead, and this will in practice require some additional legal expense. The company is actually created by filing certain documents with the Registrar of Companies and paying his registration fees and certain revenue duties. The most important documents are described below.

1   *The memorandum of association.* This contains the company's name, the capital of the company and the shares into which the capital is divided, and whether and if so in what way the liability of the members is limited. The memorandum must be signed by at least two persons if the company is a private company and at least seven persons if the company is

86

a public company; these persons must each agree to take and pay for at least one share in the company, and they will be the first members of the company. [31] It is thus a most important document. Two points are worthy of special note. The statement of the company's sphere of activity, as set out in the memorandum of association, should be wide enough to suit the wishes of the members; although a purported contract made outside those purposes might be binding on the company in favour of an innocent third party contracting with it,[32] persons who have committed the company to this irregular activity would be liable to the company for any damage suffered by it in consequence. Secondly, the capital of the company can lawfully be fixed at any sum from, say, 2p (two members each of whom agree to take one share worth 1p) to, say, one million pounds, though under European influence it seems probable that the minimum capital necessary to launch the company will ere long be increased to a sum amounting to several thousand pounds. Thought should therefore be given to how much capital the company is likely to require (authorised or nominal capital—the maximum permissible) and how much of this the members are now prepared to pay or undertake to pay by buying shares in the company now (the issued capital). These shares must be paid for either in cash or in money's worth, thus, for example, a farmer owning a farm worth £20,000 and livestock worth £10,000 might sell the farm and livestock to a company formed by him (with at least one other member) in return for 30,000 shares of £1 each. The land would be conveyed by deed to the company. He could if desired (e.g. to save estate duty provided he lives a good while thereafter) give away most of the shares to the younger members of his family. Once capital has been paid by the members to the company in return for their shares it is unlawful for them to take any capital back again out of the company unless with leave of the court under section 66 or on dissolution of the company. The company uses the capital to finance its trade, and pays yearly or more frequent dividends to its members out of the profits of its trading. The member may, of course, sell his shares to a third party (but see *post*, page 92). including another member, for whatever price that person is willing to pay.

Where a co-operative farming organisation is registered as a company under the Companies Act, then in view of the rule of law that a company cannot reduce its capital at will it is impossible, save by an expensive application to the court and compliance with certain other requirements, [33] to repay the share capital of a member who ceases to do business with the company and whose interest in the company thereby becomes that of an investor alone. In a registered society under the Industrial and provident Societies Act, 1965 (*post*, pages 94–102), there is often provision in its rules for the repayment of share capital to inactive members. 'The mobility of capital is the mark which most clearly distinguishes a co-operative from a commercial company, and which above all makes registration under the Industrial and Provident Societies Act more appropriate for co-operatives than registration under the Companies Act. A co-operative company must make special provisions. . . to ensure that control shall not pass into the hands of ex-participants and their heirs or successors, since the principle of capital maintenance forbids repayment of the capital of companies registered under the Companies Act except in very special circumstances.'[34]

As regards a co-operative company registered under the Companies Act, the participant's capital contribution, other than a single share, will often take the form of a loan in order to make it lawful to return capital to him upon his retirement.

2 *The articles of association.* These govern the internal working of the company, e.g. rules concerning directors and meetings.

3 *The statement of the nominal capital.* Since stamp duty at the rate of 50*p* per £100 is payable on this,[35] it is advisable to restrict the nominal capital to what is necessary in the near future. The company can subsequently resolve to increase its capital,[36] should this prove desirable later.

On receipt of these and other less important documents the Registrar of Companies will issue a certificate of incorporation which is conclusive evidence that the company is now in existence. Companies other than public companies (see *post*, pages 92–4) may then commence trading.

How the company resolves to act

The company, as we have seen, is a distinct legal person from its members; such a person can only resolve to act through the agency of human beings. The possible organs for taking decisions within the company are:

(a) the board of directors,
(b) the managing director(s),
(c) the members of the company in general meeting.

A member acting individually and in his capacity as member has no power whatever to bind the company.

The precise division of powers between these possible organs will depend on the terms of the constitution of the individual company. A private company must by law have at least one director, and a public company at least two;[37] although this minimum requirement must be satisfied, beyond that the number of directors which it is desirable to have must depend upon the scope of the company's activities and the wishes of the participants in the enterprise. A sole director is likely to be willing to give full-time attention to the affairs of the company, but if there are several directors it is questionable whether all will be willing to do so, and in such a case a managing director may be appointed to work full time and be paid a salary commensurate with his labours, leaving the larger board of directors to meet, say, monthly to take major decisions (always by majority vote) and investigate progress.

The company must by law convene an annual general meeting of its members,[38] and may convene other general meetings as and when required. The decisions of the general meeting are arrived at by resolutions of the members as to what shall and shall not be done. For most resolutions a simple majority of those voting suffices, but the constitution of the particular company could require a three-quarters majority of those voting, and for certain matters (e.g. to alter the articles of association under section 10) the Companies Act, 1948, requires this larger majority. Voting is initially by show of hands, with one vote *per member* voting, but in general a member or members dissatisfied with the result may demand a poll which will normally result in one vote for *each share* held, and the result of the poll will prevail over the show of hands. The number of members required in order to demand a poll, or the number of shares. which the member or members making the demand must hold, depends on the constitution of the individual company so far as consistent with the Companies Act, 1948; any five members with voting rights, or members holding one-tenth or more of the total voting rights, or holding shares with voting rights on which an aggregate sum has been paid of at least one-tenth of the total sum paid up on all the shares carrying voting rights, can demand a poll, and the constitution of the individual company can make it easier but not more difficult than this to demand a poll.[39]

A member can appoint a proxy to vote at the meeting on his behalf. A proxy so appointed cannot vote upon a show of hands unless the constitution expressly empowers him to do so; he can however vote upon a poll,[40] and the instrument appointing a proxy is deemed to empower the proxy to join in demanding a poll.[41]

Although shares *prima facie* carry equality as regards return of capital on dissolution, right to dividends and voting (although of course if I own more shares than you I shall have more votes, etc., for that reason) this presumption of equality can be rebutted by the articles of the particular company which could, for example, provide that each of my shares shall carry 100 votes and each of your shares one vote. A father who wishes to retain management control of his farming company and yet give away the great bulk of his shares to his family to avoid estate duty on his death could employ this device of weighted voting, but he must not be voted unduly large remuneration for his management services or otherwise absorb an unrealistic proportion of the company's income or he will be charged to estate duty on that ground alone. [42]

The first directors are usually appointed by those who create the company. Later appointments are governed by the articles, which usually provide for their being appointed by the members in general meeting. It therefore follows that a person who owns more than half of the shares (assuming no weighted voting) would be able to elect or dismiss the entire board of directors and, in general meeting, prevent all resolutions being passed of which he disapproved and, conversely, pass all simple majority resolutions by his own vote! The practical distribution of the voting strength is a cogent thought to be borne in mind when deciding what influence one is likely to be able to exercise in the affairs and destiny of the company, and conversely what influence is likely to be exercised *against one* by the various factions which may inhabit the company! Factions within the company are not infrequently locked in prolonged internecine warfare with one another.

Care should also be taken in deciding how much power should be given to the directors by the company's constitution and how much to the general meeting. The directors are entitled to exercise the powers conferred on them without any regard to the wishes of the general meeting. [43] The general meeting can alter this state of affairs by altering the articles to reduce the powers of the directors; to achieve this a three-quarters majority of the votes cast is needed [44] and may not be easy to obtain. Alternatively the members may decline to re-elect the directors when the time comes if the constitution of the company provides that the directors shall retire at a specified date unless re-elected. They could also dismiss the directors by ordinary resolution, [45] but in this case the directors will be entitled to damages if they hold long-term service contracts with the company which are broken by the dismissal.

Borrowing by the company

A company frequently desires, in addition to the capital paid in by the members in return for their shares (share capital) to raise further money by borrowing (loan capital); the loan creditor often obtains security by taking a mortgage upon the company's assets. It should be noticed that a company is usually in a position to offer a more extensive range of assets to secure the loan than an individual if he were to own the same assets. The reason for this is that whereas both may mortgage their land, an individual is unable to offer his goods (livestock, machinery, etc.) as additional security for the loan without paralysing his trade, since each time he wished to sell anything he would need the consent of his mortgagee, plus various other legal complexities. But a company is permitted by law to include its goods as part of the security offered by creating what is known as a floating charge on the goods, and to dispose of the goods freely until the mortgagee becomes entitled and chooses to enforce his security. The mortgage will then attach to whatever goods happen to be owned by the company *at the time when the security is enforced* (usually by seizure and sale of the goods). Inclusion of the goods as part of the security increases the value of the assets available to the lender if he has to enforce it and hence tends to induce him to lend more.

Since the company is a separate legal entity from its members (*ante*, pages 84–5), it follows that a farmer who considers his enterprise to be a risky one can form a company with limited liability and sell his business to it in exchange for shares and, mainly, a mortgage on the company's assets; the value of the shares and the mortgage should, of course, equal the value of the business. Should the company later trade unsuccessfully and become unable to pay its debts, he, by virtue of his security, will rank ahead of at any rate most of the company's creditors in claiming such assets as the company has up to the amount of his secured debt.

Liquidation of the company

Liquidation is the process which leads to the dissolution of the company, and may be commenced in one of two ways. It may be done compulsorily by order of the court; such a court order may be granted on a number of grounds, such as that the membership has fallen below the minimum which is requisite, or that it is just and equitable to place the company in liquidation, but the most frequent ground is that the company is unable to pay its debts. Alternatively the liquidation of the company may be set in motion voluntarily, by resolution of the members to commence liquidation. Usually a three-quarters majority of those voting will be required to pass the resolution. On liquidation a person, who is called a liquidator, will be appointed to gather in and sell the company's assets, pay its debts and distribute any surplus to the members in accordance with their rights.

Distinction between private companies and public companies

Private companies. These must have a minimum of two members[46] and a maximum of fifty excluding past and present employees of the company[47] (it will be remembered that for partnerships the maximum is twenty). Such companies are in economic reality (but not in law) sole traders or partnerships trading with limited liability for all members (unless, of course, they elect to form an unlimited company). Being a relatively small group of persons in close personal association, they must by law prohibit any invitation to the public to subscribe either share or loan capital,[48] thus the members must find the share capital and any loan capital by private arrangement. They must also restrict in the articles of association the right of a member to transfer his shares[49]; this is to prevent an outsider being brought into the group of members without the concurrence of the group expressed in some fashion. The law does not state what form the restriction is to take; restrictions often employed are either that no transfer of shares may be made without the consent of the directors, who are given an absolute discretion whether to grant or to refuse the transfer, or that before transferring the shares to a non-member the members must first be given a chance to buy the shares at a fair price. The form of restriction employed deserves attention, since it obviously affects the marketability, and hence often the value, of the shares; the effect could be drastic in each case.

Private companies will suffice as the vehicle for most farming enterprises, unless the enterprise is very large or it is desired that the public should take a proportion of the benefits and the risks. Until recent times it might well have been thought that only those persons with grandiose schemes should indulge in creating a public company solely for the purpose of farming land. But owing to the great increase in the value of farm land which has taken place of late and the heavy capital requirements of modern farming, it may well be that even the financing of an ordinary farm will increasingly require to be done through the medium of a public company; alternatively a private company could be formed and a minority shareholding sold to, for example, a large institutional investor such as an insurance company.

Public companies. The only likely purpose in creating such a company is to persuade the investing public at large to take up shares in the company and subscribe capital accordingly. Since so large a body of members could not exercise any detailed surveillance over the company's affairs, much power will be placed in the hands of the directors, and at least one managing director will probably be essential. The calibre of the directors will largely determine the success or otherwise of the company. At the annual general meeting the members will, in theory at any rate, be able to hold the directors to account for their stewardship of the company during the year previous to the meeting; the theoretical control of the members is often thought to be little exercised in reality.

The principal features which distinguish a public company from a private one are:

1 If the public are to be invited to take up shares, clearly the existence of the proposed issue of shares must be brought to the public attention, and this can only be done by circulating a document (known as a prospectus) by newspaper advertisement, leaving quantities with bankers and stockbrokers to distribute to their customers, etc. The bankers and stockbrokers will have to be paid a small commission, known as brokerage, for this service. If the law did not step in here, the document might be couched in unduly vague but glowing terms concerning the assets and prospects of the company. The law does step in, and prescribes an extensive amount of factual information concerning the company which must be included in the prospectus, [50] and the directors and others authorising the issue of the prospectus are in general liable both criminally and in civil actions for damages by dissatisfied shareholders who successfully applied to the company for shares in reliance on a prospectus containing an untrue statement. [51] Criminal liability, and probably liability for damages, also attaches in respect of omission to disclose the prescribed information. [52] The cost of preparing, printing, advertising and circulating the prospectus should not be under-estimated.

2 A Stock Exchange quotation for the company's shares will usually be desirable in order to improve the marketability of the shares and so enhance the attractiveness of the issue. Before granting a quotation the Stock Exchange will investigate and want to be satisfied about the affairs of the company. It is not unknown for companies to be formed with the sole, albeit unavowed, purpose of defrauding the company's shareholders, or the company's creditors, or both.

3 The directors must by law make an estimate of the capital sum required to carry on the company's business effectively. If the public do not collectively subscribe this sum in response to the prospectus, the attempted issue has by law failed *totally* and all money subscribed in response to the prospectus must be repaid to the applicants for the shares,[53] thus all the expenses of the issue have been wasted. The directors may seek to insure against a disaster of this kind by approaching persons called underwriters and asking them to agree to take up whatever shares comprised in

the issue are not taken up by the public. The directors should make sure that the underwriters have sufficient financial resources to meet their commitment. In return for this service, the underwriters will be paid a commission calculated on the value of the entire issue. The rate of commission will, of course, depend on the underwriter's assessment of the likely extent to which he is on risk, but by law the maximum commission payable must not exceed 10 per cent or the rate prescribed by the company's articles, whichever is the less. [54] The underwriter would, of course, decline to underwrite if he thought the likely extent of his risk was greater than his commission.

4   A large public company is, of course, by nature a pretty impersonal thing. Any restriction imposed by the *general* law on the right of a member to transfer his shares freely would clearly be quite out of place here, and is only appropriate to private companies (see *ante*, page 92). A member of a public company has therefore an unrestricted right to transfer his shares except where this right is cut down by the articles of association of his particular company.

5   A public company cannot begin trading or make binding contracts until the Registrar of Companies grants it a trading certificate; compliance with various matters must be proved to the Registrar before he will grant it. [55]

6   A public company must convene an initial meeting of its members, known as the statutory meeting, not less than one nor more than three months after the company became entitled to commence business, and must furnish each member with a detailed report, called the statutory report, on the position of the company up to the time of the report; [56] a private company need do none of this. In practice a company which is ultimately intended to be a public company can evade the need to hold the statutory meeting and circulate the statutory report by commencing its existence as a private company and subsequently, after having carried on business for the requisite length of time, altering its articles by special resolution to delete one or more of the three essential requirements of a private company (*ante*, page 92), thus automatically turning into a public company.

Co-operative societies

Instead of trading as a partnership or a company, it is possible to register as a society under the Industrial and Provident Societies Act, 1965. As will appear subsequently, it is doubtful whether registration as a company has any advantage nowadays over registration as a society. An agricultural co-operative need not seek any form of corporate status by registration under this or the Companies Act unless it has more than twenty members and is formed for the purpose of carrying on a business which has for its object the acquisition of gain; a lesser number might elect to trade as a partnership. A mutual organisation (see *post*, pages 104–6) need not be registered regardless of the number of members since its object is not the acquisition of gain.

Registration and entitlement to register

Co-operatives registered under the Industrial and Provident Societies Act, 1965, are corporate bodies with limited liability.[57] The rules of the society may authorise it to carry on any industry, business or trade.[58] A society can be registered if it is shown to the satisfaction of the Registrar that the society is a *bona fide* co-operative society and the rules of the society make provision for the matters set out in Schedule 1 of the Act.[59] A society which carries on business in order to make profits mainly for the payment of interest, dividends or bonuses on money invested or lent to the society is not within the Act.[60]

The Registrar has issued a memorandum indicating some of the criteria which he will apply in deciding whether a body qualifies for registration. These include open membership: 'there must be no artificial restriction of membership with the object of increasing the value of proprietory rights or interests'. Moreover 'a rule providing that any person should have more than one vote might suggest *prima facie* that the society was not a true co-operative society. The return on share and other capital must not exceed a moderate rate which may vary according to circumstances, but should approximate to the minimum necessary to obtain such capital as is required to carry out the primary objects of the society. The society must so conduct its business as to show that its main purpose is the mutual benefit of its members, and that the benefit enjoyed by a member depends upon the use which he makes of the facilities provided by the society and not upon the amount of money which he invests in the society.'

The society must have at least seven members,[61] or at least two members if the membership consists solely of other registered societies.[62] The society must be registered at the central office established under the Friendly Societies Act, 1896, and various documents such as the application to register the society, amendments to its rules and certain resolutions passed by the society must be registered at the central office and are open to public inspection. The Registrar will prevent a society from be-coming registered with an undesirable name, and the word 'Limited' must in general be the last word in the society's name. [63] An application to register a society must in general be signed by seven members and the secretary and be sent to the Registrar together with two printed copies of the rules. [64] Upon registration the society becomes a corporate body which can sue and be sued in its corporate name. [65] Every registered society must have a registered office, [66] and all communications and no-tices must be addressed to the registered office.

Matters to be dealt with in the society's rules

Among the matters which must be provided for by the rules of the society are its name, its objects, the place of its registered office, the terms of admission of its members, the mode of holding meetings and voting, the mode of altering the rules, the appointment and removal of a committee and of managers or other officers and their respective powers and remu-neration, the amount of each member's interest, not exceeding £1,000, in the shares of the society which any member other than a registered soci-ety may hold, whether the society may borrow money or take it on deposit from members or others and on what conditions, whether shares shall be transferable and whether and how members may withdraw from the society, provision for the claims of the representatives of deceased members, the audit of the accounts and the mode of application of the society's profits and whether and in what manner any part of the society's funds may be invested. [67]

The binding effect of the rules

The rules of the society bind the society and all members and persons claiming through them as if each member had signed his name and affixed his seal to the rules and as if the rules contained a promise by each member and those claiming through him to conform to the rules. [68] How-ever a member is not in general bound by any amendment to the rules requiring him to take up more shares or to increase the sum payable on his shares unless he consents in writing to the amendment. [69] Subject to this restriction, the rules can be amended in the manner laid down by the existing rules, and such an amendment must be made in good faith.

96

The capital of the society

The rules of the society need make no provision concerning the number or value of the shares which it may issue and unless such provision is in fact made the share capital will vary from time to time. It may be that the Industrial and Provident Societies Act permits the Registrar to approve society rules making possible the issue of preference shares and non-voting shares; the 'matters to be provided for in the society's rules' include 'determination whether the shares or any of them shall be transferable, . . . determination whether the shares or any of them shall be withdrawable, . . .'. From this it is clear that some distinction at least is permissible between different shares of the same society. No member, except another registered society, may have any interest exceeding £1,000 in shares of the society. [70] The power of the society to borrow or to receive money on deposit from its members or others depends on what is stated in its rules; members are free to provide as much loan capital (as distinct from share capital) as they choose without any legal maximum so long as this accords with the rules of the society. 'It is quite usual for the recently formed marketing co-operatives to limit shareholding to a single share per member, but to require from every member a "qualification loan" in proportion to service provided'. [71]

The management of the society

The rules of the society must provide for the appointment of a committee, whatever called, and of managers and other officers and their respective powers and remuneration. [72] Each society must have a committee and a secretary. If the rules of the society vest the control of its business in the committee of management, then the members of the society cannot exercise such control in general meeting. [73]

The admission and liability of the members

The rules of the society must set out the terms of admission of members. [74] A register of the names, addresses, number of shares and the amount paid thereon of each member, with the dates on which he became or ceased to be a member, must be kept at the registered office of the society. [75] A member is personally liable for the debts of the society to the extent of any sum unpaid on the shares still held by him, or as a past member for the sum unpaid on the shares which he held within a year before the commencement of the winding up of the society's affairs, and insofar as his contribution is required to pay debts or liabilities of the society contracted while he was a member and which would not be met by the contributions of the existing members. [76]

Withdrawal and nomination

It seems that the rules may prevent a member from withdrawing from the society; the rules must provide whether and how members may withdraw. [77] The rules must also provide for the claims of representatives of deceased members. Moreover a member of the society may during his lifetime send a written and signed statement to the society nominating a person or persons to become entitled on his death to the whole or a specified part of his property in the society. [78] In general the committee of the society must, on receipt of proof of the member's death, transfer or pay the value of the ex-member's property to the nominated person; [79] if the property consists of shares in the society, this duty applies even if under the rules the shares are not transferable, except insofar as the transfer of the shares would raise the share capital of the nominee above the maximum permissible under the rules. [80]

The amount of property which could be disposed of in this way is limited; the Administration of Estates (Small Payments) Act, 1965, raises the limit to £500. [81] This signed statement is not a will, hence the formalities relating to wills (*post*, pages 112–13) do not apply.

Meetings and voting

The rules must provide for the mode of holding general meetings; [82] the Act does not state how often the meetings should be held, but it is advisable that there should be at least an annual meeting and the Registrar might not accept a rule which did not provide for the holding of a meeting with reasonable frequency. The Chief Registrar may, with the consent of the Treasury, call a special meeting of a registered society on the application of one-tenth of its members, or of one hundred members if the membership exceeds one thousand members. Evidence of good reason for holding the meeting must be given in support of the application, and the expenses of the meeting are payable by the applicants, the society or its members or officers in such proportions as the Chief Registrar may direct. [83]

The rules must provide for the scale and right of voting; [84] a rule which provides that a member may have more than one vote may *prima facie* be taken to indicate that the society is not a true co-operative society.

Investment of funds and distribution of profits

The society must provide in its rules whether and in what manner any part of its capital may be invested; the rules must also provide for the application of the society's profits.[85] The Registrar requires that the rate of interest on the capital of the society must by the rules be limited to that which approximates to the minimum necessary to obtain the capital needed to carry out the society's objects, but the rules may provide for a further distribution of profits among the members provided that this further amount which each member is permitted to receive is related to the profit made by the society in respect of that member's purchases from the society or use of the marketing or other facilities provided by the society. The Committee of Inquiry on Contract Farming[86] summarised the position thus. Payment of interest on shares is not excluded, but the rate is restricted. This provision is in accordance with the principle that, in a co-operative, the shareholding function is (or should be) secondary to the main purpose of subscribing to a commercial service, whereas in the non-co-operative organisation the main reason for making an investment is to obtain a financial return. This difference in objectives is fundamental, and has had many important consequences. In particular it has meant that capital accumulation has been more difficult for co-operatives than for their commercial counterparts—since members are naturally unwilling to accept low returns on capital which they are free to withdraw and invest elsewhere, and there is no incentive for non-members to invest at all (even if this was allowed under the rules). . . . It must be recognised that U.K. co-operatives are not in the same position for attracting and retaining capital as either their counterparts in many places abroad or even their non-co-operative rivals within the U.K. We therefore advocate measures sufficient to redress the disadvantages of the present co-operative position . . . . We are insistent . . . that grouped farming operations in the U.K. have, in the past, suffered from a chronic shortage of equity investment (mainly through fiscal and tax policies which have inhibited profit retentions in either the private or the co-operative sectors to anything like the extent which has been possible in most other countries.)' [87]

Accounts and audit

Every society must cause to be kept proper books of account with regard to its transactions, assets and liabilities, and establish and maintain a satisfactory system of control of its books of account, its cash holdings and its receipts and remittances.[88] Every revenue account of a society must, for the period to which the account relates, give a true and fair view of the income and expenditure of the society as a whole if the account deals with the affairs of the society as a whole; if the account deals with a particular business conducted by the society, it must give a true and fair view of the income and expenditure of the society in respect of that business. Every society must, with regard to each year of account, cause to be prepared either a revenue account dealing with the affairs of the society as a whole for that year, or two or more revenue accounts for the year which deal separately with particular businesses conducted by the society. Every balance sheet of a society must give a true and fair view of the state of its affairs as at the date of the balance sheet. A society must not publish any revenue account or balance sheet unless it has been previously audited by the appointed auditor, it incorporates a report by the auditor stating whether it is a true and fair view, and it has been signed by the secretary of the society and by two members of the committee of the society acting on behalf of their committee. [89]

In general every society must in each year of account appoint a qualified auditor or auditors to audit its accounts and balance sheet for that year. But a society may if it wishes employ unqualified auditors to audit the accounts if the receipts and payments of that society in respect of the preceding year of account did not in the aggregate exceed £5,000, the number of its members at the end of that year did not exceed five hundred, and the value of its assets at the end of that year did not in the aggregate exceed £5,000. [90] An auditor is not qualified unless he is a member of certain professional bodies or is an approved auditor appointed by the Treasury; [91] an officer or servant of the society or the partner or employee of such a person is disqualified, as is a body corporate. [92]

Disputes

The rules of the society may make provision for the manner in which disputes between the society and its members are to be settled. If so the procedure laid down by the rules must be followed; however those in dispute may, unless expressly forbidden by the rules of the society, consent to refer a dispute to the Chief Registrar. [93]

Conversion, cancellation or dissolution of the society

A registered society can convert itself by special resolution into a company registered under the Companies Act; [94] the special resolution must be passed by a majority of not less than two-thirds of the members of the society who are entitled to vote and who have voted at a general meeting of which notice, specifying the intention to propose the resolution, has been duly given according to the rules, and confirmed by a majority of the members entitled to vote who have voted at a subsequent general meeting of which due notice has been given, held not less than fourteen days nor more than a month after the day of the meeting at which the resolution was first passed. [95] Conversely, a company registered under the Companies Acts may by passing a special resolution under those Acts convert itself into a registered society. Such a resolution must appoint seven persons out of the membership of the company who, together with the secretary, must sign the rules of the society into which the company is to be converted. [96]

The Registrar may cancel the registration of the society if the number of members has fallen below seven, or if an acknowledgement of registration has been obtained by fraud or mistake, or the society has ceased to exist, or the society has wilfully and after notice from a Registrar violated any of the provisions of the Act, or if it appears to him that the society is not a *bona fide* co-operative society; cancellation on the last two grounds requires the approval of the Treasury. [97] If the society carries on more than one third of its trade with persons who are not members of the society the Registrar may seek to cancel the registration of the society.

A registered society may be dissolved either by a court order to wind up the society or by a resolution for its winding up passed in the same way as companies can resolve to wind up, or by the consent of three-quarters of the members testified by their signatures to an instrument of dissolution. [98] If an instrument of dissolution is the chosen method, the instrument must set out the assets and liabilities of the society, the number of members and their interests in the society, the claims of the creditors and the provisions to be made for them, and the intended division of the funds and property of the society. The instrument must be registered with the Registrar. [99]

The Working Party on Agricultural Co-operative Law noted in their Report that 'the retired farmer will be the keener to withdraw his co-operative capital when the return on it compares unfavourably with that receivable on a similar sum invested elsewhere, and in a period of growing inflation he is extremely conscious that he cannot expect any capital appreciation of his co-operative shares . . . because those shares can always be bought from the co-operative at par, though the balance sheet may reveal that on a distribution of assets to members (on dissolution) or on a reconstruction the holder would be entitled to much more than the nominal value of his holding. This contrast between prices and values is dangerous, for it may tempt members to dissolve or reconstruct, against the best interests of the co-operative and the agricultural community which it is intended to serve, for the sake of capital appreciation which would otherwise be denied them. Recognition of this danger had led the Registrar of Friendly Societies to agree to the issue of bonus shares in some registered societies. . . but such bonus shares have been issued in proportion to the recipients' trade, not to their share capital'.

It should be noted that a farmer who injects part of his capital into a farming co-operative instead of his own farm may suffer a disadvantage at the hands of the Inland Revenue in consequence. If a farmer invests in farm land, farm buildings and machinery, on his death estate duty will only be charged on 55 per cent of the value of those assets when he died (*post*, pages 163–4), but if he invests his capital in a farming co-operative which in turn invests the money in such assets, the farmer obtains no relief on his death as regards his investment since he owns shares and not the agricultural assets which are owned by the co-operative.

Likely effect of European Community on agricultural co-operatives

A draft Community Regulation (*post*, pages 374–5) for producers' groups which is in course of preparation defines 'producers' group' in a manner which does not require the group to be a co-operative, nor debars a minority of the producer members from exercising a majority of the votes, nor the annual profit from being distributed on the basis of the shareholdings of the members rather than on their use of the services provided. A 'producer' must however be a farmer of an undertaking situated on Community territory engaged in the production of scheduled products. The 'producers' group' must apply common rules for producing and marketing, and all the members produce which is of the type handled by the 'producers' group' must be marketed through the group, except in so far as the group itself makes exemptions. 'Producers' groups' must give proof of 'sufficient economic activity' at a level still to be decided, and will be subject to inspection to ensure that the financial aids given have been properly used. The financial aids envisaged are a subsidy to encourage the establishment of new groups, investment aids relating to supply and preparation for sale, and guarantees or loans contracted for the above purposes. It appears that the European trend is towards producers marketing the whole of their produce through the group or organisation to which they belong.

It is to be noted that the above Regulation is in draft form only, and might be greatly modified before becoming legally binding or might even

102

never come into effect at all. But the Committee of Inquiry on Contract Farming [100] state in their Report that in Community legislation 'the emphasis is on the professional aspect of the organisations which are to be fostered; they must be composed of producers and owned by them, but how these producers divide control and profits among themselves is regarded as their own affair. Inevitably, it would seem, the U.K. will have to adapt itself to this same concept. We shall expect therefore to see a gradual process whereby the present emphasis on the specifically co-operative character of the producer bodies now being encouraged under present Government policy is diminished and replaced by a wider policy of encouraging producer bodies of all kinds. Very often, of course, these bodies will be co-operative—but of their own volition and not as a condition of any government aid they have received' (pages 50 and 51 of the Report).

Trusts

The business of farming can be conducted through the medium of a trust, whereby trustees are appointed (*ante*, pages 14–15) to handle the affairs of the trust for the benefit of the beneficiaries of the trust. The trustees may carry on farming with the trust funds if empowered to do so by the document creating the trust, and the terms of the power may also be drafted to permit the trustees to continue farming even if the farming shows a loss. Under a power to farm the trustees can employ managers and other staff to carry on the farming business, thus a farmer could, for example, buy a farm and let it to a trust under which the farmer is a beneficiary and is then employed by the trustees to manage the farm.

The trust may empower the trustees to accumulate the income for a certain period of time restricted by law, instead of distributing that income during the period. At the end of the period the accumulated income is distributed in the manner specified in the instrument creating the trust. The income of the trust can be accumulated during the minority of an infant alive when the trust was created, but the most useful accumulation period allowable by law is usually that of twenty-one years from the date of the creation of the trust. [101] The benefit of accumulating the income in this way is chiefly where the income would have been liable to a very high rate of tax owing to the high income of the beneficiaries of the trust had it been distributed to them; if the income is accumulated it will not suffer tax at more than the normal rate during the period of accumulation.

A discretionary trust may be created under which the trustees have discretion to pay the income as they see fit among the persons named as beneficiaries in the trust instrument, and this can be advantageously combined with a power to accumulate the income if the trustees see fit instead of distributing it; under such an arrangement the trustees have great flexibility either in distributing the income or retaining and accumulating it according to the tax situation and the needs of the trust for obtaining further funds for carrying on the farming business out of the accumulated income after it has borne tax at the normal rate. Under the Finance Act, 1969, estate duty will be charged on the trust funds on the death of a discretionary beneficiary under the trust, the amount of the charge being based on the proportion of income which that beneficiary has received in relation to the total income of the trust and computed over the period which the Act states to be relevant (*post*, page 171).

The trustees of two or more trusts could enter into partnership with one another. A farm owned by a trust could be managed by a limited company, thus restricting liability for losses incurred in the running of the farming business.

Mutual organisations

Where persons contribute to a common fund for their mutual benefit, as for example to finance a club run solely for the benefit of its members, any surplus paid out to the members on the division of this fund is not taxable. This principle of mutuality can be advantageously employed by farmers and the like wishing to form a farming co-operative in order to acquire buildings and equipment to be used for the provision of facilities to the members of the society.

This doctrine of mutuality was developed in cases concerning the business of mutual insurance associations, and was first clearly established in *New York Life Insurance Company* v. *Styles* [102] There all members of the company were policy holders who benefited from the surplus of any year's trading by way of a reduction in future premiums or a bonus added to their policies. The House of Lords held by a majority that the surplus was not a taxable profit, being merely the excess of the premiums paid by the members over the expenditure for which they were responsible. 'When a number of individuals agreed to contribute funds for a common purpose . . . and stipulate that their contributions, so far as not required for their purpose, shall be repaid to them, I cannot conceive why . . . contributions returned to them should be regarded as profits' (*per* Lord Watson). 'I do not understand how persons contributing to a mutual fund in pursuance of a scheme for their mutual benefit—having no dealings or relations with any outside body—can be said to have made a profit when they find that they have overcharged themselves, and that some portion of their contributions may be safely refunded' (*per* Lord MacNaghten). It was immaterial that a separate legal entity, the company, had been created as part of the machinery for carrying out the joint enterprise.

In *Municipal Mutual Insurance Ltd.* v. *Hills*[103] it was said that 'The essence of the matter is that a number of persons who are exposed to some contingency . . . associate themselves together as contributors to a common fund on the footing that if the contemplated contingency befalls any contributor he or his representatives shall receive a compensatory payment out of the common fund . . .. As the common fund is composed of sums provided by the contributors out of their own monies, any surplus arising after satisfying claims obviously remains their own money. Such a surplus resulting merely from miscalculation or unexpected immunity cannot in any sense be regarded as taxable profit . . .. The cardinal requirement is that all the contributors to the common fund must be entitled to participate as a class in the surplus and that all the participators in the surplus must be contributors to the common fund; in other words, there must be complete identity between the contributors and the participators. If this requirement is satisfied, the particular form which the association takes is immaterial' (*per* Lord Macmillan). Although these remarks were uttered in the context of insurance, similar considerations would apply concerning the surplus arising from the creation of a common fund for the provision of any other service. If a mutual association trades with non-members, the profits derived from this are taxable.[104] Whether the mutuality rule applies to an agricultural co-operative will probably depend on both constitutional and operational factors. It would appear that the contributors to the common fund must have ultimate control over it, and that their contributions may be made either in cash or in kind. The establishment of a reserve for future contingent claims on the fund is permissible provided the reserve is not excessive. If the co-operative association engages in a multiplicity of different types of trading activity it would in practice be difficult to prove that the requirements of mutuality were satisfied in respect of each separate activity.

In *Fletcher* v. *Income Tax Commissioner*[105] a club owned a beach and members of the club were entitled to use the beach in return for a subscription; other persons, including those staying at the local hotels, could buy a ticket entitling them to use the beach. Subsequently a new class of member was created, called the 'hotel members', of whom there were in fact only three or four, and whose subscription to the club was based on the number of guests staying at the hotels and entitled those guests to use the beach. The question was whether the subscriptions of the hotel members were trading receipts of the club assessable to tax. The club contended that there was no liability to tax on these because of the mutuality principle; on the facts this contention failed. The question was stated to be 'is the activity, on the one hand, a trade, or an adventure in the nature of trade, producing a profit, or is it, on the other, a mutual arrangement which, at most, gives rise to a surplus? . . . The proposition of the appellant is that so long as there is common membership—each member having membership rights, i.e. at least the right to vote, and a proprietory share in assets—mere inequality of rights or obligations does not take the case out of mutuality and into trading . . . . Their Lordships are of opinion that, except in the simplest cases, no single criterion is likely to be decisive. They accept that mutuality is not necessarily excluded by the fact that some "members" are corporate bodies, or even corporate bodies engaged in trade. But the relevance of facts such as these must vary with the nature of the activity . . . . If mutuality is to have any meaning there must be a reasonable relationship, contemplated or in result, between what a member contributes and what, with due allowance for interim benefits of enjoyment, he may expect or be entitled to withdraw from the fund: between his liabilities and his rights' (*per* Lord Wilberforce).

Agricultural associations and the Restrictive Trade Practices Act, 1956

The Agricultural and Forestry Associations Act, 1962, was passed in order to exempt agricultural co-operatives from the Restrictive Trade Practices Act, 1956; its effect is that certain agreements of agricultural co-operatives which might otherwise require to be registered under Part I of the 1956 Act are exempt from registration. However, the 1962 Act did not refer to agricultural co-operatives by name. An agreement was to be exempt from registration if made by any association of persons occupying land used for agriculture or forestry or both, provided (a) the association is registered under the Industrial and Provident Societies Act, or being a company within the meaning of the Companies Act, 1948, contains in its memorandum or articles of association such provisions as may be prescribed by order of the Ministers with regard to the number of members, number of shares held by members, distribution of rights, voting rights or other matters; and (b) at least 90 per cent of the voting power is attached to shares held by persons occupying land used as previously mentioned; and (c) the only or principal business carried on by the association is the marketing of preparation for market of produce produced by members of the association on land occupied by them (with or without similar pro-

106

duce not so produced), or the supply to such members of goods required for the production of such produce on such land, or in the case of an association of persons occupying land for forestry the carrying out of forestry operations for such members on such land, or any combination of these; an association of associations satisfying these conditions is also exempted. [106] Ministerial Orders amplifying the matters which a company must, if it is to be exempted, contain in its memorandum or articles of association are the Agricultural and Forestry Associations (Exceptions) Order 1962 [107] as amended by the Agricultural and Forestry Associations (Exceptions) Amendment Order 1964. [108] The principal conditions laid down are that the profits of the association, after providing for such a return on share capital not exceeding $7\frac{1}{2}$ per cent per annum as may be specified in the memorandum or articles of association, shall, so far as divided among the members, be divided in proportion to the use made by the members of the facilities provided by the association, and that any distributed reserves shall be similarly divided; a provision that every member shall be entitled to one vote only at any meeting or alternatively that if he is entitled under the constitution to more than one vote he shall not at any meeting be entitled to exercise more than one-tenth of the total votes which could be exercised by all the members voting at the meeting if each member had one vote; a provision that the business of the association must be so conducted that in any period of three consecutive financial years of the association the value of the produce bought from or marketed for persons who are not members of the association or of goods supplied to such persons or of services rendered to them must not exceed one-third of the values of all the produce marketed, goods supplied and services rendered by the association, and a provision that the members of the association shall have equal rights to market their produce through the association and to obtain goods and services from it. The Agriculture (Miscellaneous Provisions) Act, 1968, section 44, extends the effect of the 1962 Act and the Orders made under it to any co-operative association, regardless of whether it complies with (a) to (c) above, which has as its object or primary object to assist its members in carrying on the business of agriculture or forestry or both on land occupied by them; 'Co-operative association' is defined as a body of persons having a written constitution from which the Minister is satisfied, having regard to the provision made as to the manner in which the income of the body is to be applied for the benefit of its members and all other relevant provisions, that it is in substance a co-operative association.[109] It seems that in deciding whether to grant approval the Minister will apply the same tests as does the Registrar in deciding whether to register a society under the legislation relating to industrial and provident societies.

Notes

1 Report of the Committee of Inquiry on Contract Farming; HMSO Cmnd. 5099.
2 Report of the Committee of Inquiry on Contract Farming, *ante*.
3 Partnership Act, 1890, section 1.
4 Companies Act, 1948, section 434.
5 (1931) 16 T.C. 187.
6 Section 5.
7 Section 8.
8 Section 10.
9 Section 28.
10 Section 30.
11 Section 29.
12 Section 24.
13 Section 24.
14 Section 24.
15 Section 24.
16 Section 25.
17 Sections 26 and 32.
18 Section 33.
19 Registration of Business Names Act, 1916, section 1.
20 Partnership Act, 1890, section 35.
21 Section 32.
22 Section 39.
23 Section 44.
24 Limited Partnership Act, 1907, section 4.
25 Section 8.
26 Section 11.
27 Section 6.
28 Companies Act, 1948, sections 124 and 127.
29 [1897] A.C. 22.
30 Companies Act, 1967, section 47.
31 Companies Act, 1948, sections 1 and 2.
32 European Communities Act, 1972, section 9.
33 Companies Act, 1948, section 66.
34 Report of the Working Party on Agricultural Co-operative Law, July 1971. Central Council for Agricultural and Horticultural Co-operation.
35 A different system of levying duty on the capital of companies seems likely to come into effect before long (Finance Bill, 1973, clauses 39 to 41

and Schedule 18); this Bill is, however, not law as yet.
[36] Section 61.
[37] Section 176.
[38] Section 131.
[39] Section 137.
[40] Section 136.
[41] Section 137(2).
[42] Finance Act, 1940, section 46; *post*, pages 177–8.
[43] *John Shaw and Sons (Salford), Ltd.* v. *Shaw* [1935] 2 K.B. 113.
[44] Companies Act, 1948, section 10.
[45] Section 184.
[46] Companies Act, 1948, section 1.
[47] Section 28.
[48] Section 28.
[49] Section 28.
[50] Section 38 and the Fourth Schedule.
[51] Sections 43 and 44.
[52] Section 38 and *Re South of England Natural Gas and Petroleum Co. Ltd.* [1911] 1 Ch. 573; compare *Nash* v. *Lynde* [1929] A.C. 158.
[53] Section 47.
[54] Section 53.
[55] Section 109.
[56] Section 130.
[57] Industrial and Provident Societies Act, 1965, section 3.
[58] Section 1.
[59] Section 1(1).
[60] Section 1(3).
[61] Section 2(1).
[62] Section 2(2).
[63] Section 5.
[64] Section 2(2).
[65] Section 3.
[66] Section 1(1).
[67] Section 1(1), 6(1) and Schedule 1.
[68] Section 14(1).
[69] Section 14(2).
[70] Section 6(1)
[71] Report of the Working Party on Agricultural Co-operative Law.
[72] Section 1(1) and Schedule 1.
[73] *Alexander* v. *Duddy* (1956) S.C. 24.
[74] Section 1(1) and Schedule 1.

[75] Section 44(1).

[76] Section 57.

[77] Section 1(1) and Schedule 1.

[78] Section 23.

[79] Section 24(1).

[80] Section 24(2).

[81] Administration of Estates (Small Payments) Act, 1965, section 2.

[82] Industrial and Provident Societies Act, 1965, section 1(1) and Schedule 1.

[83] Section 49.

[84] Section 1(1) and Schedule 1.

[85] Section (1) and Schedule 1.

[86] Report of the Committee of Inquiry on Contract Farming, (HMSO Cmnd 5099).

[87] Report of the Committee of Inquiry on Contract Farming. (HMSO Cmnd 5099).

[88] Friendly and Industrial and Provident Societies Act, 1968, Section 1.

[89] Section 3.

[90] Section 4.

[91] Section 7.

[92] Section 8.

[93] Industrial and Provident Societies Act, 1965, section 60.

[94] Section 52.

[95] Section 50.

[96] Section 53.

[97] Section 16(1).

[98] Section 55.

[99] Section 58.

[100] HMSO Cmnd 5099.

[101] Perpetuities and Accumulations Act, 1964, section 13.

[102] (1889) 14 App. Cas. 381.

[103] (1932) 48 T.L.R. 301.

[104] *Carlisle and Silloth Golf Club* v. *Smith* [1913] 3 K.B. 75.

[105] [1972] A.C. 414

[106] Agricultural and Forestry Allocation Act, 1962, section 1.

[107] S.I. 1962 No. 1892.

[108] S.I. 1964 No. 14.

[109] Agriculture (Miscellaneous Provisions Act, 1968, section 44, incorporating Finance Act, 1965, section 70.

4 Wills and Intestacy

This chapter is prefaced by a warning that it is most inadvisable for a layman to make his own will, at any rate unless his property is very small; this is because a layman is unlikely to appreciate that the words he uses often bear technical legal meanings, and his own draftmanship may well either fail to carry out his wishes or give rise to lengthy and expensive litigation concerning the interpretation of the words used. The chapter is merely designed to provide an outline understanding of the law of wills and of intestacy, and of the procedure for dealing with the estate of a deceased person.

Wills

Capacity to make a will

A will made before 1970 by a person under the age of twenty-one is invalid;[1] since 1969 a person who has reached the age of eighteen can make a valid will.[2] Soldiers and seamen may in certain circumstances make a privileged will, either formally or informally, despite being under age.

A person must have testamentary capacity in order to make a valid will. This means that he must have an understanding of the nature of the testamentary act and its effect, a recollection of the property he intends to dispose of and of the persons who are the objects of his bounty and the manner in which the property is to be distributed.[3] A person suffering from mental disorder can make a valid will during a lucid interval in which he satisfies the above requirements.[4]

A particular insane delusion will not preclude the testator from making a valid will except insofar as the delusion affects a particular clause or clauses of his will or unless it affects the testator's general faculties.[5]

The burden of proving the testator's capacity is on the person seeking to establish the will; but if a will, rational on the face of it, is shown to have been executed and attested in the manner required by law, it is presumed, unless there is evidence to the contrary, to have been made by a person of sufficient mental capacity.[6]

If the testator is so infirm as to raise a doubt concerning capacity, it may be advisable to enlist the services of a medical practitioner to examine the testator and furnish evidence concerning this.

The Lord Chancellor or a nominated judge has power to execute a will for a mentally disordered person who is believed incapable of making a will.[7]

The court will not uphold the will of a blind or illiterate testator unless the court is satisfied that the will was read over to the testator before its execution or that the testator knew its contents at the time of execution;[8] it is advisable to show this by the terms of the attestation clause (see *post*, page 113), although sworn evidence given by anyone having knowledge of the facts is admissible.

Undue influence

A will executed under the pressure of undue influence is invalid as to the whole or any part of the will affected by it; influence is not undue unless it amounts to fraud or coercion,[9] and mere persuasion of the testator falling short of coercion is not sufficient.[10]

Once it has been proved that a will has been executed with due solemnity by a person of competent understanding and apparently a free agent, the burden of proving that it was executed under undue influence is on the person alleging this.[11]

Formalities for making a will

The will of a testator made within the United Kingdom must, if the testator had his permanent home and habitual residence at all times within the United Kingdom, comply with the following formal requirements. The will must be in writing and signed at the foot or end thereof by the testator, or by some other person in his presence and by his direction.[12] The signature need not be of the testator's name; thus, for example, the making of a mark on the will by the testator will be sufficient so long as the court is satisfied that the testator intended this mark to operate as his signature of the will.

Although the testator's signature must be at the foot or end of the will, this bears a liberal interpretation under the Wills Act Amendment Act, 1852, but any provisions in the document which follow the testator's signature either in time or in space are invalid. Thus if a will is signed at the foot of the first page, but for lack of space the testamentary dispositions are continued on to the other side of the page, the provisions on the other side are invalid unless some express reference is made to them above the testator's signature on the first page so as to work an incorporation of them on to the first page above the signature.

The testator must make or acknowledge his signature in the presence of two or more witnesses present at the same time, and those witnesses must then attest and subscribe the will in the presence of the testator.[13] Hence if the will is not signed in the presence of at least two witnesses, the testator must acknowledge his signature to such witnesses; the witnesses need not be informed of the nature or contents of the document, but the testator must produce the document and request the witnesses to attest his signature and the witnesses must either see or have the chance to see the testator's signature.

Both witnesses must be present at the time when the testator makes or acknowledges his signature and before either witness attests and signs the will, and the testator must be present when the witnesses attest and sign. 'Presence' requires both mental and physical presence. Mental presence requires an awareness of what is happening, and physical presence requires the ability to see what is happening had the person chosen to look; thus where the testator had signed the will in the presence of the witnesses, and the witnesses then left the testator in that room and went to an adjoining room where they signed their names on the will, the door between the two rooms being left open but the testator not being at an angle where he could see the witnesses through the door, the attestation by the witnesses was held to be bad as not having been made in the testator's presence.[14]

A blind person cannot witness a will.[15]

A witness can sign by using his name, his initials or a mere mark.

If a beneficiary under the will or the spouse of a beneficiary witnesses the will, then his witnessing of the will is valid but the gift to the beneficiary who witnessed or to his spouse is void.[16] To this rule there are a number of qualifications; moreover a gift is not invalidated by the attestation of a beneficiary or his spouse if the will is sufficiently witnessed without his or her attestation.[17] It is advisable that the will should contain a clause showing that the formalities regarding attestation have been complied with.

Revocation

It is inherent in the nature of a will that it shall be revocable by the testator at any time up to the moment of his death. This is true, so far as the law of wills is concerned, even if the testator entered into a binding contract during his lifetime not to revoke his will, although his breach of bargain may give rise to a claim for breach of contract or for breach of trust.

A will can be revoked by any one of three methods. It may be revoked by another will or 'codicil' (i.e. a supplementary testamentary document by which the testator adds to or varies his will) or by some other written instrument executed like a will or codicil and declaring an intention to revoke the will. [18] A will usually contains a clause expressly stating that the testator is revoking all previous testamentary dispositions made by him and that this document is his last will; merely to describe the document as 'the last will and testament' of the testator does not in itself manifest a sufficient intention to revoke former testamentary instruments, except to the extent that the earlier dispositions cannot stand with those made by the later documents. [19] The dispositions made by a later testamentary document operate as an implied revocation of earlier testamentary dispositions made by the same testator so far as the later dispositions are inconsistent with the former, but the earlier dispositions will be valid except insofar as they are inconsistent. [20] If however the court takes the view that the testator only intended to revoke his will conditionally upon the truth of some fact or event which subsequently turns out to have been unfounded, then in contemplation of law there is no revocation since the condition which was in the mind of the testator is not fulfilled. [21]

Another method of revoking a will is by burning, tearing or otherwise destroying it by the testator or by some other person in the testator's presence and by his direction with the intention of revoking the will. [22] There must be an actual physical destruction of the will or of a vital part such as the testator's signature; merely to strike the words through with a pen, without obliterating the words, is not a sufficient destruction. [23] The physical destruction of two or three non-vital lines of a will have been held a revocation by destruction of those lines only. [24] The destruction must be carried out by the testator or by some person in the testator's presence and by his direction; a destruction carried out without the testator's presence is of no legal effect, nor can the testator make what was done out of his presence effective by expressing his subsequent approbation. The testator must have the intention of revoking the will by means of its destruction, thus an accidental destruction of the will does not revoke it. [25] Verbal evidence is admissible to prove the contents of a will which has been destroyed without having been revoked.

As already seen with regard to revocation of a will by a later document, so also as regards an alleged revocation by destruction the court may find that the testator intended his revocation to be conditional, so that if the condition goes unfulfilled there is no revocation. Thus where the testator destroyed his will by burning it in the mistaken belief that should he die without making a will his widow would take the whole of his property, it

114

was held that the will had not been revoked. [26]

The third method of revocation is that a will is automatically revoked by the testator's subsequent marriage;[27] to this principle there is a minor exception which in some circumstances saves the exercise by the will of the testator of a power of appointment, and a more important one in that the Law of Property Act, 1925, section 177, provides that a will made after 1925 and expressed to be made in contemplation of marriage is not revoked by the solemnisation of the marriage contemplated. Section 177 does not save a will which was only expressed to be made in contemplation of marriage generally,[28] since in order to be saved the will must express the fact that the testator contemplates marriage to a particular person[29] and the will must sufficiently indicate the identity of that person.

Alterations to the will

Alterations to a will are presumed to have been made after the will was executed. [30] If the alteration constitutes an actual obliteration of some of the words of the will, then it takes effect as a revocation by destruction of those words. Alterations falling short of obliterations are ineffective, and thus the original words stand, unless the alteration or a memorandum referring to it is signed by the testator and the witnesses;[31] in practice it is sufficient if the testator and the attesting witnesses initial the will alongside the alteration. [32]

Revival of wills

A will which has been revoked can be revived either by re-execution, or by a duly executed codicil showing an intention to revive the will. [33] In one case the testator made a will leaving all his property to Miss E.P.H. whom he married subsequently; the will had not been expressed to be made in contemplation of marriage, and was thus revoked by the marriage. Having been told of this fact, the testator made a signed and duly witnessed statement on the envelope containing his will 'the herein-named E.P.H. is now my lawful wedded wife', and the court held that this was a codicil which sufficiently showed the testator's intention to revive his will since the statement could have had no other purpose. [34]

A will revoked by destruction cannot be revived. Moreover the intentional destruction of a revoking instrument is not sufficient to revive a revoked will. [35]

Appointment of executors

An executor is a person whom the testator appoints to handle the testator's estate upon his death and to carry out the provisions of his will; sometimes however a person can become an executor without having been appointed by the deceased, inasmuch as the court may in certain limited circumstances appoint an executor and, more importantly, an executor of a sole or last surviving executor of the testator becomes the executor of that testator. [36] This last example means that an executor must also take on any unfinished executorships of his testator, but this chain of representation, as it is known, only applies to and through an executor who proves the will (*post*) of his testator.

An executor may be appointed to act as such either expressly or by implication; an implied appointment is made when the testator directs that some named person is to carry out the administration of the testator's estate, but without expressly stating that he is to be executor.

The testator need only appoint one executor, but he may appoint any number he chooses, although the court will not grant probate (see *post*) to more than four executors in respect of the same property.[37]

A person who has been appointed executor may decline to act as such even if, during the testator's lifetime, he agreed to accept the office; after the death of the testator the court has power to require any person appointed as executor to elect whether he will accept the office or not. If an executor enters upon the administration of the estate he impliedly accepts the office and will not as a rule be allowed to change his mind afterwards.

An executor who is not debarred from renouncing office under the above rules may do so by writing signed by him and recorded in the Probate Registry, and if so his rights in respect of the executorship altogether cease.

Obtaining probate of the will by the executor(s)

An executor derives his title from the will of his testator, and the testator's property vests in the executor immediately upon the death of the testator. [38] He may therefore at once enter upon the administration of the estate, but in general he cannot establish in court his rights as executor or make any formal proof of his title unless he has proved the will of his testator and he produces a copy of the will certified under the seal of the court. The acquisition of this formal proof of the testator's authority is known as obtaining probate of the will; only an executor can obtain probate.

116

In general probate cannot be obtained until seven days have elapsed since the testator's death;[39] conversely monetary penalties may be imposed on any person who administers a dead person's estate without obtaining probate within six months after the death.[40]

The normal method of obtaining proof of a will is by bringing it into the Principal Probate Registry or a district Probate Registry, together with an Inland Revenue affidavit (i.e. sworn written testimony) concerning the extent of the deceased's estate; the proving executor must also swear an oath that he believes that the will is the last will of the testator, that he is the person appointed executor in it, that he will administer the estate according to law and render just and true accounts whenever required, and that the gross value of the estate amounts to a specified sum. If the will is shown to be in order probate will then issue.

An alternative method of obtaining probate is by bringing a court action to have the will pronounced valid, or by successfully defending an action to have it pronounced invalid. The executor might consider it advisable for his own protection to have the validity of the will established in this way if he thinks it is likely to be contested. Legislation has been passed making a grant of probate or administration (*post*, pages 120—2) unnecessary in order to deal with certain very small estates.

Intestacy

A person dies intestate to the extent that he does not dispose of his property by will; thus a person may die wholly testate, or wholly intestate, or, where he leaves a will disposing of only part of his property, partly testate and partly intestate.

The property in respect of which a person dies intestate, insofar as it does not already consist of money, is to be held, by those administering his estate, on trust to sell it and convert it into money, though 'personal chattels', (*post*, page 119) are not to be sold except for special reasons.[41] After meeting the liabilities of the deceased and the expenses of administration, the rest of the intestate property of a person dying intestate after 1969 is to be distributed as follows.[42] (It is however as well to bear in mind that the intestacy laws are altered from time to time and that the alterations do not always attract much publicity when they occur, hence a person satisfied with the rules set out below might nevertheless ponder the advisability of making a will, whereby he might also gain by exercising his right to appoint a suitable executor.)

If the intestate leaves a surviving spouse but no issue, no parent or brother or sister of the whole blood or issue of such brother or sister, then the surviving spouse takes the whole estate absolutely.

If the intestate leaves a surviving spouse and issue, the surviving spouse takes the 'personal chattels' (see *post*, page 119) absolutely and £ 15,000 after the costs and estate duty relating to this sum have been paid out of the rest of the estate, together with interest at £4 per cent per annum on the £15,000 from the date of death until date of payment; the surviving spouse also takes a life interest (which the spouse may elect to have redeemed and be paid its capital value) in one-half of what is left of the intestate property, and the remainder of the intestate property is held on the statutory trusts for the intestate's issue. The 'statutory trusts' mean that the property is held for the benefit of the children of the intestate, and the issue of deceased children, who are alive or of whom their mother is pregnant at the date of the intestate's death, and who attain the age of eighteen or marry under that age; the surviving children of the deceased take in equal shares, and the issue of deceased children of the deceased take amongst them in equal shares the share their parent would have taken had he been alive at the date of the intestate's death. The 'statutory trusts' relating to relatives other than issue (*post*, page 119) are in essence similar, except that members of the class of relatives in question are substituted for issue.

If the intestate leaves no issue but leaves a surviving spouse and at least one of any of the following—a parent, a brother or sister of the whole blood or issue of such brother or sister—then the surviving spouse takes the personal chattels absolutely, £40,000 after the costs and estate duty relating to this sum have been paid out of the rest of the estate, together with interest at £4 per cent per annum on the £40,000 from the date of death until the date of payment, and half of the remainder of the intestate property absolutely; the other half of what is left of the intestate property is to be held in trust for the surviving parent or parents absolutely, and if there is no surviving parent is to be held on the statutory trusts for the brothers and sisters of the whole blood of the intestate.

If the intestate leaves issue but no surviving spouse the intestate property is to be held on the statutory trusts for the issue of the intestate.

If the intestate leaves no surviving spouse and no issue but leaves a parent or parents, then the intestate property is to be held on trust for the surviving parent, or surviving parents in equal shares, absolutely.

If the intestate leaves no surviving spouse, no issue and no parent, then the intestate property is to be held in trust for the following persons living at the death of the intestate and in the following order:

(a) on the statutory trusts for the brothers and sisters of the whole blood of the intestate; but if none, then

(b) on the statutory trusts for the brothers and sisters of the half-blood of the intestate; but if none, then

(c) for the grandparents of the intestate, and if more than one in equal shares; but if none, then

(d) on the statutory trusts for the uncles and aunts of the intestate (being brothers or sisters of the whole blood of a parent of the intestate); but if none, then

(e) on the statutory trusts for the uncles and aunts of the intestate (being brothers or sisters of the half blood of a parent of the intestate).

In default of any person taking an absolute interest as above, the intestate property is to go to the Crown or the Duchy of Lancaster or the Duke of Cornwall.

The 'personal chattels' which are not to be sold without special reason and to which a surviving spouse is entitled include indoor and outdoor furniture and effects, motor cars, jewellery, plate, books and consumable stores, but excluding chattels used for business purposes, money or securities for money. [43] A herd of cattle on a farm has been held to be 'used for business purposes' although the farm made no profit. [44]

If the intestate property includes an interest in a dwelling house in which the surviving spouse was resident at the time of the intestate's death, the surviving spouse can compel those administering the deceased's estate to transfer the matrimonial home at a proper valuation in satisfaction or part satisfaction of the spouse's interest under the intestacy; [45] in certain circumstances set out in the Second Schedule to the Act, including those where the dwelling house is held with agricultural land and an interest in the agricultural land is comprised in the residue of the estate, the spouse's right cannot be exercised unless the court is satisfied that its exercise is not likely to diminish the value of assets in the residue of the estate (other than the interest in the dwelling house) or make disposal of them more difficult.

If the dwelling house is worth more than the surviving spouse's interest in the deceased's estate, those administering the estate have power to appropriate to the survivor an interest in the house in which the survivor was resident at the time of the death; this appropriation is to be done partly in satisfaction of the survivor's interest and partly in return for payment by the survivor of the rest of the value of the dwelling. [46]

If a decree of judicial separation is in force and the separation is continuing, then if, after 1 August 1970, either party to the marriage dies wholly or partly intestate the property of the deceased spouse will devolve as if the other party to the marriage were already dead. [47]

Partial intestacy

If a person dies partly testate and partly intestate, the property in respect of which he dies intestate will be distributed in accordance with the intestacy rules set out above. [48] But the children or remoter issue of such a person must bring into account any benefit acquired by them under the deceased's will before they can claim any benefit under the partial intestacy; [49] other persons (except a surviving spouse) are not required to bring into account on a partial intestacy any benefit which they receive under the will. If a surviving spouse takes a beneficial interest (other than in personal chattels (*ante*, page 119) specifically left to the spouse by the will) under the deceased's will, then the spouse's right to the sum of £15,000 or £40,000, as the case may be, with interest is to be taken as a reference to that sum, diminished by the value at the date of death of the benefit taken under the will, with interest calculated accordingly. [50]

Administration

Where the deceased did not appoint an executor to deal with his estate or the executor declines to act, a grant of administration must be obtained in order to deal with his estate. Unlike an executor, an administrator derives his title wholly from the grant of administration to him, although when the grant is made it relates back to the time of the deceased's death for the purpose of protecting the estate from wrongful injury done between the date of the death and the date of the grant. The 'personal representative(s)' of the deceased is a descriptive legal expression which includes both his executor(s) and administrator(s).

The general principle is that the grant will be made to the person who has the greatest beneficial interest in the estate if that person chooses to act. Thus if there is a total intestacy, the surviving spouse (if any) is the first person entitled to take out a grant, followed by the persons entitled to succeed to the estate in the order of priority set out above (*ante*, pages 118—19). If several persons are entitled in the same degree of priority, as for example where the deceased left several children but no surviving spouse, the usual practice is to make the grant to the first of these persons who applies for it; if several persons in the same degree of priority should apply for the grant, the grant will be made to that person who is most likely to use it to the benefit of the estate and those interested in the estate, [51] and if there seems no reason to distinguish between the applicants on that ground the grant will be made to the member of the group having priority who has the largest interest or whom the majority of the group favour. [52]

A joint grant may be made to not more than four persons; if a minority or life interest arises under the intestacy, the grant must be made to at least two individuals or to a trust corporation (*ante*, page 10).[53]

Grant of administration where there is a will but no proving executor

Where the deceased left a will but there is no executor who obtains probate (*ante*, pages 116–17) of the will, a grant of administration with the will annexed must be obtained. Here again the general principle is to grant administration to the person who has the greatest interest in the estate of the deceased, should that person choose to apply; there are detailed provisions concerning the priority of entitlement. [54] If there are a number of claimants for a grant the court will select from amongst them on the same principles as those applicable to a grant on a total intestacy (see *ante*, pages 120–1).

Death of executor or administrator before completing the administration

If all the persons to whom a grant of probate or administration has been made die before the estate of the deceased has been completely administered, and if 'the chain of representation' (*ante*, page 116) applicable to executors is not continued, a grant of administration to the unadministered assets will have to be taken out in favour of a new administrator in order that the administration may be completed. The same rules as are applicable to original grants of administration will be observed.

Procedure when seeking a grant of administration

In general a grant may be sought at any Probate Registry or sub-registry. The grant will not normally be issued until at least fourteen days after the death of the deceased. [55]

The Inland Revenue affidavit containing particulars of the deceased's estate must be delivered for revenue purposes; the applicant for a grant of administration must swear an oath duly to administer the estate, and stating such matters as the place and time of the deceased's death and whether there is a life interest or a minority arising in the estate. The

Probate Registrar may in certain circumstances require a guarantee, with two sureties, to the gross amount of the estate as sworn.

Revocation of grant of probate or administration

If it appears to the court that the grant of probate or administration ought not to have been made or contains an error, the court may revoke it; this would be done, for example, where the grant was obtained by fraud on the court, or where a later will is discovered, or where the grant was made to the wrong person, or the supposed testator or intestate subsequently turns out not to be dead. A minor error can be corrected without a revocation of the grant.

Notwithstanding any subsequent revocation or variation of the grant of probate or administration, all conveyances of any interest in property already made to a purchaser by a person to whom the grant was made remain valid. [56]

Restriction on the freedom of testamentary disposition

Where a person who had his permanent home in England or Wales dies on or after 1 January 1969, an application may be made by or on behalf of certain dependants (*post*) of the deceased for maintenance out of the deceased's estate; if the court thinks that the disposition of the deceased's estate made by his will, or the law relating to intestacy, or the combination of both, is not such as to make reasonable provision for the maintenance of that dependant, the court may order such reasonable provision as it thinks fit to be made out of the deceased's net estate for the maintenance of the dependant.[57]

The application by the dependant must normally be made within six months of the date on which the grant of probate or administration to the deceased's estate was first taken out, although the court has power to extend the time. The dependants of the deceased who may apply comprise the surviving spouse; a daughter who has never been married or who is, because of some mental or physical disability, incapable of maintaining herself; a son who has not attained the age of twenty-one or who is, because of some mental or physical disability, incapable of maintaining himself.

Provision for maintenance under the court order is normally made by way of periodic payments, and must cease not later than the death of the dependant or, in the case of the spouse, the remarriage of that spouse; in the case of a daughter who has not been married or who is under a disability, on her marriage or cesser of disability whichever is the later; in the case of a son who is not yet twenty-one on his reaching that age or, if under a disability, on the cesser of his disability. [58] The court may if it thinks fit make an order providing that maintenance shall be wholly or partly paid by way of a lump sum. [59] The court may make an interim order if the dependant appears to be in immediate need of financial assistance but it is not yet possible to determine what order should finally be made.

An order can only be made if reasonable provision has not been made for the maintenance of the dependant. What is reasonable must depend on the circumstances of the dependant, the circumstances of the testator or intestate, the amount of his estate, the claims of others on his bounty, and all the surrounding circumstances including the conduct of the dependant himself. [60] The court must have regard to the deceased's reasons, so far as ascertainable, for not making any provision or any further provision for the dependant; the court must also have regard to the nature of the property comprised in the deceased's net estate, and should not order a provision to be made which would necessitate a sale of the property which would be improvident having regard to the interests of the deceased's dependants and of the person who, apart from the court order, would be entitled to the property. [61] 'Net estate' in general means the property which the deceased could dispose of on his death less the amount of his liabilities and the administration expenses and estate duty payable on his death.

If an order is made under the Act, then the deceased's will or the intestacy law, or both, are to have effect, as regards his estate, subject to the variations specified in the order. [62]

Notes

1   Wills Act, 1837, section 7.
2   Family Law Reform Act, 1969, sections 1 and 3(1).
3   *Banks* v. *Goodfellow* (1870) L.R. 5 Q.B. 549.
4   *In the Estate of Walker* (1912) 28 T.L.R. 466.
5   *Banks* v. *Goodfellow* (1870) L.R. 5 Q.B. 549.
6   *Symes* v. *Green* (1859) 1 Sw. and Tr. 401.
7   Administration of Justice Act, 1969, section 17.
8   Non-Contentious Probate Rules, 1954, r. 11.
9   *Boyse* v. *Rossborough* (1857) 6 H.L.C. 2, 48.

10 *Parfitt* v. *Lawless* (1872) L.R. 2 P. and D. 462.
11 *Craig* v. *Lamoureux* [1920] A.C. 349.
12 Wills Act, 1837, section 9.
13 Wills Act, 1837, section 9.
14 *Doe* v. *Manifold* (1813) 1 M. and S. 294.
15 *In the Estate of Gibson* [1949] P. 434.
16 Wills Act, 1837, section 15.
17 Wills Act, 1968, section 1.
18 Wills Act, 1837, section 20.
19 *Re Hawksley's Settlement* [1934] Ch. 384.
20 *Re Murray* [1956] 1 W.L.R. 605.
21 *In b. Hope-Brown* [1942] P. 136.
22 Wills Act, 1837, section 20.
23 *Stephens* v. *Taprell* (1840) 2 Curt. 458.
24 *Re Nunn* (1936) 52 T.L.R. 322.
25 *Re Booth* [1926] P. 118.
26 *In the Estate of Southerden* [1925] P. 177.
27 Wills Act, 1837, section 18.
28 *Sallis* v. *Jones* [1936] P. 43.
29 *In the Estate of Langston* [1953] P. 100.
30 *In b. Sykes* (1873) L.R. 3 P. and D. 26.
31 Wills Act, 1837, section 21.
32 *In b. Blewitt* (1880) 5 P.D. 116.
33 Wills Act, 1837, section 22.
34 *In b. Davis* [1952] P. 279.
35 *Major* v. *Williams* (1843) 3 Curt. 432.
36 Administration of Estates Act, 1925, section 7(1).
37 Judicature Act, 1925, section 160(1).
38 *Woolley* v. *Clark* (1822) 5 B. and Ald. 744.
39 Non-Contentious Probate Rules, Rule 5.
40 Stamp Act, 1815; Customs and Inland Revenue Act, 1881.
41 Administration of Estates Act, 1925, section 33(1).
42 Administration of Estates Act, 1925, section 46, as amended by the Intestates' Estates Act, 1952, the Family Provision Act, 1966, the Family Law Reform Act, 1969 and the Family Provision (Intestate Succession) Order 1972 S.I. 1972 No. 916.
43 Administration of Estates Act, 1925, section 55(1).
44 *Re Ogilvy* [1942] Ch. 288.
45 Intestates' Estates Act, 1952, section 5 and Second Schedule.
46 Administration of Estates Act, 1925, section 41; Intestates' Estates Act, 1952, Second Schedule.

Matrimonial Proceedings and Property Act, 1970, section 40.

Administration of Estates Act, 1925, section 49.

Administration of Estates Act, 1925, section 49(1), as amended by the Intestates' Estates Act, 1952, sections 3 and 4 and First Schedule and the Family Provision Act, 1966, section 1(2).

Intestates' Estates Act, 1952, as amended by the Family Provision Act, 1966, section 1.

Warwick v. *Greville* (1809) 1 Phill. 123.

Budd v. *Silver* (1813) 2 Phill. 115.

Judicature Act, 1925, section 160.

Non-Contentious Probate Rules, rule 19.

Non-Contentious Probate Rules, rule 5.

Administration of Estates Act, 1925, section 37.

Inheritance (Family Provision) Act, 1938, section 1(1), as amended by the Intestates' Estates Act, 1952, Part II and Third and Fourth Schedules, and the Family Provision Act, 1966, section 2.

Inheritance (Family Provision) Act, 1938, as amended by Family Law Reform Act, 1969.

Inheritance (Family Provision) Act, 1938, section 1(4).

Re Ducksbury [1966] 1 W.L.R. 1226.

Family Provision Act, 1966, Third Schedule.

Inheritance (Family Provision) Act, 1938, section 3, as amended by Intestates' Estates Act, 1952.

5 Taxation

Taxation of self-employed persons: Schedule D

Tax under Schedule D is charged on the profits of a trade or profession carried on wholly or partly in the United Kingdom.[1] Whether or not a person is trading (a term henceforth often used compendiously, unless otherwise stated, to embrace the pursuit of a trade or profession; the word 'trade' is used in a similar sense) is a mixed question of law and fact; the repeated purchase and sale of goods or the rendering of services by a person in return for monetary reward is clearly trading by him, but a mere isolated transaction can be a difficult borderline matter. In *Martin* v. *Lowry*[2] a person previously unconnected with the linen trade bought from the government a vast quantity of surplus linen after the close of the war. Having failed to resell it as one lot, he set up his own trading organisation and sold the linen in smaller quantities during a period of about a year at a profit of close on £2 million; he was held to be trading in the linen.

In *Rutledge* v. *I.R.C.*[3] the plaintiff, while abroad in pursuance of a business venture of a totally different nature, made a single purchase of a million rolls of toilet paper for £ 1,000; soon after returning to this country he sold the entirety to another person at a gain of over £ 10,000. This was held to be trading, although his dealing in this line of business was confined to the single purchase followed by the single sale. It is important to note that the sheer bulk of the purchase made it self-evident that it must have been bought for resale and as a commercial venture.

If the taxpayer has carried out repeated transactions of the same type, this is an important factor weighing in favour of the view that he has been trading.[4]

The local Inspector of Taxes initially decides whether the transaction in question constitutes trading, but the taxpayer has the right of appeal against his decision to the Commissioners, the burden of proof resting on the taxpayer to prove that the Inspector is wrong. Further appeal lies to the High Court by case stated for the opinion of the Court on a point of law; this includes, in addition to the construction of Acts of Parliament relating to revenue matters, the question whether the decision of the Commissioners was reasonably supported by the findings of fact as made by the Commissioners and set out in the case stated for the opinion of the Court.[5]

Tax is charged on the annual profits obtained from trading, i.e. the total of taxable receipts (*post*) from the trade less the legally deductible expenses. The yearly profits of a trade are normally computed for tax purposes on the earnings basis; this involves taking account of the sums earned (whether or not paid) less the deductible expenses incurred (whether or not paid) during the tax year in question. As regards those carrying on professions, the tax authorities may permit profits to be calculated on the cash basis by reference to the actual sums received and paid out during the period in question, although the taxpayer could insist on being taxed on the earnings basis if he chose.

Only profits from the trade which are of an income nature are liable to income tax (although capital profits may be liable to capital gains tax, *post*, pages 151–9). Thus if a farmer were to buy a new farm and sell his old farm at a profit, the profit thus made would not in general be liable to income tax since the farmer would not as a rule be trading in farms but only in farming stock and produce. A person who carried on a trade of buying and selling land would be liable to tax on the profits made from the sale of the land since these would be of an income nature. The distinction between what is a capital profit and what is an income profit therefore lies in the nature of the business carried on by the person whose liability to tax is called in question, and not in the nature of the asset which is realised at a profit.

In ascertaining the profit from the trade, it is necessary to take into account the value of the stock-in-trade with which he begins and the stock-in-trade with which he ends the accounting period in question, and any enhanced figure at the end of the period will be an item of profit. The stock-in-trade is to be valued, item by item, on the basis of either its cost price or its market price if the market value is lower and the taxpayer so elects,[6] and the taxpayer's choice of the basis of valuation can be varied as between the different items so that one item could be valued at market value and another item valued at cost. The result is that if an unrealised item of stock has risen in value the trader will postpone any liability to pay tax on the increase by continuing to value the stock at cost, whereas conversely if an item of his stock has fallen in value below cost price he will probably elect to reduce the computation of his profit for the year by valuing that item at its diminished current market value.

Agreement has been reached between the National Farmers Union and the Inland Revenue that a farmer, when valuing his livestock at cost, may regard cost as being 60 per cent (previously 75 per cent) of the market

128

value of homebred cattle and 75 per cent of the market value of sheep and pigs. This method of valuation is merely a rough and ready one, and does not preclude the farmer from proving that cost was in fact lower than this or seeking to persuade the Inspector of Taxes that some other basis would, as for example in the case of pedigree cattle, be a truer reflection of cost.

Animals kept by a farmer for the purposes of his farming are to be treated as trading stock, except where the farmer elects that animals forming part of production herds shall be treated on the herd basis.[7] An election for the herd basis must be made in writing to the Inspector, and applies to all production herds of the class in respect of which the election is made. Generally speaking the election for the herd basis must be made within two years from the end of the first Revenue year in respect of which the farmer is chargeable to tax or allowed loss relief under Schedule D in respect of his farming, although the period is extended if the whole or a substantial part of a production herd kept for farming is slaughtered by a public body under the law relating to diseases of animals and compensation is payable to the farmer in respect of this; an election for the herd basis is irrevocable. The farmer will, however, be given a further opportunity to elect to be treated on the herd basis if Clause 35 of the Finance Bill, 1973, should become law, as seems likely; if so he will be entitled to make his election for the herd basis at any time between the passing of the Act and 5 April 1976. Such an election will take effect, if made by a farming company, for the accounting period in which it is made and all subsequent periods, but if made by a sole trader or partnership it takes effect for the Revenue year during which it is made and the accounts on which the assessment for that Revenue year is based (normally the preceding year basis; *post*, pages 132–4), and for all subsequent years.

The effect of electing to be treated on the herd basis is that the initial cost of the herd and of any additions to it and the value of the herd are left out of account for Schedule D purposes, thus changes in market value do not affect the position under that head. Replacements to and sales from the herd are to be brought into account under Schedule D, although there are special rules concerning the computation of the consequent receipts or expenses. If the herd is sold as a whole and another production herd of the same class is acquired, the above rules apply as though a number of animals equal to the number in the original herd or in the newly acquired herd, whichever is the less, had been sold from the original herd and replaced in it. If, without acquiring another production herd of the same class, the herd is sold or substantially reduced in number by sale either all at once or over a period not exceeding a year, then in general any profit or loss arising from such a transaction is not to be taken into account under

Schedule D.[8] There are a number of detailed rules concerning the herd basis which are applicable to particular cases.

To realise the assets of a trade after it has been permanently discontinued does not constitute trading,[9] but notwithstanding this it is now expressly required by statute that on discontinuance any trading stock belonging to the trader must be valued at the amount it would fetch on a sale in the open market at the time of discontinuance, thus taxing any rise in value. But an open market valuation is not required if the trade is discontinued by reason of the death of a sole trader [i.e. a person trading on his own account (with or without employees), and hence not in partnership], or if the stock is sold for valuable consideration to a person who trades or intends to trade in the United Kingdom so that the cost of acquisition by the latter is a deductible expense in computing his profits; in the latter case the trader who has just discontinued brings into account the actual sum he has received for the transfer. [10]

If a trader, instead of selling part of his stock-in-trade, appropriates it for his own use or enjoyment or for that of his family, he must bring the market value of the stock at the time of appropriation into his accounts for tax purposes.[11] The defendant in *Sharkey* v. *Wernher* owned a stud farm for horses, which was admittedly a trade, and also owned racing stables which were admitted to be a purely recreational activity. The defendant transferred some horses from the farm to the racing stables, and the case was fought to decide what value should be attributed to the horses for the purpose of the trade accounts. It was held that the value to be thus attributed was not the cost of breeding the horses, but their market value at the time of their transfer. Thus a farmer who uses his own produce or livestock for domestic consumption must, when preparing his accounts for tax, treat these articles as if they had been sold in the normal course of trade at the retail value. But this rule only applies to the disposal of stock-in-trade, and articles which have never been part of the trader's stock do not come within it.

Deduction of expenses of the trade

In computing the profits of the trade, the general principle is that only expenses wholly and exclusively incurred for the purpose of the trade are deductible. [12] Generally speaking, such expenses as are incurred in the actual earning of profit are deductible; this expenditure must be of an income and not of a capital nature, as well as being incurred wholly and exclusively for the purpose of the trade. As to the former, it has been said that 'When an expenditure is made, not only once and for all, but with a view to bringing into existence an asset or an advantage for the enduring benefit of the trade, I think that there is very good reason. . . for treating such an expenditure as properly attributable not to revenue but to capital'. [13] Thus the cost of acquisition of the business premises, such as the acquisition of the farm or thé construction of farm buildings, is not deductible (though capital allowances may be claimed in respect of the latter; *post,* pages 138–9).

As regards the requirement that the expenditure must be incurred wholly and exclusively for the purpose of the trade, the expenses of maintenance of the taxpayer, his family or establishment, or any sums expended for his domestic or private purposes are expressly disallowed. [14] It has been ruled that the furtherance of the trade must be the sole purpose of the expenditure, although if this is the sole purpose the fact that some other incidental consequence ensues will not disqualify the expenditure; [15] in strictness, therefore, when expenditure is incurred partly for business and partly for private purposes none of this expenditure is deductible, but the tax officials frequently allow deduction, on a concessionary basis, of a proportionate sum in respect of that part of the expenditure which was incurred in furtherance of the trade purpose.

Where a trader claimed to deduct medical expenses incurred in regaining his health on the ground that he would be unable to pursue his trade unless he did so, the expense were disallowed since they were not wholly and exclusively incurred for the purpose of the trade but also for the advantage and benefit of the taxpayer as a living human being. [16]

If rent is paid in respect of the business premises on which the trade is carried on, such rent is clearly deductible, and if the rented building is used partly for trade and partly for private purposes the Revenue allow a deduction in respect of that part of the rent which is referable to the trade. [17]

Money spent in carrying out repairs to assets of the business is a deductible expense so long as it is a revenue rather than a capital expense. Where a trader bought a ship in bad repair, the cost of subsequent repairs to the ship was held to be capital expenditure so far as the cost was attributable to the extent of disrepair existing at the time of its purchase. [18] But where a trader bought a cinema in disrepair at the date of its purchase, though the disrepair had no bearing on the purchase price, and the trader repaired the cinema at a cost which the accountancy profession would regard as revenue expenditure, it was held that the expense was deductible as revenue expenditure when computing profits. [19] In order to be deductible, the expenditure must be incurred in carrying out repairs as distinct from effecting improvements. It has been judicially stated, albeit in a different context, that 'Repair is restoration by renewal or replacement of subsidiary parts of a whole. Renewal, as distinguished from repair, is reconstruction of the entirety, meaning by the entirety not necessarily the whole but substantially the whole subject-matter under discussion'. [20]

The cost of fines, such as a fine incurred for a speeding offence committed by a farmer on the way to the market, is not deductible since the fine is not paid in order to earn a profit. [21]

The cost of a tax appeal launched by the trader against a disputed assessment by the tax authorities of his trading profit is not deductible, [22] but the fees paid to an accountant in respect of the preparation of the computation of the taxpayer's trading profit are allowed, as are most legal expenses incurred in the conduct of the trade, such as commencing an action to recover a trade debt. The expense of entertaining business customers is expressly disallowed unless the customer is an overseas customer. [23]

The cost of travelling from one place of business to another by the taxpayer is deductible. but the expense of travelling between home and a place of business is not deductible, [24] unless it can be proved on the facts that the taxpayer's home was itself the base for his business operations.[25]

The interest paid on a loan, such as a bank overdraft, borrowed for the purpose of the business is deductible. [26] Payments to provide pensions for the taxpayer's employees are deductible if this is done wholly and exclusively for the purpose of the trade, as are, subject to certain rather complex conditions, payments made to provide pensions in the future for the employees.

The basis of assessment

The income tax year runs from 6 April of one year to 5 April of the succeeding year; where a person is charged to tax on the profits of his trade or profession the tax so charged is payable in two equal instalments on 1 January and 1 July. The basis on which the amount chargeable to tax is calculated for the year in which the charge to tax is actually levied is usually arrived at on what is known as the preceding year basis; this means that since the trader or professional man is required to make up his account of profit or loss for a period of one year at a time (though the starting and closing dates of the trader's accounting year are not required to coincide with the starting and closing dates of the Revenue year from 6 April to 5 April) the trader's profit which is liable to tax in the current Revenue year is that which the trader made during the trader's own accounting year which came to a close during the preceding Revenue year.

Thus if a trader is being assessed to tax for the Revenue year running from 6 April 1973 to 5 April 1974, and if the trader's own private accounting period runs from, say, 10 January in each year to 9 January in the following year, the trader's liability to tax for the Revenue year 1973–74 would normally be based on the trader's figure of profit or loss made during the period from 10 January 1972 until 9 January 1973.

The preceding year basis naturally is incapable of application to the first year in which the trader commences his business, but the special rules relating to the computation of profits on commencement of a business usually extend to the first three Revenue years relating to it. Hence the charge to tax for the first Revenue year will be based on the profits from the date of commencement of the business up to the following 5 April; if the trader's own first accounting year covers a period extending beyond 5 April, as will probably be the case, the computation of his profit between the date of commencing the business up to 5 April must be made by apportioning the profits of his first accounting year in relation to how much of it falls before 5 April and how much after that date. The amount of profit taxed during the second Revenue year is based on the actual profits of the first accounting year of trading, and for the third Revenue year is found by using the normal preceding year basis which, as explained above, means the profits of the trader's own accounting year which falls within the Revenue year previous to the year as regards which the computation of the taxable sum is being made. However as regards the second and third Revenue years (both or neither), the taxpayer has the option of having his assessments to tax based on the actual profits of the trading from 6 April to 5 April in each of those years; in practice this computation is made by apportioning on a time basis the profits shown by the trader's accounts over any trading periods part of which fall within those Revenue years. This option is exercisable by notice to the Inspector of Taxes within seven years from the end of the second tax year and can be revoked at any time within that period.

The operating of the above rules may be illustrated with the aid of an example. Assume that a trader commences business on 6 October 1968. Assume that his profits for the first three years of trading are as follows:

	£
Accounting year ending 5 October 1969	1,800
Accounting year ending 5 October 1970	2,400
Accounting year ending 5 October 1971	3,600

The assessments to tax would usually be:

For the Revenue year 1968–69, 6/12ths of the actual profits
during the year ending 5 October 1969   £ 900

For the Revenue year 1969–70, actual profits of the year ending
5 October 1969   £1,800

For the Revenue year 1970–71, actual profits of the year ending
5 October 1969   £1,800

For the Revenue year 1971–72, actual profits of the year ending
5 October 1970   £2,400

For the Revenue year 1972–73, actual profits of the year ending
5 October 1971   £3,600

Should the taxpayer elect to be taxed during the second and third
Revenue years on the basis of the actual profits made during those
years the assessments would be made as follows:

Revenue year 1969–70:	6 April 1969 to 5 October 1969: 6/12ths × £1,800 = £900 6 October 1969 to 5 April 1970: 6/12ths × £2,400 = £1,200	£2,100
Revenue year 1970–71:	6 April 1970 to 5 October 1970: 6/12ths × £2,400 = £1,200 6 October 1970 to 5 April 1971: 6/12ths × £3,600 = £1,800	£3,000

It will be apparent that the computation of profits for tax purposes
during the opening years of the business is likely to differ considerably
from the actual profits made during those years; since the actual profits of
the first year's trading will figure in the computation of taxable profit for
the first three Revenue years (unless the taxpayer elects to be assessed on
a current year basis), it is desirable for tax purposes that the profits of the
first trading year should be kept low.

The rules for assessment during the opening years of the business are
contained in sections 115–117 of the Income and Corporation Taxes Act,
1970.

Discontinuance of business

If the trade is permanently discontinued, the computation of tax for the
final Revenue year in which business is carried on is based on the actual
profits from 6 April of the year of discontinuance up to the date of
discontinuance. As regards the penultimate and pre-penultimate Revenue
years, assessments to tax for these years will already have been made on

the preceding year basis. If the combined total of the actual profits of these two years exceeds the combined total of profits as computed on the preceding year basis, the tax ultimately payable must be adjusted by reference to those actual profits. The actual profits are found by apportioning on a time basis the profits of the trader's accounting periods which relate wholly or partly to the Revenue year in question.[27]

If there is a change in the persons who carry on a trade, the amount of the profits or gains on which tax is chargeable and the persons on whom it is charged must be decided as if the activity had been permanently discontinued at the date of the change and a new activity had then been begun[28] (for the position where there is a change of partners carrying on a business, see *post,* page 136). Thus if a trader sells his business as a going concern to another trader, the outgoing trader will be assessed on the basis of the rules regarding computation of taxable profits which apply to a discontinued business, and the incoming trader will be assessed on the basis of the exceptional rules relating to commencement of a business. But this rule only applies if the business itself continues, and thus not to a person who merely takes over the assets of the trade from an outgoing trader without taking over the business itself;[29] it may be a difficult question of fact to decide which of these events has occurred.

Taxation of partnerships

The date on which the partnership comes into existence or ceases to exist for tax purposes must be decided as a mixed question of fact and law;[30] declarations of the partners concerning the date of inception or of termination are not conclusive on the point. The income of the partnership is ascertained by applying the rules appropriate to individuals, thus tax will be levied on a trading partnership in accordance with the rules of Schedule D. A single return showing the whole of the partnership income must be made to the Inspector of Taxes by a partner, and this task usually falls on the partner who is first named in the partnership agreement.[31] The tax payable by each of the partners will then be established, and the total due from all the partners is also set out in a joint assessment of tax made in the partnership name by the Inspector of Taxes. Each partner is liable to the Revenue for the whole of the firm's tax;[32] normally the firm pays the tax to the Revenue and each partner contributes his share.

Partnership income must for tax purposes be divided between the partners by reference to the share of profits to which each partner is entitled during the Revenue year in question; this is so notwithstanding the fact that the profits of the current Revenue year may well be computed on the preceding year basis (*ante*, pages 132–4) and may have been divided between the partners on a different basis in the year in which those profits were actually earned. If a partner is paid a salary by the firm, or is paid interest on capital contributed to the firm by him, such payments do not reduce the profits of the firm but are regarded merely as modes of distributing those profits between the partners.

If the partnership suffers a loss, that loss must be apportioned between the partners in the same way that profits are apportioned between them. Each partner is entitled to claim relief separately in respect of his share of the loss and may take his relief under whichever of the available methods (*post*, pages 137–8) he elects.

Effect of change of partners

If a partner dies or retires, or a new partner is admitted to the firm, or a sole trader takes another person into partnership with him, then the amount of the profits of the trade, profession or vocation on which tax is chargeable and the persons on whom it is chargeable are to be determined as if the business had been permanently discontinued at the date of the change and a new business had then been commenced;[33] the rules relating to the assessment of profits on newly established and on discontinued business have been discussed previously (*ante*, pages 132–5). But if a business passes on death to the trader's spouse and they have been living together, the rules relating to discontinuance are not enforced unless the taxpayer so desires, though unexhausted losses and capital allowances (*post*, pages 138–9) pertaining to the deceased trader cannot be carried forward for the benefit of the spouse.

The provisions relating to deemed discontinuance and commencement normally applicable on a change of partnership can be excluded so long as at least one person who was a partner prior to the change continues in the partnership after the change, and all the partners before and after the change (including the personal representatives of a dead partner) elect to treat the partnership as a continuing business; this election must be made by written notice signed by the above persons and sent to the Inspector within two years after the date of the change.[34] In deciding whether to exercise this option much depends on the personal circumstances of each of the partners, but it will often be advantageous to exercise the option if profits have been rising and are expected to continue to do so. If an election to be treated on a continuing basis is made, the apportionment of profits between the partners for the year in which the change is made will usually be based on the length of time for which they have been partners.

If a person sustains a loss in any trade or profession carried on by him either solely or in partnership, he may carry the loss forward and offset it against profits of the same business in subsequent years of assessment. The loss must be offset against the first available profits from the same business, but if the profits of the first available year are insufficient to exhaust the loss the surplus loss can be carried forward and set against the next available profits, and so on until the loss is finally exhausted. [35]

If a business is carried on by an individual or a partnership of individuals, and the business is then sold to a company in return wholly or mainly for the allotment of shares in that company, then the individuals continuing to hold those shares throughout the Revenue year in question may set off any unrelieved loss incurred before the conversion of the business into a company against any income derived by the individuals from the company by way of dividend or otherwise as if this income were income of the business. [36]

Since a business which is assessed on the preceding year basis (*ante*, pages 132–4) and which makes a loss must inevitably show no taxable profit from that business in the next year of assessment, the person who incurred the loss may prefer to seek immediate tax relief rather than postpone the taking of such relief. It is provided that where a person suffers a loss in any trade or profession carried on by him either solely or on partnership, he may by written notice given within two years after the year of assessment in which the loss was incurred claim relief in respect of the loss by setting it off against any other income which he may have either in that year or in the following year of assessment, taking the relief against the income of the earlier year insofar as such income is available. [37] It will be noted that this relief is not restricted to income derived from the same business. However, this type of relief cannot be claimed unless it is proved that, in the Revenue year in which the loss was sustained, the business was being carried on on a commercial basis and with a view to the realisation of profit; the fact that the business was being carried on so as to afford a reasonable expectation of profit is conclusive evidence that it was being carried on at that time with a view to the realisation of profit. [38] The object of this provision is to prevent persons with a very high income, and hence a very high rate of tax, from carrying on business merely for pleasure and setting the losses thereby incurred against their other income, thereby in effect defraying the losses substantially at the expense of the Revenue. It is further provided that if loss is incurred in the trade of farming or market gardening, and in each of the previous five years a loss

137

was incurred in carrying on that trade, then relief against the former loss can only be claimed by way of set-off against subsequent profits of the same business;[39] in practice the Revenue do not seek to enforce this provision.

Loss on discontinuance of business

If the business has been permanently discontinued, a loss sustained during the last twelve months of its continuance can be set against the profits of the three years preceding the year in which the discontinuance took place, unless relief against the loss has been obtained under some other provision; if carried back in this way, the relief must first be taken against profits, if available, of the most recent of the three years and carried back further if need be.[40]

Capital allowances

The relief obtainable where a capital allowance is claimable is by way of deduction from the profits of the trade or profession.

Capital allowances are available in respect of, amongst other things, machinery and plant used for carrying on a business and for agricultural or forestry buildings and works.

An allowance, known as 'a first-year allowance' is available to a person carrying on a trade or profession on which he expends capital in providing machinery or plant.[41] The first-year allowance in relation to expenditure incurred after 21 March 1972 is an amount equal to the whole of the expenditure.[42] First-year allowances do not apply to capital expenditure on the provision of mechanically propelled road vehicles other than commercial and certain other vehicles.[43]

Insofar as the trader elects not to claim the first-year allowance for which he is eligible, he is in general entitled to writing-down allowances for machinery or plant used for the purposes of the trade and belonging to him (including articles taken by him on hire-purchase). The writing-down allowances are given on the cost of the machinery or plant less the first-year allowance, are given in every year other than the first year until the value of the machinery or plant is exhausted, and are calculated by allowing in each year 25 per cent of the cost of the article reduced by any allowances already given.

Where a number of items of plant or machinery are purchased by the trader, there are provisions for aggregating the various items and treating them as one for the purpose of applying the writing-down allowances.

If the machine is later sold for an amount which exceeds its written-down value, the trader is liable to a 'balancing charge' on an amount equal to the excess.

The first-year and writing-down allowances are available whether the article is purchased new or second-hand.

Capital allowances are also available in respect of certain buildings. Thus if the owner or tenant of any agricultural or forestry land incurs any capital expenditure on the construction of farm houses, farm or forestry buildings, cottages, fences or other works, he can claim writing-down allowances during a period of ten years starting with the chargeable period in which the expenditure was incurred.[44] The expenditure must be incurred for the purposes of husbandry or forestry on the land in question, and as regards expenditure on the farm house one-third of the cost is the maximum which can qualify.[45] The unexpired allowance can be transferred to a successor in title.

Taxation of employees: Schedule E

Tax is charged under Schedule E on the emoluments of the offices and employments which fall within that Schedule of the Income and Corporation, Taxes Act, 1970. 'Office' includes a directorship,[46] a trusteeship and an executorship. The tests for determining what is an 'employment' seem to be akin to the tests for deciding who is a servant in order to determine whether his master has vicarious liability for torts committed by the servant (see *post,* pages 318–20). The same person may come under both the rules of Schedule D and of Schedule E if he carries on both a trade and an employment, each as part-time activities, during the same Revenue year, in which event the gains and expenses of each branch of his activities must be separately ascertained in order to arrive at his tax liability in respect of Schedule D on the one hand and Schedule E on the other,[47] unless the Revenue permit some relaxation of this for the sake of convenience.

Emoluments arising from the office or employment

Only emoluments which are derived from an office or employment become liable to tax under Schedule E. Any money received is not liable to tax unless it was paid with reference to the services rendered by virtue of the employment, and as a reward for the performance of those services at some point of time; the money received need not have been paid by the employer but may have come from a third party, as for example when a

139

customer tips a waitress in a restaurant. Thus where a company guaranteed its employees against loss on the sale of their houses in order to promote their mobility to other areas where they might be useful to the company, it was held that such a payment was not liable to tax because, although the company would not have made the payment save to an employee, it did not make the payment to him in respect of his services.[48]

If the payment made relates to services rendered during the previous year or years, it must be taxed as an emolument of the year or years during which the services were rendered and not of the year when actually paid.[49]

A gift to an employee is taxable if it is made because of his services, but not if made because of his personal qualities.

Taxation of benefits in kind

Taxable emoluments include not only payments in cash, but also benefits in kind which are convertible into money and payments made to third parties in order to discharge a monetary obligation of the employee; benefits which are not convertible into cash, such as free meals provided by the employer, a free uniform which remains the employer's property, or free travel, board and lodging are not taxable. As regards payments to third parties, where a company paid the bills for rates, heating, light and the upkeep of a residence which the company requested its director to occupy in order to uphold the company's prestige, it was held that these sums were taxable since they discharged monetary obligations which would fall to be paid by the director had they not been paid by the company.[50] And if an employer pays the income tax on his employee's salary for him, the tax so paid must be regarded as an emolument of the employee and further tax paid on it.

Where an employer purchases an article and gives it to his employee, the sum chargeable to tax is the value of the gift to the employee and not the sum paid by the employer. In *Wilkins* v. *Rogerson*[51] the employer gave a suit to his employee inasmuch as the employer paid the bill of the tailor who made the suit. The contract to make the suit was between the employer and the tailor and not between the tailor and the employee. The employee was taxable on the second-hand value of the suit since this was the sum for which he could cash the suit; had the employee ordered the suit from the tailor and the employer paid the tailor's bill, the employee would have been chargeable to tax on the sum so paid.

If the employee is obliged by the terms of his contract of employment to occupy premises for the more efficient discharge of his duties, he is not liable to tax on the annual value of these premises since his occupation of them cannot rightly be considered an emolument of his employment.[52] If the employee is merely entitled, though not obliged, to occupy premises provided by reason of that person, or of that person's spouse, holding an office or employment, and the rent paid is less than the annual value of the premises, then the annual value of the premises, less any rent actually paid for them, is treated as a taxable emolument of that person.[53] The annual value is the rent which might reasonably be expected to be obtained if the premises were let on a yearly tenancy and the tenant paid the usual tenant's rates and taxes and the landlord paid for repairs, insurance and maintenance.[54] The employee is regarded as paying a rent equal to the annual value so long as the rent paid by him was a full rent when the tenancy was granted, despite the fact that the rent remains unchanged and rental values have now increased or that the landlord could now obtain a higher rent.[55]

The reimbursement to an employee by his employer of expenses incurred wholly, exclusively and necessarily in the performance of the employee's duties is not an emolument of the employee. A reasonable, though estimated, expense allowance is not treated as a taxable emolument, but there are special provisions relating to this as regards directors and certain other employees (*post*, pages 142–3).

Termination of employment

A sum payable to a person on termination of his employment and to which he is contractually entitled by virtue of the terms on which he undertook the employment is a taxable emolument under Schedule E.[56] Other payments made in connection with the termination of the holding of the office or employment or any change in its terms are chargeable to tax under Schedule E, whether the payment is made to the employee or to his personal representative or to the employee's spouse, relative or dependent.[57] A payment is exempt from tax unless it exceeds £5,000, in which event the excess over £5,000 is taxable; payments made in connection with the termination of the employment by the death of the employee or office-holder or made by reason of injury to or disability of such a person are in any event exempt from this taxing provision.[58] Insofar as a payment is taxable, there are extremely complex provisions for determining the exact amount of tax payable, the effect of which is to reduce the rate of tax which would otherwise be payable.

Pension contributions

Contributions paid by the employee, either into a pension fund set up by the employer or to an insurance company which has agreed with the employer that it will provide pensions to the employees, are not deductible when computing the employee's taxable emoluments unless the pension scheme is an 'exempt approved scheme' (i.e. one approved by the Revenue and established under irrevocable trusts).[59]

Contributions paid by the employer to a scheme for providing pensions for his employee or the employee's dependents are deemed to be income of the employee and chargeable to tax in the Revenue year during which the sum is paid[60] unless the scheme is an approved or statutory scheme.[61] Pensions actually paid under an approved scheme are liable to tax under Schedule E and are usually treated as earned income.

Deductible expenses under Schedule E

Expenses incurred by the holder of an office or employment are only deductible from his taxable emoluments if the expenses have been incurred wholly, exclusively and necessarily in the performance of his duties.[62] Expenses incurred in fitting the employee to perform his duties, as distinct from their actual performance, are not deductible within this test; an employee bound by the terms of his employment to attend certain evening classes was therefore not entitled to deduct the expenses incurred in so doing, since it was the employer rather than the work done during employment which necessitated the expense of attending the classes.[63] Indeed it has been judically said that the allowable expenses under Schedule E are 'notoriously rigid, narrow and restricted in their operation.[64] Thus the cost of travel from the employee's home to the employee's place of work is not normally deductible. But it is otherwise if the employee's duties have actually begun before he leaves home; where a doctor employed by a hospital was required by the terms of his appointment to be available in his home for emergencies and to be ready there to receive calls, some of which might necessitate the doctor coming to the hospital to treat the patient, it was held that the doctor's travelling expenses between his home and the hospital in response to such calls were deductible expenses since he was performing his duties in both his home and the hospital.[65]

Directors, whatever they are paid, and employees whose gross emoluments including all benefits in kind and expense allowances exceed £ 2,000 per annum are dealt with more rigorously than other employees as regards taxation of benefits in kind and expense allowances. They are in general liable to tax under Schedule E on all benefits in kind and all expense allowances which they, their spouses, family, servants, dependants and guests[66] receive, although they may deduct such expenses as are wholly, exclusively and necessarily incurred in the performance of their duties; certain matters, such as the provision of meals in the staff canteen, are exempt from being thus taxed under Schedule E.[67] A case which illustrates the application of the general principle is *Westcott* v. *Bryan*.[68] There a company required its managing director to occupy a larger house than the managing director would himself have desired in order that the company's business customers could be entertained there, and the company paid the bills relating to insurance, maintenance and the like concerning the house; it was held that this expenditure should be apportioned between that incurred for the company's benefit and that incurred for the director's benefit, and that the director must pay tax on the latter under Schedule E.

It is to be noted that the deductions allowable as above are less than those permitted under Schedule D, Case 1, (*ante*, pages 130–2); this, and the tax rules relating to directors, should be borne in mind when considering whether to conduct a business through the medium of a company of which one is to be a director or to be employed with emoluments exceeding £2,000 per annum.

Deduction of tax under Schedule E

All persons liable to pay tax under Schedule E are given a code number by the Revenue; the code number is determined by the amount of reliefs and allowances which the taxpayer is entitled to offset against his taxable income. The employer is supplied with tax tables and is bound to deduct tax at the appropriate rate from each payment of salary, and must account for the tax to the Collector of Taxes within fourteen days after the end of each month.

Income from land: Schedule A

Income arising from the ownership of land is normally taxable under Schedule A. This tax is charged on the annual profits or gains arising in respect of rents or other receipts (save of a capital nature) from the ownership of an estate or interest in land in the United Kingdom;[69] exceptionally, rent payable under a furnished letting is *prima facie* not chargeable under Schedule A, but is taxed under Schedule D, Case VI.[70]

Receipts of a capital nature are not chargeable to tax under Schedule A.

Schedule A tax is not levied on the rents themselves, but on the profits or gains arising in respect of them, thus certain expenditure is deductible before computing the profit liable to tax. On the other hand, the tax is *prima facie* leviable on the rents which the taxpayer is entitled to receive, irrespective of whether or not he actually receives them;[71] relief from this harsh provision is however claimable if the taxpayer waived receipt of the money to avoid hardship and acted reasonably in doing so, or if failure to receive the rent was attributable to the default of the tenant and the taxpayer proves that he has taken such reasonable steps as were available to try to enforce payment.[72]

Although tax under Schedule A is levied on a current year basis, it is necessary that the assessment should first be made on a preceding year basis (see *ante*, pages 132–3), followed by an adjustment when the profits of the current year are finally agreed.[73]

Since a premium (i.e. a capital lump sum payment) is not an annual profit or gain, it is necessary to have special rules bringing a premium into charge to tax, otherwise the landlord would be inclined to let premises at a premium rather than a rent. When a premium is required under the terms of the lease and the duration of the lease does not exceed fifty years, the landlord is to be treated as becoming entitled on the grant of the lease to an amount of rent (in addition to any actual rent) equal to the amount of the premium less one-fiftieth of that amount for each complete year of the lease other than the first year.[74] Any sum paid in connection with the grant of the tenancy is presumed to have been paid as a premium unless other sufficient value for it is proved to have been given.[75] Thus the longer the lease, the less the tax on the premium; if the lease exceeds fifty years there is no tax on the premium, and if the lease does not exceed this period the discount on the taxable sum increases with the length of the lease.

Work done by the tenant enhancing the value of the landlord's interest in the premises

If the terms of the lease oblige the tenant to carry out work on the premises, the lease is deemed to have required the payment of a premium to the landlord (in addition to any other premium) of an amount equal to that by which the value of the landlord's estate or interest immediately after the commencement of the lease exceeds what its value would then have been if the lease did not so oblige the tenant.[76] Thus where the landlord grants a lease in return for the payment of rent and an undertak-

144

ing by the tenant to carry out improvements to the property, the increased value of the landlord's interest resulting from the tenant's undertaking is regarded as a premium and is taxed accordingly. The discounting rules relating to the length of the lease mentioned above will apply, and the enhancement in value to the landlord's interest will also diminish according to the length of time which must elapse before he can regain possession of the premises.

There are a number of complicated statutory provisions designed to catch artificial transactions entered into in order to avoid the rules relating to tax on premiums.

Capital gains tax (*post,* pages 151–9) may be chargeable on that part of a premium which does not attract liability to tax under Schedule A.

Tax where lease granted at an undervalue is assigned

If a lease not exceeding fifty years was granted on terms less favourable to the grantor than he could, having regard to land values prevailing at the time of the grant, have required, so that the landlord has in effect forborne to exact a premium which he could have required, then on every subsequent transfer of the lease for a value greater than that which the transferor himself gave the transferor is himself taxable on the excess, treated as a premium, until the combined total of the sums thus taxable in the hands of the transferors reaches that sum which the landlord forbore to exact for himself;[77] this charge is levied under Schedule D, Case VI, and not under Schedule A. This provision is designed to catch cases where the landlord seeks to avoid tax by letting the land at an undervalue to a crony who then transfers the lease at a premium which would, apart from this provision, not be taxable under the main premium taxing provision which relates only to the grant of the lease;[78] however the terms of this anti-avoidance provision catch innocent lettings at an undervalue as well.

Sale of land subject to a right of reconveyance

The provisions relating to tax upon premiums could *prima facie* be avoided by selling the land outright with a clause that it shall be reconveyed to the grantor at a lower price at the end of such period as is agreed. To prevent this it is provided that where the terms subject to which an estate or interest in land is sold stipulate that the land shall or may be required to be reconveyed at a future date to the vendor or to someone connected (widely defined to include his spouse and relatives, his partners, their spouses and their relatives, and any company or companies either under his control or under the control of himself or those acting in concert with him or under their directions)[79] with him, the vendor is to be charged to tax on the amount by which the sale price exceeds the reconveyance price, this difference being discounted as if it were a premium and as if the land had been leased for a period starting with the date of its actual sale and ending with the earliest date on which it is liable to be reconveyed.[80]

Calculation of tax payable on taxable premiums

An individual, but not a company, who is charged to income tax on a premium or other amount treated as a premium is relieved as follows from incurring a very high rate of tax on the chargeable sum; basically this is done by dividing the chargeable sum by the number of years for which the lease was granted, and the rate of tax on the yearly sum so found is then calculated as if that yearly sum were the top part of that taxpayer's income; tax is then charged at the rate so found on the whole of the chargeable sum.[81]

Allowable deductions from rents and receipts

In computing taxable profits or gains, various deductions are allowed from the rents, receipts, and from the premiums received insofar as these are treated as rent.[82] The taxpayer may deduct payments made by him in respect of maintenance, repairs, insurance or management, or of rates or other charges on the occupier which the taxpayer was obliged to pay, or in respect of any rent or rentcharge in respect of the land, or in respect of services provided under the terms of the lease unless the taxpayer receives a separate payment in respect of such services.[83] Loss resulting from the fraudulent misappropriation of rent by the taxpayer's agent was held not to be an expense of management but rather an expense arising from mismanagement.[84]

A distinction must be drawn between expenditure on maintenance and repairs, which is allowable as a deduction, and expenditure on improvements and additions which is not thus allowable. Where expenditure on improvements and alterations removes the need for what would otherwise be necessary expenditure upon maintenance and repairs, then the estimated cost of the maintenance and repairs which are thus avoided is allowed as a deduction when computing the sum taxable.

In general, deductible expenses must relate to expenditure incurred during the lease, and, in the case of maintenance and repairs, to dilapidations which occur during the lease.[85] Exceptionally, however, if successive leases are granted at full rents, an excess of allowable expenses under the old lease may be carried forward and deducted from rent payable under the later such lease or leases, but this right to carry expenses forward is broken by the grant of a lease which is not at a full rent or by a period of owner-occupation of the property. Premises are let at a full rent if the rent (including that part of any premium payable which is treated as rent) is adequate, taking one year with another, to meet the cost to the landlord of fulfilling his obligations under the lease and of any expenses on maintenance, repairs, insurance and management of those premises for which he is responsible.[86] Further, if the landlord lets two or more properties separately and rent payable under a lease at a full rent is inadequate to absorb the landlord's expenditure on the premises included in that lease, the excess expenditure may be set off against rent derived from other leases which do not oblige the tenant to maintain and repair those premises.[87]

Companies as landlords

If a company lets its property as an investment, taxable gains from this are computed under the rules of Schedule A as previously set out, but here the cost of managing the company, and not merely the cost of managing the property let, is allowable as a deductible expense.[88]

Income from woodlands

Tax on the occupation of woodlands in the United Kingdom which are managed on a commercial basis and with a view to profit is normally chargeable under Schedule B. The tax is charged on the occupier on an amount equal to one-third of the annual value of the woodlands; the annual value is determined as if the land, instead of being woodlands, were to be let on a yearly letting in its natural and unimproved state, and is fixed by reference to the rent which a tenant might reasonably be expected to pay if he were responsible for the cost of repairs, insurance and maintenance.[89]

A person who occupies woodlands managed by him on a commercial basis and with a view to profit may elect to be charged to tax under Schedule D instead of under Schedule B;[90] he will then be charged on the basis of profits made and not on the basis of annual value. The election must comprise all such woodlands on the same estate; woodlands planted or replanted within the ten years prior to the election can, if the occupier so wishes, be treated as forming a separate estate. The election is effective for the Revenue year to which it relates and for all subsequent years as long as the woodlands are occupied by the person who made the election. If such woodlands are currently unproductive of profit, as for example when they are young, it is better to be taxed under Schedule D because relief may be claimable for losses currently incurred in their management (*ante*, pages 137–8), and relief may be claimable for certain kinds of capital expenditure in connection with woodlands (*ante*, pages 138–9). When the woodlands reach maturity, they can then be sold to a new occupier who would automatically be taxed under Schedule B (and thus without reference to the profits made), unless he otherwise elected. By this procedure, tax advantages in relation to the woodlands may be gained in addition to the estate duty advantages (*post*, pages 164–5).

If the taxpayer does more than market the timber from the woodlands, as where he manufactures the timber into boxes and crates at a mill some distance away, he is liable to be adjudged to be trading under Schedule D in respect of this further activity.[91]

General liability to income tax

The 'total income' of any person means his total income from all sources estimated in accordance with the provisions of the Income Tax Acts.[92] Income received under deduction of tax, such as dividend income, must in computing total income be calculated at the gross figure before tax was deducted. From his total income an individual may deduct such personal reliefs as are appropriate to his individual circumstances. Income tax is levied at the basic rate upon this net figure and, where the net figure is high enough, at higher rates. An individual is also surcharged at a further rate of 15 per cent on the amount by which his investment income, which means any income other than earned income, exceeds £2,000. An annuity paid to a retired partner or his widow is not regarded as earned income.

These rules are embodied in the Finance Act, 1972, section 66, which provides:

> Income tax for the year 1973–74 shall . . . be charged at the basic rate of 30 per cent; and
> (a)   in respect of so much of an individual's total income as exceeds £ 5,000 at such higher rates as are specified in the Table below; and
> (b)   in respect of so much of the investment income included in an individual's total income as exceeds £ 2,000 at the additional rate of 15 per cent.

TABLE

Part of excess over £5,000	Higher rate
The first £1,000	40 per cent.
The next £1,000	45 per cent
The next £1,000	50 per cent
The next £2,000	55 per cent
The next £2,000	60 per cent
The next £3,000	65 per cent
The next £5,000	70 per cent
The remainder	75 per cent

Personal reliefs are initially disregarded in determining the total investment income of an individual; once his investment income has been quantified, personal reliefs must be treated as reducing his earned income until such income is thereby exhausted before any excess of reliefs can be regarded as reducing his investment income;[93] the effect of this principle is to keep the investment income surcharge as high as possible.

Deduction for interest paid by the taxpayer

In general interest paid by the taxpayer is deductible from his total income except as regards the first thirty-five pounds of interest so paid by him in any year of assessment to tax.[94] If interest is paid at a rate in excess of a reasonable commercial rate, the excess is not allowed as a deduction.[95] The disallowance for relief of the first thirty-five pounds so paid in each Revenue year does not apply to interest paid as a business expense, or on loans incurred for the purchase or improvement of land or to acquire an interest in a close company or partnership, or for the purchase of machinery or plant used by a partnership or in an office or employment, or interest on certain loans to pay estate duty.[96]

Husband and wife

Generally speaking the income of a married woman living with her husband is regarded as his income for income tax purposes, thus the income of the spouses must be aggregated for the purpose of determining total income. A married woman is regarded as living with her husband for tax purposes unless they are separated under a court order or a deed of separation, or they are in fact separated in such circumstances that this is likely to be permanent.[97] But either spouse may apply for a separate assessment, the effect of which is that each spouse becomes responsible for payment of the amount of tax attributable to that spouse's income and that the reliefs and allowances are apportioned between them; it does not, however, result in any reduction in the total amount payable by them, since for the purpose of determining this their incomes remain aggregated as before. Hence it is further provided that a man and his wife living with him may jointly elect for any year of assessment that the earnings of the wife, meaning roughly her earned income, shall not be aggregated with other income of the spouses in determining their liability to tax;[98] an election not to aggregate would obviously be desirable if the wife has earned income and the combined income of the spouses is high.

If the wife has earned income, the husband is entitled to an additional deduction from total income of £595 or the amount which the wife earns, whichever is the less; this deduction is not allowable if the spouses elect that the wife's earnings shall not be aggregated with the rest of their income.[99]

Parent and child

The income of an infant child is treated as the child's income and not as the income of his parent,[100] unless the income of the child is derived from a settlement (which for tax purposes embraces not only settlements within the land law (*ante*, pages 7–12) but a great many other transactions besides)[101] made by his parent. If the child's income exceeds £115 in the Revenue year, the claim of his parent to a personal relief in respect of the child is curtailed.

Life insurance relief

This relief is given in respect of premiums paid by the taxpayer on a policy of insurance effected after 22 June 1916, and which secures a capital sum payable on death, provided the insurance is made by the claimant and is taken out on the life of the claimant or on that of his wife. If the premiums total more than £20, the relief is a deduction equal to income tax at half the basic rate on the amount of the premiums; if the premiums total less than £20, the relief is a deduction equal to income tax at half the basic rate on the amount of the premiums or on £10, whichever is the less. But relief is only given insofar as the total premiums do not exceed one-sixth of the claimant's total income, and no relief will be given on the excess of any premium over 7 per cent of the capital sum payable on death.[102] Moreover as regards policies effected after 19 March 1968,

150

the premiums will not qualify for relief unless the policy is a 'qualifying policy';[103] this means that the policy must run for a minimum period of ten years or until earlier death, the premiums must be spread out reasonably evenly throughout the duration of the policy, and the capital sum payable on death must be at least three-quarters of the total premiums payable under the policy.

Personal reliefs generally

There are a large number of personal reliefs which may or may not be claimable according to the individual circumstances of the taxpayer; the details of those reliefs is outside the scope of this work.

Payment of interest: deduction of tax

Interest is usually paid in full without deduction of tax by the payer, but if yearly interest is paid by a company, or by a partnership of which a company is a member, or by any person to another person whose usual place of abode is outside the United Kingdom, then the person by or through whom the payment is made must pay the money net by first deducting income tax from it at the basic rate for the year in which the payment is made;[104] an account of the deduction must be rendered to the Inspector of Taxes.[105] But interest payable in the United Kingdom on a bank overdraft (whether the interest is 'yearly' or not), must be paid gross without deduction of tax.[106] 'Yearly' in this context refers to the degree of permanence of the loan and thus to whether the obligation to pay interest is to last for more than a year; it does not refer to the frequency with which the interest is calculated and payable.

Capital gains tax

General principles

Capital gains tax is levied on the total chargeable gains which a person makes on disposing of a capital asset in a Revenue year of assessment, after deducting allowable losses incurred on the disposal of other capital assets (see also *post*, pages 152–6); the chargeable gain or allowable loss is ascertained in accordance with the provisions of the Finance Act, 1965, Schedule 6, and is broadly (see also *post*, pages 155–6) the difference between the cost of acquisition of the asset and the price received when selling it, though sometimes the market value of the asset on 6 April 1965, is taken to be its acquisition cost.

The amount of the tax is 30 per cent on the chargeable gains made by the taxpayer during the Revenue year of assessment in which the gain accrues, after deducting any allowable losses;[107] exceptionally, however, chargeable gains of companies are charged with corporation tax (though the effective rate of corporation tax is for this purpose reduced approximately to the rate of capital gains tax) and not with capital gains tax. Moreover if the gain of an individual does not exceed £5,000, he is instead chargeable to income tax on one-half of the amount of the gain if this would be to his benefit; marginal relief is given if the gain somewhat exceeds £5,000.[108] In applying this alternative, the half of the gain must be added to that person's other income and treated as the top part[109] of his income (thus attracting the highest tax) and as investment income.[110] This alternative will clearly be advantageous to those paying tax at the normal rate, but would not be suitable for a taxpayer with a very high income.

A person who is neither resident nor ordinarily resident nor trading within the United Kingdom in the year of assessment is not liable to capital gains tax on the gains which he makes during that year.[111]

The charge to capital gains tax arises when the disposal of a chargeable asset takes place;[112] disposal includes a part disposal, and where the asset is disposed of or acquired under a contract the disposal or acquisition is usually treated as taking place at the time when the contract is made. If a capital sum is received by way of compensation for damage, injury or destruction to a chargeable asset or under a policy of insurance against such a risk, this is to be regarded as a disposal of the asset taking place at the time when the capital sum is received;[113] however there will not be a disposal provided, in the case of an asset not wholly destroyed, the capital sum is applied in restoring it, or, if the asset is wholly lost or destroyed, the capital sum received is within one year of receipt applied in acquiring a replacement, and in either case the taxpayer claims this relief.[114] The destruction of an asset is to be treated as a disposal of the asset whether or not any money is received in this respect by the owner,[115] and if a building is destroyed the person deemed to dispose of the building is to be treated as if he had also disposed of its site at the market value at that time.[116]

The transfer of an asset by way of mortgage and its retransfer on the redemption of the mortgage is not an acquisition or a disposal.[117]

If there is a bonus or rights issue of shares or debentures in a company which the share or debenture holders receive in proportion to their existing holdings, the new shares or debentures are to be treated as if the holders had acquired them when they acquired their original holdings, and the total holding of each share or debenture holder is treated as acquired at a price equal to the price paid for the original holding plus any price paid for the new holding. [118]

If the shares or debentures of company A are acquired by company B in exchange for shares or debentures in company B, and if company B will thereafter have control of company A, the shareholders of company A are not regarded as having made any new acquisition or disposal of their shares. [119]

A transfer of a business as a going concern together with the whole of its assets to a company is not treated as a chargeable disposal of any of the assets so far as the consideration for the transfer consists of shares issued by the company. [120] This provision enables an individual trader or a partnership to convert the business into a company without being considered to have disposed of the assets.

If a spouse disposes of an asset to the other spouse while they are living together, the acquiring spouse is in general regarded as having acquired the asset at the same price as that which the disposing spouse is regarded as having paid for it, thus no charge to capital gains tax arises. [121]

If a person disposes of an asset by way of gift or otherwise than by way of *bona fide* bargain, this is regarded as if a disposal and an acquisition had taken place at a price equal to the market value of the asset at that time. [122] The donor or the seller at an undervalue is chargeable with any tax which thus becomes payable, but sometimes the person taking the gift or the purchaser at an undervalue can be made to pay the tax. [123]

On the death of an individual, the assets of which he had power to dispose are deemed to be acquired on his death by his personal representatives or other person on whom they devolve (*ante*, Chapter 4) for a price equal to their market value at the date of the death, but no charge to capital gains tax arises on the death. [124] This principle is thus as a rule beneficial to the individual. If a person acquires an asset as a beneficiary under the will or the intestacy of the deceased, no charge to capital gains tax arises and the beneficiary is treated as acquiring the asset at the date when the personal representatives acquired it and at its market value at that time. [125] But if the personal representatives sell the assets, as for example to pay estate duty, they are chargeable to any gain which accrued between the date of the death and the date of the disposal.

Settled property

'Settled property' means property held in trust except where the trustee holds it on trust for another person absolutely entitled as against the trustee or who would be absolutely entitled as against the trustee if that person were not under a disability. (i.e. were not an infant or mental patient). [126]

Where property is placed in settlement this is regarded as a disposal of the property, regardless of whether the person making the disposal is interested as a beneficiary or as a trustee;[127] placing property in settlement is thus likely to give rise to a taxable gain or allowable loss. The trustees of the settlement are to be regarded as a single and continuing body of persons,[128] thus an actual change of trustees and transfer of assets to the new trustees does not give rise to a disposal. If the trustees sell the settled property, this is likely to produce a taxable gain or an allowable loss. Moreover when a person becomes absolutely entitled to any settled property as against the trustees, then all the assets forming part of the settled property to which he becomes so entitled are deemed to have been disposed of by the trustees and immediately reacquired by the trustees at a price equal to the market value of the asset;[129] any subsequent disposal by the trustees will be treated as if it were a disposal by the beneficiary absolutely entitled. The above general rule has now been modified by the Finance Act, 1971, Schedule 12, whereby if a person becomes absolutely entitled to assets forming part of the settled property on the termination by death of a person entitled to a life interest therein, no taxable gain arises on the disposal to the person who is now absolutely entitled, but he is deemed to have acquired the assets at their value at the date of the disposal. Moreover on the termination of a life interest in possession in all or part of the settled property, the whole or a corresponding part of the assets which continue to be settled property are deemed to have been disposed of and reacquired by the trustees at the market value at that time, although no charge to capital gains tax arises by reason of the deemed disposal. [130]

Any capital gains tax which may arise on a disposal or deemed disposal of the settled property is assessed on the trustees, although a beneficiary to whom the asset or its proceeds is transferred may in certain circumstances be assessed.

154

Gifts liable to estate duty

If estate duty is chargeable on a gift made during a person's lifetime and if the donee still owns the asset at the time of that person's death, the asset is deemed to have been disposed of and reacquired at the date of death by the donee at a price equal to its then market value, but no taxable gain arises on the disposal;[131] where the value chargeable to estate duty of the property given is reduced because it was given more than four years before the donor's death, the rules relating to the notional disposal and reacquisition by the donee are only to be applied to that proportion of the asset which the value on which estate duty is chargeable bears to the market value of the asset at the time of the donor's death.[132]

Rules for calculating gain or loss

If the asset is acquired after 6 April 1965, there may be deducted from the amount received on the disposal of the asset:

(a)   the cost of acquisition of the asset, including incidental costs, or the expenditure incurred in producing the asset;

(b)   expenditure incurred to enhance the value of the asset which is reflected in its state at the time of disposal, and expenditure incurred in establishing, preserving or defending the taxpayer's title to or right over the asset;

(c)   the incidental costs of making the disposal, such as fees paid to estate agents or professional advisers.

Insurance premiums on a policy to cover a risk of damage or loss or depreciation of the asset are not deductible, nor is any deduction allowed for expenditure borne by the Crown or any public authority; interest is in general not deductible. [133]

No provision is made by the legislation for taking account of the effect of inflation in arriving at the taxable gain;[134] this is obviously deplorable in a highly inflationary society such as ours now is.

As regards wasting assets with a predictable useful life not exceeding fifty years, and excluding leasehold land but including plant and machinery which is always regarded as having such a life, the expenditure incurred on its acquisition is to be treated as written off to nil at a uniform rate day by day over the predictable life of the asset; expenditure incurred on its improvement is to be regarded as written off in the same way from the date when the expenditure was first reflected in the state of the asset. [135]

With regard to leasehold interests either in land or in other property, the asset is deemed to waste at a rate which accelerates as the end of the period of the lease draws nigh; a lease of land for more than fifty years is not treated as a wasting asset. [136]

If an asset is sold at a price payable by instalments, the price received for the disposal is taken to be the capitalised value of the payments. [137]

As regards assets held on 6 April 1965, then if the asset consists of quoted shares the gain or loss is normally calculated by reference to the quoted market value on that date, but the original cost of acquisition is taken if this would result in a smaller gain or loss. [138]

As regards other assets, the gain or loss is deemed to accrue at a uniform rate throughout the period of ownership, so that only the proportion of deemed gain which occurs after 5 April 1965 is chargeable; the taxpayer can however elect to have his gain or loss ascertained by reference to the actual value of the asset on 6 April 1965, although his loss relief is restricted to the loss actually incurred. [139]

Capital gains tax is charged on the total amount of chargeable gains accruing to the taxpayer in the year of assessment, after deducting any allowable losses.[140] Any surplus allowable losses which occur in a year of assessment can be carried forward and set against chargeable gains of future years. [141]

Exemptions

Certain assets are not chargeable to capital gains tax, thus no taxable gain or allowable loss arises on their disposal. [142] These include private motor cars, savings certificates, winnings from betting and from prizes, or sums obtained by way of compensation for any injuries suffered by an individual to his person, profession or vocation. [143] If a person takes out a life insurance policy either on his own life or on that of another person, there is no liability to capital gains tax if the policy monies are paid to the person who took out the policy or to his estate; this exemption does not however apply in favour of a person who buys the policy from the person who takes the policy out.[144]

A person is not liable to capital gains tax if the total net amount received by him as the price of all his disposals made during the year does not exceed £500. [145]

A gain made by an individual on disposing of his dwelling house is not taxable if the house was his only or main residence throughout the period of his ownership, or throughout that period except all or part of the last twelve months of such ownership; certain other periods of absence may be disregarded.[146] A person who owns two or more houses may nominate one

156

of these as being his main residence. The exemption extends to a disposal by trustees of a settlement of a house which is the only or main residence of a person entitled to occupy it under the terms of the settlement.[147] But no exemption is allowed if the dwelling house was acquired wholly or partly for the purpose of realising a gain from its disposal.

A gain which results from the disposal of an item of tangible property other than land is not taxable if the price paid on the disposal does not exceed £1,000; conversely if such an article purchased for more than £1,000 is disposed of for less than £1,000, the allowable loss is calculated as if the article had been sold for £1,000. [148] These provisions cover such articles as furniture, pictures and the like if within the above financial limits. If two or more articles form part of a set, and are disposed of by the same seller to the same buyer or to different buyers who are acting in concert, then the two or more transactions are to be treated as a single transaction disposing of a single asset; the value of the assets is thus added together in order to decide the price obtained. [149]

Gains resulting from the disposal of works of art and similar objects which are both exempted from estate duty and given to a public body are not chargeable to capital gains tax; the same applies if such an article is disposed of by a gift or settlement, provided an undertaking similar to that applicable as regards the securing of exemption from estate duty is given. The capital gains tax exemption is withdrawn, as is the estate duty exemption, if the article is subsequently sold (unless the sale is to a public body) or if the undertaking is broken; the tax will fall on the seller or the owner who breaks the undertaking.[150] Any capital gains tax payable is allowed as a deduction from the amount chargeable to estate duty.

Postponement of tax where business assets are replaced

If business assets are sold and replaced by others, the trader is permitted to deduct any gain thus made from the cost of acquisition of the replacement; the same process can be repeated as often as need arises, thus payment of the tax is deferred until business assets are disposed of and are not replaced. This may be done by a person carrying on a trade or profession, and including the occupier of woodlands on a commercial basis. [151] But the option of postponed payment is only available if the whole of the price which such a person receives for the disposal of assets used only for the purposes of the trade or profession throughout the period of his ownership is applied by him in acquiring other assets which when acquired are used only for the purposes of the trade or profession;[152] there is limited relief if only part of the price obtained on selling the assets is so applied. The relief is normally given only if the acquisition of the new assets takes place or an unconditional contract to acquire them is made within a year before or not more than a year after the disposal of the old assets, or such further period as the Revenue permit.[153] Moreover if Clause 37 of the Finance Bill, 1973, should become law the basic period within which the new assets must be acquired will be extended, as regards assets acquired on or after 6 April 1973, to their acquisition within three years instead of one year.

If less than the whole price obtained for the old assets is applied in buying new ones, but an amount not less than the gain (whether taxable or not) on the disposal of the old assets is so applied, the amount of the gain on which payment of tax may be postponed is the taxable gain on the sale of the old assets less any part of their sale price which is not applied in buying the new assets.[154]

By a Revenue concession owner-occupiers of farm land whose land is acquired under a compulsory purchase order will be allowed one year, starting from when they finally quit the holding, in which to acquire the new assets; the moment from which the year starts to run is thus deferred until after the date of the forced sale of their holding, so long as the land is temporarily let or licensed back to them for farming purposes.

The assets which may be thus sold or acquired comprise any building or structure in the nature of a building occupied and used only for the purposes of the trade and any land so occupied and used, fixed plant and machinery, ships, aircraft, goodwill and hovercraft.[155] No relief is given if the new assets are bought for the purpose of realising a gain on their disposal.[156] If the new assets acquired are of a wasting nature (including for example leases), there are complex provisions whose effect is greatly to curtail the above relief.[157]

Disposal of a business on retirement

If a person over the age of sixty disposes of a business which he has owned throughout the ten years ending with the disposal, some relief will be given in respect of the capital gains tax arising on the disposal. If this person has reached the age of sixty-five the amount of gain exempted from tax is £10,000, and if he retires between the age of sixty and sixty-five a proportionate part of this relief is given. The relief is given on the assets used for the purpose of his trade or profession but excluding assets held as investments. The relief is also applied in certain circumstances where a person over the age of sixty disposes on retirement of shares in a company which has been a trading company during the ten years ending with his death and of which he has been a full-time working director. [158]

Position of companies

The gains or allowable losses of a company are computed in the same way as those of an individual for the purpose of applying the capital gains tax. Its capital gains are however liable to corporation tax and not to capital gains tax, and the alternative basis of charge whereby an individual may be charged to income tax on half the gain instead of capital gains tax (*ante*, page 152) is of course inapplicable to a company since it never pays income tax.

Corporation tax

The profits of companies are liable to corporation tax. Under the system introduced by the Finance Act, 1972, the company pays corporation tax on all its profits; when distributing its profits to the shareholders in the form of dividends, the company makes an advance payment of corporation tax to the Revenue at a rate equal to three-sevenths of the amount distributed in dividend. The members are regarded for the purpose of computing their own income tax liability as having received an amount of income equal to that of the dividend paid plus the tax which the company has paid to the Revenue on that dividend. Advance payments of corporation tax made in respect of dividends and other distributions to the members in an accounting period are set against the liability to corporation tax of the company on its profits (excluding chargeable capital gains; see *post*, pages 159–60) for the period. The effect is that the company pays corporation tax on all its profits whether distributed or not.

Corporation tax is levied by reference to financial years commencing on 1 April and ending on 31 March in each following year. Corporation tax was charged at the rate of 40 per cent for the financial year 1972 which ended on 31 March 1973; the rate of corporation tax for the financial year ending on 31 March 1974 has yet to be fixed, but is expected to be at the rate of 50 per cent.

A company whose taxable profits (including chargeable capital gains) do not exceed £15,000 in the accounting period will pay corporation tax at a lower rate known as the 'small companies rate'. Marginal relief is given if the company's profits are between £15,000 and £25,000. [159]

The chargeable gains of the company are to be taxed at a lower rate than the corporation tax rate, and this will be done by excluding a proportion of such gains from the charge to corporation tax;[160] the effective rate thus charged will be seven-ninths of the rate of corporation tax, which rate has not yet been fixed, as regards the financial year 1973 ending on 31 March 1974.

The rate of tax with which the company is chargeable is ascertained by reference to the financial year running from 1 April to 31 March, but the assessments to corporation tax are made on the company by reference to the company's own accounting period; where the latter does not coincide with the financial year, the taxable sum must be calculated by apportioning the profits of the accounting period between the financial years in which the period falls.[161] The company's own accounting period cannot for tax purposes be longer than twelve months, and corporation tax is generally payable within nine months from the end of the accounting period.

Interest paid by a company out of the company's profits chargeable to corporation tax is usually allowed as a deduction from the total profits of the company for the accounting period in which the interest was paid;[162] but a payment of interest is not regarded as deductible from the company's profits if either the payment is charged to capital, or is not ultimately borne by the company, or is not made under a liability incurred for valuable and sufficient consideration (save that certain donations to charities are allowable deductions).

Corporation tax is charged on the company's profits, meaning its income and chargeable capital gains (though at a lower rate on the latter; *ante*) which arise in the accounting period, less allowable deductions. The amount of income is for corporation tax purposes to be computed in accordance with income tax principles.[163] 'Income tax law' means the law which applies to the charge of income tax on individuals.[164]

Corporation tax, not capital gains tax, is charged on the chargeable gains less allowable losses which arise in any accounting period of the company; its chargeable gains are ascertained by reference to the principles which apply to capital gains tax.[165]

There are provisions relating to the grant of relief for losses made by companies which are broadly similar to those applicable to individual traders and their income tax.[166]

Where a company begins to carry on a trade which was previously carried on by another company, the trade is regarded as continuing in the same ownership if on or at any time within two years after the change the trade or an interest amounting to not less than a three-quarters share in it

160

belongs to the same persons as the trade or such an interest belonged to at some time within a year before the change;[167] for this purpose the company's trade may be regarded as belonging to the persons owning the ordinary share capital of the company in the same proportion as their shareholdings.[168] If the above applies, losses and capital allowances (*ante*, pages 138–9) are in general treated as if no change had taken place, though there are provisions aimed at counteracting the avoidance of tax through the abuse of this principle.

Provisions exist whereby a company within a group of companies can surrender its claim to capital allowances or to relief against losses to another company within the group;[169] companies are within a group if one company owns three-quarters of the ordinary share capital of the other, or if a third company owns three-quarters of the ordinary share capital of both the others.

A payment of advance corporation tax by a company in respect of any distribution made by it in an accounting period can be set against the company's liability to corporation tax on any of its income charged to corporation tax for that accounting period,[170] but it cannot be offset against the company's chargeable gains since these attract a lower rate of corporation tax than the other profits of the company. There are further restrictions on the right to offset a payment of advance corporation tax where the company makes a distribution which is in excess of its profits of the accounting period in which the distribution was made.[171]

The members of a company are treated as having borne income tax at the basic rate by reason of the company's liability to account to the Revenue for advance corporation tax. Members whose income is high and whose tax liability is in consequence not restricted to tax at the basic rate will be liable to higher rate income tax on dividend income and to the investment income surcharge. Hence wealthy shareholders in companies would often prefer that the company should not distribute its profits by way of dividend but should retain the profits within the company so that the company would only pay corporation tax on them; alternatively a wealthy shareholder who is also a director might prefer to have the profits utilised in paying large remuneration to the directors which they would take as earned income and hence avoid the investment income surcharge. Legislation has been passed to restrict these manoeuvres, but it is only applicable to companies whose control is vested in a few persons only, such companies being known as 'close companies'.

A 'close company' is a company resident in the United Kingdom which is under the control either of five or fewer participators, or of participators who are also directors.[172] A person has control of a company if he exercises or is able to acquire control over the company's affairs, whether by having the majority of the votes or the majority of the shares or being entitled in a winding up to the majority of the assets available for distribution; in deciding whether he has control, there can be attributed to him any rights of a person who is his nominee, or the rights of any company of which he has control, or the rights of his associates. [173] A 'participator' means a person having a share in any capital or income of the company, including a loan creditor other than a bank lending money to the company in the ordinary course of its business. [174] The word 'associate' in relation to a participator includes most of the participator's relatives and also any partner of his. [175]

The following are not 'close companies': a company which is not resident in the United Kingdom; a company at least 35 per cent of whose shares with voting rights and not restricted to a fixed rate of dividend are held by the public and whose shares have within the preceding year been quoted and dealt in on a recognised Stock Exchange; [176] a company which is controlled by another company which is not itself a close company; a registered industrial provident society (see *ante*, pages 94—102).

If the company is a close company, then any expense which it incurs in providing living accommodation, entertainment, services or other benefits to a participator, the cost of which is not reimbursed by the participator to the company, is to be treated as in the nature of a dividend paid by the company to the participator; 'participator' in this context includes the participator's associates. [177] Moreover interest paid by a 'close company' to its directors or their associates is sometimes treated as payment of a dividend by the company. [178] Loans made by a 'close company' to a participator in the company or his associate expose the company to corporation tax on a sum equal to the rate of advance corporation tax on the amount of the loan; [179] if the participator subsequently repays the loan the amount of tax is refundable. [180] Even more importantly, there are provisions, the details of which are too complex for inclusion here, applicable where a close company fails to distribute its income among its members although the retention of the income is not justified by the requirements of the company's business; in such a case the Revenue may issue directions with the effect that the members of the company are taxed as if the income which it is unnecessary for the company to retain had in fact been distributed among the members. [181]

Estate duty

General principles

Estate duty is charged on all property which passes on the death of a person.[182] Such property is valued at the price which, in the opinion of the Commissioners of Inland Revenue, the property would fetch if sold in the open market at the time of death (*post*, pages 178–9). The property passing includes all property which the deceased owned absolutely, either solely or, so far as his interest extended, as a joint tenant or as a tenant in common (*ante*, page 14); it also includes property over which the deceased had a general power of appointment, or property which he gave away less than seven years before his death (or less than one year if given for public or charitable purposes), or property in which he had a life interest or which was charged with payment of an annuity to him.

The rates of estate duty currently applicable are laid down by Part I of Schedule 17 to the Finance Act, 1969, and set out in Appendix IV to this book (*post*, page 393). There is no duty unless the estate exceeds £15,000; duty is levied on every slice of value above this figure at rates of duty which increase substantially with each slice of higher value. Since different persons may have to pay (*post*, page 180) and bear (*post*, pages 181–2) the duty, it may be necessary to find the amount of duty attributable to each item of dutiable property. This is done by finding the estate rate, which is the percentage proportion which the total duty payable on the estate bears to the total value of the property in the estate.[183]

Reduced rate of estate duty on certain property

Where an estate includes agricultural property, duty is charged on the 'agricultural value' of the agricultural property at only 55 per cent of the estate rate (*ante*); no such reduction is allowed as regards any additional value which the property might have if it were to be used for a non-agricultural purpose. 'Agricultural property' means agricultural land, pasture and woodland, and also includes such cottages, farm buildings, farm houses and mansion houses (together with the land occupied therewith) as are of a character appropriate to the property.[184] Buildings used in the intensive rearing of livestock on a commercial basis in order to produce food for human consumption are by concession regarded as agricultural property.[185] The 'agricultural value' of agricultural property means the value which the property would bear if it was subject to a perpetual covenant prohibiting its use other than as agricultural property, and disregarding the value of any timber, trees or underwood growing on the land.[186]

The reduced agricultural rate of estate duty is applied to land held upon trust for sale (*ante*, pages 12–13), but capital money arising under the Settled Land Act, 1925, although 'land' for the purposes of disposition and devolution (*ante*, page 10) is nevertheless personal property and hence disentitled to the reduced agricultural rate of charge; the Settled Land Act is not concerned with taxation.[187]

If a person is at the time when he dies under contract to sell his agricultural land, such property is not regarded as agricultural land when determining the liability of his estate for estate duty. Conversely if a person is under a contractual obligation to purchase agricultural land at the time when he dies, then in computing the estate duty payable on his death the reduced rate is only applicable to the market value of the agricultural land at the time of his death less the unpaid balance of the purchase money.[188]

If agricultural property is subject to a mortgage which is deductible for estate duty (see *post*, page 179), the deduction must be apportioned between the agricultural value and the non-agricultural value of the property.[189]

Estate duty is also payable at only 55 per cent of the estate rate on industrial hereditaments, machinery and plant which is used for the purposes of a business which is dutiable on the death.[190]

Aggregation

The general principle is that all property which passes on the deceased's death must be aggregated so as to form one estate in order to determine the rate of duty appropriate to the estate. Exceptionally, certain types of property are exempt from aggregation. These are:

1   Unsettled property not exceeding £15,000; for this purpose the definition of settled property excludes property settled by the deceased himself or a settlement made at his expense, and property of which the deceased was competent to dispose and has disposed. Marginal relief is given if the value of the unsettled property slightly exceeds £15,000.
2   Where property which passes on death includes land on which timber, trees or underwood are growing, the value of the underlying land only is taken into account when deciding the aggregate value of the estate. The value of all timber, trees or underwood passing on the death is regarded as a separate estate and is dutiable only when they are sold; underwood is how-

164

ever exempted from duty even if sold. The dutiable amount on a sale is in practice limited to the value of the timber at the date of the deceased's death. The rate at which duty then becomes payable on the timber is the estate rate appropriate to the last estate in which the timber passed, without aggregating the timber. A wealthy man who is thus potentially liable to a high rate of estate duty can avert much of this by investing substantially in timber, since the estate rate of duty payable on his death will be decided with reference to his remaining property only and no duty at all will be payable on the timber until it is sold; there are also income tax advantages regarding timber (*ante*, pages 147–8).

3   Duty on works of art, including pictures, prints, books and manuscripts can be remitted if they appear to the Treasury to be of national, scientific or historic interest and are given or left by will for national purposes or to various public bodies;[191] property given to certain museums and public galleries may be exempt.[192] Moreover, if these objects appear to the Treasury to be of national, scientific, historic or artistic interest, they are exempt from duty regardless of whether they are given to a public body or to a private individual, but exemption is only conferred if undertakings to properly preserve the object, not to export it, and the like are given to the Treasury and performed. If the object is sold, duty normally becomes payable on the proceeds of sale; if an undertaking is broken, duty becomes payable on the value of the object at that time. If duty becomes payable within three years after the death, the proceeds of sale or value of the object are to be aggregated with the rest of the deceased's estate so as to increase the duty payable on every item of property passing on his death; if duty becomes payable more than three years after the death, duty is payable on the proceeds or the value of the object, as the case may be, aggregated with the rest of the deceased's estate in order to determine the rate of duty on the object but leaving the rate of duty on all the other property of the deceased unchanged. Thus a wealthy man may save a good deal of duty by investing in certified works of art, provided the beneficiaries of his estate neither sell the works nor break the undertakings until more than three years after the death.

Insurance policies taken out before 20 March 1968, are exempted from aggregation with the rest of the deceased's property, provided the aggregate value of the policies does not exceed £25,000; a proportionate part of this relief is given if the aggregate value exceeds £25,000.

General exemptions from estate duty

Property given to the National Gallery, the British Museum and certain

165

other like public bodies is ignored in arriving at the principal value of an estate. Property given to charities up to a limit of £50,000 and property up to a limit of £15,000 given to or devolving upon the deceased's widow or widower is similarly ignored. [193] 'Gift' includes gift by will.

Quick succession relief

If estate duty would *prima facie* be payable twice within five years on the same property, and the property has not been sold between the two deaths in respect of which the duty becomes payable twice, the amount of duty payable on the property on the second death is reduced in accordance with a sliding scale so that the reduction diminishes as the period between the two deaths grows. If the value of the property has fluctuated between the two deaths, relief is in general restricted to the lower value of the property on either of the deaths. [194]

Gifts

The topic of gifts is of such practical importance as to merit reasonably extensive discussion. In order to escape duty, the gift must have been made at least seven years before the deceased's death (or at least a year before the death as regards gifts made for public or charitable purposes; though gifts to charity of up to £50,000 are often exempted from duty regardless of when the gift is made) and the donee must have taken immediate possession and enjoyment of the property given to the entire exclusion of the donor or of any benefit to him by contract or otherwise. [195] If *immediate* possession and enjoyment of the property given was not so taken by the donee to the entire exclusion of the donor, then in order to escape duty such possession and enjoyment must have been taken for at least seven years before the donor's death (or at least a year as regards a non-exempt gift made for public or charitable purposes). If however the donor dies more than four years after the making of such a gift some relief is given in that the principal value of the property given will be reduced for estate duty by 15 per cent if the donor's death occurs during the fifth year after the gift was made, by 30 per cent if death occurs during the sixth year thereafter, and by 60 per cent if the death occurs during the seventh year.

The requirement that the donee must have assumed immediate *bona fide* possession and enjoyment of the property upon the making of the gift is fulfilled not merely by an outright transfer to the donee or to trustees for the donee upon such terms, but also where the donor binding-

166

ly declares himself trustee for the donee; in the case of a trust concerning land the trust must be evidenced in writing signed by the person declaring the trust,[196] and a disposition of a subsisting beneficial interest under a trust must be made in writing signed by the person making it;[197] written evidence of other types of trusts, while not legally essential, is highly desirable in order to facilitate proof that the trust did in fact come into existence upon the date alleged.

If the donor reserves to himself a beneficial interest in property and then gives the donee only the beneficial interest which is left after satisfying the donor's interest, the reservation of the donor's interest will not detract from the donor's exclusion from the property given since the donor never gave that interest away in the first place; thus where a farmer carried on a farming business in partnership with his children, although at that time the farmland itself was not partnership property but was in the exclusive ownership of the farmer, and subsequently the farmer transferred the farmland to his children, the farming partnership continuing as before, it was held that the gift was of land already subject to the partnership and hence the donor had not retained any interest in the property which he gave.[198] But where a father gave land to his son outright, and some time afterwards the father and son entered into a partnership agreement to conduct farming on that land, it was held the father had not been excluded from possession and enjoyment of the property given (irrespective of whether or not the father gave full value for his rights in the partnership), hence the land was dutiable on the father's death which occurred some eighteen years after he gave away the land. (*Chick* v. *Commissioner of Stamp Duties*).[199] But it has now been enacted that, if the property given consists of land or chattels, actual occupation or possession thereafter of the land or chattels by the donor shall be disregarded if the donor gives full consideration in money or money's worth for such occupation or possession;[200] the effect of this provision is to restrict the operation of the principle laid down in *Chick's Case, ante.*

As regards the requirement that the donee must take the property 'to the entire exclusion of the donor, or of any benefit to him by contract or otherwise', it seems that the words 'by contract or otherwise' require the existence of a legally enforceable bargain. Thus in *Att.-Gen.* v. *Seccombe*[201] the owner of a farm gave it to his nephew. The nephew took over the headship of the property, but the donor of the farm continued for the rest of his life to reside in the farm house and be supported by the nephew; there was however no express antecedent bargain between them that this should be so. On the death of the donor many years afterwards, it was held that the gift fulfilled the requirements for exemption from estate duty, although the decision has its critics who argue that a factual exclusion of the donor from the property is required; hence it may be unwise to rely on this decision.

Dispositions for an inadequate consideration

In general a transfer of property in return for a price which is less than its value will be regarded as a sale unless there was a deliberate element of bounty in the transaction.[202] But if a disposition at an undervalue is made in favour of a relative, this is in general to be treated as a gift of the balance to the relative.[203]

The property which is dutiable

If the gift is one of cash, the money given is dutiable.

If the gift is of property other than cash, then if the donee retained the property at the date of the donor's death the property given is dutiable and is valued at the date of the donor's death. If the donee parted with the property before the donor's death, then if he did so at a full value paid in money the money is dutiable; if he did so at a full value in exchange for property other than money, the property received in return is dutiable and is valued at the date of the donor's death. If the donee has parted with the property at an undervalue or by way of gift, the property thus disposed of is dutiable and is valued at its market value at the date on which he parted with it.

If the donee had settled the property given to him, the donor is to be regarded as having settled the property himself. If the donor makes a dutiable gift by way of a settlement, then if the settlement was still in force at the date of the donor's death the duty is charged on the property in the settlement at the date of his death except insofar as the property is derived from other sources; if the settlement had ended before the donor's death, the duty is charged on the property which was in the settlement at the time when it ended and valued at that date.

The provisions for identifying the dutiable property and the date at which it is to be valued are contained in the Finance Act, 1957, section 38.

Gifts exempted from estate duty

1 *Gifts in consideration of marriage.* If a gift is made in consideration of marriage and is either an outright gift to a descendant of the deceased, or

the deceased was either a party to the marriage or the ancestor of such a party and the gift was either an outright gift to the other party to the marriage or a settled gift, then estate duty is only charged on any excess value of the gift over £5,000; a gift made in consideration of marriage which does not satisfy the above is only chargeable to estate duty on the excess over £1,000. [204]

In order for a gift to be made in consideration of marriage, it must be made on the occasion of a marriage, must be conditional upon the marriage taking place and must be made for the purpose of or to encourage the marriage. [205] Moreover a gift is not to be treated as having been made in consideration of marriage except, in the case of an outright gift, insofar as it is a gift to a party to the marriage; in the case of any other gift, such as a settled gift, the persons entitled to benefit must in substance be confined to the parties to the marriage, the issue of the marriage and their spouses, and persons becoming entitled on the failure of trusts in favour of the issue. [206]

2 *Gifts paid from income.* A gift is exempt from estate duty if it is shown that the gift was part of the normal expenditure of the deceased, that he made the gift out of his income and, after allowing for all gifts forming part of his normal expenditure, he was left with sufficient income to maintain his usual standard of living. [207] The payment by the deceased of premiums on a policy of life insurance for the benefit of a donee, such as a Married Woman's Property Act policy (*post*, page 364), will often be exempt under this provision.

3 *Gifts not exceeding £500 in aggregate as regards the individual donee.* Such gifts are exempt provided that the property given to the donee did not include any interest in settled property, and that the donee took *bona fide* possession or enjoyment of the property immediately upon the gift and retained it to the entire exclusion of the deceased or of any benefit to him by contract or otherwise. [208] Gifts which are already exempted from estate duty on other grounds are disregarded in determining whether the £500 limit has been exceeded. If the gift exceeds £500, marginal relief is given by restricting the duty payable to the excess over £500 if this is less favourable to the Revenue.

4 *Gifts not exceeding £100 in aggregate to any individual donee.* Such gifts will normally fall within the £500 limit, but are free from the restrictive conditions which occasionally disqualify gifts from being exempt within this higher limit and which are set out above. [209]

5 *Gifts to surviving spouse.* Property given to the deceased's widow or widower is exempt up to £15,000.[210]

6 *Gifts to charities.* Gifts to charities up to a limit of £50,000 are, subject to certain conditions, exempt from estate duty. [211]

Settled property

Duty is charged on settled property if at any time during the seven years ending with the deceased's death the property was settled and the deceased was entitled to an interest in it for his benefit; duty is also chargeable if the deceased terminated or disposed (whether for value or not) of such an interest in such property unless he did so at least seven years before his death and was throughout that period entirely excluded from possession and enjoyment of the property and from any benefit to him by contract or otherwise (see *ante*, pages 166–8).[212] Exceptionally, duty is not chargeable under the above rules if the settlement had come to an end before the death because the deceased had attained full age or had become absolutely entitled to the property, nor, as regards part of the property, if that part was disposed of in order to pay any tax or duty which is properly payable out of the settled property.

By a rule akin to that applicable to gifts, the value of the settled property on which duty is chargeable is reduced by 15 per cent if the deceased terminated or disposed of his interest between four and five years ending with his death, by 30 per cent if between five and six years prior to his death, and by 60 per cent if between six and seven years prior to his death.

If the deceased's interest conferred a right to receive a variable part of the income of the property in which his interest subsisted, a portion of that property is dutiable and is calculated by reference to the proportion which the aggregate sum received by the deceased because of his interest during the seven years ending with his death or the date of the earlier termination or disposal of the interest bears to the aggregate income produced by the property during that period.[213] But if the deceased's interest gave a right to receive a non-variable part of the income of the property, the dutiable part of the property is fixed by reference to the proportion borne by the deceased's part of the income from the property at the date of his death or of the earlier termination or disposal of his interest.

170

Discretionary trusts

If property is held on trusts under which the trustees have power to distribute the income to one or more amongst a specified class of beneficiaries as the trustees see fit (known as property held on 'discretionary trusts'), the general rule is that on the death of a beneficiary under such a trust duty becomes chargeable on a slice of the property producing the income; the slice is ascertained by reference to the proportion which the trust income paid to or applied for the benefit of the beneficiary during a period of seven years bears to the total income produced by the trust property during that time;[214] there are, however, complex rules for determining exactly what is the period above referred to, and the application of these can sometimes result in a heavy charge to duty although the deceased beneficiary has not received much income under the trust.

Enlargement of life interest

If a life tenant shortly before his death buys out the interest of the remainderman (ante, page 6) in the settled property, the result would prima facie be to diminish the estate duty payable; this is because, had the property remained in settlement, the whole capital value of the settled property would have been dutiable plus the private funds of the deceased, whereas by making the purchase the whole of the property previously settled remains dutiable but the private funds of the deceased are diminished to the extent of the purchase money which he has paid away and the total charge to estate duty would thereby be reduced. This manoeuvre is however nullified from the estate duty aspect by a provision that if the remainder was purchased within a period of seven years before the deceased's death (or within one year if purchased from a body established for public or charitable purposes only), estate duty is also to be charged upon the amount or value paid for the purchase of the remainder.[215] If the deceased survived the purchase for more than four years, a measure of relief is given akin to that concerning gifts (ante, page 166).

Exemption from duty on death of surviving spouse

No duty is payable on settled property on the death of the surviving party to a marriage, provided duty has or would but for the smallness of the estate have been paid on that property on the death of the other party to the marriage, and provided the surviving spouse has not been competent to dispose of the settled property at any time since the settlement.[216] The most common instance of this useful exemption is that where property has borne duty on the death of one spouse who leaves a life interest only to the surviving spouse, there is no duty on the death of the surviving spouse. The exemption applies whether the settlement was created before the death of the first spouse or by his will or on his intestacy, or even if the settlement was created by a third party. It also applies in favour of a divorced ex-spouse since such a person will still have been 'a party to the marriage'. The requirement that the surviving party must at no time during the settlement have been competent to dispose of the property is satisfied despite the conferment of a power of appointment on the survivor so long as the terms of the power prevent the survivor from appointing the property to himself or taking the property in default of appointment. [217]

Postponement of payment of estate duty until death of surviving spouse

Where the settlor creates a life interest, no duty is payable on the revertes of the property to the settlor in his lifetime by reason of the death of the life tenant, provided no other interest is created by the settlement. [218] Furthermore, payment of estate duty on an 'interest in expectancy' (which is defined (Finance Act, 1894, section 22) as including a reversion or remainder) may be made, at the choice of the person who is to pay it over, either when the duty is paid on the rest of the property or when the interest in expectancy falls into possession. [219] If payment of duty is not postponed, the interest in expectancy must be valued at the date of death of the person in respect of whom duty is payable; if payment is postponed, the value of the interest in expectancy at the date of the death of the person in respect of whom duty is payable must be ascertained at his death and aggregated with the rest of the property in order to determine the rate of estate duty on the other property, but when the interest in expectancy falls into possession it must be revalued at that date and aggregated with the rest of the estate in order to determine the rate of duty on the property comprised in the interest in expectancy itself.

The rules concerning the exemption from estate duty as regards property reverting to the settlor and the right to postpone payment of estate duty on an interest in expectancy may be combined with advantage by a spouse who wishes to provide for the surviving spouse and to defer payment of duty until both spouses are dead. Thus if one spouse settles property on the other for life (thus leaving himself with the reversion), then if the other spouse dies first the reverter to settlor exemption applies and no duty is payable on that spouse's death; if the spouse creating the settlement survives seven years and then dies, his reversion becomes dutiable but those administering his estate can elect to postpone payment of the duty until his reversionary interest falls into possession on the death of the other spouse.

Remuneration of trustee

Although the strict legal position is debatable concerning the liability to duty of property charged with payment of remuneration to a trustee for his services, it appears that, in practice at any rate, duty will not be charged on reasonable remuneration for those services paid in such a manner.

Partnerships

Where a father and his sons made a partnership agreement by which the sons were to take over the father's share of goodwill on his death without any cash payment in return, the sons being required under the agreement to devote their time to the partnership business meanwhile, it was held that on the father's death no duty could be charged on the share of goodwill which passed to the sons, since there is an exemption from duty applicable where property passes by reason only of *bona fide* purchase from the person under whose disposition the property passes and the purchase was made for full value for money or money's worth paid to the vendor, [220] and the sons had purchased the goodwill for full value in money's worth in the shape of the services which they had rendered. [221] The exemption will not apply unless the value rendered in return for the purchase is the full corresponding value. [222] (It should be noted that the exemption relating to '*bona fide* purchase from the person under whose disposition the property passes' is a narrow one, since if property is purchased absolutely and the purchaser subsequently dies, the property passes on his death by virtue of his will or intestacy and not by virtue of the previous disposition from the vendor, hence the exemption does not apply.)

Property held in joint ownership

If property is held in joint ownership, that property must be subject to a trust (*ante*, page 14). Estate duty is chargeable according to the extent to which the deceased held an interest in the property for his own benefit,

173

and it is thus irrelevant that he held an interest in the property as trustee except insofar as he also held that interest for his own personal benefit. In deciding who is entitled to the benefit of the property, one should bear in mind that if a person buys property and places the title in the joint names of himself and a stranger, there is a legal presumption that the stranger holds the property merely as trustee for the person who bought it; this presumption is of course rebuttable by contrary evidence. If however a person buys property and transfers it to his wife, child or someone for whose welfare that person's conduct has shown an intention to undertake the responsibility, the presumption is that the transferee was intended to take the property for his own benefit. Again the presumption is rebuttable by contrary evidence, and it will be noted that no such presumption arises when a wife transfers property to her husband or to her children, unless her conduct has shown an intention to undertake responsibility for their welfare.

Where a presumption arises that the transferee is to take a benefit in the property transferred, then if the property is land he is presumed to take the benefit immediately and absolutely, whereas if property other than land, such as shares, is bought in joint names the presumption appears to be that the transferee is to take the capital for his benefit on the death of the transferor should he survive that death, but that meanwhile the income from the property is to be taken solely by the transferor.[223] Thus where property other than land is purchased in joint names and this presumption holds, the whole of the property is charged with duty when the buyer dies, whereas no duty at all is chargeable if the other person dies first since he had never had possession and his interest is only a contingent one.

Duty being chargeable on the beneficial interest, it is frequently difficult in the case of husband and wife to find out exactly what the beneficial interest of each spouse in the property was. If both have contributed to the purchase of property and there is not sufficient evidence to show how much each has contributed respectively, they are frequently regarded as having provided the purchase money equally. If both spouses contribute to the funds in a joint bank account in their names, then a credit balance on the account will be presumed to belong to the spouses equally unless there is positive evidence to show the proportion in which each contributed to it.

Policies of life insurance

Policies owned by the deceased at his death, whether taken out on his own life or on the life of another, are dutiable on his death as property of which he was competent to dispose at that date.[224] As regards policies which the deceased did not own when he died but on which he nevertheless paid the premium or premiums in order to keep up the policy for the benefit of another person, then for estate duty purposes the payment of premiums is to be treated as a gift to that other person of rights under the policy, and the property given is regarded as having at the deceased's death a value equal to the proportion of the value of the policy which the premium paid bears to the aggregate of all relevant premiums;[225] if the policy was kept up by the deceased until his death, all premiums are relevant premiums. The above provision does not apply if the gift made by the deceased is one of money, as might well be so if the deceased paid the sum required to keep up the policy directly to the person whom he wished to benefit and not to the insurance company. The normal exemptions and reliefs applicable to gifts apply here also, particularly those relating to gifts made seven years before the deceased's death (*ante*, pages 166–8), gifts forming part of the deceased's normal expenditure and reasonable (*ante*, page 169), and graduated reliefs for gifts made at least four years before the deceased's death (*ante*, page 166).

If the deceased took out a policy on his life and gave it away within seven years prior to his death, the property dutiable is to be valued at the deceased's death at a sum equal to that proportion of the value of the policy which the total premiums paid under the policy before the deceased gave it away bears to the total of all the premiums payable under the policy.[226]

Controlled companies

A controlled company is one which is under the control of not more than five persons. For this purpose relatives (as defined) count as a single person, as do partners, or a person and his nominee, or beneficiaries under a trust of the company's shares or debentures. If five or fewer persons (as above defined) are able to exercise or entitled to acquire control over the company's affairs, whether by the exercise of voting power or otherwise, or possess or are entitled to acquire more than half of the issued share capital of the company, they are considered to control the company. To escape this definition there must be at least ten 'persons' in the company and no five of them in 'control' of it, which means that none of them must have a casting vote; in practice nearly all family companies are inevitably caught by the definition.

When a person dies owning shares and debentures in a controlled company, these may be required to be valued, not at their market value, but by reference to that part of the value of the company's net assets which is proportionate to that which the deceased's own holding of shares and debentures in the company bears to the total of its issued shares and debentures;[227] valuation on an assets basis will usually produce a much higher figure than a valuation by reference to the market value of the deceased's shares and debentures in the company.

Valuation on an assets basis is required by the Revenue if the company was a controlled company at any time during the seven years prior to the deceased's death, and the deceased had control of the company at any time during the seven years; he is deemed to have had control if he controlled the power of majority voting on any matter affecting the company as a whole, or could have obtained such control by the use of a power exercisable by him.[228] Control which the deceased had only in the capacity of trustee is to be disregarded, unless the deceased himself made the disposition under which the trusteeship arose.[229] An assets valuation can also be required: (a) if, during a continuous period of two years falling within the seven years prior to death, the deceased had powers equivalent to control (such powers include the ability to control the exercise of the powers of the board of directors or power to control the composition of the board);[230] or (b) if, during a continuous period of two years within the seven years prior to the deceased's death, his share of dividends declared and debenture interest paid exceeded half the total dividends and debenture interest paid by the company during that period;[231] or (c) if, at any time during the seven years ending with his death, the deceased was entitled in possession for his own benefit to at least half of the issued shares and debentures of the company.[232]

As regards (a) to (c) above, assets valuation is only required if, immediately after the deceased's death, a person with control or powers equivalent to control of the company, either alone or together with his relatives, is beneficially entitled in possession to the shares or debentures, or immediately before and after the death the shares or debentures are held by the trustees of some trust who have control of the company by virtue of their trustee shareholdings.[233] In the case of a gift of the shares or debentures by the deceased, a requirement is that immediately after the death or since the gift the donee must have had control or powers equivalent to control of the company, either alone or together with his relatives.[234]

Under an assets valuation the assets are valued on the basis of what they would fetch if sold in the open market at the time of the deceased's death. But assets used or occupied for the purpose of a trade carried on by the company are to be valued on the basis that they can only be used for the

176

purpose of that business,[235] though this cannot be used to bring the estate duty valuation below the market valuation of the shares or debentures.

Valuation on an assets basis does not apply to shares or debentures in which permission to deal has been granted by a recognised Stock Exchange and provided dealings in the shares in the ordinary course of business have been recorded during the year ending with the deceased's death; this step can be taken by the controller of the company in order to avoid what might otherwise be a very heavy charge to duty.

If shares or debentures valued on the assets basis are sold to a non-relative at arms length within three years after the death, then, subject to any adjustment for different circumstances arising after the death,[236] the sale price will be substituted if less than the assets valuation. Nor does an assets valuation apply if the shares or debentures were given away before the deceased's death into the absolute ownership of an employee or ex-employee of the company or his widow or orphan, provided the donee was not a relative of the deceased and did not have control or powers equivalent to control of the company either alone or with his relatives at any time since the making of the gift.[237]

If the company is engaged in agriculture or forestry, duty is charged at 55 per cent of the estate rate (see *ante*, page 163) on that part of the net value of the deceased's shares or debentures as is attributable to the agricultural value of agricultural property occupied by the company for the purposes of agriculture or forestry; this relief is not obtainable if the company does not itself occupy the property, such as where the company has let the property to someone else. Similar relief is given as regards the value attributed to the deceased's shares or debentures in respect of industrial hereditaments or machinery and plant occupied or used by the company for the purpose of its business.[238] Relief in respect of these assets is not granted where the deceased died owning shares which are not valued on an assets basis, hence sometimes valuation on an assets basis is desirable in order to obtain the above reliefs.

Benefits from controlled companies

A person might transfer his business to a controlled company, give away his shares in the company and survive at least seven more years, and yet continue to draw an income akin to the total income of the business by taking it in the form of director's remuneration and analogous benefits. It is however provided that where a person has transferred property to a controlled company and has received benefits from the company prior to his death, a slice of the company's net assets is deemed to pass on his death in the proportion which the aggregate benefits to the deceased during the seven accounting years of the company prior to his death bear to the net aggregate income of the company during those years. [239] In computing the benefits to the deceased, reasonable remuneration for his services is excluded. [240] It is only necessary that the company should have been controlled at any time between the date when the property was transferrred and the date of death. [241] The duty is payable by the company and is a charge on the company's assets. [242]

Valuation of property for estate duty

Estate duty is payable on dutiable property of the deceased; the property is valued at the price which it would fetch if sold in the open market at the time of his death.[243] When the 1973 Finance Bill becomes law, persons accountable for estate duty on shares or debentures quoted on a recognised Stock Exchange or on holdings in authorised unit trusts will in general be able to choose to have these valued for estate duty either at the date of the death or at the time of their sale provided the sale takes place within twelve months following the death.

The time of death means the moment immediately after death, thus where a farm was leased to a partnership of which the deceased was a member, and the partnership came to an end with the deceased's death (*ante*, page 82), it was held that the deceased's ownership of the farm should be valued on the basis that it was saleable with vacant possession. [244] Exceptionally, shares and debentures in controlled companies may sometimes fall to be valued upon the assets basis (*ante*, pages 175–7). Property which could be sold with vacant possession on the deceased's death must be valued as if it was in fact sold thus, regardless of what is actually done with the property.

A reduction in value must be made if the property can be shown to have depreciated in value by reason of the deceased's death, [245] as for example in the case of a business whose prosperity was largely dependent on the personal qualities of the deceased.

If the property is sold on the open market soon after the deceased's death, this will be some evidence of its value at the date of death, due allowance being made for any change in prevailing market conditions or relevant circumstances.

The existence of a 'special purchaser', such as an adjoining farmer who might be willing to pay a very high price to acquire the deceased's farm and add it to his own, is a relevant factor in deciding the market value of that farm; although it would not generally be assumed that he would need to pay the full value which he is prepared to give before knocking out the other bidders, yet the other bidders might often be expected to know of the existence of the special purchaser and therefore to bid more with a view to reselling the property to him than they would otherwise be prepared to give, thus the market value would often be something around midway between the value which the property would make if there were no special purchaser and the highest figure which the special purchaser would be prepared to give.

If property is held subject to a restriction on its transfer, such as shares in a private company (*ante*, page 92), this property must be valued on the assumption that it could be sold to anybody but that the hypothetical buyer would take subject to the same restrictions as bound the deceased and would take that into account in deciding how much to pay for the property;[246] this will result in a higher valuation than the deceased could himself have got for the property. Similarly, if the deceased had granted an option to a third party to purchase the property at a price below its market value, the estate duty valuation must be based on its open market value.

If the land is held in co-ownership, a 10 per cent reduction is allowed in recognition of the difficulties inherent in co-ownership.

As regards cottages occupied by farm workers, no account is to be taken of any value attributable to the fact that the cottages are suitable for letting probably at a higher rental, to persons other than farm workers.[247]

Where the value of property is found for estate duty purposes, that value is to be taken as its value for the purpose of capital gains tax also (*ante*, pages 151–9), unless the estate duty valuation is made on some special basis such as the valuation of shares on the assets basis (*ante*, pages 175–7).

Deductions

Reasonable funeral expenses are deductible from the estate. Debts incurred by the deceased are deductible if he received full value in money or money's worth in return for the creation of the debt and if there is no enforceable right to reimbursement from a third party in respect of it.[248] Illegal or unenforceable debts are not deductible.

If the debt was not created by the deceased, but he or his property are liable to pay it, the debt is deductible whether or not created for full value, provided there is no enforceable right to reimbursement from a third party.

179

Capital gains tax owed by the deceased is deductible from the value of his estate.

Persons liable to pay the duty to the Revenue

The person to whom the Revenue looks for payment of the duty is not necessarily the person who ultimately bears the duty. Those administering the deceased's estate are accountable to the Revenue for duty on land situate outside Great Britain and on all property other than land wherever situate, provided such property was owned by the deceased at his death or he had power to appoint the property in his own favour. [249] As regards other property the Revenue can, generally speaking, look either to the beneficiary or beneficiaries of it, or every trustee or other person in whom any interest in the property or its management is at any time vested, or every person who derives title to the property other than a *bona fide* buyer without notice of the liability to estate duty; [250] where property is vested in a trustee, he is by Revenue practice primarily accountable for the duty. Controlled companies are sometimes accountable for duty [251] (*ante*, pages 177–8).

Payment of estate duty

The deceased's estate cannot be dealt with without a grant of probate or administration (*ante*, pages 116–22), and in order to obtain such a grant the person wishing to deal with the estate must, among other things, prepare an Inland Revenue affidavit with full particulars concerning all dutiable property of the deceased, and must deliver the affidavit within six months after the death; duty is paid initially on the value of the property as set out, and any necessary adjustments are made subsequently.

Time of payment of estate duty

Duty on property other than land which was owned by the deceased at his death or which he could then have appointed to himself must be paid when the Inland Revenue affidavit is delivered or within six months after the death, whichever is earlier. [252]

Duty on land may, at the option of the person accountable, be paid either on delivery of the affidavit or by eight equal yearly instalments or sixteen half-yearly instalments with interest, the first instalment not being due and interest not starting to run until one year after the death. [253] This option to pay by instalments has now been extended to shares or debentures which are valued on the assets basis, and to other shares not quoted on the Stock Exchange, if the Commissioners think that the duty cannot be paid at once without undue hardship or in certain other circumstances, and to leaseholds or to a business insofar as the duty is attributable to the net value of the business.[254]

In general unpaid estate duty carries interest at 3 per cent each year without deduction of tax and from the date when the duty became payable. As to the persons by whom the duty is ultimately borne, the testator may in his will provide as he pleases concerning the person by whom the duty shall ultimately be borne, and thus the will may contain a clause that the beneficiary under it is to take the property 'free of duty'. The interpretation of such a clause depends on its context in the particular will, but *prima facie* it will be construed to apply only to the duty payable on the testator's death and not to duty payable on the subsequent death of the inheritor of the property or of an interest in it.[255]

In the absence of such a provision, the duty on the deceased's property (including leaseholds and legacies except insofar as paid out of the proceeds of land) other than land is regarded as an expense of administering the estate, provided the property was situate in Great Britain and was either owned by the deceased at his death or he could have appointed the property to himself at that time. The result is that the duty on such property will *prima facie* be borne by any property of which the deceased did not dispose by his will, and if there is no such property will be borne by his residuary estate.[256] (Certified works of art form an exception to this principle; *ante*, page 157). If the testator leaves a will giving 'my shares in X Ltd. to A, my farm Blackacre to B, and the rest of my property to C', the dispositions to A and B are specific and that to C is residuary.

The estate duty on all other property is a charge on the property itself, and therefore must be borne by the beneficiary who takes that property unless the testator otherwise provides.

These rules specifying the property out of which estate duty is *prima facie* to be paid should be borne in mind by the testator when drawing up his will and in considering whether he wishes to make any special provision in it concerning this matter.

If land is held upon a statutory trust for sale for tenants in common (see *ante*, page 14), the interest of a deceased tenant in common is treated as land for all estate duty purposes.[257] But if there is an express trust for sale this interest is treated as personalty as regards incidence, with consequent effect as regards ascertaining the person by whom the duty falls to be borne.

Disputes concerning estate duty

Disputes concerning the valuation of land are decided by the Lands Tribunal, with further appeal on a point of law to the Court of Appeal. [258] Apart from this, any person against whom a claim for duty has been made or is likely to be made may apply to the Chancery Division of the High Court to have his liability decided. [259] Alternatively, any person aggrieved by a decision of the Commissioners as regards estate duty may appeal to the High Court, or to the County Court if the value of the property in dispute does not exceed £10,000. [260] In general the duty in dispute must be paid first as a condition of the appeal, and in practice this procedure is little used. Finally, any person sued by the Crown for unpaid estate duty can always defend the lawsuit.

Value added tax

General example of its operation

Before going into detail, the operation of value added tax may be illustrated by an example. Thus if a manufacturer of a lawn mower wished to sell it to a retailer at a price which, ignoring value added tax, would leave the manufacturer with £50, he would, so long as value added tax remains at its current rate of 10 per cent, [261] charge the retailer £55; he would send to the retailer two invoices, one for £50 and the other a value added tax invoice for £5. If the retailer in his turn wished to sell the mower to a customer at a price which would be £70 were there no such thing as value added tax, he would in fact charge the customer £77, of which £7 would be value added tax at the rate of 10 per cent and computed on the price which the retailer would charge for the article but for the tax. The retailer does not, however, have to account to the Revenue for tax of £7 on this transaction, but only for tax of £2; this is because he can offset the value added tax of £5 which has been charged to him on this transaction (known as his 'input tax') against the tax of £7 charged by him (known as his 'output tax') for which he would otherwise have been accountable to the Revenue, leaving him with a balance of £2 of value added tax payable to the Revenue. Similarly the manufacturer in the example can offset any value added tax charged to him in his business operations against his liability to account to the Revenue for value added tax charged by him.

General effect of the tax upon farmers and growers

Any items of expenditure by the farmer or grower on goods and services, apart from a few exceptions, are now subject to value added tax; the introduction of this tax within this country was an inevitable consequence of entering the European Economic Community, and indeed the tax does not at present exist outside Europe.

Farmers and growers receive special treatment in respect of their production of food in that they are entitled to reclaim all value added tax which they pay on the supply of taxable goods and services to them for use in the farming business, whereas the supply of food produced by them is free from the tax; this system is technically known as zero-rating. The result is that a farmer who himself only supplies edible products will not charge value added tax, whereas conversely he can usually claim a refund of the tax charged on the supply of taxable goods and services, such as fertilisers and machinery, to him. He is thus in effect drawn into the new tax system as regards form filling and paper work, but is in other respects outside it in the ultimate financial result as regards his business activities. A farmer who makes or intends to make only zero-rated supplies can ask the Commissioners of Customs and Excise to be exempted from registration, [262] and if his request is granted he will not be able to reclaim any tax charged to him by his suppliers. Moreover farmers whose total sales are less than £5,000 per annum could if they wished decide not to register (see *post*, page 184) and thus avoid the form filling, but if they did they would have to bear personally the value added tax on the supply of taxable goods and services to them. These farmers ought to have weighed up the cost of the tax against the cost of the additional paper work. If most of the farm expenditure is on zero-rated items such as livestock, feeding stuffs and most seeds then the additional paper work involved in becoming registered may not be worthwhile; many small farmers would however probably find themselves involved in the receipt of a number of business goods or services subject to the value added tax.

Farmers and growers supplying non-edible products (other than a person whose total sales are less than £5,000 per annum and who elects not to register) will have to charge the value added tax on the price of goods of the above type or of services which they supply and account periodically for the tax to the Customs and Excise after deducting any value added tax paid by them in respect of the business.

Value added tax must be collected and paid over to the Customs and Excise by taxable persons; 'person' here includes partnerships, companies and the like as well as individuals. 'Taxable person' usually means a registered person, but also includes any person who ought to be registered although he has not in fact registered. [263] A person who supplies only goods and services which are exempt from the value added tax is not required to register. A person who intends to supply goods or services which are liable to the value added tax must in general register with the Customs and Excise. If his annual turnover (not his profit) in taxable goods or services is less than £5,000 per annum he is not required to register, but he may do so if he chooses.

Every registered taxable person is sent a certificate of registration by the Customs and Excise showing his value added tax registration number.

The value added tax is payable on supplies (other than 'exempt supplies' see *post*, page 186) of goods and services by way of business.[264] 'Supplies' means transactions such as sales or hire-purchases, and the performance of services. A business includes any trade, profession or vocation. [265]

The value added tax is collected at each stage of the process of production or distribution of goods and services. The tax is ultimately borne by the consumer. At each stage, the taxable person is charged by his suppliers with value added tax on the goods and services they supply to him for his business. Those goods and services are called his inputs, and the tax on them is his input tax. When he in turn supplies goods and services, not necessarily the same ones, to his customers, he charges the customers with value added tax; the goods and services he supplies are called his outputs, and the tax he charges is his output tax. At intervals he is required to make a return to the Customs and Excise; he then adds up all his output tax and all his input tax and deducts the smaller amount from the greater, and the difference between them is the amount which he either has to pay to or can reclaim from the Customs and Excise. If a taxable person supplies some goods and services which are exempt from the value added tax and others which are not, there will have to be an apportionment in order to determine how much of his input tax he may deduct when arriving at his tax liability to the Customs and Excise. [266]

It will be seen that every registered person who supplies taxable goods or taxable services is required to act as an unpaid tax collector for the Customs and Excise, but does not bear any value added tax himself as regards those supplies.

The computation of the tax

The tax is a tax on the ultimate consumer, although the method of collection is extremely complicated; basically a person will pay the tax on all goods and services supplied to him, except as regards such goods and services, as food, as are exempt from the tax; where there is a chain of transactions, as in the sale several times of the same taxable article which thus passes through several pairs of hands, the tax is levied on the element of enhanced value which occurs on each separate sale, and each person making the sale is accountable to the Customs and Excise in respect of the tax levied on the extent to which the price of the article was enhanced by him when it left his hands. Thus if A and B are taxable persons and C is not, and A sells a taxable article to B for £10 excluding tax, and B resells the article to C for £20 excluding tax, the article then being permanently retained by C, A will be liable (assuming value added tax at a rate of 10 per cent) to the Customs and Excise for tax of £1; he will supply B with an invoice stating the amount of the tax and will charge B a total of £11. B will also be accountable to the Customs and Excise for £1 of tax, this being 10 per cent of the amount which B added to the price of the goods, and B will charge C a total of £22 pounds; B is not obliged to give C an invoice for £2, the total tax charged, because C is not a taxable person. Since C permanently retains the goods he cannot pass any of the tax on to a third party and must bear it himself; the whole of the tax can thus be seen to fall upon the ultimate consumer. Even if C later changes his mind and sells the goods he will not even then be able to pass any of the tax on since he is not a taxable person (see *ante*, page 184) and therefore also will not charge value added tax on the sale by him. It will also be seen that the value of the goods or services on which the value added tax is calculated is usually the price paid, excluding the value added tax itself, by the person to whom the goods or services are supplied. If the customer does not pay money but indulges in a transaction of barter (see *post*, page 277), the value on which the value added tax has to be charged is the open market value of the supply. [267]

If machinery is acquired on hire-purchase, credit-sale or conditional sale agreement within the financial limits of the Hire-Purchase Acts (*post*, pages 293, 301—2) the value added tax is charged on the cash price stated in the agreement and is payable in a lump sum. If such an agreement falls outside the financial limits set out in the Hire-Purchase Acts, then the value added tax is charged on the total sum payable under the agreement including interest, and not merely on the cash price.

If a machine is merely rented, the tax is chargeable on each rental payment.

Time when value added tax becomes chargeable

The tax on a supply of goods and services becomes chargeable at a definite time, called the tax point. The rate of tax to be charged is the rate in force at the tax point, and the supply must be recorded in the tax period in which the tax point occurs. As regards goods, the basic tax point is the date when the goods are removed to give effect to the transaction, but if the supplier issues a tax invoice within fourteen days after the basic tax point then the date when the invoice is issued becomes the actual tax point. A taxable person can elect by written notice to the Customs and Excise not to follow the latter rule, if he prefers to adopt the basic tax point. Where periodic payments are made in return for goods on hire or rental, there is a tax point connected with each payment. As regards services, the basic tax point is the date when the service is performed, but if the supplier issues a tax invoice within fourteen days after the basic tax point, the date when the invoice is issued becomes the actual tax point unless the taxable person elects not to follow this rule and to adopt the basic tax point. [268]

Exempt supplies

The purchase of land, the purchase of grazing or mowing rights, bank charges and bank interest, insurance, and local authority and water rates are among the matters altogether exempt from the value added tax system. Rents, apart from rents due in respect of the letting of holiday accommodation, are also exempt. [269]

Zero-rated supplies

Where the supply is zero-rated no tax is charged on the supply, but in all other respects the supply is treated as a taxable supply. [270]

Zero-rated items include the erection of new buildings (though not the maintenance and repair of buildings), most seeds, water, petrol, fuel oil and electricity. [271] Although the sale of a farm animal is zero-rated, the value added tax will be chargeable on the auctioneer's commission.

Examples of supplies which are subject to the tax

Items taxable at the standard rate of 10 per cent include wool, flowers, flower seeds and bulbs, agricultural contracting, the hire of machinery, holiday accomodation and meals and the provision of camping facilities, and agistment. Also included are the value of trees when sold, and the hiring of a machine in return for a payment in cash or in kind.

Particular transactions

1   *Repairs to buildings.* The cost of repairs to buildings is subject to the value added tax. Where such expenditure is incurred on the farm house, the farmer will be allowed to reclaim the value added tax in respect of that proportion of the expenditure which is agreed as being referable to the business use of the premises rather than private use. When negotiating this one should bear in mind the exemption of the taxpayer's private dwelling house from capital gains tax, which cannot be claimed for that part of the house which is used for business purposes.

2   *Motor vehicles.* A trader is not given a tax credit for the value added tax payable on the purchase of a passenger car even where the car is used in his trade, and no value added tax is chargeable on the proceeds of the subsequent sale of that car by the trader except insofar as the amount of the value added tax would exceed the tax paid on the purchase of the car. The above rule does not apply to the purchase of a Land Rover used for business purposes.

3   *Imports and exports.* Value added tax is payable on imported goods, whether the importer is a taxable person or not, though it is not payable on services obtained from abroad. Exports of goods are zero-rated, [272] but value added tax will be payable by the importer if the goods are shipped to another country within the European Economic Community.

4   *Wages and contractor's services.* An employee's service to his employer is not subject to the value added tax. The services of an agricultural contractor are however subject to the tax, unless the contractor is a small trader who has elected not to register (see *ante,* page 184).

5   *Discount.* Where the amount payable for goods or services is to be reduced if payment is made immediately or within a specified time, the value added tax is charged on the net price whether or not the discount is claimed. Where a discount is given for quantity or a rebate is made calculated on the annual turnover, the value added tax is charged initially on

the gross price and an adjustment can be made later when the discount or rebate is shown to have been earned.

6 *Second-hand goods.* Second-hand goods are usually chargeable with value added tax on the price at which they are supplied, but if a car dealer sells a second-hand car the tax in only charged on the dealer's profit.

7 *Bad debts.* A trader who has paid value added tax in respect of taxable goods or services supplied by him cannot reclaim the amount if the debt subsequently turns out to be a bad debt.

8 *Returnable containers.* If goods are sent out in returnable containers, even if a deposit is paid on the containers, the value of the container or the deposit is not taken into account in determining the value of the supply unless the container is not returned.

9 *Artificial transactions.* If a taxable person sells goods to an exempt person at an artificially low price because of the relationship between them, the Customs and Excise may serve notice on the taxable person directing that the value of his supplies be regarded as not less than their open market value.

Value added tax invoices

A taxable person must keep a copy of any value added tax invoice issued by him. A tax invoice must in general be issued when goods or services taxable at the standard rate are supplied to another person who is a taxable person. The issue of tax invoices for zero-rated supplies and for supplies to customers who are not taxable persons is optional. The invoice must contain an identifying number and date, the date of supply, the supplier's name, address and value added tax registration number, the customer's name (or trading name) and address, the type of supply (such as whether it is a sale or a hire-purchase or credit-sale transaction; *post,* pages 277–302), a description sufficient to identify the goods or services supplied, the quantity and amount payable (excluding the tax) for each such description, the total amount payable (excluding the tax), the rate of any cash discount offered, and the rate and amount of the value added tax charged. Value added tax invoices are required to be issued if the goods or services in question are taxable at the standard rate and are supplied to a taxable person. The Customs and Excise have power to approve the use of less detailed tax invoices in circumstances where it is not reasonably practicable to issue invoices showing all the particulars which are usually required. Moreover a retailer or other taxable person supplying goods or services direct to the general public need not issue a tax invoice, not even to another taxable person, unless the customer asks for one. If a tax invoice is requested, then provided the amount payable for the individual supply does not exceed £10 (including value added tax) the supplier may issue a less detailed tax invoice showing only the supplier's name, address and value added tax registration number, the date of supply, a description sufficient to identify the goods or services supplied, the amount payable (including value added tax), and the rate of value added tax in force at the time of the supply. Zero-rated or exempt supplies must not be included in this less detailed tax invoice. Copies of these invoices need not be kept by the supplier.

Taxable persons must make sure that they obtain and preserve tax invoices, since without such an invoice it will not be possible to claim deduction of input tax. Exceptionally, however, as regards certain kinds of taxable supply input tax may be deducted without a tax invoice, provided that the cost, including value added tax, of the goods or services was not more than £10, and so long as there is no doubt that the supply was made by a registered taxable person.

Keeping accounts and records

Every taxable person must keep records and accounts of all goods and services he receives or supplies in the course of his business, and must do so in sufficient detail to allow him to calculate correctly the amount of value added tax that he has to pay or can reclaim and to complete the necessary tax returns. The period covered by a taxable person's tax return is known as the tax period, and the standard tax period is three months, but if the taxable person declares that he expects his input tax regularly to exceed his output tax (as where most of his outputs are zero-rated) he will be given a tax period of one month, thus enabling him to obtain earlier repayments.

For each tax period a taxable person must summarise his records of output tax, deductible input tax and any tax adjustments affecting the amount due or repayable; these summaries must be entered in a special book and must show the tax due to the Customs and Excise, the tax deductible, and the net amount for payment or repayment. The records and accounts must be kept in a form which will enable Customs and Excise officers to check the completeness and accuracy of the returns. These accounts and all related documents and other documents relating to the business must be kept for three years from the last date to which they refer, and must be produced when required for inspection by officials from the Customs and Excise.

Two or more corporate bodies may apply to be treated as members of a group for value added tax purposes if one of them controls each of the others, or one person (whether a body corporate or an individual) controls all of them, or two or more individuals carrying on a business in partnership control all of them. The business carried on by the various members of the group will then be treated for value added tax purposes as a business carried on by one of them, known as the representative member, who will be registered and be responsible for sending in the tax returns and paying or reclaiming the tax for the group. [273]

A registered person must inform the Customs and Excise of any change in the name or trading name of the business or in the composition of the partnership and the like.

When a registered person closes down or sells his business, he must inform the Customs and Excise in writing of this fact within ten days thereafter.

Powers of the Customs and Excise

The officials of the Customs and Excise may enter business premises at any reasonable time for the purpose of exercising their powers to see that records and accounts are in order and that the tax is being correctly calculated and paid. [274]

Where a taxable person has failed to make the required returns or to keep the required documents and to afford the facilities necessary to verify the returns, or where it appears to the Commissioners of Customs and Excise that such returns are incomplete or incorrect, the Commissioners may assess the amount of tax due from him to the best of their judgement. [275]

As a condition of being permitted to supply goods or services which are taxable supplies, a taxable person may be required by the Commissioners to provide security for the payment of any tax which may become due from him. [276]

Notes.

[1] Income and Corporation Taxes Act, 1970, sections 108 and 109.
[2] [1927] A.C. 312.

190

3 (1929) 14 T.C. 490.

4 *Pickford* v. *Quirke* (1927) 13 T.C. 251.

5 *Edwards* v. *Bairstow and Harrison* (1949) A.C. 14.

6 *I.R.C.* v. *Cock, Russell and Co. Ltd.* [1949] 29 T.C. 387.

7 Income and Corporation Taxes Act, 1970, section 139 and Schedule 6.

8 Income and Corporation Taxes Act, 1970, Schedule 6.

9 *I.R.C.* v. *Nelson* (1938) 22 T.C. 716.

10 Income and Corporation Taxes Act, 1970, section 137.

11 *Sharkey* v. *Wernher* [1956] A.C. 58.

12 Income and Corporation Taxes Act, 1970, section 130.

13 *British Insulated and Helsby Cables Ltd.* v. *Atherton* [1926] A.C. 205.

14 Section 130.

15 *Bentleys, Stokes and Lowless* v. *Beeson* (1952) 33 T.C. 491.

16 *Norman* v. *Golder* (1944) 26 T.C. 293.

17 Section 130.

18 *Law Shipping Co. Limited* v. *I.R.C.* (1924) 12 T.C. 621.

19 *Odeon Associated Theatres Ltd.* v. *Jones* [1972] 2 W.L.R. 331.

20 Per Buckley L.J. in *Lurcott* v. *Wakely and Wheeler* [1911] 1 K.B. 905.

21 *I.R.C.* v. *Alexander von Glehn & Co. Ltd.* [1920] 2 K.B. 553.

22 *Smith's Potato Estates Ltd.* v. *Bolland* [1948] A.C. 508.

23 Section 411.

24 *Newsom* v. *Robertson* [1953] Ch. 7.

25 *Horton* v. *Young* (1971) 47 T.C. 60.

26 Section 130.

27 Income and Corporation Taxes Act, 1970, section 118.

28 Section 154.

29 *Reynolds, Sons and Co. Ltd.* v. *Ogston* (1930) 15 T.C. 501.

30 *Waddington* v. *O'Callaghan* (1931) 16 T.C. 187; *ante*, page 80).

31 Taxes Management Act, 1970, section 9.

32 *Income Tax Commissioners for the City of London* v. *Gibbs* [1942] A.C. 402.

33 Income and Corporation Taxes Act, 1970, section 154.

34 Income and Corporation Taxes Act, 1970, section 154, as amended by Finance Act, 1971, section 17.

35 Section 171.

36 Section 172.

37 Section 168.

38 Section 170.

[39] Section 180.
[40] Section 174.
[41] Finance Act, 1971, section 40(1) as amended by Finance Act, 1972, section 67.
[42] Finance Act, 1971, section 41(3).
[43] Section 43.
[44] Capital Allowances Act, 1968, sections 68 and 69.
[45] Section 68(3).
[46] *McMillan* v. *Guest* [1942] A.C. 561.
[47] *Mitchell and Edon* v. *Ross* [1962] A.C. 814.
[48] *Hochstrasser* v. *Mayes* [1960] A.C. 376.
[49] *Heasman* v. *Jordan* [1954] Ch. 744.
[50] *Nicoll* v. *Austin* (1935) 19 T.C. 531.
[51] [1961] Ch. 133.
[52] *Tennant* v. *Smith* [1892] A.C. 150.
[53] Income and Corporation Taxes Act, 1970, section 185.
[54] Section 531.
[55] Section 185.
[56] *Dale* v. *De Soissons* (1950) 32 T.C. 118.
[57] Sections 187–188.
[58] Section 188.
[59] Finance Act, 1970, section 21.
[60] Finance Act, 1970, section 23.
[61] Section 24.
[62] Income and Corporation Taxes Act, 1970, section 189.
[63] *Blackwell* v. *Mills* (1945) 26 T.C. 468.
[64] *Per* Vaisey J. in *Lomax* v. *Newton* [1953] 2 All E.R. 801.
[65] *Pook* v. *Owen* [1970] A.C. 244.
[66] Section 202(2).
[67] Sections 195–203.
[68] (1969) 45 T.C. 476.
[69] Section 67(1).
[70] Section 64(1).
[71] Section 67(1).
[72] Section 87.
[73] Section 69.
[74] Section 80(2).
[75] Section 90.
[76] Section 80.
[77] Section 81.
[78] Section 80; *ante*, page 144.

[79] Section 533.
[80] Section 82.
[81] Income and Corporation Taxes Act, 1970, Schedule 3.
[82] Sections 71–77.
[83] Section 72.
[84] *Pyne* v. *Stallard-Benoyre* (1964) 42 T.C. 183.
[85] Section 72.
[86] Section 71.
[87] Section 72.
[88] Section 304.
[89] Sections 91–92.
[90] Section 111.
[91] *Collins* v. *Fraser* (1969) 46 T.C. 143.
[92] Income and Corporation Taxes Act, 1970, section 528.
[93] Finance Act, 1971, section 34.
[94] Finance Act, 1972, section 75.
[95] Section 75.
[96] Section 75 and Schedule 9.
[97] Income and Corporation Taxes Act, 1970, section 42.
[98] Finance Act, 1971, section 23 and Schedule 4.
[99] Finance Act, 1971, section 23 and Schedule 4.
[100] Finance Act, 1971, section 16.
[101] Income and Corporation Taxes Act, 1970, section 454(3).
[102] Income and Corporation Taxes Act, 1970, section 21.
[103] Income and Corporation Taxes Act, 1970, Schedule 1, Part 1.
[104] Income and Corporation Taxes, Act, 1970, section 54 as amended.
[105] Section 54(3).
[106] Section 54(2).
[107] Finance Act, 1965, sections 19 and 20.
[108] Finance Act, 1965, section 21.
[109] Section 21(2) (c).
[110] Section 21.
[111] Section 20.
[112] Section 19.
[113] Sections 22 and 45.
[114] Schedule 6.
[115] Section 23(4).
[116] Section 23(5).
[117] Section 22(6).
[118] Schedule 7.
[119] Schedule 7.

[120] Finance Act, 1969, Schedule 19.
[121] Finance Act, 1965, Schedule 7.
[122] Schedule 7.
[123] Schedule 7.
[124] Finance Act, 1965, section 24(1) as amended by Finance Act, 1971, section 59 and Schedule 12.
[125] Finance Act, 1965, section 24(7).
[126] Finance Act, 1965, sections 22(5) and 45(1).
[127] Section 25(2).
[128] Section 25(1).
[129] Section 25(3).
[130] Finance Act, 1965, section 25(4), as amended by Finance Act, 1971, Schedule 12.
[131] Finance Act, 1971, Schedule 12.
[132] Finance Act, 1971, Schedule 12.
[133] Finance Act, 1965, Schedule 6.
[134] *Secretan* v. *Hart* (1969) 45 T.C. 701.
[135] Schedule 6.
[136] Schedule 8.
[137] Schedule 6.
[138] Schedule 6.
[139] Schedule 6.
[140] Section 20(4).
[141] Section 20(4).
[142] Section 27.
[143] Section 27.
[144] Section 28.
[145] Finance Act, 1965, section 57 and Schedule 11.
[146] Finance Act, 1965, section 29.
[147] Finance Act, 1965, section 29.
[148] Finance Act, 1965, section 30.
[149] Section 30.
[150] Section 31.
[151] Finance Act, 1965, section 33.
[152] Finance Act, 1965, section 33, as amended by Finance Act, 1971, section 60.
[153] Section 33(3).
[154] Finance Act, 1965, section 33(2).
[155] Section 33(6) as amended.
[156] Section 33(5).
[157] Finance Act, 1969, section 42 and Schedule 19.

[158] Finance Act, 1965, section 34.
[159] Finance Act, 1972, section 95.
[160] Section 93.
[161] Income and Corporation Taxes Act, 1970, section 243(3).
[162] Section 248(1).
[163] Income and Corporation Taxes Act, 1970, section 250(1).
[164] Section 250(2).
[165] Section 265(2).
[166] Section 177.
[167] Section 252(1).
[168] Section 253.
[169] Sections 258–264.
[170] Finance Act, 1972, section 85.
[171] Section 85.
[172] Income and Corporation Taxes Act, 1970, section 282(1).
[173] Section 302.
[174] Section 303.
[175] Section 303.
[176] Section 283.
[177] Section 284.
[178] Section 285.
[179] Section 286(1).
[180] Section 286(5).
[181] Sections 296–297.
[182] Finance Act, 1894, section 1.
[183] Finance Act, 1969, section 35.
[184] Finance Act, 1925, section 23(4).
[185] Revenue Concession No. E 15.
[186] Finance Act, 1925, section 23(2).
[187] *Midleton (Earl)* v. *Cottesloe (Baron)* [1949] A.C. 418.
[188] *Philipson Stow's Special Representatives* v. *I.R.C.* [1959] T.R. 23.
[189] Finance Act, 1925, section 23(3).
[190] Finance Act, 1954, section 28.
[191] Finance Act, 1894, section 15(2).
[192] Finance Act, 1972, section 121.
[193] Finance Act, 1972, section 121.
[194] Finance Act, 1958, section 30, as amended.
[195] Finance Act, 1894, section 2(1) (c).
[196] Law of Property Act, 1925, section 53.
[197] Law of Property Act, 1925, section 53; *Grey* v. *Inland Revenue Commissioners* [1960] A.C. 1.

198 *Munro* v. *Commissioner of Stamp Duties* [1934] A.C. 61.
199 *Chick* v. *Commissioner of Stamp Duties* [1958] A.C. 435.
200 Finance Act, 1959, section 35(2).
201 [1911] 2 K.B. 688.
202 *Att.–Gen.* v. *Johnson* [1903] 1 K.B. 617.
203 Finance Act, 1940, section 44.
204 Finance Act, 1968, section 36.
205 *Re Park, decd.* (*No. 2*) [1972] 2 W.L.R. 276.
206 Finance Act, 1963, section 53(1).
207 Finance Act, 1968, section 37(1).
208 See *ante*, pages 166–8; Finance Act, 1949, section 33.
209 Finance (1909–10) Act, 1910, section 59.
210 Finance Act, 1972, section 121; see *ante*, page 166.
211 Finance Act, 1972, section 121.
212 Finance Act, 1894, section 2(1)(b), as amended by Finance Act, 1969.
213 Finance Act, 1969, section 37.
214 Finance Act, 1969, section 37.
215 Finance Act, 1969, section 38.
216 Finance Act, 1894, section 5 as amended.
217 *Re Penrose* [1933] Ch. 793.
218 Finance Act, 1896, section 15.
219 Finance Act, 1894, section 7.
220 Finance Act, 1894, section 2.
221 *Att.–Gen.* v. *Boden* [1912] 1 K.B. 539.
222 *Re Clark* (1906) 40 Ir.L.T. 117.
223 *Fowkes* v. *Pascoe* (1875) L.R. 10 Ch. 343.
224 Finance Act, 1894, section 2(1)(a).
225 Finance Act, 1959, section 34.
226 Finance Act, 1959, section 34.
227 Finance Act, 1940, section 55.
228 Finance Act, 1940, section 55.
229 Finance Act, 1940, section 58.
230 Finance Act, 1954, section 31.
231 Finance Act, 1954, section 29.
232 Finance Act, 1954, section 29.
233 Finance Act, 1954, section 29.
234 Section 29.
235 Finance Act, 1960, section 66.
236 Finance Act, 1954, section 30.
237 Section 30.

238 Finance Act, 1954, section 28.
239 Finance Act, 1940, section 46.
240 Section 51.
241 Section 58.
242 Section 54.
243 Finance Act, 1894, section 7.
244 *I.R.C.* v. *Graham's Trustees* (1970) 49 A.T.C. 365.
245 Finance (1909–10) Act, 1910, section 60.
246 *I.R.C.* v. *Crossman* [1937] A.C. 26.
247 Finance Act, 1911, section 18.
248 Finance Act, 1894, section 7.
249 Finance Act, 1894, section 8 as amended by Finance Act, 1962, section 28.
250 Finance Act, 1894, section 8.
251 Finance Act, 1940, section 5̄4.
252 Finance Act, 1894, section 6.
253 Section 6.
254 Finance Act, 1971, section 62.
255 *Re Paterson's Will Trusts* [1963] 1 W.L.R. 623.
256 Administration of Estates Act, 1925, Schedule 1, Part II.
257 Law of Property Act, 1925, section 16.
258 Lands Tribunal Act, 1949.
259 Administration of Justice (Miscellaneous Provisions) Act, 1933, section 3.
260 Finance Act, 1894, section 10.
261 Finance Act, 1972, section 9.
262 Finance Act, 1972, Schedule 1.
263 Finance Act, 1972, section 4.
264 Finance Act, 1972, Section 2(2).
265 Section 45.
266 Section 3.
267 Section 10.
268 Section 7.
269 Schedule 5.
270 Section 12.
271 Schedule 4.
272 Section 12.
273 Section 21.
274 Section 37.
275 Section 31.
276 Section 32(2).

6 Town and Country Planning and Compulsory Purchase

Town and country planning

General administration

The Town and Country Planning Act, 1971, is now the principal Act governing planning; the details of planning law are however often found in subordinate legislation made by officials under the authority of this and other Acts, rather than in the Act itself. The central authority for the administration of planning control is the Department of the Environment; central control over all matters relating to town and country planning in England and Wales is now handled by the Secretary of State who heads the Department of the Environment.[1] Detailed administration is the task of the local planning authorities; these are county councils and county borough councils.[2] Regulations have been made authorising or requiring county councils to delegate some of their functions to non-county borough, urban or rural councils within their areas.[3]

Survey

Each local planning authority must institute a survey of its area, or sometimes of part of the area, if it has not already done so; when so doing, its duty is to examine those matters which may be expected to affect the development of the area or the planning of its development. The survey must include such matters as the principal physical and economic characteristics of the area, the size, composition and distribution of the population of the area and the communications and traffic of the area. These matters must be kept under constant review. The local planning authority may if it wishes institute a fresh survey of its area at any time and must do so if the Secretary of State so directs.[4]

The structure plan

Having made this survey of their area, the local planning authority must then prepare and send to the Secretary of State a report of the survey together with a structure plan for the area and seek his approval to the plan. The structure plan must be in the form of a written statement, and must contain or be accompanied by such diagrams, illustrations and descriptive matter as the local planning authority think appropriate for the purpose of explaining or illustrating the proposals in the plan. The written statement must formulate the local planning authority's policy and general proposals as regards the development and other use of land in their area, including measures for the management of traffic, and must state the relationship of those proposals to general proposals for the development and other use of land in neighbouring areas which may be expected to affect their own area. The proposals must indicate any part of the area selected for commencement of comprehensive treatment by development, redevelopment or improvement[5]; such an area is called an 'action area'. Publicity must be given to the making of the structure plan and an opportunity given to the public to make objections.[6]

Local plans

The local planning authority may also prepare a local plan or plans; such a plan consists of a map and a written statement, and must formulate in such detail as the authority think appropriate its proposals for the development and other use of land in that part of their area.[7] The local planning authority must afford an opportunity for objections to be made to them.[8] A local plan cannot be adopted unless it conforms generally to the structure plan as approved by the Secretary of State.[9] A local plan is thus a detailed statement of an aspect of town and country planning which is dealt with in a more general fashion in the structure plan.

Importance of the plans

The main purpose of the development plans is to guide the local planning authorities in their subsequent decisions. To the farmer the structure and local plans may have a dual significance. Firstly, he can by consulting the plans obtain guidance as to whether future development, such as the extension of a town or the creation of a motorway, is likely to affect his own land. Secondly, should he himself wish to carry out development on his land and need planning permission to do so (*post*, pages 201–6), the plan

200

may give him some general guidance concerning the likelihood of such permission being granted; the local planning authority must 'have regard to the provisions of the development plan, so far as material to the application' when dealing with any application for planning permission to develop.[10]

The development plan system of structure and local plans introduced by the 1971 Act is being gradually brought into force within different localities by means of Orders made by the Secretary of State.

Any two or more local planning authorities may apply to the Secretary of State for his consent to their areas being treated as a combined area, and with such consent may institute a joint survey and prepare a joint report and a joint structure plan for the combined area.[11]

Development

Planning permission must be obtained before carrying out any development. 'Development' is defined as 'the carrying out of building, engineering, mining or other operations in, on, over or under land, or the making of any material change in the use of any buildings or other land'.[12] Building operations include rebuilding and structural alterations of or additions to buildings; building includes any structure or erection or any part of a building, but plant and machinery inside a building are not included. Engineering operations include the formation or laying out of means of access to highways.[13]

The use of what has previously been a single dwelling house as two or more separate dwelling houses is a material change of use of that building,[14] and the use for the display of advertisements of an external part of a building which is not normally so used involves a material change in the use of that part.[15] But development does not include the carrying out of works for the maintenance, improvement or other alteration of a building, provided the works affect only its interior or do not materially affect its external appearance.[16]

Development thus consists of either carrying out an 'operation', or making a 'material change of use' of the land; it has been held that to place an egg-selling machine on a roadside verge near a farm involves a material change of use.[17] But where the Secretary of State has made an Order setting out certain uses of land in classes, then change of use to another use within the same class will not constitute development although change to a use within a different class would do so;[18] the Town and Country Planning (Use Classes) Order,[19] specifies a number of classes for this purpose. Nor is it development to use land for the purposes of agriculture or forestry, or to use for those purposes any building occupied together with land so used.[20] Agriculture includes horticulture, fruit growing, seed growing, dairy farming, the breeding and keeping of live-stock and market gardening.[21]

A person who is doubtful whether his proposals amount to 'development' may make a written request to the local planning authority to decide the point.[21a] Even where the proposed activity constitutes development, the Secretary of State may make Development Orders which grant an automatic blanket permission to all persons to carry out the forms of development specified in the Order.[22] Under the Town and Country Planning General Development Order,[23] a general permission is granted by the Order itself for a number of types of development including the following: the carrying out on agricultural land having an area of more than one acre and comprised in an agricultural unit of building or engineering operations requisite for the use of that land for the purposes of agriculture (other than the placing on land of structures not designed for those purposes or the provision or alteration of dwellings), provided the ground area covered by any building erected pursuant to this permission does not, either by itself or after the addition thereto of the ground area covered by any existing building or buildings (other than a dwelling house) within the same unit erected or in course of erection within the preceding two years and wholly or partly within 90 metres of the nearest part of the said building, exceed 465 square metres, the height of any building or works does not in general exceed 12 metres, and no part of any buildings (other than movable structures) or works is within 25 metres of the metalled portion of a trunk or classified road; the erection or construction and the maintenance, improvement or other alteration of roadside stands for milk churns, except where they would abut on any trunk or classified road; the winning and working, on land held or occupied with land used for the purposes of agriculture, of any minerals reasonably required for the purposes of that use, including the fertilisation of the land so used and the maintenance, improvement or alteration of buildings or works thereon which are occupied or used for the purposes aforesaid, provided no excavation is made within 25 metres of the metalled portion of a trunk or classified road, and subject to certain other conditions; the carrying out, on land used for the purposes of forestry (including afforestation), of building and other operations (other than the provision or alteration of dwellings) requisite for the carrying on of those purposes, and the formation, alteration and maintenance of private ways on such land—subject to certain conditions.

As regards the first permission listed above, the Town and Country

Planning (Landscape Areas Special Development) Order,[24] imposes a further condition relating to such development within the areas specified in the Schedule to the Order; the condition is that no building other than a movable structure shall be erected, altered or extended in pursuance of this permission until at least fourteen days after the local planning authority had been given written notice of intention to do so, including a short description of the proposed building or extension and of the materials to be used, and a plan indicating the site; and, if within that period a notification to that effect is sent to the applicant, the approval of the local planning authority must be obtained with respect to the design and external appearance before any development is commenced. As regards the exercise of this power, Ministry Circular No. 39/67 points out that modern and efficient farming practice depends increasingly on the use of buildings, some of which, such as tower silos and grain drying and storage buildings, must of necessity be tall; in the circular the central government asks local planning authorities to bear in mind the needs of the agricultural industry and to use their powers primarily as a means of securing the acceptable siting and design of farm buildings, rather than of refusing permission for their erection.

Application for planning permission to develop

Any person may apply for planning permission to develop land, even if he is not the owner of the land. But the local planning authority must not entertain an application for permission unless it is accompanied by a certificate signed by or on behalf of the applicant and stating either that (a) the applicant is the owner in fee simple or the tenant of that land; or (b) he has given notice of the application twenty-one days before its date to all persons who were then owners (including a tenant with a tenancy for a fixed term with at least ten years to run) of the land, or that the applicant is unable to comply and has taken such steps as he reasonably can. Further, the certificate must either state that none of the land in question forms part of an agricultural holding, or that the applicant has given notice of the application to every person who twenty-one days beforehand was a tenant of an agricultural holding forming part of the land in question.[25] The local planning authority must take into account any representations made to them by either an owner or agricultural tenant of the land.[26]

An application for planning permission may relate to buildings or works constructed or to a use of land instituted before the date of the application.[27]

Outline applications

In order to save the expense of making a detailed application until he knows whether his proposal is likely to meet with approval in general principle, the person seeking to develop may make what is known as an 'outline application', expressed to be such, for permission to erect buildings. If such an application is granted development must not be commenced until subsequent planning approval has been obtained with regard to such matters as siting, design, external appearance, means of access and landscaping of the site as were reserved by the local planning authority when they granted permission in response to the outline application. Unless the planning authority fix a longer or shorter time, application for planning approval regarding the matters so reserved must be made within three years from the grant of outline planning permission, and the development must actually be commenced within five years from the date when outline permission was granted or two years from the date of final approval of the reserved matters, whichever is the later.[28]

The decision whether to grant permission and on what conditions

The decision of the local planning authority upon an application for permission to develop must be notified within two months, otherwise the application is treated as having been refused.[29]

In deciding whether to grant planning permission, the local planning authority must have regard to the provisions of the development plan, so far as material to the application, and to any other material considerations; the authority may grant planning permission, either unconditionally or subject to conditions, or may refuse it.[30] Such conditions may include the regulation of the development or use of any land under the control of the applicant, even if the application did not relate to that land, and may require the carrying out of works on such land so far as the local planning authority think this expedient in connection with the development authorised by the grant of planning permission; the conditions may also require the removal of any buildings or works authorised by the permission or the discontinuance of any use of land so authorised at the end of the specified period and the carrying out of any works required for reinstatement of the land at the end of that period.[31]

'Although the planning authorities are given very wide powers to impose "such conditions as they think fit", nevertheless the law says that those conditions, to be valid, must fairly and reasonably relate to the permitted development. The planning authority are not at liberty to use

204

their powers for an ulterior object, however desirable that object may seem to them to be in the public interest. If they mistake or misuse their powers, however *bona fide,* the court can interfere . . .' (*per* Denning L.J. in *Pyx Granite Co. Ltd.* v. *Ministry of Housing and Local Government*).[32] If a condition which is later held to be invalid is attached to the grant of planning permission, it seems that if the condition in question is of fundamental importance the whole grant of permission is invalidated, but that this result will not ensue if the condition is only of minor importance;[33] judicial utterances upon this topic have not however all been entirely harmonious.[34]

In *Wilson* v. *West Sussex County Council*[35] it was held that a grant of planning permission to erect an 'agricultural cottage' limited the occupation of the building to someone mainly engaged in agriculture.

In *Fawcett Properties Ltd.* v. *Buckingham County Council*[36] the local planning authority had granted the previous landowner permission to develop part of the land by building a pair of cottages subject to a condition that 'the occupation of the houses shall be limited to persons whose employment or latest employment is or was employment in agriculture . . .' and stating that the reason for this condition was 'because the council would not be prepared to permit the erection of dwelling-houses on this site unconnected with the use of the adjoining land for agricultural . . . purposes'. The cottages had been so occupied in the past, but the present owners, who had bought the land subsequently, sought a declaration that it was beyond the power of the council to impose the condition or that the condition was void for uncertainty. It was held that the condition was a reasonable one to impose in furtherance of the planning policy of protecting the green belt by limiting the kind of buildings that should be built there and the kind of occupier that should occupy them, and the validity of the clause was upheld.

A condition may state the period within which the development must begin or must be completed, and may grant permission to endure for a specified period only.

A grant of planning permission is impliedly subject to the condition that development must be commenced within five years after the date on which permission was granted, unless the planning authority fix a longer or a shorter time.[37] Moreover if development has been begun within the stipulated period but has not been completed within that time, and the local planning authority think that it will not be completed within a reasonable period, the authority may serve notice on those affected stating that the planning permission will cease to have effect as regards development carried out after the end of the period specified in the notice, such period being at least a year after the notice comes into effect on confirmation by the Secretary of State.[38]

A grant of planning permission to develop is, except insofar as its terms indicate to the contrary, made for the benefit of the land and of all persons who are for the time being interested in the land.[39]

Appeal against refusal of permission or the conditions imposed

When an application for planning permission is either refused or granted subject to conditions, the applicant may, within six months thereafter, lodge notice of appeal with the Secretary of State who may deal with the application as if it had been made to him in the first instance and whose decision is final.[40]

An appeal to the Secretary of State places before him the whole of the application for planning permission and not just that part of the local planning authority's decision which displeases the applicant, thus the Secretary of State could make a decision which is even more onerous to the applicant.

Provision has been made for certain appeals to be heard and decided by an inspector appointed by the Secretary of State.[41] The Secretary of State may by regulation prescribe certain appeals to be dealt with in this manner; in pursuance of this power the Secretary of State has made the Town and Country Planning (Determination of Appeals by Appointed Persons) (Prescribed Classes) Regulations,[42] which sets out various classes of appeal which are to be decided thus. In other cases the inspector hears the appeal, and the Secretary of State decides the appeal after receiving the inspector's report. A decision made on appeal can only be challenged by an application made to the High Court within six weeks thereafter on the grounds that the decision is not within the powers of the Act or that the interests of the applicant have been substantially prejudiced by a procedural defect.[43]

Compensation for refusal of permission, or the conditions attached, in certain cases

If planning permission is refused, or granted only subject to conditions, for certain types of development including (a) carrying out, on land used for the purposes of agriculture or forestry, of building or other operations required for the purposes of that use except operations for the erection, enlargement, improvement or alteration of dwelling houses or buildings used for the purposes of market gardens, nursery grounds or timber yards or for other purposes not connected with general farming operations or with the cultivation of trees; (b) the winning and working, on land held or occupied with land used for the purposes of agriculture, of any minerals reasonably required for the purposes of that use, including the fertilisation of the land so used and the maintenance, improvement or alteration of buildings or works thereon which are occupied or used for those purposes,[44] then the local planning authority must pay compensation to a person whose interest in the land is of less value than it would have been if permission had been granted or granted without conditions.[45]

Remedies against unauthorised development

Enforcement notice. If the local planning authority think that development has been carried out after 1963 without planning permission or in breach of the conditions subject to which permission was granted, the authority may, if they think it expedient, serve an enforcement notice on the owner and (if different persons) the occupier of the land, requiring the breach to be remedied. Where the breach consists of carrying out operations without permission, or breach of a condition attached to the grant of permission, or changing without planning permission the use of a building to use as a single dwelling house, the enforcement notice must be served within four years after the date of the breach. But if the development involves only change of use, then, with the single exception mentioned above, there is no time limit within which the notice must be served. The notice must specify the matters alleged to constitute the breach, the steps which the authority require to be taken in order to remedy the breach, and the period within which those steps must be taken. The notice itself takes effect from the date stated therein, which must be at least twenty-eight days after the notice was served.[46] Any person interested in the land may appeal in writing to the Secretary of State against the notice at any time before it comes into effect, and if this is done the notice will not take effect until the appeal has been decided. The appeal can be made on any of seven grounds set out in the Act, such as that planning permission ought to be granted, or that the notice is served out of time, or that the requirements of the notice are excessive or give too little time for compliance.[47] The Secretary of State must arrange a hearing before an inspector if either side so desires, and the Secretary may either grant planning permission or uphold, alter or quash the notice; an appeal lies from his decision to the High Court on a point of law. In addition to prosecuting for failure to comply, the local authority may also in the event of non-compliance enter on the land and carry out the steps prescribed by the notice, other than discontinuance of any use, and recover from the person who is then the owner the reasonable costs so incurred.[48] A current owner of the land who has to pay the costs although he did not himself carry out the unauthorised development can in turn recoup himself from the person who originally carried out the development;[49] it may not always be easy to ascertain who was the original developer.

Compliance with the terms of an enforcement notice does not discharge the notice.[50] Hence the resumption of the use of land, after that use has been discontinued in compliance with an enforcement notice, will consitute a further contravention of the notice;[51] the same is true if development of land by way of reinstating buildings or works which have been demolished or altered in compliance with an enforcement notice is carried out.[52] Unless a successful appeal is made, the owner of the land or, if the breach relates to its use, any person who uses or causes or permits the land to be used in contravention of planning control, is liable on conviction before the magistrates to a fine of up to £400 and to a further fine of up to £50 for each day that the breach continues after the first conviction.[53]

Stop notice. Having served an enforcement notice, the local planning authority may before it takes effect serve in addition a stop notice prohibiting any person on whom it is served from carrying out or continuing any further specified operations on the land which are alleged to be a breach of planning control; the notice must specify the date on which it is to take effect, which must be at least three days after it was served. The stop notice procedure does not apply to development which involves only change of use, except where the alleged breach of planning control is the deposit of refuse or waste materials. Failure to comply with a stop notice is punishable as with an enforcement notice (*ante*). The stop notice ceases to have effect when the enforcement notice comes into effect or is quashed on appeal.[54]

Revocation of planning permission
The local planning authority can, if they think it expedient, revoke or modify a planning permission already granted. This power can be exercised at any time before the operations or change of use for which permission was granted have been carried out, and is not to affect so much of the operations as have already been carried out.[55] Compensation must be paid for any abortive expenditure and any loss of development value.[56]

Power to require authorised development to be discontinued
A local planning authority may by order confirmed by the Secretary of

State require the alteration or removal of any authorised building or the discontinuance of any authorised use of land,[57] but compensation must be paid for the cost of compliance and for abortive expenditure and for loss of development value.[58] To continue to use land in breach of such an order is a criminal offence punishable by a fine.[59]

Listed buildings: building preservation notices, etc.

The Secretary of State must compile or approve lists of buildings of special architectural or historic interest, and must supply local authorities with copies relating to their areas. The county borough or county district council for the area must then notify owners and occupiers of such listed buildings.[60]

In deciding whether a building should be listed, the Secretary of State may take into account not only the building itself but also its relationship to other buildings and the desirability of preserving features associated with it but not actually forming part of the building itself.[61]

In general it is a criminal offence, punishable with a fine or imprisonment or both, to cause such a building to be demolished or altered so as to affect its character without first obtaining consent from the local planning authority or the Secretary of State unless the work needs to be done urgently.[62] Even if a building is not listed, the local planning authority may confer a temporary protection upon it by means of a building preservation notice. This comes into force immediately it has been served and is effective for up to six months thereafter; during this period the same restrictions as if the building were in fact a listed building apply,[63] and the local planning authority will seek to persuade the Secretary of State that the building should be listed.

A 'listed building enforcement notice' may be served by the local planning authority if they think that works have been or are being executed to a listed building in contravention of the provisions relating to the protection of such buildings; the notice must state the alleged contravention and require it to be remedied. Unless a successful appeal is made to the Secretary of State, failure to comply with the notice results in a fine on the person who owned the building when the notice was served and the local authority may carry out the steps required by the notice and recover the cost from the person who owns the land at the time this is done.[64]

If it appears to the Secretary of State that reasonable steps are not being taken for the proper preservation of a listed building, he may authorise the appropriate local authority (whether or not the local planning authority) to acquire the building and any requisite adjacent land compulsorily.[65] At least two months before compulsory purchase is commenced a 'repairs notice' must have been served on the owner of the building specifying the works which are considered reasonably necessary for its preservation and explaining the consequences of non-compliance;[66] (the notice must explain the effect of section 116 also). Application may be made to the magistrates to stay proceedings on the compulsory purchase order; they may grant the stay if satisfied that reasonable steps have been taken for preserving the building.[67]

If a listed building is compulsorily acquired the compensation to be paid to the owner will in general disregard any depressing effect on its value due to its having been listed.[68] But if the acquiring local authority are satisfied that the listed building has been deliberately allowed to fall into disrepair in order to justify its demolition and the development or redevelopment of the site, they may ask the Secretary of State to include in the compulsory purchase order a direction for minimum compensation, which if granted means that compensation is to be assessed on the basis that planning permission would not be granted for any development or redevelopment of the site.[69]

The Secretary of State for the Environment may make grants towards the upkeep of buildings appearing to be of outstanding historic or architectural interest and their contents; a condition may be imposed that these shall be open to the public at stated times.[70]

Tree preservation orders

When granting planning permission for development, a local planning authority must impose conditions and make tree preservation orders whenever appropriate to secure the preservation or planting of trees.[71] Moreover if the local planning authority think it expedient in the interests of amenity to provide for the preservation of trees or woodlands in their area, they may make a tree preservation order with regard to such trees or groups of trees as are mentioned in the order; the order may prohibit the cutting down, topping, lopping or wilful destruction of trees except with the consent of the local planning authority, and may secure the replanting of any part of a woodland area which is felled in the course of operations permitted under the order. The order does not take effect until confirmed by the Secretary of State, who must first consider any objections and representations made by the owners and occupiers of land affected by the order. No order can prevent the cutting down, topping or lopping of trees which are dying, dead or dangerous, or insofar as this is required for the prevention or abatement of a nuisance;[72] (for nuisance, see *post*, pages 312–4). Subject to any exceptions and conditions specified in the order, compensation will be payable by the local planning authority to any person in respect of damage or expenditure incurred by reason of the fact that any consent required by the order to be obtained is either refused by the authority or only granted subject to conditions.[73] The order if contested must first be confirmed by the Secretary of State, but if it appears expedient to the local planning authority they may include in the order a direction that the order shall take effect provisionally and without confirmation on a date specified in the order; if so the order remains in force for a maximum period of six months prior to confirmation.[74]

Application may be made for consent to interfere with protected trees, using much the same procedure as when applying for planning permission.

If a tree protected by an order, other than a tree to which the order applies as part of a woodland, is removed or destroyed either in contravention of the order or by virtue of the provisions relating to dying, dead or dangerous trees, it becomes the duty of the land owner, unless the planning authority dispense with this requirement, to plant another tree of an appropriate size and species at the same place as soon as reasonably practicable, and the tree preservation order shall apply to the new tree in the same way as it applied to the original tree.[75]

A person who contravenes a tree preservation order is liable to be fined.[76] If he fails to comply with a condition requiring a felled tree to be replaced, the local planning authority may within four years thereafter serve a notice to plant upon the owner of the land. Unless a successful appeal is made to the Secretary of State, failure to comply with the notice enables the authority to enter the land and take steps to remedy the breach and to recover the reasonable cost from the owner.[77] Alternatively, an injunction may be obtained to restrain a breach of a tree preservation order.[78]

The Forestry Act, 1967

Although in strictness related more to the husbanding of timber resources rather than town and country planning, it is here convenient to mention that under the Forestry Act, 1967, a felling licence granted by the Forestry Commissioners must in general be obtained before felling trees; exceptions to this need for a licence include (a) a person felling trees on land occupied by him or by his tenant provided the aggregate cubic content of the felled trees does not exceed 825 cubic feet in any quarter of a year, and provided the aggregate cubic content of the trees so felled which are sold by that person does not exceed 150 cubic feet in any quarter or such larger quantity as the Forestry Commissioners may allow; (b) any felling which is done to prevent danger or to prevent or abate a nuisance (*post*, pages 312–4) or is in compliance with any obligation imposed by Act of Parliament, or because the tree obstructs an electricity line or a development for which planning permission has been granted.[79]

If an application for a licence is made, the Commissioners must grant it unconditionally unless they think it expedient to refuse in the interests of good forestry or agriculture or of the amenities of the district, or for the purpose of complying with their duty of promoting the establishment and maintenance in Great Britain of adequate reserves of growing trees.[80] If the application is refused, any person who is for the time being the owner of the trees is entitled to compensation for any depreciation in their value attributable to their deterioration because of the refusal.[81] Claims for compensation may be made from time to time in respect of the deterioration, but no such claim can be made in respect of deterioration taking place more than ten years before the date of the claim, and a claim in respect of felled trees must be made within one year after their felling.[82]

The Commissioners may grant the licence subject to such conditions as they think expedient for securing the restocking or stocking with trees of the land on which the felling is to take place, or of such other land as may be agreed between the Commissioners and the applicant, and the maintenance of those trees in accordance with the rules and practice of good forestry for a period not exceeding ten years.[83]

If the Commissioners do not notify their decision within three months after receipt of the application, the application is treated as refused.[84]

If an application is made to the Commissioners for a felling licence in respect of trees to which a tree preservation order (see *ante*; pages 210–11) relates, and consent under the order is required for the felling of the trees, then the Commissioners, if they propose to grant the licence, must give notice in writing to the authority by whom the order was made, and if the authority object the matter must be referred to the Secretary of State.[85]

Anyone who fells a tree without first obtaining a felling licence where such a licence is required is guilty of a crime and liable to a fine.[86]

If the Commissioners think it expedient, in the interests of good forestry or for purposes connected with their duty of promoting adequate reserves of growing trees, that any growing trees should be felled in order to prevent their deterioration or to improve the growth of other trees, they may give directions to the owner of the trees requiring him to fell them within a specified period of not less than two years thereafter.[87] A person to whom such directions are given may if aggrieved apply to the Minister of Agriculture, Fisheries and Food to refer the matter to a committee of three persons; any ultimate action must accord with the report of this committee.[88]   A person who is exposed to a net loss by reason of the directions may require the Minister to acquire his interest in the land affected, or if he has the right to sell the trees for immediate felling require the Commissioners to buy the trees to which the directions relate; the Minister then has the option of either revoking or modifying the directions, or referring the notice to the committee in order to determine whether the person who served the notice is in fact involved in a net loss.[89]   Otherwise the felling directions will cease to have effect, and the Commissioners shall be deemed to have contracted to buy the trees or the Minister to have served notice to acquire the land in accordance with the terms of the notice.[90]

If work required to be carried out in accordance with the conditions of the felling licence or any directions to fell given by the Commissioners is not complied with, the Commissioners may give the person responsible a notice requiring such steps as are specified in the notice to be taken in order to remedy the default within the period stated in the notice; if the notice is not complied with the Commissioners may enter on the land and take those steps and recover any expenses reasonably incurred from the person to whom the notice was given, and that person is also liable to a fine.[91]   Appeal lies against such a notice to the Minister who will refer the matter to the committee for their report.

Land incapable of reasonably beneficial use; service of purchase notice

Where an application for planning permission is refused or granted only subject to conditions, then if the owner of the land claims that the land has become incapable of reasonably beneficial use in its existing state, and cannot be made capable of such use by development in accordance with conditions imposed or by carrying out any other development for which planning permission has been granted or is undertaken to be granted, he may serve on the council of the county borough or county district in which the land is situate a notice requiring the council to purchase his interest in the land.[92]   The council must then state to the owner whether they or another public body are willing to comply with the notice, and if unwilling that a copy of the notice has been transmitted to the Secretary of State.[93]   The Secretary of State must then either grant permission or direct that it be granted for development which would render the land capable of reasonably beneficial use, or confirm the notice.[94]   These provisions apply where planning permission is subsequently revoked or modified by imposing conditions under section 45 (*ante*, page 208), or an order is made under section 51 requiring discontinuance of the use of land or the alteration or removal of buildings or works (*ante*, pages 208–9), or application for consent to demolish, alter, or extend a listed building is refused or granted only on conditions, and in each case the land is incapable of reasonably beneficial use in its existing state or for a purpose which would be permitted.[95] Land is not incapable of reasonably beneficial use in its existing state merely because it would have been worth much more had planning permission to develop it been granted,[96] thus this remedy is not likely to be of widespread application.

Waste land injuring amenity

If the local planning authority think that the amenity of any part of their area or an adjoining area is seriously injured by the condition of any garden, vacant site or other open land in their area, the authority may serve notice on the owner and occupier of the land requiring such steps to be taken for abating the injury as are specified in the notice; the notice comes into effect at the date specified therein, which must be at least twenty-eight days after the notice was served.[97]

A person on whom the notice has been served may appeal to the magistrates on the ground that the factual conditions requisite before serving it have not been satisfied or that the remedial steps described by the notice are excessive.[98] Unless there is a successful appeal, failure to comply with the notice is a criminal offence punishable with a fine,[99] and the local planning authority may in the event of non-compliance enter the land and do the work itself and recover the reasonable cost from the owner.[100]

In *Stephens* v. *Cuckfield Rural District Council* [101] the plaintiff owned land on part of which he had some years ago erected structures for the purpose of a sawmill; the land surrounding the structures had been used as a sawmill yard. Subsequently the land was let to car breakers, who used the premises for that purpose. The land was surrounded on three sides by other land belonging to the plaintiff and on the fourth side by a public road. The local authority then served notice on the plaintiff under section 65 ordering the removal of all cars, car bodies and machinery from the land. The plaintiff sought a declaration that the land was not 'a garden, vacant site or other open land'. The Court held that whether a piece of land falls within those words is to be decided by the exercise of common sense in the circumstances of each case. Here the land was fenced and used for the purpose of a business of a car breaker's yard, part of the business was carried on within a building on the land, and looking at the matter as a whole the plot was not open land.

Control of advertisements

The Secretary of State is empowered to make regulations restricting the display of advertisements so far as he thinks this expedient in the interests of amenity or public safety. The regulations may make different provision with respect to different areas, and may make special provision as regards areas of special control, these being either rural areas or other areas which appear to the Minister to require special protection on the grounds of amenity. [102] Planning permission is deemed to have been granted for the display of advertisements which comply with the regulations. [103]

The Town and Country Planning (Control of Advertisements) Regulations 1969, [104] as amended by the Town and Country Planning (Control of Advertisements) (Amendment) Regulations 1972 [105] embody the detailed rules relating to the display and control of outdoor advertisements.

A local planning authority may require the removal of any advertisement displayed or the discontinuance of the use of any advertising site used in contravention of the advertisement regulations. A person who displays an advertisement in contravention of the regulations is liable to a fine. [106] A person is deemed to display an advertisement if it is displayed on land of which he is either the owner or the occupier or if it publicises his goods, trade, business or other concern, unless he proves that it was displayed without his knowledge or consent. [107]

The word 'advertisement' is defined to mean 'any word, letter, model, sign, placard, board, notice, device or representation, whether illuminated or not, in the nature of and employed wholly or in part for the purposes of advertisement, announcement or direction . . . and . . . includes any hoarding or similar structure used or adapted for use for the display of advertisements . . . '.[108]

The regulations apply to the display of advertisements on land or buildings (including any structure or erection) subject to certain exceptions; the principal exceptions comprise an advertisement on enclosed land provided the advertisement is not readily visible from outside the enclosure or from within any such part of the enclosure as carries a public right of way or to which the public have access, or an advertisement within a building, or displayed upon or inside a vehicle, or incorporated in and forming part of the fabric of the building.[109]

Each local planning authority must consider whether any part of its area should be defined as an area of special control; the general rule within such an area is that no advertisements whatsoever can be displayed, although exceptions can be made.[110]

Outside areas of special control, the general principle is that no advertisements may be displayed without consent; the consent required may either be express consent granted by a local planning authority or by the Secretary of State, or 'deemed consent' which is deemed to be granted by the regulations themselves.[111] There is deemed consent for all advertisements displayed on 1 August 1948;[112] this includes the use of a site for the display of advertisements, so long as there is no substantial increase in the extent, or substantial alteration in the manner, of its use for such display on 1 August 1948,[113] and for certain other classes of advertisements as set out in regulation 14. All such advertisements are subject to certain standard conditions set out in the regulations. Moreover the local planning authority can require the discontinuance of the display of any advertisement which has deemed consent if they think discontinuance expedient in the interest of amenity or public safety.[114] The discontinuance notice must be served on the advertiser and on the owner and occupier of the premises, and any such recipient of the notice may appeal to the Secretary of State against the notice.[115]

An application for express consent to the display of an advertisement may be made, and in considering whether to grant consent the local planning authority must consider the interests of amenity and public safety.[116] The grant of express consent must be for a fixed period which cannot exceed five years unless the Secretary of State approves; if no period is specified the consent takes effect for five years.[117] A local planning authority must decide whether to grant express consent within two months after the application unless this period is extended by written agreement with the applicant;[118] if the decision is not given within this time the application is treated as refused.[119] Every local planning authority is to keep a register containing particulars of their decisions on applications for express consent.[120] An applicant for express consent who is aggrieved by a refusal or by the conditions imposed may appeal to the Secretary of State within one month thereafter.[121]

An advertisement must only be displayed with the permission of the owner of the land or other person entitled to grant permission.[122] Breach of this condition is itself a contravention of the regulations and is a criminal offence.[123]

Where in order to comply with the regulations a person carries out works to remove an advertisement which was being displayed on 1 August 1948, or to discontinue the use for the display of advertisements of any site which was being thus used upon that date, he may claim compensation as regards expenses reasonably incurred by him in carrying out necessary works. The claim must be made in writing to the local planning authority within six months from the completion of the works.[124]

Conservation areas

The local planning authority must decide whether within its territory there are any 'areas of special architectural or historic interest the character or appearance of which it is desirable to preserve or enhance' and if so must designate them as conservation areas. In such an area special attention must be paid to the desirability of preserving or enhancing its character or appearance by appropriate use of the powers conferred by the Act.[125]

Caravan sites

Control of caravan sites is achieved both by the need for planning permission whenever any development is involved (*ante*, pages 201–2), and also by the requirement of a site licence from the local authority which can control in detail the use of the site.[126] Under the 1960 Act the general rule is that no land may be used as a caravan site unless and until a site licence has been issued by the local authority (i.e. outside London the council of a borough or rural district council)[127] to the occupier of the land comprising the site.[128] If an occupier of land contravenes this requirement he is liable on the first offence to a fine of £100 and on a second or subsequent offence to a fine of £250.[129]

A 'caravan site' is any land on which a caravan is stationed for human habitation and land used in conjunction therewith;[130] sites used merely for the storage or display of unoccupied caravans are not within the scope of the 1960 Act, though the general town and country planning law will be applicable.

An application for a site licence must be made in writing by the occupier of the land to the borough or district council in whose area the land is situated,[131] and must give[132] the particulars required by the Secretary of State in the Caravan Sites (Licence Applications) Order, 1960.[133] Provided there has been a grant of planning permission otherwise than under and by virtue of a Development Order (*ante*, pages 202–3), and unless the applicant has had a site licence revoked within the previous three years, the local authority must issue a site licence within, usually, two months of receiving the particulars.[134] Thus a site licence will only be issued if the requisite planning permission to use the land as a caravan site has already been formally granted by the local planning authority, who must have consulted the site licensing authority before doing so.[135] The general rule under the 1960 Act is that if such planning permission has been granted, a site licence must be issued; the importance of the 1960 Act usually lies not in the granting or withholding of the site licence, but in the number and type of conditions which may be attached to the grant.

A register of site licences is to be kept by every site licensing authority and open to public inspection.[136]

The holder of a site licence who ceases to occupy the site may, with the consent of the local authority, transfer it to the new occupier;[137] certain formalities must be complied with.

In general a site licence cannot be issued for a limited period, but if the governing planning permission to use the land as a caravan site is for a limited period then the site licence must expire when the planning permission expires.[138]

The local authority have a wide discretion to attach conditions to a site licence, but these must be such as the authority think it necessary or desirable to impose on the occupier in the interests of the caravan dwellers on the site, or of any other class of persons, or of the public at large;[139] in deciding what conditions to impose the local authority must have regard to the 'Model Standards for Caravan Sites' issued by the Secretary of State under the Act.[140]

Without prejudice to their general power to impose conditions, the authority is specifically authorised to do so restricting the occasions on which caravans are stationed on land for human habitation, or the total number of caravans so stationed at any one time; controlling, whether by reference to size, state of repair or any other feature (other than the materials of which the caravans are constructed), the types of caravan stationed on the land; regulating the positions in which caravans are stationed on land for human habitation, and prohibiting, restricting, or otherwise regulating the placing or erection on such land, at any time when caravans are so stationed, of structures and vehicles of any description whatsoever and of tents; securing the taking of any steps for preserving or enhancing the amenity of land on which caravans are so stationed, including planting and replanting the land with trees and bushes; securing that, at all times when caravans are stationed on land, proper measures are taken for preventing and detecting the outbreak of fire, and adequate means of fighting fire are provided and maintained; securing that adequate sanitary facilities and such other facilities, services or equipment as the local authority may specify are provided for the use of persons dwelling in caravans and that, at all times when cara-

218

vans are stationed on land for human habitation, such facilities and equipment are properly maintained.[141]

A condition must be attached to a site licence requiring a copy to be conspiciously displayed on the site unless the site is restricted to three caravans or less. [142]

A condition of the licence may require the doing of works on the site by the occupier within a specified period; it may also prohibit the bringing of caravans on the site until such works are completed to the satisfaction of the local authority.[143] If in the former case the works are not completed within the period, the local authority may do them and recover the cost from the occupier. [144]

Within twenty-eight days after its issue, a person aggrieved by a condition of the licence may apply to a magistrate's court to cancel or vary the condition if the court thinks it unduly burdensome.[145]

If the occupier fails to comply with any condition attached to a site licence, he is liable to a fine; on a third or subsequent conviction for breach of a condition the court may make an order revoking the licence. [146] If the licence is revoked the local authority cannot issue a further licence to that occupier until three years thereafter.[147]

A local planning authority may at any time, after giving the licence holder an opportunity of making representations, alter the conditions of the licence or impose new ones, [148] and the licence holder may himself apply for this to be done. The holder of the licence may if aggrieved appeal to the magistrate's court in respect of these matters.[149]

There are a number of caravan sites for which a site licence under the 1960 Act is not required; these include the use of agricultural land as a caravan site for seasonal accommodation of agricultural workers employed on land in the same occupation, or for seasonal accommodation of forestry workers employed on land in the same occupation, or for the accommodation of persons employed in connection with building or engineering operations on the same or adjoining land.[150]

An authorised officer of a local authority may in connection with the discharge of its powers enter upon a caravan site or upon land for which an application for a site licence has been made, having first given twenty-four hours notice to the occupier; any person wilfully obstructing such an officer is liable to a fine. [151]

Compulsory purchase of land and compensation

The Act which confers the power of compulsory acquisition

Numerous Acts of Parliament empower public authorities to take land compulsorily from private individuals for a wide variety of purposes; as an example, the Secretary of State may authorise the appropriate local authority to acquire compulsorily any land within their area if he is satisfied that the land is required in order to secure its treatment as a whole by development, redevelopment or the like, or that it is expedient that the land should be held together with land so required, or that it is expedient to acquire the land immediately for a purpose necessary to the proper planning of an area in which the land is situate.[152]

The procedure by which this power is applied to the land in question.

Although the procedure for exercising the power of compulsory acquisition varies with the provisions of the Act which confers the power, yet by far the most frequent method nowadays is by means of a compulsory purchase order made in accordance with the Acquisition of Land (Authorisation Procedure) Act, 1946. If the acquiring body are a local authority, the first step is for the local authority to make a compulsory purchase order; the order must describe by reference to a map the land to which it applies, and must be in the form prescribed by regulations. Before submitting the order for confirmation to the confirming authority, the acquiring body must publish a notice of the order in one or more local newspapers for two successive weeks and serve a similar notice on every owner, lessee and occupier of any land comprised in the order; the notice must be in the form prescribed by the regulations and must, among other things, specify the time (not being less than twenty-one days from the first publication or service of the notice) within which and the manner in which objections to the order may be lodged with the confirming authority. The confirming authority is the relevant Minister. If the Minister is himself seeking to acquire the land, the Minister acts as both the acquiring and confirming authority.[153]

The Minister may disregard objections from persons other than owners, lessees or occupiers; he may also require any person to state the grounds of his objection in writing, and may disregard the objection if satisfied that it relates exclusively to matters which can be dealt with by the tribunal by whom the compensation is to be assessed.[154] Those matters include the amount of compensation, the apportionment of rent payable under a lease which includes both land which is and land which is not to be acquired compulsorily;[155] whether part of a house, park or garden can be taken without serious detriment to the remainder;[156] whether the remaining agricultural land is reasonably capable of being farmed separately from that part of the agricultural land proposed to be taken.[157]

220

If no objection is duly made, or if all objections are withdrawn or are such as the Minister is entitled to disregard, the Minister may confirm the order with or without modifications; otherwise the Minister must, before confirming or finally making the order, either cause a public local inquiry to be held or give any owner, lessee or occupier who has made such an objection an opportunity of appearing before and being heard by a person appointed by the Minister; the Minister must, before confirming or finally making the order, consider the objections and the report of the person who holds the inquiry or hearing. Notice of the confirmation of the order must be published in one or more local newspapers and must be served, with a copy of the confirmed order, upon the persons to whom notice of the making or preparation of the order had to be given initially. Within six weeks thereafter a person aggrieved may apply to the High Court and challenge the validity of the order on the grounds that it was not within the powers of the relevant Act or that the interests of the applicant have been substantially prejudiced by failure to comply with the requirements of the Act or of the Tribunals and Inquiries Act, 1971, or of any rules and regulations made under either of those Acts; apart from this the validity of the order cannot be challenged in any legal proceedings whatsoever. [158]
In *Smith* v. *East Elloe Rural District Council*[159] it was held that these words preclude the court from upholding a challenge to the validity of the order if the challenge is commenced after the six-week period has been allowed to go by; some members of the Court also said that the order cannot be challenged even within the six-week period on the ground that the order was made or confirmed in bad faith. However in *Anisminic* v. *Foreign Compensation Commission* [160] it was held that somewhat similar words contained in another enactment did not preclude the court from enquiring whether the decision embodied in a document is in fact a nullity; the Court tended to place a narrow interpretation on what was actually decided in Smith's Case (*ante*).

Buying out holders of an interest in the land

The procedure to be followed after the compulsory purchase order has come into effect is usually governed by the Compulsory Purchase Act, 1965; the Act applies [161] to any compulsory purchase to which the Acquisition of Land (Authorisation Procedure) Act, 1946, First Schedule, is applicable (*ante*, page 220).

After the compulsory purchase order has been confirmed, it is lawful for the acquiring authority to agree to purchase for money any estate or interest in the land which is subject to the order;[162] this provision enables the authority to acquire by agreement, if they can do so without resorting to the actual exercise of compulsion, land which they are entitled to acquire compulsorily by virtue of the order.

Failing agreement, the powers of compulsory purchase must be exercised within three years from the date when the compulsory purchase order became operative;[163] service of notice to treat (*post*) is a sufficient exercise of the powers for this purpose.

When the acquiring authority require to purchase any of the land subject to compulsory purchase, they must give notice (known as a 'notice to treat') to all the persons interested in the land, so far as known to the acquiring authority.[164]

Every notice to treat must:

(a) give particulars of the land to which the notice relates;
(b) demand particulars of the recipient's estate and interest in the land, and of the claim made by him in respect of the land; and
(c) state that the acquiring authority are willing to treat for the purchase of the land, and as to the compensation to be made for the damage which may be sustained by reason of the execution of the works.[165]

No notice to treat need be served if the acquiring authority only wish to destroy rights in property, such as easements (*ante*, pages 19–24), and not to acquire them; the persons who owned these rights must seek to establish a right to compensation for injurious affection.[166] (Where the acquiring authority merely wish to acquire easements over the land, it depends on the substantive provisions of the Act under which they operate whether they must acquire the land over which the easement runs or whether they need merely acquire the easement.)

If any of the land subject to compulsory acquisition is in the possession of a person having no greater interest in the land than as tenant for a year or from year to year, then if that person is required to give up possession (*post*, page 223) of such land before the expiration of his interest he is entitled to compensation for the value of his unexpired interest and for any just allowance which ought to be made to him by an incoming tenant, and for any loss or injury which he may sustain.[167] If only part of the land is thus compulsorily acquired, he is also entitled to compensation for the damage done to him in his tenancy by severance or injurious affection.[168] If a person claiming a greater interest than as a tenant at will (i.e. a tenancy subsisting only so long as both landlord and tenant so desire) claims compensation in respect of any unexpired interest under any lease or grant of the land which is subject to compulsory purchase, the acquiring authority may require him to produce the lease or grant or the best evidence of it which is in his power; if after written request this is not produced within twenty-one days thereafter, he is to be considered as a tenant holding only from year to year and to be entitled to compensation accordingly.[169]

These provisions are construed to mean that a notice to treat need not be served upon a tenant who has no greater interest than as a yearly tenant or with an unexpired period of his tenancy of no more than a year; such a person can either be required to give up possession before the expiration of his interest and be paid compensation,[170] or can be required to yield up possession—in general without compensation—when his tenancy expires either by lapse of time or by reason of notice to quit served by his landlord or served by the acquiring authority after they have become landlord by having purchased the interest of the person who was the landlord prior to the acquisition. But as regards compensation:

1 There are additional provisions governing the rights of holders of business tenancies which are not tenancies of an agricultural holding.[171]

2 Persons in lawful possession of non-agricultural land who are displaced on or after 17 October 1972, in consequence of its compulsory acquisition or of certain other actions by public bodies, and who have no interest for which they are entitled to compensation under any other Act of Parliament, are in general entitled to a 'disturbance payment'.[172] The amount of such a payment is in general the reasonable removal expenses of the person entitled to the payment, plus any loss sustained by him in consequence of the disturbance of any trade or business which he was conducting on the land.[173]

3 Tenants of agricultural holdings who have no greater interest than as tenant for a year, or from year to year, are in general entitled to elect to be treated as if they had been required to give up possession of the land before the expiration of their interest, thus preserving a right to compensation (in accordance with the Compulsory Purchase Act, 1965, section 20; *ante*). Moreover when such an agricultural tenant is served with notice to quit relating to only part of his holding, he may in general serve notice on the acquiring authority claiming that the rest of the holding is not reasonably capable of being farmed as a separate agricultural unit, and if the notice is upheld the acquiring authority are regarded as having taken possession of the rest of the holding prior to the expiration of the notice to quit, thus entitling the tenant to compensation in respect of that part also.

These results are achieved by virtue of the following provisions. Where a person in occupation of an agricultural holding, having no greater interest than as tenant for a year or from year to year, is served with notice to quit the holding after an acquiring authority have served notice to treat on the landlord of the holding or, being an authority possessing compulsory purchase powers, have agreed to acquire the landlord's interest in the holding, and:

(a)   either section 24(1) of the Agricultural Holdings Act, 1948, (*ante* page 55) does not apply to the notice by virtue of the land being required under section 24(2)(b) of the 1948 Act (*ante*, page 55) for a non-agricultural use for which planning permission has been granted; or

(b)   the Agricultural Land Tribunal have consented to the operation of the notice and stated in the reasons for their decision that they are satisfied that the land is required for a non-agricultural use falling within section 25(1)(e) of the 1948 Act (*ante*, page 59) although not within section 24(2)(b) of that Act, then the following provisions apply. If the person served with the notice so elects and gives up possession of his holding to the acquiring authority on or before the date on which his tenancy terminates in accordance with the notice, then section 20 of the Compulsory Purchase Act, 1965 (*ante*, pages 222–3) and section 12 of the Agriculture (Miscellaneous Provisions) Act, 1968 (*post*, page 240) take effect as if the notice to quit had not been served and the acquiring authority had taken possession of the holding in pursuance of a notice of entry under section 11(1) of the Compulsory Purchase Act, 1965 (*post*, pages 245–6) on the day before that on which the tenancy terminates in accordance with the notice to quit; the provisions of the Agricultural Holdings Act, 1948 relating to compensation of a tenant on the termination of his tenancy and sections 9 and 15(2) of the Agriculture (Miscellaneous Provisions) Act, 1968 (additional payment and compensation in cases of notice to quit) shall not have effect in relation to the termination of the tenancy by reason of the notice to quit. This election cannot take effect if, before the expiration of the notice to quit, an acquiring authority take possession of the land in pursuance of an enactment providing for the taking of possession compulsorily. The election must be made by notice in writing served on the acquiring authority not later than the date on which possession of the holding is given up, and can be made in relation to a notice to quit part of an agricultural holding in the same way as in relation to a notice to quit the entire holding.[174]

Where a notice to quit in respect of which a person is entitled to make an election as above relates to only part of an agricultural holding and that person does so elect within two months after the date of service of notice to quit or, if later, the decision of the Agricultural Land Tribunal, he may also within the period serve notice on the acquiring authority claiming that the remainder of the holding is not reasonably capable of being farmed, either by itself or in conjunction with other relevant land, as a separate agricultural unit. If the acquiring authority do not agree in writing to accept this notice as valid, either the claimant or the authority may refer the matter to the Lands Tribunal for decision. If the notice is either accepted or held to be valid, and if before the end of twelve months thereafter the claimant has given up to the acquiring authority possession of the part of the holding to which the notice relates, then section 20 of the Compulsory Purchase Act, 1965, and section 12 of the Agriculture (Miscellaneous Provisions) Act, 1968 take effect as if the acquiring authority had taken possession of that part in pursuance of a notice of entry under section 11(1) of the 1965 Act (*post*, pages 245–6) on the day before the expiration of the year of the tenancy which is current when the notice is so accepted or declared valid. Any notice of election served as above ceases to have effect if, before the expiration of notice to quit, an acquiring authority take possession of the land in pursuance of an enactment providing for the compulsory taking of possession.[175]

If a person served with a notice to treat does not within twenty-one days thereafter state the particulars of his claim or treat with the acquiring authority in respect of it, or if agreement is not reached as to the amount of compensation, the question of disputed compensation must be referred to the Lands Tribunal.[176]

After notice to treat has been served on him the owner of the land may still sell his interest in the land subject to the notice, but cannot create a new interest whose nature would increase the burden of compensation falling on the acquiring authority.

Service of notice to treat does not of itself create a contract of sale or change the ownership of the land in any way, but it gives either party the right to have the compensation assessed and then to have the purchase completed, and binds the acquiring authority to take the land unless the notice is withdrawn by agreement between the parties or where an Act expressly permits withdrawal. Section 31(1) of the Land Compensation Act, 1961, enables the acquiring authority to withdraw a notice to treat within six weeks after receiving written particulars of the claim for compensation; if those particulars are not submitted they may, unless they have entered into possession of the land, withdraw the notice within six weeks after the claim has been finally adjudicated.[177] Compensation must be paid for any loss or expenses occasioned by the giving and withdrawal of the notice.[178]

Once the compensation has been ascertained, a relationship comes into existence between the parties analogous to that of vendor and purchaser under an ordinary contract for the sale of land, and their respective rights and duties are governed accordingly. The owner must show good title to the land and be prepared to execute the conveyance. But it seems that the vendor cannot be required to give any covenants concerning his title. The costs of all conveyances of the land subject to compulsory purchase and of proving title to the land must be borne by the acquiring authority.[179]

Owner's refusal to convey the land

If the owner of any interest in the land purchased by the acquiring authority refuses to accept a tender of the compensation agreed or awarded, or neglects to make out a title to or refuses to convey the land, the acquiring authority may pay the compensation money into court to the credit of the parties interested in the land.[180] Having done this, the authority may then execute a deed poll describing the land and declaring the circumstances under which, and the names of the parties to whose credit, the payment into court was made.[181] On execution of the deed poll all interests in the land of the persons for whose use the compensation was paid into court vest absolutely in the acquiring authority, and the authority is entitled to immediate possession of the land as against those persons.[182]

Compulsory acquisition of part of property; owner's right to require more to be taken in some circumstances

1 No person can be required to sell a part only of any house, building or manufactory, or of a park or garden belonging to a house, if he is able and willing to sell the whole, unless the Lands Tribunal (post, page 229) determine that (a) in the case of a house, building or manufactory the part proposed to be acquired can be taken without material detriment to the remainder, or (b) in the case of a park or garden the part proposed to be acquired can be taken without seriously affecting the amenity or convenience of the house.[183] When deciding this the Tribunal must take into account not only the effect of the severance but also the use to be made of the part proposed to be acquired and, in a case where the part is proposed to be acquired for works or other purposes extending to other land, the effect of the whole of the works and the use to be made of the other land.[184] If the Tribunal decide against the owner, they must award compensation for any loss due to the severance of the part proposed to be acquired, in addition to its value; the party interested is then required to sell the part to the acquiring authority.[185] It seems, judging from the

interpretation of an earlier Act containing similar provisions, that a person served with notice to treat relating to only part of the premises should serve a counter-notice requiring the acquiring authority to take the whole, and that the authority are then entitled, even after a decision by the Lands Tribunal which goes against the authority on the question of detriment, to elect either to abandon the notice to treat or to take the whole.

2   If any land not situated in a town or built upon is cut through and divided by the works so as to leave a quantity of land which is less than half an acre, the owner of this may require the acquiring authority to purchase it along with the land subject to compulsory purchase; this does not apply if the owner has other adjoining land into which the land so left can be thrown and be conveniently occupied together, in which event the acquiring authority must, if so required by the owner, at their own expense throw the piece of land so left into the adjoining land by removing the fences and levelling the site, and by soiling it in a satisfactory and workmanlike manner.[186]

3   Where an acquiring authority serve notice to treat in respect of agricultural land on a person (whether in occupation or not) having a greater interest in the land than as tenant for a year or from year to year, and that person has such an interest in other agricultural land comprised in the same agricultural unit as that to which the notice relates, the person on whom the notice is served ('the claimant') may, within two months after the date when the notice to treat was served, serve on the acquiring authority a counter-notice:

(a)   claiming that the other land is not reasonably capable of being farmed, either by itself or in conjunction with other relevant land, as a separate agricultural unit; and
(b)   requiring the acquiring authority to purchase his interest in the whole of the other land.

If he does this the claimant must also within the same period serve a copy of the notice on any other person who has an interest in the land to which the requirement in the counter-notice relates, but failure to comply with this does not invalidate the counter-notice. The 'other relevant land' referred to above means land comprised in the same agricultural unit as the land to which the notice to treat relates, and land comprised in any other agricultural unit occupied by the claimant on the date of service of the notice to treat, being land in respect of which he is then entitled to a greater interest than as tenant for a year or from year to year; it however excludes any such land in respect of which the acquiring authority have served another notice to treat which is not withdrawn.[187]

If the acquiring authority do not within two months after the date of service of a counter-notice agree in writing to accept it as valid the claimant or the authority may, within two months after the end of that period, refer it to the Lands Tribunal for a decision; if the counter-notice is accepted by the authority or declared to be valid by the Lands Tribunal the authority are deemed to be authorised to acquire compulsorily the claimant's interest in the land to which the requirement in the counter-notice relates, and to have served notice to treat in respect of it. The claimant may however withdraw his counter-notice at any time before the compensation payable in respect of compulsory acquisition in pursuance of the counter-notice has been determined by the Lands Tribunal or at any time before the end of six weeks beginning with the date on which the compensation is so determined.[188] If under this counter-notice procedure the acquiring authority become entitled to a lease of any land but not to the interest of the landlord, the authority must offer to surrender the lease to the landlord on such terms as the authority consider reasonable; the question of what terms are reasonable may be referred to the Lands Tribunal by either party, and if the parties have not agreed the terms within three months after the authority's offer the authority must refer the question to the Tribunal if the reference has not been made already. If the question is referred to the Tribunal the landlord is deemed to have accepted the surrender of the lease one month after the date of the Tribunal's decision or on such other date as the Tribunal may direct, and to have agreed with the authority on the terms of surrender which the Tribunal has held to be reasonable.[189] Any terms as to surrender contained in the lease itself are to be disregarded in considering the reasonableness of the terms on which the authority offer to surrender the lease to the landlord.[190]

Right of acquiring authority to take further land

If the owner of any land cut through and divided by the works requires the acquiring authority, under the provisions of the empowering Act, to make any bridge, culvert or other communication between the land so divided and:

(a)   the land is so divided as to leave, either on both sides or on one side, a quantity of land which is less than half an acre, or which is of less value than the expense of making the communication between the divided land; and

(b)   the owner has no other land adjoining that piece of land, the acquiring authority may require the owner to sell them the piece of land. Any dispute as to the value of the piece of land, or as to the expense of making a communication between the divided land, must be determined by the Lands Tribunal.[191]

Compensation: general

Where land is authorised to be acquired compulsorily, any question of disputed compensation is to be referred to the Lands Tribunal.[192] The Lands Tribunal is appointed by the Lord Chancellor. It consists of a President and such number of other members as the Lord Chancellor may determine; the President must have held judicial office or be a barrister of at least seven years standing, and the other members must either be barristers or solicitors of similar standing or be persons having experience in the valuation of land.[193] Any one or more of the members may exercise the powers of the Tribunal, and the President of the Tribunal may select a member or members to deal with a particular case or class of cases.

The Tribunal sits in public and in general not more than one expert witness on either side may be heard, unless with special leave from the Tribunal; a member of the Tribunal dealing with the proceedings is entitled to enter on and inspect the relevant land.[194] Evidence is given orally and on oath. The Tribunal's decision must be written and reasoned, and is final save that appeal on a point of law may be taken directly to the Court of Appeal, and thence with leave to the House of Lords.

If either the acquiring authority have made an unconditional offer in writing of a specified sum as compensation to any claimant and the sum awarded by the Tribunal to that claimant does not exceed the sum offered, or the Tribunal is satisfied that a claimant has failed to deliver to the acquiring authority, in time to enable them to make a proper offer, a notice in writing stating the exact nature of the interest in respect of which compensation is claimed and giving details of the compensation claimed, distinguishing the amounts under separate heads and showing how the amount claimed under each head is calculated, then the Tribunal must, unless there are special reasons, order the claimant to bear his own costs and to pay the costs of the acquiring authority so far as they were incurred after the offer was made or the notice should have been delivered. Conversely where a claimant has delivered a notice with sufficient particulars of his claim in adequate time and has made an unconditional offer in writing to accept a specified sum as compensation, then if the sum awarded to him by the Tribunal is equal to or exceeds the sum claimed the Tribunal must, unless there are special reasons, order the acquiring authority to bear their own costs and to pay the costs of the claimant so far as these were incurred after his offer was made.[195]

Heads of claim for compensation

A person whose land has been compulsorily acquired may be entitled to compensation for (a) loss of the land itself; (b) damage caused by severance of the land from other land previously held with the land acquired; (c) injurious affection of his remaining land; (d) disturbance; he is also entitled to interest on the compensation monies.

Compensation for the land itself

It seems that compensation is not to be assessed by reference to values prevailing at the date of notice to treat, but that in general the appropriate date is when possession is taken or when the agreement for or the assessment of compensation is made, whichever is the sooner.[196]

The ascertainment of the interest to be valued, on the other hand, is a different issue to the valuation of that interest after it has been ascertained. In *Rugby Joint Water Board* v. *Shaw-Fox*[197] it was held that the interest to be valued on a compulsory acquisition is the interest which existed at the date of the notice to treat. Exceptionally, however, upon a compulsory acquisition or taking possession of an agricultural holding or any part of it, any assessment of the compensation to be paid upon the acquisition of the interests of either landlord or tenant must disregard any right of the landlord to serve a notice to quit or any notice already served by him which would be ineffective if section 24(2) (b) of the Agricultural Holdings Act, 1948 (land required for non-agricultural use for which planning permission has been granted; *ante*, page 55) and section 25(1)(e) of that Act (proposed termination of the tenancy for the purpose of the land being used for a non-agricultural use not falling within section 24(2) (b); *ante*, page 59) excluded any reference to the land being required or used by an acquiring authority;[198] the tenant's compensation is to be reduced by the amount of any reorganisation compensation (*ante*, pages 64–6) paid to him under the Agriculture (Miscellaneous Provisions) Act, 1968, section 12.[199] The whole of the exception is inapplicable to compensation which falls to be assessed by reference to prices current on a date before 23 May 1973.[200]

Compensation for the land must be assessed in accordance with the following rules. No allowance can be made on account of the acquisition being compulsory (it was at one time the practice to add 10 per cent

230

because of this). The value of land is in general to be the amount which the land if sold in the open market by a willing seller might be expected to realise, though this is not to affect the assessment of compensation for disturbance (*post* pages 236–40) or any other matter not directly based on the value of land [201] In *Watson* v. *Secretary of State for Air* [202] the court said that when assessing the compensation to be paid on the compulsory acquisition of a tenancy of a farm the profit made by the claimant farmer is a very material consideration, because it might well be that the notional purchaser buying the claimant's interest in the land would fix the price he was prepared to pay on the basis that he also would be likely to make such a figure of profit by farming.

The special suitability or adaptability of the land for any purpose must not be taken into account if that purpose is a purpose for which it could be applied only in pursuance of statutory powers, or for which there is no market apart from the special needs of a particular purchaser or the requirements of any authority possessing compulsory purchase powers. [203] The acquiring authority are not to pay any increase in the value of the land if the increase can be said to have been brought about by the scheme of development which gives rise to the need for the compulsory purchase. [204] The scheme of development is regarded as covering any development carried out in any part of an [action area] (*ante*, page 200) for which a [local plan] (*ante*, page 200) is in force, or in any part of an area delineated as the site of a new town or delineated in a [structure or local] plan (*ante*, page 200) as an area of town development.[205]

Secondly, if on a compulsory purchase of land the scheme of development causes an increase in value of other contiguous or adjacent land belonging to the same owner, this increase is to be deducted from the compensation. [206] But any diminution in the value of the land which is caused by the threat of compulsory purchase is to be ignored.[207]

The market value of land is governed by the use which can lawfully be made of it (but see also *post*, pages 232–3), hence it is important to know for what types of development planning permission is likely to be granted When assessing compensation for the compulsory purchase of land certain assumptions concerning planning permission must be made. [208] Any planning permission in existence at the date of the notice to treat is to be taken into account. [209] Moreover it is to be assumed that planning permission would be granted for such development as is considered to fall within the existing use under town and country planning law, [210] unless compensation has become payable under planning law in respect of a refusal to permit this or because of conditions imposed. [211] Also where land is acquired for purposes which involve the carrying out of proposals of the acquiring authority for its development, and there is not in force an actual planning permission for that development at the date of the notice to treat, it is to be assumed that planning permission would be granted for such development as accords with the proposals of the acquiring authority.[212]

Apart from the land being in an [action area for which a local plan is in force], if the land to be acquired consists of or forms part of a site defined in the [structure or local] plan as the site of proposed development of a particular kind, it is to be assumed that planning permission would be granted for that development;[213] if the land consists or forms part of an area shown in the plan as one allocated primarily for a specified use or range of uses, it must be assumed that planning permission would be granted for any development which is for the purpose of that use or within the range of uses, and for which planning permission might reasonably be expected to be granted.[214] Moreover if the land to be acquired is land in an [action area for which a local plan is in force] it must be assumed that planning permission would be granted for any development for a use falling within the range of uses planned for the whole [action] area (whether or not it is the use indicated by the plan for the particular land to be acquired) for which planning permission to develop the land might have been expected to be granted in defined hypothetical circumstances; the hypothetical circumstances are those which would have existed if the whole area had not been defined in the plan as an [action] area, and no particulars or proposals relating to any land in that area had been contained in the plan, and if no development or redevelopment of the area in accordance with the plan had taken place before the notice to treat.[215]

Throughout the above paragraph it is to be assumed that any planning permission granted would be made subject to such conditions as might reasonably be expected in the circumstances to be imposed by the authority granting permission, and, if it appears from a programme map or statement in the plan that permission would only be granted at a future time, it must be assumed that the permission would be granted at that time;[216] references to development for which planning permission might reasonably have been expected to be granted are to be construed as references to such development if the relevant land were not proposed to be acquired compulsorily.[217]

The [structure or local] plan might reserve the land for a public purpose of a financially unattractive nature, such as an open space, and if so the provisions of the plan will be of no financial assistance to the owner. Hence it is provided that if the land does not consist or form part of an area defined in a [structure or local] plan as an [action area for which a local plan is in force], or is not in an area shown in the plan as being allocated primarily for residential, commercial or industrial uses, either the owner or the acquiring authority may apply to the local planning authority for a certificate of appropriate alternative development.[218] Application for the certificate should be made before any dispute concerning compensation has been referred to the Lands Tribunal, since after such a reference the application can only be made with consent in writing of the other party or with leave of the Lands Tribunal.[219]

An application for a certificate under section 17 must specify one or more classes of development which the applicant alleges to be appropriate if the land were not to be acquired for public purposes, and must be accompanied by a statement specifying the date on which a copy of the application has been or will be served upon the other party.[220] The planning authority must issue to the applicant a certificate stating the kind or kinds of development which might reasonably have been expected to be permitted for the land, had it not been proposed to acquire the land under compulsory powers, or that no development could reasonably have been expected to be permitted other than the development (if any) which is proposed to be carried out by the acquiring authority;[221] if permission would only have been granted subject to conditions, or at a future time, the certificate must state this.[222] In deciding what development is permissible for the purpose of the certificate, the planning authority is not to exclude development by reason only that such development would not accord with the provisions of the [structure or local] plan,[223] such as where the plan reserves the land for an unremunerative purpose.

Either party to the acquisition can appeal to the Secretary of State against the certificate issued, and notice of appeal must be given within one month after receipt of the certificate.

There are complex provisions which, broadly speaking, ensure that compensation for the land acquired is neither increased nor reduced by the effect of development carried out or proposed to be carried out under the scheme of development underlying the acquisition, provided such development would not have been likely to have been carried out otherwise.[224]

In *Camrose (Viscount)* v. *Basingstoke Corporation*[225] the Lands Tribunal, in valuing a large area of land subject to compulsory purchase and situated near to the town of Basingstoke, had only attributed a 'hope' value to over two hundred acres of land which were some distance from the existing town centre; the tribunal took the view that development of that land for residential purposes was in the normal course of things unlikely in the foreseeable future. The court held that the basis of valuation adopted by the Lands Tribunal was correct because 'even though the two hundred and thirty-three acres are assumed to have planning permission, it does not follow that there would be a demand for it. It is not planning permission by itself which increases value. It is planning permission coupled with demand. The tribunal thought that the demand for these 233 acres was so far distant as to warrant only a "hope" of development, and valued them accordingly. I see nothing wrong with this method of calculation' (*per* Denning M. R.).

Claim for compensation other than for loss of land taken compulsorily

Where only part of the land is taken, the owner may suffer damage to his remaining land either because it is cut in two, as by the making of a road through his farm, or because his farm is not as convenient a size and shape as it was prior to the loss of the land which has been compulsorily acquired from him; a claim for 'severance' may arise in respect of this. His remaining land may also be rendered less valuable by the erection of, for example, a sewage treatment plant on the land compulsorily acquired from him, which is scarcely calculated to enhance the amenity and enjoyment of his remaining land; this may give rise to a claim for 'injurious affection'. Whether he is entitled to compensation for these things depends on the provisions of the particular enactments governing the compulsory purchase of land from him. Nearly all compulsory acquisitions are governed by the Compulsory Purchase Act, 1965,[226] which states that when assessing compensation regard must be had not only to the value of the land to be purchased by the acquiring authority, but also to the damage, if any, to be sustained by the owner of the land by reason of the severance of the land purchased from his other land, or the injurious affection of that other land by the exercise of the statutory powers.[227] A right to compensation for injurious affection only arises if the injury is caused by a proper exercise of statutory powers; if it is caused by acts that are beyond those powers the remedy is by an action for damages and/or an injunction.[228] In settling the compensation all subsequent damage that can be reasonably foreseen should be taken into account. Compensation is claimable for damage arising from the use made of the works as well as from their construction. Moreover when land is acquired or taken from any person for the purpose of works which are to be situated partly on that land and partly elsewhere, compensation for injurious affection of the land retained by that person is to be assessed by reference to the whole of the works and not only to the works which are situate on the land acquired or taken from him;[229] this provision is however inapplicable to any compensation which fell or falls to be assessed by reference to prices current on a date prior to 17 October 1972.[230]

Compensation is also claimable for disturbance in having to vacate the premises. In *Harvey* v. *Crawley Development Corporation*[231] a displaced householder, who had been compensated for expenses incurred in removal of furniture and for adjustments to curtains and carpets in order to make them fit a new house, claimed also as compensation for disturbance the surveyor's fees, legal costs and travelling expenses incurred, firstly, in an abortive proposed purchase of a new home, and secondly, in the successful purchase of a new home. It was held that any loss flowing from the compulsory acquisition can properly be the subject of compensation for disturbance, provided it is not too remote and is the natural, direct and reasonable consequence of the dispossession. All these items, including those for which payment had already been made, were properly claimable under the above head; any losses or expenses incurred in the removal of fixtures and fittings from business premises, or from loss of business in consequence of being turned out, or from loss of goodwill would similarly be claimable. It was however said that if a house was compulsorily acquired from a person who owned the house as an investment, and that person were to reinvest the compensation received for the house in stocks and shares, he could not claim as an item of compensation the brokerage paid by him to the stockbroker, because this would be too remote; it would not be the consequence of the compulsory acquisition, but rather the result of his own choice in putting the money into stocks and shares instead of putting it on deposit at the bank. Similarly if he chose to buy another house as an investment, he would not get the solicitor's costs of investigating title on buying the new house, since these would be incurred as the result of his own choice of investment and not as the result of the compulsory acquisition. A householder who paid a higher price for the house bought as a replacement would not be compensated merely because he paid a higher price inasmuch as he would be presumed to have got value for the excess payment in the shape of a better new house.

The reasonable cost of preparing the claim for compensation can be included in the claim.[232] The owner cannot claim the value of his land for a different use (within the range allowed; see *ante*, pages 231–3) than that for which it is at present used and claim for disturbance as well, since he would have to undergo disturbance in order to obtain the enhanced value attributable to the different use;[233] he must therefore accept whichever basis of claim is more favourable to him.

Compensation for disturbance where business carried on by person over the age of sixty

If a person is carrying on a trade or business on any land and in consequence of the compulsory acquisition of the whole of that land is required to give up possession to the acquiring authority, then subject to certain conditions the compensation payable to him in respect of the compulsory acquisition of his interest in the land or under the Compulsory Purchase Act, 1965, section 20 (*ante*, pages 222–3) shall, so far as attributable to his disturbance, be assessed on the assumption that it is not reasonably practicable for him to carry on the trade or business or, as the case may be, the part of the trade or business of which he has retained the goodwill, elsewhere than on that land. The conditions to be satisfied if this is to apply are:

(a)   that he must have attained the age of sixty on the date on which he gives up possession in consequence of the compulsory acquisition;

(b)   that the annual value of the aggregate of his land which forms the subject of a single entry in the rating valuation list must not exceed the amount prescribed by an order made by the Secretary of State; and

(c)   that he has not disposed of the goodwill of the whole of the trade or business, and he enters into undertakings with the acquiring authority that he will not dispose of the goodwill or, as the case may be, of the part of the trade or business of which he retains the goodwill, and that he will not, within such an area and for such a period as the acquiring authority may require, directly or indirectly engage in or have any interest in any other trade or business of the same or substantially the same kind as that carried on by him on the land acquired.

If an undertaking given as above is broken the acquiring authority may recover from the person compensated a sum equal to the difference between the amount paid to him and the amount which would have been payable if it had been assessed without regard to these special rules.

The above rules apply to a trade or business carried on in partnership as if references to the person by whom it is carried on and to the undertakings to be given referred to all the partners, and, subject to certain conditions relating to the ages and undertakings of the shareholders can apply to a trade or business carried on by a company. [234]   The whole of this special rule relating to a business carried on by a person over the age of sixty does not however apply to any compensation which fell or falls to be assessed by reference to prices current on a date prior to 17 October 1972. [235]

Additional payments to certain persons displaced from land

Home loss payments. Where a person is displaced from a dwelling in consequence of the compulsory acquisition of an interest in the dwelling or of certain other actions by public bodies, he is, subject to certain conditions, entitled to receive a payment (a 'home loss payment') from the appropriate authority. He is not treated as displaced in consequence of the compulsory acquisition if he gives up occupation of the dwelling before the date on which the acquiring authority were authorised to acquire an interest. He is not entitled to a home loss payment unless throughout a period of not less than five years ending with the date of displacement he has been in occupation of the dwelling, or a substantial part of it, as his only or main residence; he must also have been in occupation by virtue of an interest in the dwelling, or under a right to occupy the dwelling as a statutory tenant within the meaning of the Rent Act, 1968 (*ante,* pages 69–70), or under a contract of employment or certain other provisions. No home loss payment can be claimed if the compulsory acquisition is made in consequence of the service of a 'blight notice' (*post,* pages 249–52). The right to a home loss payment only applies if the date of displacement is on or after 17 October 1972.[236]

The amount of a home loss payment in England and Wales is (a) seven times the rateable value of the dwelling if the date of displacement is before 1 April 1973, or (b) three times the rateable value of the dwelling where the date of displacement is on or after 1 April 1973; the amount of the home loss payment is also subject to a maximum payment of £1,500 and a minimum payment of £150. The Secretary of State may from time to time prescribe different multipliers and a different maximum or minimum.[237]

If the date of displacement is before 23 May 1973, the home loss payment must be claimed within six months after that date; in other cases the payment must be claimed within six months beginning with the date of displacement. The claim must be made in writing and be accompanied or supplemented by such particulars as the authority responsible for making the payment may reasonably require. The home loss payment must be made within three months after the date on which a claim is made as above or, if those three months end before the date of displacement, on the date of displacement.[238]

The provisions relating to home loss payments are applied with modifications to a person residing in a caravan on a caravan site who is displaced from that site, provided no suitable alternative site for stationing a caravan is available to him on reasonable terms.[239]

Farm loss payments. Where land constituting or included in an agricultural unit is land in respect of which the occupier has either a 'freehold interest' (which seems to mean an interest other than leasehold) or a tenancy granted or extended for a definite term of years of which not less than three remain unexpired at the date of displacement, then if in consequence of the compulsory acquisition of his interest in the whole of that land ('the land acquired') he is displaced from the whole of that land and not more than three years after the date of displacement he begins to farm another agricultural unit ('the new unit') elsewhere in Great Britain, he is, subject to certain conditions, entitled to receive a payment (a 'farm loss payment') from the acquiring authority. He is only regarded as displaced in consequence of the compulsory acquisition of his interest if he gives up possession:

(a)   on being required to do so by the acquiring authority;
(b)   on completion of the acquisition; or
(c)   where the acquiring authority permit him to remain in possession of the land under a tenancy or licence of a kind not making him a tenant as defined in the Agricultural Holdings Act, 1948 (*ante*, pages 41–2), on the expiration of that tenancy or licence;

references to the date of displacement are references to the date on which the person concerned gives up possession as above. No farm loss payment is to be made to any person unless on the date on which he begins to farm the new unit he is in occupation of the whole of it by virtue of a freehold interest or tenancy, not having been entitled to any such interest or tenancy before the date on which the acquiring authority were authorised to acquire his interest in the land acquired. No farm loss payment is to be made to a person whose interest is compulsorily acquired in consequence of his having served a 'blight notice' (*post*, pages 249–52), nor to a person entitled to a payment of reorganisation compensation (*ante*, pages 64–6) under the Agriculture (Miscellaneous Provisions) Act, 1968,[240] in consequence of the acquisition of an interest in or the taking of possession of that land. A farm loss payment can only be claimed if the date of displacement is on or after 17 October 1972.[241] If an interest in land is acquired by agreement by an acquiring authority with compulsory purchase powers, the authority may make a payment corresponding to a farm loss payment.[242]

The amount of the farm loss payment is a sum equal to the average annual profit derived from the use for agricultural purposes of the agricultural land compulsorily acquired; that profit is to be computed by reference to the profits for the three years ending with the date of displace-

238

ment, or for the period during which the person concerned has been in occupation of the land if that period is less than three years. There are further and complex detailed provisions relating to the exact computation. Where the value of the agricultural land which was compulsorily acquired exceeds the value of the agricultural land comprised in the new unit the amount of the farm loss payment is to be proportionately reduced. The amount of a farm loss payment is not to exceed the amount (if any) by which (a) the payment (calculated apart from this provision) together with compensation for the acquisition of the interest in the land acquired (including any sum included as compensation for disturbance) exceeds (b) the compensation actually payable for the acquisition of that interest. Any dispute concerning the amount of a farm loss payment is to be determined by the Lands Tribunal. [243]

A farm loss payment must be claimed by the person entitled to it before the expiration of one year beginning with the date on which the person displaced began to farm another agricultural unit; if, however, he began to do so before the 1973 Act was passed the period for making the claim is one year beginning with 23 May 1973. The claim must be made in writing and be accompanied or supplemented by such particulars as the acquiring authority may reasonably require. Where the agricultural unit containing the land acquired is occupied for the purposes of a partnership firm the provisions relating to farm loss payments are to have effect in relation to the firm and not to the partners individually, and any interest of a partner in the land acquired is to be treated as an interest of the firm, save that the requirements as to the new agricultural unit are to be regarded as complied with in relation to the firm as soon as they are complied with by any one of the persons who were members of the firm. Where a person who would have been entitled to a farm loss payment dies before making a claim, his personal representative (*ante,* page 120) is entitled to make the claim within the period originally available for doing so. The authority making a farm loss payment must also pay any reasonable valuation or legal expenses incurred by that person in connection with his claim, subject to the powers of the Lands Tribunal in respect of the costs or expenses of proceedings before the Tribunal. A farm loss payment carries interest, at the rate prescribed from time to time, from the date of the making of a complete claim until the date of payment. [244]

Reorganisation compensation for agricultural tenants. Where an acquiring authority compulsorily purchases the interest of a tenant of an agricultural holding, reorganisation compensation under section 9 of the Agriculture (Miscellaneous Provisions) Act, 1968 (*ante,* pages 64—6) is in general payable as if the acquiring authority were the landlord and compensation for disturbance had become payable. [245] But in general reorganisation compensation is not payable where the acquiring authority require the land for the purposes of agricultural research or experiment, or demonstrating agricultural methods, or for the purposes of the enactments relating to small holdings, or where the Minister acquires the land under powers to ensure the full and efficient use of it for agriculture. [246] Nor is reorganisation compensation payable by the acquiring authority if the tenant was neither in possession nor entitled to possession of the land immediately before the acquiring of his interest or the taking of possession by the authority; in deciding whether the tenant is in possession or entitled to possession at that date, any agreement relating to the land such as is mentioned in section 2(1) (*ante,* pages 41–2) of the Agricultural Holdings Act, 1948, and which has not taken effect as an agreement for the letting of the land for a tenancy from year to year is to be disregarded.[247]

Where the tenancy is for a period of two years or upwards, reorganisation compensation is only payable if the amount payable to the tenant by the acquiring authority in consequence of the acquisition is exceeded by the aggregate of the amounts which, if the tenancy had been from year to year, would have been so payable by way of compensation and as reorganisation compensation, and even then is restricted to an amount equal to the excess.[248]

Disturbance payments. Persons who, though without any compensatable interest, were in lawful possession of non-agricultural land become in general eligible for a 'disturbance payment' if displaced from that land upon its acquisition. [249]

Compensation where occupier is rehoused. The amount of compensation payable in respect of an interest in land which is compulsorily acquired is not to be reduced on account of the fact that the acquiring authority have provided or undertaken to provide, or that another authority will provide, residential accommodation under any Act of Parliament, for the person entitled to the compensation;[250] this provision does not however affect any compensation which fell or falls to be assessed by reference to prices current on a date prior to 17 October 1972.[251]

Right to advance payment of compensation

Where an acquiring authority have taken possession of land the authority must, if an appropriate request is made, make an advance payment on account of any compensation payable by them for the compulsory acquisition of any interest in that land. A request for advance compensation must be made by the person entitled to compensation; it must be made in writing; must give particulars of the claimant's interest in the land (so far as not already given pursuant to a notice to treat), and must be accompanied or supplemented by such other particulars as the acquiring authority may reasonably require to enable them to estimate the amount of compensation in respect of which the advance payment is to be made. The amount of the advance payment is in general 90 per cent of the agreed compensation if the acquiring authority and the claimant have agreed the amount of compensation, and if they have not agreed the amount then 90 per cent of the amount of compensation estimated by the acquiring authority. The advance payment must be made within three months from the date on which a proper request for payment was made as above, or, if those three months end before the date on which the acquiring authority take possession of the land to which the compensation relates, on the date on which they take possession. There are provisions relating to the eventual adjustment of an advance payment when the amount of the compensation is finally assessed.[252]

Injurious affection where no land is taken

The possible heads of claim where land is taken from the claimant have been set out above. If no land is taken from the claimant, some Acts do and some do not provide for compensation for injurious affection, thus the success of a claim will initially depend on the relevant Act or Acts which govern the compulsory acquisition.

If the Compulsory Purchase Act, 1965, applies, as will usually be the case, compensation for injurious affection is claimable provided:

(a)   the injury is the consequence of a lawful exercise of the statutory powers (otherwise the remedy is by bringing an action in tort for nuisance);[253]
(b)   the damage arises from acts which would, apart from the statutory powers, have given rise to a cause of action;
(c)   the damage results from a physical interference with a public or private right which is incident to the land affected;
(d)   the damage is from the construction of the works and not from their user; test (d) is based on the express words of the Act.[254]

An example of injurious affection would be the destruction of easements hitherto enjoyed by the claimant over the land acquired. If the acquiring authority destroys an easement or breaks a restrictive covenant binding the land when carrying out the authorised works in accordance with statutory powers, the injured party must seek his remedy by way of compensation for injurious affection. The compensation is normally assessed on the basis of what damages would have been recoverable in an action of tort.

Compensation for injurious affection where no land is taken carries interest, at the rate prescribed from time to time, from the date of the claim until payment.[255]

The right to claim compensation has, subject to a number of restrictions, been extended to include certain claims regarding depreciated value caused by the use of public works, and not merely from their construction as outlined above. Where the value of an interest in land is depreciated by physical factors caused by the use of public works, compensation for this may be payable by the responsible authority. The physical factors are noise, vibration, smell, fumes, smoke, artificial lighting and the discharge on to the land in respect of which the claim is made of any solid or liquid substance. The public works are any highway, any aerodrome (other than an aerodrome in the occupation of a government department),[256] and any other works or land provided or used in the exercise of statutory powers. Physical factors caused by an aircraft arriving at or departing from an aerodrome are to be treated as caused by the use of the aerodrome, but apart from this the source of the physical factors must be situated on or in the public works whose use is alleged to be their cause. Compensation is not payable under these provisions in respect of physical factors caused by the use of any public works other than a highway unless immunity from actions for nuisance (*ante,* pages 312—4) in respect of that use is conferred by some relevant Act of Parliament. (But if in resisting a claim for compensation for depreciation caused by the use of public works, the authority against whom the claim is made contend that no Act of Parliament relating to the works in question confers immunity from a tort action for nuisance (*ante,* pages 312—4) in respect of the use to which the claim relates, then if compensation is not paid on the claim and the claimant subsequently brings an action for nuisance against the authority regarding the matters in respect of which the claim was made, no Act of Parliament relating to those works which was in force when the contention was made is to afford a defence to the action for nuisance insofar as the action relates to those matters.)[257] Further, compensation is not payable in respect of physical factors caused by accidents involving vehicles on a highway or accidents involving aircraft, nor is compensation payable in relation to a claim unless, if made in relation to a highway, the date on which the highway was first opened to public traffic and, if made in

242

relation to other public works, the date on which the works were first used after completion, falls in either case on or after 17 October 1969 ('the relevant date'). [258] An interest only qualifies for compensation in relation to the above type of claim if the interest was acquired by the claimant before the relevant date in relation to that claim; further, if the interest is in land which is a dwelling, then the interest must be the legal fee simple or a tenancy granted or extended for a term of years certain of which not less than three years remain unexpired on the date of service of the notice of the claim ('an owner's interest'); if and so far as the interest is in land which is not a dwelling, the claimant's interest must (a), in relation to land which forms the subject of a single entry in the rating valuation list, be that of a person who occupies the whole or a substantial part of the land by virtue of owning an 'owner's interest' (*ante*) or (b), in relation to land in an agricultural unit, the claimant's interest must be that of a person who occupies the whole of that unit and is entitled, while so occupying it, to an 'owner's interest' in the whole or any part of that land. Moreover the land in relation to which the claim is made must be or form part of either an agricultural unit, or land which forms the subject of a single entry in the rating valuation list and whose annual value does not exceed the amount prescribed by order of the Secretary of State. [259]

A claim is made by serving on the responsible authority a notice containing particulars of the land in respect of which the claim is made, the claimant's interest and the date on which it was acquired, the claimant's occupation of the land (unless irrelevant to the claim), any other interests in the land known to the claimant, the public works to which the claim relates, the amount of compensation claimed, and certain other prescribed particulars. In general a claim must be made within the 'claim period', i.e. within a period of between one and three years after the 'relevant date' (*ante,*). If the claim is valid the authority must also pay any reasonable valuation or legal expenses incurred in connection with the claim, subject to the powers of the Lands Tribunal in respect of the costs or expenses of proceedings before the Tribunal. [260]

The compensation payable on any claim must be assessed by reference to prices current on the first day of the 'claim period' (*ante*). When assessing depreciation due to the physical factors caused by the use of any public works, account is to be taken of the use of those works as it exists on the first day of the 'claim period' and of any intensification that may then be reasonably expected of their use in the state in which the works are on that date. The value of the interest in respect of which the claim is made is in general assessed by reference to the nature of the interest and the condition of the land as it subsisted at the date of service of notice of the claim (leaving out of account any mortgage or contract of sale or if made after the 'relevant date' (*ante*), for the grant of a tenancy to which the interest is subject); however there must be left out of account any part of the value of the interest which is attributable to any building or improvement or extension of a building on the land if the building or, as the case may be, the building as improved or extended, was first occupied after the 'relevant date', and also any change in the use of the land made after that date. [261] Various assumptions concerning the grant of planning permission must be made when assessing the value of the interest in respect of which the claim is made. [262] The compensation payable on a claim is in general to be reduced by an amount equal to any increase in the value of the claimant's interest in the land in respect of which the claim is made and of any interest in any other land contiguous or adjacent to that land to which the claimant was entitled in the same capacity on the 'relevant date', provided the increase is attributable to the existence of or the use or prospective use of the public works to which the claim relates. [263] Moreover compensation is not payable on any claim unless the amount of the compensation exceeds £50. [264] There are various other detailed restrictions concerning compensation. [265]

Provision is made for claims relating to alterations to public works, and also regarding changes of use of public works other than a highway or aerodrome; there are detailed provisions defining the alterations which are covered and excluding any claims relating to the intensification of an existing use. In relation to claims relating to such alterations and changes of use, the 'relevant date' is redefined to mean either the date at which the highway was first opened to public traffic after completion of the alterations to the carriageway, or the date on which the other public works were first used after completion of the alterations, or the date of the change of use, as the case may be. [266]

The requirement of section 2 that the claimant must have acquired his interest before the 'relevant date' does not apply to any interest acquired by him by inheritance from a person who acquired that interest, or a greater interest out of which it is derived, before the relevant date. For this purpose an interest is acquired by a person by inheritance if it devolves upon him by virtue only of testamentary dispositions or of the law of intestate succession (Chapter 4, *ante*), or of the right of survivorship between joint tenants (*ante*, page 14) taking effect on the death of another person or the successive deaths of two or more other persons. [267]

There are special provisions relating to the making of claims in respect of which the period during which the claim must be made has wholly or partly expired before the 'commencement date'. [268] Any disputed claims for depreciation caused by the use of public works are to be referred to the Lands Tribunal for decision.[269]

'Commencement date' means 23 June 1973.[270]

Compensation for depreciation caused by the use of public works carries interest, at the rate prescribed from time to time, from the date of service of the notice of the claim or, if that date is before the beginning of the 'claim period' (post), from the beginning of the 'claim period', until payment. [271] 'Claim period' in general means the period between one and three years after the 'relevant date'.[272]

Mitigation of injurious effect of public works

Insulation against noise. The Secretary of State may make regulations imposing a duty or conferring a power on responsible authorities to insulate buildings against noise caused or expected to be caused by the construction or use of public works, or to make grants in respect of the cost of such insulation.[273]

Power to pay expenses of persons moving temporarily during reconstruction, improvement or alteration of certain public works. Where works are carried out for the construction or improvement of a highway, or for the construction or alteration of any public works other than a highway, and the carrying out of those works affects the enjoyment of an adjacent dwelling to such an extent that its continued occupation is not reasonably practicable, the responsible authority may pay any reasonable expenses incurred by the occupier of the dwelling in providing suitable alternative residential accommodation for himself and members of his household for the whole or any part of the period during which the works are being carried out.[274]

Powers of acquiring authority to enter land subject to compulsory purchose

As regards acquisitions of land to which the Compulsory Purchase Act, 1965, applies (*ante,* page 221) the Act confers the following powers to enter on the land. The acquiring authority, after giving not less than three nor more than fourteen days notice to the owners or occupiers, may enter on the land subject to compulsory purchase, but only for the purposes of surveying and taking levels, or of probing or boring to ascertain the nature of the soil and to set out the line of the works. The owners or occupiers must be compensated for any damage; any dispute regarding the compensation goes to the Lands Tribunal.[275]

If the acquiring authority have served notice to treat (*ante,* pages 222–3) in respect of the land, they may enter on and take possession of that land not less than fourteen days after serving notice of intention to enter; any compensation agreed or awarded for the land of which possession is taken carries interest, at the rate prescribed from time to time by the Treasury [276] from the time of entry until the compensation is either paid to the owners or is paid into court under the 1965 Act. [277] This procedure is frequently used.

The acquiring authority may also enter on and take possession of any of the land by complying with the following procedure as regards every person interested in the land who has not consented to entry by the authority. The acquiring authority must pay into court by way of security the amount of compensation claimed by each such person, or a sum equal to the value of his interest as determined by an able practical surveyor appointed in writing by two Justices of the Peace acting together. The authority must also give or tender to each such person a bond with two sureties for a penal sum computed as above, and conditioned for payment to each person or into court in accordance with the Act of all the compensation which may be agreed or awarded, together with interest at the rate prescribed from the time of entry until the compensation is so paid over. [278] This procedure is rarely used.

Under the Town and Country Planning Act, 1968, [279] the acquiring authority may vest in themselves land which they are authorised by a compulsory purchase order to acquire, and may do this by means of a 'general vesting declaration'. The 'general vesting declaration' can in general be made two months after notice of the confirmation or final making of the compulsory purchase order has been published in the local press, and notice of the declaration must in general be served upon the occupiers of the land affected; the declaration must specify a period of at least twenty-eight days from the date of service of notice on the occupiers after which the land will vest in the authority, and the authority may thus obtain good title to the land, carrying with it a right (subject to certain exceptions) to enter on the land, without the need for a conveyance of it in the usual way. Compensation is payable as if the acquiring authority had taken possession of the land at the date when it became vested in them by virtue of the declaration.

Subject to the above and to any other Act conferring a power of earlier entry, the acquiring authority must not, except with the consent of the owners and occupiers, enter on any of the land subject to compulsory purchase until the compensation payable for the interests in that land has been agreed or awarded, and has been paid to the persons having those interests or paid into court in accordance with the Act. [280] If the acquiring authority, or any of their contractors, wilfully enter on and take possession of any of the land subject to compulsory purchase in contravention of the rules set out above, the acquiring authority forfeit to the person in possession of the land the sum of £10, recoverable as a civil debt, in addition to the amount of any damage done to the land; if the acquiring authority or their contractors remain in unlawful possession of any of the land after forfeiture has been adjudged, the authority are liable to forfeit the further sum of £25 for every day on which they so remain in possession. [281] If however the acquiring authority have failed to purchase an interest in the land or to pay compensation for it because of mistake or inadvertence, they are in general entitled to remain in undisturbed possession of the land provided they remedy the matter within six months from the date when they learned of it, or after the interest has been established if there is a dispute concerning this. [282]

Service of counter-notice after receipt of notice of entry relating to only part of an agricultural holding

Where an acquiring authority serve notice of entry under section 11(1) of the Compulsory Purchase Act, 1965 (*ante,* pages 245–6) on the person in occupation of an agricultural holding, being a person having no greater interest than as tenant for a year or from year to year, and the notice relates to only part of that holding, the person on whom the notice is served ('the claimant') may, within two months from the date of service of the notice of entry, serve on the acquiring authority a counter-notice:

(a)   claiming that the remainder of the holding is not reasonably capable of being farmed, either by itself or in conjunction with other relevant land, as a separate agricultural unit; and

(b)   electing to treat the notice of entry as a notice relating to the entire holding. If he serves a counter-notice the claimant must also serve a copy on the landlord of the holding, but failure to comply with this does not invalidate the counter-notice.

'Other relevant land' means (a) land comprised in the same agricultural unit as the agricultural holding, and (b) land comprised in any other agricultural unit occupied by the claimant on the date of service of the notice of entry, being land in respect of which he is then entitled to a greater interest than as tenant for a year or from year to year; it does not include land other than that to which the notice of entry relates in respect of which the acquiring authority have served a notice to treat which is not withdrawn. [283]

If the acquiring authority do not within two months after the date of service of the counter-notice agree in writing to accept it as valid, the claimant or the acquiring authority may, within two months after the end of that period, refer the matter to the Lands Tribunal for a decision. If the counter-notice is accepted or held by the Tribunal to be valid, then if before the end of twelve months after it has been thus accepted or held valid the claimant has given up possession of every part of the agricultural holding to the acquiring authority:

(a) the notice of entry is deemed to have extended to the part of the nolding to which it did not relate; and

(b) the acquiring authority are deemed to have taken possession of that part in pursuance of notice of entry on the day before the expiration of the year of the tenancy which is current when the counter-notice is either accepted or held by the Tribunal to be valid.

If the claimant gives up possession of the holding to the acquiring authority as above but the authority have not been authoriseu to acquire the landlord's interest in or in any part of that part of the holding to which the notice of entry did not relate ('the land not subject to compulsory purchase'), then neither the claimant nor the authority are under any liability to the landlord by reason of the claimant having given up possession of the land not subject to compulsory purchase or the authority taking or being in possession of it. Immediately after the date on which the authority take possession of the land not subject to compulsory purchase they must give up to the landlord and he must take possession of that land. The tenancy is to be treated as having terminated on the date on which the claimant gives up possession of the holding to the acquiring authority or, if he gives up possession of different parts at different times, when he gives up possession of the last part, but without prejudice to any rights or liabilities of the landlord or the claimant which have accrued before that date; any rights of the claimant against or liabilities of the claimant to the landlord which arise on or out of the termination of the tenancy by virtue of this (under whatever head those rights or liabilities may arise) are to be rights and liabilities of the authority, and any question as to the payment to be made in respect of any such right or liability is to be referred to and decided by the Lands Tribunal. Further, any increase in the value of land not subject to compulsory purchase which is attributable to the landlord's having taken possession of it under this provision must be deducted from the compensation payable in respect of the acquisition of his interest in the remainder of the holding. [284]

Before taking possession of part only of an agricultural holding under certain other enactments[285] the acquiring authority must serve notice of their intention to do so on the person in occupation of the holding and the above provisions relating to the service of a counter-notice after receipt of notice of entry and the effect of the counter-notice are to apply subject to any necessary modifications of terminology.[286]

Value of property diminished by its proposed acquisition for public purposes; owner's right to serve a blight notice

Property may fall in value or even become unsaleable when it becomes known, or believed, that the property will be acquired in the future for certain types of public development. There are complex provisions enabling certain owner-occupiers to force the appropriate public authority to acquire their interests in the land without delay. These provisions apply to land which is either land indicated in a structure plan (*ante,* page 200) as land which may be required for the purposes of any functions of a public body or which may be included in an action area (*ante,* page 200), or is land allocated for the purpose of any such functions or as the site of proposed development for such functions by a local plan (*ante,* page 200), or is land indicated in a structure or local plan as land on which a highway is to be constructed, altered or improved, or is land on or adjacent to the line of a highway which by certain other methods is proposed to be constructed, altered or improved, or certain other types of land.[287] References to the plans mentioned above have been extended to include, in the case of a structure plan, a plan which has been submitted to the Secretary of State although not yet in force, or proposals for alterations to a structure plan submitted to the Secretary of State after the plan has been approved, or modifications of which notice has been given and which are proposed by the Secretary of State to such plan or proposals; in the case of a local plan, to the plan or proposed alterations to it of which copies have been made available for inspection in accordance with statute, or modifications or alterations to the plan of which notice has been given and which are proposed to be made by the Secretary of State or by the local planning authority; these extensions do not in general apply if the above plans or proposals are withdrawn.[288] Further extensions embrace further types of proposal relating to land on or adjacent to the line of a highway which it is proposed to construct, improve or alter.[289] The extensions also include certain land affected by a resolution of the local planning authority as land required for public purposes or to be safeguarded for such purposes, or in respect of which the Secretary of State has directed that it be safeguarded for such purposes,[290] and also land affected by certain orders relating to the site of a proposed new town.[291] A person who has an interest in land of any kind described above, and who has made reasonable endeavours to sell that interest but, in consequence of the fact that the land or a part of it is of the type so described, has been unable to sell his interest except at a price substantially lower than that for which it might reasonably have been expected to sell if no part of the land were of that type, may serve notice upon the appropriate authority requiring the purchase of his interest;[292] such a notice is known as a 'blight notice'. (It should be noted that blight notices served before 23 May 1973—the date when the relevant provisions of the Land Compensation Act, 1973 came into operation—are governed by the law in force prior to that Act.)[293] The 'appropriate authority' means the public body suitable for acquiring the land for its proposed purpose, any dispute concerning this to be decided by the Secretary of State.[294] Generally speaking a person is not entitled to serve a blight notice unless he has occupied the land throughout a period of six months ending with the service of the notice, and owns either the fee simple (*ante,* pages 1—2) in the land or a leasehold which has at least three years to run.[295] A mortgagee who has become entitled to exercise his statutory power of sale (*ante,* pages 27—8) is also entitled in appropriate circumstances to serve a blight notice.[296] The personal representative (*ante,* page 120) of a deceased person is in general entitled to serve a blight notice if the deceased could himself have done so before his death, and if (a) the personal representative has made reasonable endeavours to sell the deceased's interest; (b) in consequence of the fact that the land was of a kind set out above, he has been unable to sell that interest except at a price substantially lower than that for which it might reasonably have been expected to sell if no part of the land were of that kind; and (c) one or more individuals are (to the exclusion of any corporate body) beneficially entitled to that interest.[297]

Where a blight notice is served in respect of an interest in the whole or part of an agricultural unit ('agricultural unit' meaning land which is occupied as a unit for agricultural purposes, including any dwelling house or other building occupied by the same person for the purpose of farming the land),[298] and on the date of serving the notice that unit or part of it contains land ('the unaffected area') which does not fall within any of the descriptions of land set out above as well as land ('the affected area') which does so, the claimant may include in the notice:

(a) a claim that the unaffected area is not reasonably capable of being farmed, either by itself or in conjunction with other relevant land, as a separate agricultural unit; and
(b) a requirement that the appropriate authority shall purchase his in-

terest in the whole of the unit or, as the case may be, in the whole of the part of it to which the notice relates.

'Other relevant land' means land comprised in the remainder of the agricultural unit if the blight notice is served only in respect of part of it, and land comprised in any other agricultural unit occupied by the claimant on the date when he served the notice and in which on that date he owned either the fee simple or a lease with at least three years unexpired.[299]

When a blight notice has been served upon the appropriate authority, the authority may then serve a counter-notice either (a) denying that a requirement essential for the service of a blight notice has been fulfilled, or (b) stating that the authority (unless compelled to do so under the blight notice provisions) do not propose to acquire any of the land in question, or (c) stating that as regards land either (i) allocated by a structure plan for the functions of a public authority as an action area or (ii) indicated in a development plan as land on which a highway is to be constructed, altered or improved, the authority (unless compelled to do so) do not propose to acquire any of the land during a period of fifteen years from the date of the counter-notice.[300] The authority can also in general serve a counter-notice on the ground that they only intend to acquire part of the area specified in the blight notice and state this in the counter-notice,[301] and if the counter-notice is upheld the blight notice will only be effective in relation to the part which the authority propose to acquire.[302] Where however a blight notice is served in respect of an agricultural unit containing both blighted and unblighted land and requiring the appropriate authority to purchase the claimant's interest in the whole of the land comprised in the notice on the ground that the unblighted land is not reasonably capable of being farmed, either by itself or in conjunction with other relevant land, as a separate agricultural unit (*ante,* page 250), the authority cannot object on the ground that they intend to acquire only part of the land unless they also object that the claim that the unblighted land cannot be thus farmed is not justified.[303]

The person who served the blight notice may, within two months after the counter-notice was served upon him, require the validity of the objection to be referred to the Lands Tribunal.[304] If no counter-notice is served, or if insofar as the Lands Tribunal do not uphold its validity, the appropriate authority are deemed to have been authorised to acquire the owner's interest compulsorily and to have served notice to treat (*ante,* pages 222–3) in respect of it.[305] A person who has served a blight notice may withdraw it at any time before the compensation payable in respect of compulsory acquisition in pursuance of the notice has been determined by the Lands Tribunal or within six weeks thereafter, unless the acquiring authority have already exercised the right of entering and taking possession of the land in pursuance of a notice to treat deemed to have been served in consequence of the blight notice.[306]

An owner who has served a blight or a purchase notice (*ante,* pages 213–4) is not prevented from claiming compensation for disturbance in accordance with the general rules (*ante,* pages 235–40) if the notice proves successful.

Notes

[1] Secretary of State for the Environment Order, 1970 S.I. 1970 No. 1681.

[2] Section 1(1).

[3] As from 1 April 1974, England and Wales are to be divided into local government areas known as counties; in those counties there are to be local government areas known as districts (Local Government Act, 1972, sections 1(1) and 20(1)). These are to have county and district councils respectively (sections 2 and 21). Borough, urban and rural district councils are to cease to exist upon that date (sections 1(10) and 20(6)). The county and the district councils are to be the planning authorities for the county and for the district respectively (section 182(1)), although a joint board may be established to deal with the planning of two or more areas (section 181(2). The detailed allocation of planning functions to these new planning authorities is dealt with in sections 182 to 185 and Schedule 16 of the Local Government Act.

[4] Town and County Planning Act, 1971, section 6.

[5] Section 7.

[6] Sections 8 and 9.

[7] Section 11.

[8] Section 12.

[9] Section 14.

[10] Section 29(1).

[11] Town and County Planning (Amendment) Act, 1972, section 1.

[12] Town and Country Planning Act, 1971, section 22.

[13] Section 290.

[14] Section 22(3).

[15] Section 22(4).

[16] Section 22(2).

[17] *Hidderley* v. *Warwickshire County Council* (1963) 14 P and C.R. 134.

[18] Section 22(2).

[19] 1972, S.I. 1972 No. 1385.
[20] Section 22(2).
[21] Section 290.
[21a] Section 53. (See *ante* p. 202).
[22] Section 24.
[23] 1973, S.I. 1973 No. 31.
[24] 1950, S.I. 1950 No. 729.
[25] Section 27.
[26] Section 29.
[27] Section 32.
[28] Section 42.
[29] Section 37.
[30] Section 29(1).
[31] Section 30.
[32] [1958] 1 Q.B. 554.
[33] *Kent County Council* v. *Kingsway Investments (Kent) Ltd.* [1971] A.C. 72.
[34] Compare *Pyx Granite Co. Ltd.* v. *Ministry of Housing and Local Government* [1960] A.C. 260; *Fawcett Properties Ltd.* v. *Buckingham County Council* [1958] 1 W.L.R. 1161; *Hall and Co. Ltd.* v. *Shoreham-by-Sea Urban District Council* [1964] 1 All E.R. 1; *Kent County Council* v. *Kingsway Investments (Kent) Ltd.* [1971] A.C. 72.
[35] [1963] 2 Q.B. 764.
[36] [1961] A.C. 636.
[37] Section 41.
[38] Section 44.
[39] Section 33.
[40] Sections 36 and 37.
[41] Section 36(8) and Schedule 9.
[42] 1970, S.I. 1970 No. 1454.
[43] Sections 242 and 245.
[44] Schedule 8, Part II.
[45] Section 169.
[46] Section 87.
[47] Section 88.
[48] Section 91.
[49] Section 91(2).
[50] Section 93(1).
[51] Section 93(2).
[52] Section 93(3).
[53] Section 89.

[54] Section 90.
[55] Section 45.
[56] Section 164.
[57] Section 51.
[58] Section 170.
[59] Section 108.
[60] Section 54.
[61] Section 54(2).
[62] Section 55(1).
[63] Section 58.
[64] Sections 96–99.
[65] Section 114.
[66] Section 115.
[67] Section 114.
[68] Section 116.
[69] Section 117.
[70] Historic Buildings and Ancient Monuments Act, 1953, section 4.
[71] Town and Country Planning Act, 1971, sections 59 and 60.
[72] Section 60.
[73] Section 174.
[74] Sections 60 and 61.
[75] Section 62.
[76] Section 102.
[77] Section 103.
[78] *Attorney-General* v. *Melville Construction Co. Ltd.* (1968) 67 L.G.R. 309.
[79] Forestry Act, 1967, section 1.
[80] Section 10.
[81] Sections 10 and 11.
[82] Section 11(3).
[83] Section 12(1).
[84] Section 13.
[85] Section 15, as amended.
[86] Section 17.
[87] Section 18.
[88] Section 20.
[89] Section 21.
[90] Section 22.
[91] Sections 24 and 26.
[92] Town and Country Planning Act, 1971, section 180.
[93] Section 181.

94   Section 183.

95   Sections 188–190.

96   *R. v. Minister of Housing and Local Government, ex parte Chichester R.D.C.* [1960] 2 All E.R. 407.

97   Section 65.

98   Section 105.

99   Section 104.

100   Section 107.

101   [1960] 2 Q.B. 373.

102   Section 63.

103   Section 64.

104   S.I. 1969 No. 1532.

105   S.I. 1972 No. 904.

106   Section 109.

107   Section 109(3).

108   Regulation 2(1).

109   Regulation 3.

110   Regulations 26 and 27.

111   Regulation 6.

112   Regulation 11.

113   Regulation 11(3).

114   Regulation 16.

115   Regulations 16 and 22.

116   Regulation 5.

117   Regulation 20(1).

118   Regulation 21(2).

119   Regulation 22(5).

120   Regulation 31.

121   Regulation 22.

122   Regulation 6(4).

123   Regulation 8.

124   Section 176 and Regulation 30.

125   Section 277.

126   Caravan Sites and Control of Development Act, 1960, section 3.

127   Section 29.

128   Section 1(1).

129   Section 1(2).

130   Section 1(4).

131   Section 3(1).

132   Section 3(2).

133   S.I. 1960 No. 1474.

[134] Section 3.

[135] Town and Country Planning Act, 1971, section 29.

[136] Section 25(1).

[137] Section 10(1).

[138] Section 4(1).

[139] Section 5(1).

[140] Section 5(6); Circular No. 42/60.

[141] Section 5(1).

[142] Section 5(3).

[143] Section 5(4).

[144] Section 9.

[145] Section 7(1).

[146] Section 9.

[147] Section 3(6).

[148] Section 8(1).

[149] Section 8(2).

[150] Section 2 and First Schedule.

[151] Section 26.

[152] Town and Country Planning Act, 1971, section 112.

[153] Acquisition of Land (Authorisation Procedure) Act, 1946, section 1 and First Schedule.

[154] First Schedule.

[155] Land Compensation Act, 1961, section 1.

[156] Compulsory Purchase Act, 1965, section 8; *post*, pages 226–7).

[157] Land Compensation Act, 1973, sections 53 and 61.

[158] Acquisition of Land (Authorisation Procedure) Act, 1946, section 1 and First Schedule.

[159] [1956] A.C. 736.

[160] [1969] 2 A.C. 147.

[161] Compulsory Purchase Act, 1965, section 1(1).

[162] Section 3.

[163] Section 4.

[164] Section 5(1).

[165] Section 5(2).

[166] Compulsory Purchase Act, 1965, section 10; Lands Clauses Consolidation Act, 1845, section 68; *post,* pages 234–5.

[167] Compulsory Purchase Act, 1965, section 20(1).

[168] Section 20(2); *post,* pages 234–5.

[169] Section 20(5).

[170] Section 20.

[171] Compulsory Purchase Act, 1965, section 20(6); Landlord and Ten-

ant Act, 1954, sections 37, 39 and 43; Land Compensation Act, 1973, section 47 (as regards compensation which falls to be assessed by reference to prices current on or after 17 October 1972).

[172] Land Compensation Act, 1973, section 37.

[173] Land Compensation Act, 1973, section 38; a non-agricultural business tenant must however elect whether to claim a disturbance payment or a payment under the Landlord and Tenant Act, 1954, section 37, (*ante*; payment where a new tenancy of business premises is refused on certain specified grounds); Land Compensation Act, 1973, section 37(4).

[174] Land Compensation Act, 1973, section 59.

[175] Land Compensation Act, 1973, section 61.

[176] *Post,* page 229; Compulsory Purchase Act, 1965, section 6.

[177] Land Compensation Act, 1961, section 31(2).

[178] Land Compensation Act, 1961, section 31(3).

[179] Compulsory Purchase Act, 1965, section 23.

[180] Section 9(1) and (2).

[181] Section 9(3).

[182] Section 9(4).

[183] Compulsory Purchase Act, 1965, section 8(1).

[184] Land Compensation Act, 1973, section 58.

[185] Compulsory Purchase Act, 1965, section 8(1).

[186] Section 8(2).

[187] Land Compensation Act, 1973, section 53.

[188] Land Compensation Act, 1973, section 54.

[189] Land Compensation Act, 1973, section 54(6).

[190] Land Compensation Act, 1973, section 54(6).

[191] Compulsory Purchase Act, 1965, section 8(3).

[192] Land Compensation Act, 1961, section 1.

[193] Lands Tribunal Act, 1949, section 2.

[194] Land Compensation Act, 1961, section 2.

[195] Land Compensation Act, 1961, section 4.

[196] *Birmingham City Corporation* v. *West Midland Baptist (Trust) Association Inc.* [1969] 3 All E.R. 172.

[197] [1972] 2 W.L.R. 757.

[198] Land Compensation Act, 1973, section 48.

[199] *Post,* pages 239–40; Land Compensation Act, 1973, section 48(5).

[200] Land Compensation Act, 1973, section 89.

[201] Land Compensation Act, 1961, section 5.

[202] [1954] 1 W.L.R. 1477.

[203] Land Compensation Act, 1961, section 5.

[204] Section 6.

205 Section 6(1) and Schedule I, Part I; Town and Country Planning Act, 1971, sections 20 and 291 and Schedule 23.

206 Section 7.

207 Section 9.

208 Section 14.

209 Land Compensation Act, 1961, section 14(2).

210 Section 15(3) and (4) of the 1961 Act; Town and Country Planning Act, 1971, Schedule 8.

211 Section 15(4) of the 1961 Act.

212 Section 15(1) of the 1961 Act.

213 Land Compensation Act, 1961, section 16(1); Town and Country Planning Act, 1971, sections 20 and 291 and Schedule 23.

214 Land Compensation Act, 1961, section 16(2) and (3).

215 Section 16(4) and (5); Town and Country Planning Act, 1971, section 291 and Schedule 23.

216 Section 16(6).

217 Section 16(7).

218 Section 17(1); Town and Country Planning Act, 1971, sections 20 and 291 and Schedule 23.

219 Section 17(2).

220 Section 17(3).

221 Section 17(4).

222 Section 17(5).

223 Section 17(7); Town and Country Planning Act, 1971, section 20.

224 Land Compensation Act, 1961, section 6 and First Schedule.

225 [1966] 1 W.L.R. 1100.

226 Compulsory Purchase Act, 1965, section 1(1).

227 Section 7.

228 *Imperial Gas Light and Coke Co.* v. *Broadbent* (1859) 7 H.L. Cas. 600.

229 Land Compensation Act, 1973, section 44.

230 Land Compensation Act, 1973, section 89.

231 [1957] 1 Q.B. 485.

232 *London County Council* v. *Tobin* [1959] 1 All E.R. 649.

233 *Horn* v. *Sunderland Corporation* [1941] 2 K.B. 26.

234 Land Compensation Act, 1961, section 46.

235 Land Compensation Act, 1973, section 89.

236 Land Compensation Act, 1973, section 29.

237 Land Compensation Act, 1973, section 30.

238 Land Compensation Act, 1973, section 32.

239 Land Compensation Act, 1973, section 33.

[240] Agriculture (Miscellaneous Provisions) Act, 1968, section 12; see *post*, pages 239–40.

[241] Land Compensation Act, 1973, section 35.

[242] Section 36(4).

[243] Land Compensation Act, 1973, section 35.

[244] Land Compensation Act, 1973, section 36; Land Compensation Act, 1961, section 32.

[245] Agriculture (Miscellaneous Provisions) Act, 1968, sections 12 and 13.

[246] Agriculture (Miscellaneous Provisions) Act, 1968, sections 13.

[247] Agriculture (Miscellaneous Provisions) Act, 1968, section 13(1).

[248] Agriculture (Miscellaneous Provisions) Act, 1968, section 12(2).

[249] Land Compensation Act, 1973, section 38; *ante,* pages 222–3.

[250] Land Compensation Act, 1973, section 50.

[251] Land Compensation Act, 1973, section 89.

[252] Land Compensation Act, 1973, section 52.

[253] *Imperial Gas Light and Coke Co.* v. *Broadbent (ante).*

[254] Compulsory Purchase Act, 1965, section 10, incorporating Lands Clauses Consolidation Act, 1845, section 68 and the decisions thereon, though without the provision in section 68 restricting claims to those exceeding £50.

[255] Land Compensation Act, 1973, section 63; Land Compensation Act, 1961, section 32.

[256] Land Compensation Act, 1973, section 84.

[257] Land Compensation Act, 1973, section 17.

[258] Land Compensation Act, 1973, section 1.

[259] Land Compensation Act, 1973, section 2.

[260] Land Compensation Act, 1973, section 3.

[261] Land Compensation Act, 1973, section 4.

[262] Land Compensation Act, 1973, section 5.

[263] Land Compensation Act, 1973, section 6.

[264] Land Compensation Act, 1973, section 7.

[265] Land Compensation Act, 1973, section 8.

[266] Land Compensation Act, 1973, section 9.

[267] Land Compensation Act, 1973, section 11.

[268] *Post*; Land Compensation Act, 1973, section 14.

[269] Land Compensation Act, 1973, section 16.

[270] Land Compensation Act, 1973, sections 19 and 89.

[271] Land Compensation Act, 1973, section 18; Land Compensation Act, 1961, section 32.

[272] Land Compensation Act, 1973, section 3(2), *ante.*

[273] Land Compensation Act, 1973, section 20.

[274] Land Compensation Act, 1973, section 28.

[275] Compulsory Purchase Act, 1965, section 11(3).

[276] Section 32.

[277] Section 11(1).

[278] Section 11(2) and Schedule 3.

[279] Town and Country Planning Act, 1968, section 30 and Schedule 3.

[280] Compulsory Purchase Act, 1965, section 11(4).

[281] Section 12.

[282] Section 22.

[283] Land Compensation Act, 1973, section 55.

[284] Land Compensation Act, 1973, section 56.

[285] The Lands Clauses Consolidation Act, 1845, section 85, the Compulsory Purchase Act, 1965, Schedule 3, or the Town and Country Planning Act, 1968, Schedule 3; *ante*, page 246.

[286] Land Compensation Act, 1973, section 57.

[287] Town and Country Planning Act, 1971, section 192.

[288] Land Compensation Act, 1973, section 68.

[289] Land Compensation Act, 1973, section 69.

[290] Land Compensation Act, 1973, section 71.

[291] Land Compensation Act, 1973, section 72.

[292] Town and Country Planning Act, 1971, section 193, as amended by the Land Compensation Act, 1973, section 77.

[293] Land Compensation Act, 1973, section 77(3).

[294] Town and Country Planning Act, 1971, section 205.

[295] Town and Country Planning Act, 1971, section 203.

[296] Town and Country Planning Act, 1971, section 201.

[297] Land Compensation Act, 1973, section 78.

[298] Town and Country Planning Act, 1971, section 207.

[299] Land Compensation Act, 1973, section 79.

[300] Town and Country Planning Act, 1971, section 194.

[301] Town and Country Planning Act, 1971, section 194(2).

[302] Section 195(5).

[303] Land Compensation Act, 1973, section 80.

[304] Town and Country Planning Act, 1971, section 195.

[305] Town and Country Planning Act, 1971, section 196; Land Compensation Act, 1973, sections 80–81.

[306] Town and Country Planning Act, 1971, section 198.

7 Contract, Sale of Goods and Hire-Purchase

Contract

A contract is an agreement made between two or more persons which is intended by them to be legally binding and which fulfils certain requirements imposed by the law.

Offer and acceptance

The first of these requirements is that a person must communicate his offer to the other contracting party, showing a definite intention to bind himself to the terms of the offer provided the other party agrees to them. The making of an offer must therefore be distinguished from a mere invitation to negotiate such as is contained in a catalogue or advertisement of merchandise; the prospective customer who notifies his willingness to buy the advertised goods thereby himself makes the offer. Likewise when goods are exhibited in a shop window or in a self-service shop with price attached it is the customer who makes the offer when he expresses his willingness to purchase the article.[1]

The next essential is that the other party should accept the offer on the terms on which it was made. If, instead, he insists on altering the terms or adding new ones, he will himself be making a counter-offer, and the legal effect of this is to destroy the original offer, thus leaving his counter-offer as the only offer now in existence.[2]

The person accepting must communicate his acceptance to the other party, unless the other party expressly indicates that he does not wish to be told of the acceptance and that it will be sufficient to accept by, for example, doing a specified act. Conversely, however, the offeror cannot force a contract on another person by stipulating in the offer that the other person shall be deemed to have accepted the offer unless he notifies his rejection within a specified time; thus where a tradesman, hoping to drum up custom, sends out unwanted goods on the terms that the recipient shall be deemed to have agreed to buy them unless he communicates his dissent and returns the goods, within, say, seven days after receipt, such terms are ineffectual to create a contract if the recipient of the goods does nothing.[3] Moreover by the Unsolicited Goods and Services Act, 1971, a person who receives unsolicited goods may, as between himself and the sender, in certain circumstances set out in the Act use or deal with the goods as if they were an unconditional gift to him, and any right of the sender to the goods is extinguished.

If the post is used as a means of communicating acceptance, the rule is that the acceptance of the offer takes place at the time when the letter is posted.[4] The revocation of an offer, on the other hand, though legally possible at any time before the offer has been accepted, will not take effect, whether communicated by post or otherwise, until notice of the revocation has reached the other party.[5]

An offer will also terminate by implication of law unless it is accepted within a reasonable length of time.

Consideration

In addition to the offer and acceptance, the contract must either be made by deed in the form of a written document signed, sealed and delivered as his deed by the person intending to enter into a binding undertaking, or it must be supported by consideration. Consideration is that which each party must either provide or promise to provide in return for the obligation which is to be performed by the other. The consideration furnished must be current and not lie in the past, thus a belated promise to pay a person £10 as a reward for services which he, without any expectation of being paid when he did so, had rendered before the promise to pay was made would not be binding; it would be otherwise if both parties expected throughout that payment would be forthcoming although the precise sum had not been agreed, and a reasonable sum would then be legally claimable or a price later agreed by the parties.[6]

There is, however, no legal requirement that the considerations furnished should be of approximately equal value on both sides, thus acceptance of an offer to sell a valuable item of farm machinery in return for £1 would in general produce a legally enforceable contract; in general it is for the parties, and not for the court, to decide whether the bargain is a fair one. On the other hand, if for example Smith is already bound to supply goods to Jones at a price of £100, then if Jones subsequently promised to pay Smith £200 in return for Smith supplying him with the identical goods already promised his promise to pay Smith the extra £100 would not be binding on him, since he would be receiving nothing extra in the way of consideration to support the promise made by him to pay the higher figure.[7] Likewise a creditor who is owed £10 and agrees to accept £5 from the debtor in full and final settlement is in general entitled to sue for the balance, notwithstanding his promise to forego it, since there was no consideration to support his undertaking not to claim it.[8] But had the debtor, at the creditor's request, paid a smaller sum than was originally owed at an earlier date than the creditor could have legally demanded it, this earlier date of payment would be a novel element in the second bargain which could be supposed to have some value to the creditor and would therefore be sufficient to constitute consideration and thus make binding his promise to forego the balance.[9] Moreover if the debtor can show that the creditor intended his promise to be legally binding, intended the debtor to act upon it, and the debtor has acted upon it in such a way as would render it unfair to permit the creditor to enforce the original bargain, the creditor will not be allowed to go back on his word.[10]

Intention to contract

If the bargain is to be legally enforceable the parties must have intended it to be legally binding. In transactions of a commercial nature it will be presumed that the parties did so intend unless the contrary is expressly stated. Thus in *Jones* v. *Vernon's Pools, Ltd.*[11] the plaintiff, alleging that he had posted a winning football pool coupon to the defendants, claimed the money he would have won from the defendants, who for their part denied receipt of the coupon. The coupon contained a clause that 'this coupon and any agreement . . . or payment made by or under it shall not . . . give rise to any legal relationship . . . or consequences whatsoever or be legally enforceable . . . but all such arrangements . . . are binding in honour only.' In consequence of this clause the plaintiff's action failed, and it was unnecessary to decide whether in fact the coupon had been posted.

As regards agreements of a merely social nature or made between members of a family, it is primarily a question of fact whether they intended to make a legally enforceable arrangement and in many instances the facts would not normally give rise to such an inference. Thus a wife, unable for health reasons to accompany her husband to his post abroad in the civil service, was unsuccessful in suing the husband for breach of his promise to pay her £30 per month as maintenance while they were living apart, because the court found that this arrangement between them was never intended to be legally enforceable.[12]

Capacity

The person whom it is sought to make liable under the contract must have had legal capacity to enter into it. A person now becomes an adult on reaching the age of eighteen. [13] In general contracts made by a person while he is an infant cannot be enforced against him. [14] An infant is however contractually bound by a contract of service, apprenticeship or education the terms of which considered as a whole are for the infant's benefit. [15] Moreover the infant is liable to pay a reasonable price (which may not be the contractual price) for 'necessaries' by which is meant 'goods suitable to the condition in life of such infant and to his actual requirements at the time of the sale and delivery'.[16] Further, if an infant contracts to acquire an interest in property of a permanent nature, such as land or shares, this contract will bind him unless he elects to repudiate it during his infancy or within a reasonable time after reaching adulthood, and even if he does repudiate he will be bound by payments, such as rent, which become due from him before he repudiated unless he can show that he received no consideration (*ante*, pages 262–3) at all in return for his payment.[17]

Mentally disordered persons and drunken persons can in general avoid liability under their contracts if it can be shown that because of such disabilities they did not know what they were doing and that the other contracting party was aware of this. They must, however, pay a reasonable price for necessaries sold and delivered to them.[18]

Form of contract

In general a contract does not have to be in writing in order to be legally enforceable, although it may well be a good idea to have the contract in writing in order to lessen the possibility of a dispute arising subsequently as to what were the terms of the contract.

Written evidence is, however, required as regards the following contracts. Firstly, a contract of guarantee must be so evidenced. [19] The essence of a contract of guarantee is that three parties—the creditor, the principal debtor and the guarantor—must be involved in the factual situation which gives rise to the making of the guarantee, and that the guarantor only binds himself to pay in the event of the principal debtor failing to discharge the liability which primarily rests on him.

Secondly, and of more frequent practical importance, any contract for the sale or other disposition of land or of any interest in land must be evidenced in writing. [20] Crops which require to be planted annually are not land, but other crops, such as fruit from trees, which do not require to be so planted may well be land if they are to remain growing, after the making of the contract of sale, for a sufficient period to obtain substantial further benefit from the soil. [21] It may be mentioned here that what is 'land' or 'goods' respectively depends on the context in which these terms are used, thus the one transaction could both be a contract for the sale of land within the meaning of the Law of Property Act, 1925, section 40(above) and a sale of goods for the purposes of the Sale of Goods Act, 1893, (*post*, pages 277–9); an example could arise concerning a contract made in the spring to sell a growing crop of apples when the apples become ripe.

Certain hire-purchase, credit-sale and conditional sale agreements must be made in writing (*post*, pages 292–303).

Contracts of guarantee and contracts relating to interests in land can only be enforced if the contract is evidenced in writing and signed by the defendant or his duly authorised agent. All the terms agreed (save that in contracts of guarantee the consideration need not be stated in the written document; Mercantile Law Amendment Act, 1856, section 3) between the parties must be evidenced in writing otherwise the writing will be insufficient, save that the plaintiff may waive a missing clause which is exclusively for his own benefit and then seek to enforce the agreement without that clause. [22] The written evidence need not be all in one document; provided a document signed by the defendant or his agent and containing part of the terms also expressly or impliedly refers to some other document relating to the transaction, oral evidence will be admitted to identify the second document and it will then be seen whether the two documents read together contain between them all the terms agreed by the parties.[23]

The effect of failure to produce written evidence of all the terms is that the contract is unenforceable and no action can be brought to enforce the sale of the land; however if a deposit has been paid or a cheque given in respect of it by the purchaser and the purchaser unjustifiably declines to proceed with the purchase, he cannot recover the deposit and may successfully be sued upon the cheque because neither of these things involve bringing an action to enforce the sale of the land. Moreover if the plaintiff has done an act, known as 'an act of part performance', which would be wholly inexplicable unless there existed some such contract for the disposal of the land as that which he alleges, and this act is of so substantial nature as to make it unfair to permit the defendant to take advantage of the absence of writing as a defence, the court may order the contract to be performed despite the want of writing; an authorised entry by the plaintiff into possession of premises belonging to the other party will be sufficient since it is not easily explicable unless he had a contract entitling him to do this, [24] and is serious in that the entry would constitute a trespass if the contract were not to be enforced. Conversely mere payment of part, or it would seem the whole, of the purchase price is insufficient since there are many plausible reasons why a person might pay a sum of money to another; moreover if the recipient of the money declines to complete the bargain, relying on the absence of writing, he must then refund the money which has been already paid to him.

Terms of the contract; conditions and warranties; representations

A statement made by one party to the other during the negotiations leading up to the formation of a contract may be either a condition, a warranty or only a representation. A condition is an obligation of vital importance as regards the fulfilment of the contract, and breach of a condition by one party usually entitles the other party to refuse to perform his side of the bargain and to claim damages in respect of the breach.

A condition is a term of the contract. A condition which is a term of the contract must be distinguished from a condition until whose fulfilment the parties intend no contractual obligation to arise; an example of the latter would be a contract for the sale of land which is made conditional on the vendor obtaining planning permission to build houses on the land.

A warranty is a less important obligation of the contract; a breach of warranty by one party entitles the other to claim damages in respect of the breach but does not entitle him to refuse to carry out his own obligations under the contract. A warranty is also a term of the contract.

A statement made during the negotiations leading up to the formation of the contract which was not of sufficient importance to be classified by the court as a condition or a warranty is not a term of the contract, but is at most a representation. A representation is a statement made by one party to the other before or at the time of contracting as regards some existing fact or past event, which is one of the causes which induces the making of the contract. Thus statements of law, statements of mere opinion, and silence in failing to mention relevant facts do not in general constitute representations in the legal sense, although the positive assertion of a half-truth may give rise to legal liability and in a few restricted classes of contract, such as those of insurance, the law imposes a positive duty to disclose all known material facts (see *post*, pages 359–60). It should be stressed that a representation is only legally significant if it was one of the causes inducing the contract, and in consequence will have no legal effect if

266

the other party did not know of it, or placed no reliance upon it, or knew it to be untrue.

If such a representation is untrue and is fraudulently made the other party may recover damages for deceit, and may also or alternatively in general elect to avoid the contract with the result that the parties are placed in the position they would have occupied had the contract never been made; a representation is fraudulent if it is made without an honest belief in its truth. [25] If the representation, though untrue, was made with an innocent state of mind, the other party is entitled to avoid the contract as above, and can also claim damages unless the person who made the statement 'proves that he had reasonable grounds to believe and did believe up to the time that the contract was made that the facts represented were true';[26] if the party whose representation proves to be untrue succeeds in proving his belief in its truth and the reasonable grounds of such belief then he is not liable to pay damages, and the other party must content himself with avoiding the contract.

Where a person has been induced by an innocent misrepresentation to enter into a contract and claims to avoid the contract in consequence, the court may instead declare the contract subsisting and award damages in lieu of avoidance if the court thinks that it would be equitable to do so.[27]

Whether the misrepresentation was innocent or fraudulent, the right to have the contract set aside is lost if it has become impossible meanwhile to restore the parties in substance to their previous position, or if the innocent party has been guilty of undue delay in seeking his remedy, [28] or has with full knowledge of his rights done some act which shows his intention to proceed with the contract, or if an innocent third party dealing in good faith and for value has meanwhile acquired rights in the subject matter of the contract, such as an innocent sub-buyer of goods.[29]

If a contract contains a clause seeking to exclude or restrict any liability to which a party to the contract might be subject by reason of any misrepresentation made by him or any remedy available to the other party because of it, the exempting clause (for exemption clauses generally, see *post*, pages 268–70) is to be of no effect except insofar as the court allows reliance on it as being fair and reasonable in the circumstances of the case.[30]

It may of course be difficult to decide whether a particular statement is a condition or a warranty or only a representation. If it is to constitute a condition or a warranty it must have been a term of the contract; if the parties conduct their negotiations orally and then subsequently draw up a written contract, it is difficult to show that anything said during the oral negotations which is not mentioned in the written contract was intended to constitute a term of the contract,[31] although this principle will not be applied if it can be shown that the parties intended that the written document should only contain part of the total contract made between them and to leave the reminder oral.[32] Another test, although by no means a conclusive one, for deciding whether the statement is a term of the contract is that it is more likely to be held to be a term if made shortly before the formation of the contract, rather than some considerable time beforehand and during the preliminary negotiations. Yet another factor is whether the person making the statement possessed special knowledge or skill concerning it compared with the person to whom it was made; if so the court is rather more likely to conclude that the statement was in fact a term of the contract.

In addition to the obligations arising out of the statements made by the parties, terms may also be implied into the contract by Acts of Parliament, such as the Sale of Goods Act, 1893, and the Supply of Goods (Implied Terms) Act, 1973 (*post*, pages 278–84); terms may also be implied into the contract by: (a) custom, such as a custom attaching to a particular trade, unless the words of the contract are such as to negative this; or (b) by the court in order to give effect to what the Court thinks must clearly have been the intention of both parties and thus to give business efficacy to their contract.[33]

Exemption clauses

A party to a contract frequently seeks to introduce into it a clause excluding or limiting what would otherwise be his liability under the contract on the occurrence of certain events. In order to succeed in making such a clause, if contained in a document, a part of a bargain between them, the person for whose benefit the clause is inserted must show that the document is one which the other person could reasonably suppose to be a document containing terms of the contract, and not, for example, expect to be a mere receipt for his money payment; if the exemption clause is especially severe, it may be that he must also show that special steps were taken to bring it to the attention of the other party.[34] Where a person hired a deck chair from the defendant council in accordance with a notice requiring him to pay two pence to the attendant and to obtain and retain for inspection a ticket evidencing this fact, and the hirer was injured when the chair collapsed under him when he sat upon it, he was held entitled to recover damages despite a clause printed on the ticket excluding liability for damage arising from the use of the chair, because a reasonable man would not expect the ticket to be anything other than a receipt for the two pence.[35]

If the document passes the above test and if the plaintiff has signed the document, then proof of the plaintiff's signature is proof that he agreed to be bound by all the terms of the document,[36] provided the defendant did not positively misrepresent the contents of the document to him.[37]

If the plaintiff did not sign the document containing the exemption clause, the clause will bind him, whether or not he actually knew of it, if reasonable steps were taken to bring it to his attention at the time of making the contract;[38] the clause will be ineffective if steps to bring it to the notice of the other party were only taken after the making of the contract.[39]

An oral undertaking given at the time of an auction concerning the fitness or quality of the article being auctioned will bind its giver notwithstanding any statement in the printed catalogue of the auction to the effect that no such undertaking will be given; the legal effect of the oral undertaking cannot be shrugged off by such a clause. Thus where a heifer was sold by auction, and the catalogue stated that no warranty given at the time of the sale concerning the animal should have any effect unless its terms appeared on the purchaser's statement of account, the vendor was held liable on his purely oral statement at the auction that there was nothing wrong with the animal and he would absolutely guarantee her in every respect, despite which the animal in fact turned out to be tubercular and died soon afterwards.[40]

Two further points worth noting are that, firstly, any ambiguity in the wording of the exemption clause must be construed strictly against the person for whose benefit the clause was introduced. Thus where the defendants took in the plaintiff's car for repairs on the terms that they would not be 'responsible for damage caused by fire to customer's cars on the premises', and the defendants by their negligence caused a fire there which damaged the car, it was held that the above words were not clear enough to exclude liability for the defendants' negligence since the words could be read as merely reminding the plaintiff that the defendants would not be liable for damage caused by a subsequent fire occurring without negligence on their part.[41] Secondly, a person who altogether deviates from the mode of performance of the contract which was contemplated by the parties, such as by contracting to store goods in one building and in fact storing them in another[42] or contracting for the carriage of goods by a specified route and taking the goods by a totally different route,[43] thereby becomes disentitled to rely on the protection of an exemption clause which would have covered him had he been carrying out the contract in the manner originally contemplated by the contracting parties.

Mistake

The existence of what a layman would regard as a mistake will in general have no legal effect upon the validity of the contract; the terms of the bargain will in general be ascertained by an objective examination of what the parties did and said rather than by attempting to peer into what was going on in their innermost thoughts. 'The dispute is as to what the seller promised to the buyer by the words which he used in the contract itself and by his conduct in the course of the negotiations which led up to the contract. What he promised is determined by ascertaining what his words and conduct would have led the buyer reasonably to believe that he was promising . . . . The test is impersonal. It does not depend upon what the seller himself thought he was promising, if the words and conduct by which he communicated his intention to the [buyer] would have led a reasonable man in the position of the buyer to a different belief as to the promise; nor does it depend upon the actual belief of the buyer himself as to what the seller's promise was, unless that belief would have been shared by a reasonable man in the position of the buyer'.[44]

Thus, for example, a shop keeper who agrees to sell an article to a customer for £20 would in general be held to his bargain despite his subsequently proving that it was only by error that he did not demand a price of £30. If however one party is aware that the other party must have made a mistake in the terms of his offer, such as might arise from a gross disparity between the value of the article and the price quoted by its vendor, then he will know there is no true agreement between them as to the terms of the bargain and therefore there will be no contract.[45] Moreover a mistake concerning the existence of the subject-matter of the contract at the time when the contract was made, or a mistake as to the identity of one of the contracting parties, may result in the supposed contract being adjudged to have been a nullity from the outset.

Mistake as to the contents of a signed document

A person who signs a document without sufficiently acquainting himself with its contents, and subsequently finds that he was in error concerning what he supposed to be the contents, can only avoid liability to an innocent person who seeks to enforce the document against him if he can

270

prove that the document was fundamentally different from what he supposed and that he was not negligent.[46]

Illegality

Contracts whose making is prohibited by Parliament, or by governmental or other bodies to whom Parliament has delegated authority to do this, are illegal. In addition certain contracts, such as contracts whose object is to defraud the Revenue,[47] are illegal by the decisions of the courts. The effect of the illegality is that no action can be brought to enforce the contract by either party, and that neither party can recover money or property transferred by him under the illegal contract unless he can make out a cause of action which is genuinely independent of the illegal contract; exceptionally, however, the plaintiff will be allowed to recover his property if the court thinks that he was less blameworthy than the defendant, or if the illegal purpose has not been substantially performed and there is genuine repentance by the plaintiff.[48]

Discharge of contract

When a contract is discharged the parties in general cease to be bound by their obligations towards each other. There are several ways in which the contract may be discharged.

1 *Discharge by performance.* The general rule is said to be that a party to the contract is not discharged by performance until he has exactly carried out that which he agreed to do; thus a builder who agreed to erect certain buildings for the defendant and abandoned the contract after doing little more than half the work was not entitled to recover any part of the price which had previously been agreed to be paid on completion of the whole.[49] But this general rule is much mitigated by a number of exceptions, of which the most important is that if the claimant has substantially performed his side of the bargain, he is liable to pay damages for any deficiency but is entitled to call on the other party to honour his side of the agreement.[50] The rule that a breach of warranty entitles the other party to damages but not to refuse to perform his side (*ante*, page 266) is in substance an embodiment of this principle.

Further exceptions to the general rule arise if the other contracting party prevents performance by the claimant, or if the other party, having an effective option of refusing the partial performance, elects to accept it, or if the contract is by its express terms divisible so that performance of a specified part of the whole by one party expressly entitles him to demand the fulfilment of a specified part of the total contractual obligations of the other.

2 *Discharge by agreement.* If something yet remains to be done by each party in order to fulfil their respective obligations, a simple agreement between them to release the other from his obligations is sufficient since it is supported by consideration on each side in the shape of the release which each grants the other. But if one party has wholly performed his side of the bargain, then any release by him of the other party from his obligations should in general be made by deed (*ante*, page 262) since there is no consideration to support the release; this rule is however modified by the further principle that if a person promises not to insist upon his legal rights, intends that promise to be acted upon and it is in fact acted upon by the other party, he will not be allowed to go back on his promise in an unfair manner.[51]

3 *Discharge by breach.* Breach of a vital obligation, which is therefore a condition of the contract (*ante*, page 266), does not discharge the party at fault who remains fully liable in damages, but does discharge the other party from performing his side of the bargain. The innocent party may however refuse to accept the breach of the other as discharging either party from a full performance, with the result that both parties remain liable to pay damages if they do not carry out their respective obligations.

Breach of warranty does not entitle the other party to treat the contract as discharged; he must perform his side of the agreement and claim damages from the party at fault (*ante*, page 266).

4 *Discharge by frustration.* After the contract has been formed, circumstances may subsequently change so radically as to make performance of the contract something totally different from what the parties had in contemplation when they made the contract, and if this is so the law will declare that the contract is frustrated and its obligations are automatically terminated on the occurrence of the frustrating event. Examples of such changes include the death or long and severe illness of a person who had contracted to render personal service, or the accidental destruction of a building whose continued existence was vital to the fulfilment of the contractual obligation.[52] It may, however, be that a lease can never be frustrated, since some assert that there the foundation of the contract is the creation of the legal term of years, which remains unaffected by any changes which may physically occur to the property.

Where frustration does occur, all sums payable or paid under the contract *prima facie* cease to be payable or are recoverable; however, if money was paid or payable before the frustrating event, the court may award the person to whom it was paid or payable, if that person has incurred expenses, the whole or part of his expenses from it, and if one party has conferred a valuable benefit on the other before the frustrating event the court may award him such sum, not exceeding the value of the benefit, as the court thinks just in all the circumstances.[53]

Remedies for breach of contract

If one party commits a breach of condition (*ante*, page 266), the other party may regard himself as discharged from performance of his own obligations and is also entitled to bring an action for any damage which he has suffered; instead of suing for damages, he may if he wishes claim the value of any work done by him before the time of discharge. For breach of warranty (*ante*, page 266) he may claim damages, but is obliged to perform his own side of the bargain.

The principal remedies which may be available to redress a breach of contract are:

1 *Specific performance.* This is a decree which is issued by the court and which orders the defendant to carry out the promise which he has made. This remedy is discretionary and will not be granted if an award of damages would adequately redress the breach, as in the case of a contract to sell goods of a kind readily obtainable on the open market in any event (*post*, page 291). A contract for the sale of land, on the other hand, would normally be enforceable by a decree of specific performance since the plot of land in question is considered to have a special value in the eyes of the intending purchaser, who could not therefore be expected to be contented with the mere award of damages. Specific performance will not be granted of a contract to render personal service, since it is considered invidious to compel two persons to remain in a close personal relationship with one another. Nor will it be granted of a contract performance of which cannot be ensured without the constant supervision of the court; the remedy will therefore not as a rule be granted as regards a contract to erect or repair buildings, an additional reason for refusal in this case being that damages will normally be an adequate remedy.

2 *An injunction.* This is a court order forbidding the defendant to commit a breach of contract, as for example if he contracts for the benefit of the plaintiff and his land not to build on the defendant's own land, or to restrain the commission of some other wrong, such as commission of

the tort of nuisance through wrongful interference with an easement (*ante*, pages 23–4). As with specific performance it is in the discretion of the court whether or not to grant an injunction.

3   *Damages*. The amount of damages recoverable is governed by the following rules. The damage must either arise in the usual course of things from such a breach, or must be such as may reasonably be supposed to have been in the contemplation of both parties, at the time when they made the contract, as the probable result of the breach.[54] Thus any extraordinary loss which does not arise in the usual course of things and which could not be reasonably thought to have been contemplated by both parties when they made the contract will not be recoverable. Hence in *Pilkington* v. *Wood*[55] the defendant, a solicitor, negligently advised the plaintiff that the title to a house situated in Hampshire was in order, whereupon the plaintiff bought the house for £6,000, having raised the money by means of a bank overdraft. The following year he obtained employment and wished to live in Lancashire, but when he sought to sell his Hampshire house the prospective purchaser declined to complete since the title was found to be bad. Because the plaintiff could not sell the Hampshire house he could not afford to buy a Lancashire house, and thus had to live in a Lancashire hotel during the week and to return each weekend to visit his wife who continued to live in the Hampshire house. In addition to successfully claiming damages from his solicitor for the difference in value between the Hampshire house with a good title at the time when he bought it and its value then with a defective title, the plaintiff also claimed damages for the interest he had paid on his bank overdraft to finance the purchase and £175 for Lancashire hotel expenses, £250 for car journeys between Hampshire and Lancashire at weekends and £50 for nightly telephone calls to his wife in Hampshire; it was ruled that none of these were recoverable, since the solicitor had no actual or constructive knowledge of the plaintiff's need to have an overdraft, and still less could he foresee that the plaintiff would take up work in Lancashire and even less that he would make nightly telephone calls from Lancashire to his wife.

Secondly, if the damages are paid in respect of a sum which would have been taxable had the contract been performed, such as damages in respect of salary lost by reason of wrongful dismissal, the damages paid must be reduced by the estimated amount of taxation which would have been incurred[56] unless the damages themselves are taxable in the hands of the recipient.[57]

Thirdly, the plaintiff must take all reasonable steps to mitigate the loss caused to him, and cannot recover compensation for any part of the damage which is caused by his failure to do so. Thus, for example, a servant who has been wrongfully dismissed will recover only nominal damages if he unreasonably refuses an offer of similar alternative employment on similar terms.[58]

Finally, the parties may contractually stipulate what damages should be payable in the event of a breach. If this sum was intended to be a genuine estimate of the probable loss, that sum will be payable in the event of a breach regardless of whether the actual loss is greater or less than the estimate. But if the sum fixed was instead intended to be a threat to be held over the other party in order to deter him from any breach of contract, it is a penalty and will not be recoverable (unless, unexpectedly, the actual recoverable loss turns out to be at least as great, in which event either the penalty or damages can be claimed); the actual recoverable loss, whose bounds are fixed by the principles already discussed, will instead be claimable. The sum stipulated in the contract as payable in the event of a breach will be ruled to be a penalty if it is extravagant and unconscionable when compared with the greatest loss which could arise from the breach, or if the contractual obligation is to pay money and it is agreed that, on failure to do so punctually, a sum shall be exacted in excess of the amount and reasonable interest; moreover if it is stipulated that a single sum shall be payable on the occurrence of one or more of several breaches, some of which may result in serious and others merely in trifling damage, there is a rebuttable presumption that this is a penalty clause, but the presumption is weakened if it is virtually impossible to prove the exact monetary loss which would arise on a breach.[59] In *Bridge* v. *Campbell Discount Co. Ltd.*[60] a hire-purchase contract in respect of a car included a clause that if the hire-purchase should be terminated for any reason before completion of the contract, the hirer should pay to the owner by way of agreed compensation for depreciation of the vehicle such sum as, with the payments already made by the hirer, would bring the total payments up to two-thirds of the hire-purchase price. Soon after the commencement of the hiring the hirer announced that he would be unable to make any more payments and would have to return the vehicle. This was held to be a breach of contract by the hirer; the minimum payment clause was held a penalty and incapable of being a genuine attempt to estimate the damage, since under the clause the hirer would have to pay most in alleged compensation for depreciation when he had kept the goods for only a short time before defaulting in his payments, at which point in time the goods would in fact have depreciated least! It was, however, said by some judges during the progress of the case through the courts that if the hirer had not broken his contract but had merely exercised a right to terminate it, the question whether the clause was a penalty would not arise since this can only be relevant in the event of a breach of contract, and therefore the hirer would be liable to pay the stipulated sum.

Time limits for suing

An action for breach of a contract made orally or in writing must be brought within six years after the date on which the cause of action arose; the action is brought when the writ which commences it is sealed by the court officer. If the contract was made under seal the action must be brought within twelve years after the date on which the cause of action arose. [61] But in all claims for damages for injury to the person the litigation must be commenced within three years after the injury was caused, [62] with some provision for extension of the period in favour of persons who were unaware of the injury until later. [63] The fact that the plaintiff did not realise he had a claim until the time limit had already expired does not in general extend the time, but if the action is based upon the fraud of the defendant or his agent, or the existence of the right of action was concealed by the fraud of such a person, or the action is for relief from the consequences of mistake in the legal sense (*ante*, pages 270–1), time does not begin to run against the plaintiff until he did or could with reasonable diligence have discovered the fraud or mistake.[64]

An extension of time is allowed for a person who is an infant or is of unsound mind at the time when his cause of action arises, and in such a case the action may be brought at any time within six years from the cessation of his disability or from his death, whichever is earlier.[65]

With regard to a claim for a debt or any other sum whose monetary value is already fixed and known, a written and signed acknowledgement, or part payment, made by the debtor or his agent will start time running afresh from that date. [66] But an acknowledgement in respect of a claim for damages, the amount of which awaits assessment by the court, will not start time running afresh.

A person who, either in addition to or instead of the remedy of damages, seeks the remedies of specific performance or injunction must be very prompt and vigilant to seek these latter remedies, otherwise they will be refused notwithstanding that he still remains within the six or twelve year period, whichever happens to be appropriate.

The sale of goods

General

Goods may be briefly defined as tangibles other than land; familiar examples include furniture, motor cars and cattle. A contract for the sale of goods is one in which the seller either transfers immediately, or agrees to transfer subsequently, the ownership in the goods in return for a money payment. [67] Where under a contract of sale the property ('property' here means ownership) in the goods is transferred from the seller to the buyer the contract is called a sale; but where the transfer of the property in the goods is to take place at a future time or subject to some condition thereafter to be fulfilled the contract is called an agreement to sell. [68] Hence it follows that contracts for the sale of goods do not include contracts for the sale of land, contracts of hire-purchase (because, as will be more fully explained later, the person who takes the goods on hire-purchase has only an option to purchase and has not 'agreed' [i.e. committed himself] to do so), or contracts of barter, i.e. exchange of goods for goods, though if a person furnishes both goods and money in exchange for goods then it is a sale of goods to him and he is the buyer.[69]

A contract for the sale of goods is actionable without any written evidence, although the existence of written evidence is of course desirable in that it reduces the possible scope for argument.

Much of the law relating to the sale of goods is contained in the Sale of Goods Act, 1893, (though many of its provisions relating to the implied conditions and warranties which arise on the sale, and the extent to which these may be excluded, are those substituted by the Supply of Goods (Implied Terms) Act, 1973, the 1973 Act applies to contracts for the sale of goods made on or after 18 May 1973.)[70] The principal function of the Sale of Goods Act is to fill in any gaps which may arise when persons enter into a contract for the sale of goods without addressing their minds to all the legal questions which may arise in consequence. For example, the parties may not give any thought to the question of the precise moment of time at which the transfer of the ownership of the goods from seller to buyer is to take place, and if so the Sale of Goods Act will determine this for them. [71] It is, however, also important to appreciate that most of the rules laid down in the Sale of Goods Act can be excluded if the parties reach an express contrary agreement concerning those matters, thus the Act expressly provides that 'where any right, duty or liability would arise under a contract of sale of goods by implication of law, it may be negatived or varied by express agreement, or by the course of dealing between the parties, or by usage if the usage is such as to bind both parties to the contract'. This, however, is subject to the provisions of the Sale of Goods Act concerning the extent to which the implied conditions and warranties arising under the Act can be excluded. [72] 'The provisions of the Act are in the main confined to statements of what promises are to be implied on the part of the buyer and the seller in respect of matters upon which the contract is silent, and to statements of the consequences of performance or non-performance of promises, whether expressed or implied, where the contract does not state what those consequences are to be'. [73] Moreover the Act includes a provision that the rules of common law, and in particular the rules relating to the effect of fraud, misrepresentation, mistake, or other invalidating cause are to continue to apply to contracts for the sale of goods except insofar as they are inconsistent with the express provisions of the Act. [74]

The issues which most frequently arise in contracts for the sale of goods comprise the following; the suitability of the goods for the needs of the purchaser; who can transfer ownership in the goods; at what moment of time the ownership passes and with what consequences, and the liability of either seller or buyer for unjustifiable refusal either to deliver or to accept delivery of the goods. These will be discussed separately.

Suitability and quality of the goods

As regards the suitability and quality of the goods, the parties may make what stipulations and representations they please during the negotiations leading up to the sale or in the contract of sale, and these if untrue will give rise to the appropriate liabilities depending on whether the statement was a condition, a warranty or a mere representation (see *ante*, pages 266–8). But, in addition, the Sale of Goods Act, 1893, as amended by the Supply of Goods (Implied Terms) Act, 1973, frequently implies certain conditions and warranties into the contract of sale for the benefit of the buyer.

Implied condition that goods must correspond with their description

In a sale of goods by description there is an implied condition that the goods shall correspond with the description, and if the sale is by sample as well as by description the goods must correspond with both sample and description. [75] The term 'sale by description' covers all cases where the buyer has not seen the goods at the time when he contracts to buy them. Thus in *Varley* v. *Whipp* [76] a second-hand reaping machine stated by the seller to be 'new the previous year and only used to cut fifty acres', was purchased in reliance on this without the buyer having seen the machine; it turned out to be a very old one and when the buyer saw it he insisted upon returning it, saying that he did not 'care about old things'. He was held entitled to do so as the goods did not correspond with the description given. It is also a sale by description where the buyer has seen the goods but cannot tell by looking at them that they deviate from the description given him.[77]

In *Beale* v. *Taylor*,[78] the plaintiff saw an advertisement offering a 'Herald Convertible, 1961' for sale. He inspected the car and then bought it. He subsequently found that the car consisted of the rear half of a 1961 Triumph Herald welded to the front half of an earlier model! The plaintiff was held entitled to damages for breach of section 13, having bought in reliance on the description of the car. It is also a sale by description when the goods, though seen, are also sold as goods answering to their description.[79] Furthermore, a sale of goods is not prevented from being a sale by description by reason only that, being exposed for sale or hire, they are selected by the buyer.[80]

In *Hill (Christopher) Ltd.* v. *Ashington Piggeries Ltd.* (*ante*) it was held that herring meal which had become contaminated and poisonous was nevertheless still correctly described as herring meal, since the toxic substance was some constituent element in the herring meal itself which had become harmful and was not a different poisonous substance added to the herring meal. 'I do not believe that the Sale of Goods Act was designed to provide metaphysical discussions as to the nature of what is delivered, in comparison with what is sold. The test of description, at least where commodities are concerned, is intended to be a broader, more common-sense, test of a mercantile character. The question whether that is what the buyer bargained for has to be answered according to such tests as men in the market would apply . . .' (*per* Lord Wilberforce).

The number of tins in a case,[81] the weight of goods in a bag[82] or the length and width of a roll of material[83] are, if specified by the seller, part of the description.

Implied conditions relating to fitness for purpose and quality

As regards fitness for purpose and quality, no implied conditions concerning these arise under the Sale of Goods Act unless the seller sells goods 'in the course of a business'; this includes a sale by a person who in the course of a business is acting as agent for another, except where the other is not selling in the course of a business and the buyer either knows this or reasonable steps were taken to bring it to the notice of the buyer before the making of the contract.[84]

Implied condition as to merchantable quality

Where the seller sells goods in the course of a business, there is an implied condition that the goods supplied under the contract are of merchantable quality.[85] 'Merchantable quality' is defined to mean that the goods 'are as fit for the purpose or purposes for which goods of that kind are commonly bought as it is reasonable to expect having regard to any description applied to them, the price (if relevant) and all the other relevant circumstances'. [86] But there is no condition of merchantable quality: (a) as regards defects specifically drawn to the buyer's attention before the contract is made; or (b) if the buyer examines the goods before the contract is made, as regards defects which that examination ought to reveal.[87]

Where foodstuffs are despatched for transit to the buyer, and although all right when sent off are found (without any abnormal incidents or delays during transit) to have deteriorated excessively on arrival so as to be unsaleable, the goods will not be considered to have been of merchantable quality when sent off unless they were in a condition to withstand the ordinary incidents of transit and to remain saleable within a reasonable time after arrival at their destination. This was laid down in the case of *Beer* v. *Walker*;[88] there a quantity of dead rabbits had been sold in London to be sent by train to Brighton, and, when found unfit for consumption on arrival in Brighton, the buyer was held entitled to refuse to pay for the goods because of breach of the implied condition of merchantable quality. Although Beer's case was decided at a time when there was no statutory definition of 'merchantable quality', it is thought to remain good law despite the new definition inserted by the 1973 Act, as set out above.

Implied condition of reasonable fitness for purpose

Where the seller sells goods in the course of a business and the buyer, expressly or by implication, makes known to the seller any particular purpose for which the goods are being bought, there is an implied condition that the goods supplied under the contract are reasonably fit for that purpose, whether or not that is a purpose for which such goods are commonly supplied, except where the circumstances show that the buyer does not rely, or that it is unreasonable for him to rely, on the seller's skill or judgement.[89]

280

It will be noted that for the implied condition to arise (a) the seller must sell goods in the course of a business, (b) the buyer must expressly or impliedly make known to the seller the particular purpose for which the goods are bought, (c) the buyer must reasonably rely upon the seller's skill or judgement. The following· decisions concerning the Sale of Goods Act, 1893, as it was originally enacted are thought to remain good law after the amendments introduced by the Supply of Goods (Implied Terms) Act, 1973, and to illustrate the above requirements. As regards (b) above, there are many goods, such as a hot water bottle,[90] whose very nature demonstrates what the purchaser wants them for, but where the purchaser wants the goods for a special purpose he should state that purpose expressly to the seller. In *Kendall (Henry) & Sons* v. *William Lillico & Sons Ltd.*[91] it was held that where groundnut meal was sold to be, as the sellers knew, resold by the buyer for compounding into cattle and poultry food, the sellers were liable to indemnify the buyer in respect of damages paid by him when the meal was later found to have contained a toxic substance which poisoned pheasants and partridges to whom it was eventually fed. In *Hill (Christopher) Ltd.* v. *Ashington Piggeries Ltd.*[92] the plaintiffs, compounders of feeding stuffs, contracted with the defendants, who were mink breeders, to compound and deliver to them an animal foodstuff known as 'King Size'; the foodstuff thus supplied resulted in the death of many of the mink because an ingredient, herring meal, which had been supplied to the plaintiffs by a third party, contained a toxic chemical which was especially harmful to mink. The defendants had worked out a formula in accordance with which the compound was to be made, and which, had the formula been observed, would not have contained the toxic ingredient. The plaintiffs sued the defendants for the price of the feeding-stuffs, and the defendants counter-claimed for, among other issues, alleged breach of a condition of reasonable fitness implied by the Sale of Goods, Act, 1893, prior to its amendment by the 1973 Act. The plaintiffs were found to be in breach of this condition, since the defendants, although relying on their own judgement concerning the suitability of the formula they had devised, relied on the plaintiffs' skill in obtaining good quality and non-toxic ingredients to be compounded in accordance with the formula and the plaintiffs knew that the compound would be used for feeding mink; the compound should thus have been reasonably fit for the purpose of feeding the mink. Hill's case illustrates the further point that if the goods are not reasonably fit for the purpose the seller incurs liability for breach of the implied condition irrespective of whether he was or could have been aware of the defect. 'It was no one's fault that the Norwegian herring meal which was an ingredient of the compound feedingstuff for mink made the food poisonous to those animals . . . . In the then state of knowledge, scientific and commercial, no deliberate exercise of human skill or judgement could have prevented the meal from having its toxic effect upon mink. It was sheer bad luck. The question . . . is: who is to bear the loss occasioned by that bad luck?' (*per* Lord Diplock).

Moreover by section 72 of the Agriculture Act, 1970, on the sale of any material for use as a feedingstuff there is an implied warranty by the seller that the material is suitable to be used as such. This warranty is restricted inasmuch as if the material is sold as suitable only for animals of a particular description, no warranty shall be implied by virtue of this provision that the material is suitable for other animals; moreover if the material is sold to be used as a feedingstuff only after being mixed with something else, no warranty shall be implied under this provision that the material is suitable to be so used without being so mixed. The provisions of the section have effect notwithstanding any contract or notice to the contrary.

On the sale of any material of a description, prescribed by regulations, for use as a feedingstuff there is implied, notwithstanding any contract or notice to the contrary, a warranty by the seller that the material does not contain any constituent ingredient of a kind prescribed by regulations, save insofar as the written particulars required by statute to accompany the transaction state to the contrary.[93]

Sales by sample

There are further implied conditions in a sale by sample. A contract is only a contract of sale by sample if there is a term in the contract, express or implied, that it shall be; merely exhibiting a sample during the course of negotiations does not necessarily make it a sale by sample. [94] In a sale by sample there are implied conditions: (a) that the bulk shall correspond with the sample in quality; (b) that the buyer shall have a reasonable opportunity of comparing the bulk with the sample; (c) that the goods are free from any defect, rendering them unmerchantable, which would not be apparent on reasonable examination of the sample.[95]

Implied terms concerning title

There are also implied conditions and warranties concerning the seller's title to the goods. Unless the circumstances show an intention that the seller should only transfer such title as there may chance to be, there is:

282

(a) an implied condition in the case of a sale that the seller has a right to sell the goods, and in an agreement to sell that he will have that right at the time when the ownership is to pass; and

(b) an implied warranty that the goods are, and will remain until the ownership is to pass, free from any charge or incumbrance (such as a mortgage) not known to the buyer before the contract is made, and that the buyer will enjoy quiet possession except insofar as disturbed by the holder of a charge or incumbrance thus known to the buyer.[96]

Where the circumstances show an intention that the seller shall only transfer such title as he may chance to have, there are implied warranties that the goods will be free from charges and incumbrances known to the seller but unknown to the buyer before the contract is made, and that neither the seller nor certain other persons will disturb the buyer's quiet possession of the goods.[97] Any clause in any contract seeking to exclude the implied conditions and warranties concerning title, freedom from charges and incumbrances, and quiet possession as set out above is a void clause.[98]

The application of the conditions and warranties above may be illustrated by decisions, which appear to remain good law, concerning earlier and somewhat similar legislation. As regards the implied condition concerning title, if this condition is broken the plaintiff can recover the whole of the purchase price from the seller notwithstanding that the plaintiff may have had the use of the goods in question for some considerable time; this is because the plaintiff paid his money to get ownership of the goods, not the mere use without ownership, and he has got no ownership whatsoever.[99] As regards the implied warranty that the buyer shall have quiet possession of the goods, in *Mason* v. *Burningham*[100] the defendant purported to sell a typewriter to the plaintiff for £20; the plaintiff spent upwards of £11 on repairs to the typewriter, and subsequently discovered it to be owned by a third party to whom it had to be returned. The plaintiff sued the defendant for breach of the warranty of quiet possession, and was held entitled to recover as damages the whole amount expended, including the cost of repairs, since the wasted expenditure was reasonably incurred and was a direct and natural result of the defendant's breach of warranty.

Exclusion of the implied conditions and warranties

It is not possible to exclude the implied conditions and warranties relating to the seller's title, the buyer's quiet possession and the freedom of the goods from charges and incumbrances not known to the buyer. The position regarding exclusion of the conditions implied by the Sale of Goods Act, 1893 (as substituted by the 1973 Act) relating to description, merchantable quality, fitness for purpose and sales by sample depends upon whether or not the sale in question is to be classified as a 'consumer sale'. 'Consumer sale' is defined to mean a sale of goods (other than a sale by auction or by competitive tender) by a seller in the course of a business where the goods: (a) are of a type ordinarily bought for private use or consumption; and (b) are sold to a person who does not buy or hold himself out as buying them in the course of a business; the task of proving that a sale is not a consumer sale rests on the person who alleges this.[101]

As regards a 'consumer sale', any clause seeking to exclude the conditions implied by the 1893 Act regarding description, merchantable quality, fitness for purpose and sales by sample is a void clause. As regards a non-consumer sale, any clause seeking to exclude those implied conditions is not enforceable to the extent that it is shown to be unfair or unreasonable to allow the seller to rely on the clause; in deciding this regard must be had to all the circumstances, and in particular to the following:

(a) the relative strength of the bargaining positions of the seller and buyer towards each other, including taking into account the availability of suitable alternative products and sources of supply;
(b) whether the buyer received an inducement to agree to the exemption clause, or in accepting it had an opportunity of buying the goods or suitable alternatives from any other source of supply and without such a clause;
(c) whether the buyer knew or ought reasonably to have known of the existence and extent of the exemption clause;
(d) whether it was reasonable at the time of the contract to expect that it would be practicable to comply with the condition from which the clause seeks to exempt the seller;
(e) whether the goods were made, processed or adapted to the special order of the buyer.[102]

The buyer's remedies for breach of the implied terms

A warranty is a term collateral to the main purpose of the contract; a breach of warranty entitles the other party to claim damages but not to reject the goods and treat the contract as repudiated. [103] A condition is thus by inference a vital term whose breach *prima facie* entitles the buyer to reject the goods and to claim damages. The buyer may, however, elect if he chooses to treat a breach of condition as if it were a breach of warranty, and if so will have to keep the goods and content himself with damages only. In addition, section 11(1)(c) of the Act provides that the buyer must treat a breach of condition as if it were a breach of warranty, with the above consequences, if the contract is not severable and the buyer has accepted the goods or part thereof. A contract of sale is not severable unless expressly stated to be so, so that attention centres on when the buyer will be taken to have 'accepted' the goods. The buyer will be taken to have accepted the goods:

(a)   when he intimates to the seller that he has accepted them; or

(b)   when the goods have been delivered to him and he does any act in relation to them which is inconsistent with the seller's ownership (e.g. reselling them), subject to the overriding proviso that he will not be deemed to have accepted the goods until he has had a reasonable chance to examine them; or

(c)   where the buyer keeps the goods beyond a reasonable time without notifying the seller that he has rejected them.[104]

Who can transfer ownership

The general rule is that only the person who owns the goods, or someone whom the owner has authorised to sell the goods on the owner's behalf, can pass the ownership on. Thus it follows that in general the innocence of the purported buyer avails him not at all should he chance to deal with someone who, although perhaps the possessor of the article, is neither the owner nor has the owner's authority to sell it. To this general rule there are a number of exceptions too lengthy and complex to merit detailed treatment here; the most important is to be found in section 25(1) of the Sale of Goods Act, 1893, whereby if a person, having sold goods, remains in possession of the goods or documents of title to them, then any delivery or transfer by him of the goods or documents by way of sale or other disposition will give a good title to a person who takes in good faith and without notice of the previous sale; similar provisions apply to validate dispositions made by persons who have bought or agreed to buy the goods, and who obtain possession of the goods or the documents of title to them with the seller's consent.[105]

A further exception is that a mercantile agent may be able to pass title to goods with whose possession he has been entrusted by his principal for a mercantile purpose. A mercantile agent is an 'agent having in the customary course of his business as such agent authority either to sell goods, or to consign goods for the purpose of sale, or to buy goods, or to raise money on the security of goods'.[106] This covers persons whose business it is to have the goods of others with authority to dispose of them, such as a second-hand car dealer selling the cars on commission.[107]

Where a mercantile agent is, with the consent of the owner, in possession of goods or of the documents of title to them, then any sale, pledge or other disposition of the goods made by him when acting in the ordinary course of business of a mercantile agent is as valid as if he were expressly authorised by the owner of the goods to do so; provided that the person taking under the disposition acts in good faith, and has not at the time of the disposition notice that the person making the disposition has no authority to do so.[108] Compliance with the section thus enables the mercantile agent to pass a good title to the goods to an innocent third party notwithstanding any breach of instruction as between the mercantile agent and the person who entrusted him with the goods, such as a restriction on the price at which the goods were to be sold. This provision however only applies if the mercantile agent is entrusted with possession of the goods or documents of title in his mercantile capacity, thus it will not apply if the articles are handed over to him merely in his capacity as a friend,[109] or if a car is sent to the garage of a mercantile agent merely for the purpose of repair. Moreover the mercantile agent can only pass a good title under this provision if the disposition by him was made in the ordinary course of business of a mercantile agent; this means that he must act as if he were carrying out a transaction which he was authorised to carry out, and within business hours at a proper place of business, and in other respects in the ordinary way in which a mercantile agent would act, so that there is nothing to give rise to suspicion in the person dealing with him.[110] In general a sale of a car without its log book is not a sale in the ordinary course of business, and if title is to be passed under the Factors Act the mercantile agent must have possession in his mercantile capacity and with the owner's consent of both car and log book.[111]

The time at which ownership of the goods is transferred

It is often extremely important to determine the time at which transfer of the ownership takes place; reasons for its importance include the fact that, as has just been shown, in general only the owner can pass the ownership further. Moreover if the goods are stolen, or destroyed without fault, as for example in a transit collision which occurs without negligence, the loss usually falls on whoever owned the goods at that point in time. Again, if ownership has passed the seller of the goods may sue the buyer for the price, but if not the seller's remedy is damages only.

For these and other reasons it is often vital to know where the ownership lies. If the parties to the contract of sale address their minds to the question they can make what rules they choose as to when the ownership shall pass, but if, as is frequent, they never think about it the Sale of Goods Act, 1893, will fill the gap through the rules laid down in section 18 of the Act.

First, there are specific goods, meaning goods identified and agreed upon by both parties at the time when the contract of sale is made.[112] Examples of such goods include 'this car', 'this chair', provided both parties have identified the precise article in question at the time when the contract of sale is made; to identify them afterwards would not make them specific goods. It excludes even articles defined in the contract with some degree of particularity, such as 'a 1971 Mark VI Lugubrious sports car', unless the parties have agreed on the precise car which is to be delivered in fulfilment of the contract; it is not sufficient that they have agreed on the precise make of the car. It also excludes a contract to sell some articles from out of a larger bulk, such as 'a dozen bottles of champagne out of my stock of a thousand bottles', unless in this example the parties had at the time of making the contract identified the exact dozen bottles which were to be used in its fulfilment.

When there is an unconditional contract for the sale of specific goods in a deliverable state, the ownership in such goods passes at the time when the contract of sale is made; it is immaterial that the time of delivery or payment is postponed.[113] Goods are in a 'deliverable state' when in such a state that the buyer would, under the contract, be bound to take delivery of them.[114] It should be particularly noted that ownership in such goods passes although delivery or payment or both are not to take place until later.

Where there is a contract for the sale of specific goods and the seller is bound to do something to them in order to put them into a deliverable state, the ownership does not pass until this has been done and the buyer has notice thereof.[115]

Where there is a contract for the sale of specific goods in a deliverable state, and the seller is bound to weigh, measure, test or do some similar thing with reference to the goods for the purpose of ascertaining the price, the ownership does not pass until this has been done and the buyer has notice thereof.[116]

All goods which are not specific are known as unascertained or future goods. The ownership in such goods passes when goods of the contract description and in a deliverable state are unconditionally appropriated to the contract by either party with the express or implied assent of the other party.[117] 'Unconditional appropriation' seems to mean an irrevocable selection of particular goods in fulfilment of the contract. In *Aldridge* v. *Johnson* [118] a person contracted to buy a quantity of barley out of a large heap of barley, and left a number of his sacks to be filled with barley by the seller; the seller duly filled some of the sacks with barley from the heap, and later changed his mind and poured the contents of the sacks back on to the heap. It was held that the ownership of the barley in the filled sacks passed to the buyer at the time of their filling.

Where the buyer writes to or telephones the seller and asks him to send the goods to the buyer, it seems clear that the buyer thereby gives his consent to the seller appropriating goods in fulfilment of the contract, thus ownership of such goods, if in a deliverable state, will pass once the seller has irrevocably done so.

Finally if goods are sent 'on approval' or 'on sale or return' or other similar terms they are governed by a special rule. The ownership of such goods passes to the buyer when he signifies his approval or acceptance to the seller, or does any other act adopting the transaction (such as reselling the goods), or if he keeps the goods beyond the time fixed for their return, or if no time has been fixed he keeps them longer than is reasonable. [119]

As already mentioned, in general the risk of the loss of the goods due to their theft, or by reason of their being destroyed without fault, must be borne by whoever was owner of the goods at the time when these events occurred. But if either the seller or the buyer has the custody of the goods, and the goods are destroyed because of his negligence, then *prima facie* he must bear the loss because of his negligent custodianship. Also if delivery of the goods is delayed by the fault of either party, the goods are at the risk of the party at fault as regards any loss which might not otherwise have occurred. [120] Thus when the defendant contracted to buy a large quantity of apple juice from the seller, and owing to the defendant's failure to issue instructions concerning delivery despite repeated requests from the seller to do so a substantial quantity of the juice went bad, the loss was held to fall on the defendant because of his delay in taking delivery of the juice. [121]

Performance of the contract

Stipulations as to time of payment for the goods are not of 'the essence' of a contract for the sale of goods unless the contrary is shown by the terms of the contract. [122] *Prima facie*, therefore, the buyer's failure to pay for the goods on the date stipulated does not without more entitle the seller to treat the contract as discharged. Conversely in contracts for the sale of goods the date of delivery is often of the essence,[123] particularly as regards purchases in bulk where the goods are likely to be required for resale, thus if the seller fails to deliver the goods on the agreed date the buyer is often entitled to treat the contract as at an end.

If the seller has contracted to send the goods to the buyer and no time for delivery was fixed by the contract he must send them within a reasonable time.[124]

'Delivery' means transfer of possession and, subject to contrary agreement, does not connote delivery at the buyer's home or place of business. Thus section 29 of the Act states that, unless otherwise agreed, the place of delivery is the seller's place of business if he has one, and failing this his residence; the only exception relates to specific goods (*ante*, page 287). which both parties knew when making the contract to be elsewhere than at the seller's residence or place of business, in which event the place where those goods then were is the place of delivery.

Unless otherwise agreed, delivery of the goods and payment of the price are concurrent conditions to the extent that neither of these can be demanded unless the demandant is willing to perform the other,[125] thus the seller must be ready to hand over the goods in exchange for the price and, conversely, can assert his lien (*post*) over the goods until the price is tendered to him.

Remedies of the unpaid seller

A seller is unpaid if the whole of the price has not been paid or tendered, or if he has taken a cheque or other similar instrument as conditional payment and the instrument has been dishonoured.[126] An unpaid seller who remains in possession of the goods sold may retain them (his 'lien') until the price has been paid if no period of credit has been agreed, or if the duration of credit agreed has expired, or if the buyer is insolvent;[127] a buyer can be insolvent without being bankrupt, and is so if he has ceased to pay his debts in the ordinary course of business or cannot pay his debts as they become due.[128]

The seller loses his right to retain possession of the goods if either he delivers the goods to a carrier or other person for transmission to the buyer without reserving the right of disposal, or if the buyer or his agent lawfully obtains possession of the goods, or if the seller waives his right.[129]

If the goods are in course of transit towards the buyer and the seller learns that the buyer is insolvent, the seller has the right to instruct the carrier to stop the transit and redeliver the goods to the seller, thus enabling the seller to retain possession of them until the price has been paid.[130] Moreover the unpaid seller, once he has exercised his lien or his right to stop the goods in transit, may resell the goods if either he expressly reserved the right to do so in the original contract of sale, or if the goods are of a perishable nature, or if he gives notice to the buyer of his intention to resell and the buyer does not within a reasonable time pay or tender the price.[131] If he does resell in these circumstances the effect is to set aside the first contract of sale,[132] though if the resale price is less than the purchase price under the first contract the seller may sue the first buyer in damages for the difference.[133] Since the effect of the resale is to set aside the first sale it follows that any increase in price obtained on the second sale will belong to the seller.

In addition to exercising the above remedies through the medium of the goods themselves, the seller may also sue the defaulting buyer personally. An action by the seller for the price of the goods lies if either the ownership in the goods has passed to the buyer or if in the contract of sale the price was expressed to be payable on a fixed date irrespective of delivery of the goods.[134] If ownership in the goods has not passed to the buyer and the contract price was not expressed to be payable on a fixed date, the seller's remedy against the buyer is a claim only for damages for breach of contract, and the damages are almost certain to be a great deal less than the contract price. The measure of damages is the estimated loss directly and naturally resulting, in the ordinary course of events, from the buyer's breach of contract.[135] Where there is an available market for the goods, the measure of damages is *prima facie* the difference between their price under the contract of sale and the market price at the time when the goods ought to have been accepted, or, if no time was fixed for acceptance, then at the time when the buyer wrongfully refused to accept them. In *W. L. Thompson Ltd.* v. *Robinson (Gunmakers) Ltd.*[136] the defendant buyer wrongfully refused to take delivery of a new car which he had ordered from the plaintiff, a dealer in cars; the dealer managed to persuade the manufacturers to release him from his own obligation to take the car. Nevertheless the dealer sued the buyer for damages resulting from the buyer's wrongful refusal to take delivery; he was entitled to recover the loss of the profit which he would have made had the buyer taken delivery of the car, because supply of cars of that type exceeded the demand for them in the locality at that time and thus the dealer's loss of profit was the natural and ordinary consequence of the buyer's breach of contract. But in *Charter* v. *Sullivan*[137] the facts were similar to those of Thompson's case except that here at the relevant time demand for cars of the type in question exceeded their supply and the seller could sell every car of that type which he could get; he thus lost no profit, despite the buyer's breach, because he promptly sold every car of that type anyway, and was thus entitled to nominal damages only.

The buyer's remedies against the seller

If the seller breaks a condition or a warranty of the contract then the buyer will have the appropriate remedies against him (*ante*, pages 284–5).

By section 52, the court has discretion, in an action for breach of a contract to deliver specific (see *ante*, page 287), or ascertained goods (i.e. goods identified by the parties after the time when the contract for sale was made), to order specific performance (see *ante*, page 273), so that the goods are delivered *in specie* to the buyer. Such an order will not be granted if damages would be an adequate remedy, and damages will be adequate if such goods are readily obtainable by purchase elsewhere, [138] but specific performance may be granted if the goods in question are of a rare or unique nature.

If the seller wrongfully fails to deliver the goods the buyer may sue him for damages; the general principles which govern the amount of damages recoverable are analogous to those already discussed concerning the seller's right to sue the buyer for damages for non-acceptance. Thus since only the damage which normally flows from the breach of contract is recoverable, it follows that any specially large profit which the buyer would have made by reselling the goods, and which he now loses by reason of the seller's failure to deliver the goods to him, will normally be irrecoverable as such [139] and the damages will be limited to the difference between the contract price and the market price. But if the seller actually knew of the probable resale at the time when he contracted to sell, then the loss of the extra profits of the sale could well flow normally from the seller's breach of contract in view of his enhanced knowledge of the probable consequences. [140]

There is throughout the law of contract a general duty on the contracting parties to minimise their loss so far as they reasonably can (*ante*, pages 274–5). Insofar therefore as a person suffering from another person's breach of contract could reasonably have averted his own loss, he will not be allowed to recover damages for a loss which he could himself have prevented.

Hire-purchase

General

Hire-purchase transactions are at present widespread and popular in this country because they enable the person hiring the goods to obtain the use and enjoyment of them before he has paid for them, although ultimately he may find himself paying dearly for this privilege in that the rate of interest charged on hire-purchase transactions is usually rather high. In view of the ferocious terms imposed by some hire-purchase agreements in the past, Parliament has intervened and nowadays the contents of the agreement and the rights of the hirer are to a considerable extent regulated by statute.

Section 1 of the Hire-Purchase Act, 1965, defines a 'hire-purchase agreement' as 'an agreement for the bailment of goods under which the bailee may buy the goods, or under which the property in the goods will or may pass to the bailee'. 'Bailment' means the transfer of possession of the goods for a particular purpose, and 'the bailee' is the person having possession of the goods for that purpose. Generally speaking, the basis of a hire-purchase agreement is the transfer of possession of the goods to the hirer, coupled with an option in the hirer to purchase the goods if he so chooses; the agreement usually states that this option is exercised on his making the last of all the payments which are mentioned in the agreement. A hire-purchase of goods is thus to be distinguished from a sale of them; in the latter case the buyer has contractually bound himself from the outset to pay the whole price for them. Nevertheless, in merely monetary terms the distinction is somewhat unreal, since the payment of the final sum needed to exercise the option and to complete the purchase of the goods is usually only of small amount.

It is important to remember that the dealer whose showrooms stocked the article which is the subject-matter of the hire-purchase agreement is not in general the person who enters into a hire-purchase agreement with the customer; the dealer usually sells the article in question to a finance company and it is the finance company who enter into a hire-purchase agreement with the customer; the customer may sometimes be required to provide a guarantor (see *ante*, page 264). 'The difficulty and the artificiality about hire-purchase cases arises . . . from the fact that the member of the public involved imagines himself to be buying the article by instalments from the dealer, whereas he is in fact hirer of the article from a finance company with whom he has been brought willy nilly into contact, of whom he knows nothing, and which on its part has never seen the goods which are the subject-matter of the hire' (*per* Harman L.J. in *Ycoman Credit, Ltd.* v. *Apps*).[141] Thus there will be no contract of sale between the dealer and the customer and consequently no recourse by the customer against the dealer in respect of alleged defects in the article in question,[142] although sometimes the dealer may be liable to the customer if he makes an express representation concerning the goods which subsequently turns out to be incorrect. In *Andrews* v. *Hopkinson*[143] the plaintiff approached the defendant, a garage proprietor, with a view to buying a second-hand motor car on hire-purchase. The defendant said 'It's a good little bus. I would stake my life on it'. This the hirer came close to doing, since soon after he hired it the steering snapped and he collided with another vehicle, suffering serious injuries; he had agreed to hire the car from a finance company to whom the dealer sold it. It was held that the dealer was liable under a secondary contract between himself and the hirer; the consideration for this secondary contract seems to be that the dealer warrants the condition of the vehicle in return for the hirer agreeing to enter into a hire-purchase agreement with the finance company, to whom the dealer would otherwise be unable to dispose of the car.

Where the owner lets goods under a hire-purchase agreement within the 1965 Act, any representations with respect to these goods made to the hirer by a person other than the owner in the course of antecedent negotiations conducted by that other person are deemed to have been made by him as agent of the owner;[144] any clause to the contrary contained in the hire-purchase agreement is void.[145] Consequently representations made by the dealer are treated as if made by the owner, who will be the finance company, and the finance company will be liable accordingly. The hirer's remedies will vary according to the nature of the representation. If the court holds the representation must be taken as having been intended to be a term of the contract, it may be either a condition or a warranty (see *ante*, page 266). If neither a condition not a warranty, it will depend on whether the representation was fraudulent, negligent or neither of these (*ante*, pages 266–8).

Agreements governed by the Hire-Purchase Act, 1965

The Hire-Purchase Act, 1965, governs all hire-purchase agreements where the hire-purchase price does not exceed £2,000;[146] there is one exception to this, which is that the Act does not apply where the hirer is a body corporate.[147]

Any deposit, whether paid in money or in goods, or other initial payment by the hirer under the hire-purchase agreement forms part of the hire-purchase price.[148]

Formalities when making the agreement

The Act lays down various formalities relating to the formation of the agreement which must be complied with. Before the agreement is made, the cash price of the goods must be notified to the hirer, but it is sufficient if the hirer had made a previous inspection of the goods with labels clearly showing the cash price affixed, or if he selected the goods from a catalogue, price list or advertisement clearly stating the cash price.[149] The agreement must be signed by the hirer personally, and by or on behalf of all other parties.[150] The agreement itself must contain a statement of the cash price, the hire-purchase price, the amount of each instalment and the dates on which they are payable, a list of the goods and a statement of the hirer's right to terminate the agreement under section 27 and the restrictions which the Act imposes on the owner's right to recover the goods.[151]
The hirer must be given at least one copy (and in some circumstances a second copy) of the agreement. An owner who fails to comply with the formalities *prima facie* cannot enforce the agreement or any guarantee or security given in relation to it nor can he recover the goods from the hirer,[152] but the court may dispense with compliance with any of these formalities, other than that of stating the hirer's right to cancel the agreement under section 11 (see *post*), if satisfied that it would be just and equitable to do so and that the hirer has not been prejudiced.[153]

Hirer's right to cancel the agreement under section 11

In order to put some brake upon the activities of door to door salesmen when they succeed in committing the hirer to enter into a hire-purchase agreement without sufficient meditation, section 11 of the Act permits the hirer, where the hire-purchase agreement is not made 'at appropriate trade premises', to serve notice of cancellation upon the owner within a short period after the making of the agreement, and this cancellation will be efficacious and the agreement is deemed never to have had any effect. The period within which notice of cancellation may be served is within four days beginning with the day on which the hirer receives the copy of the agreement[154] which the owner is required to post to the hirer within seven days after the making of the agreement.[155]

Implied conditions and warranties

Subject to appropriate changes of terminology whereby 'seller', 'buyer', 'sale' and the like are substituted by 'owner', 'hirer', 'hire-purchase' and the like the conditions and warranties implied into hire-purchase agreements by the Supply of Goods (Implied Terms) Act, 1973, and the extent to which they may be excluded are analogous to the provisions applicable to the sale of goods.[156] It must be noted that, as with contracts of sale of goods, this is only true of contracts of hire-purchase made on or after 18 May 1973; contracts of hire-purchase made before that date will continue to be governed by the law in force prior to the 1973 Act, and details of that law are not included in this book.

If the purported 'owner' should subsequently turn out not to have been in fact the owner, thus breaking the condition which is normally implied regarding his title, the hirer may repudiate the agreement and recover what has already been paid, and need make no allowance in respect of his enjoyment of the goods in the meantime; this ruling was given in a case where the condition as to title arose irrespective of legislation.[157]

Decisions of the judges show that various conditions and warranties will, irrespective of any enactment by Parliament, be implied into a hire-purchase agreement unless otherwise agreed by the parties; the validity of an exemption clause seeking to exclude these non-statutory implied conditions and warranties is governed by the ordinary law of contract (*ante*, pages 268–70). One such condition is that the person who lets the goods is their owner at the time when he hands over possession to the hirer.[158] It is, moreover, fundamental to the contract of hiring that the goods hired out must correspond with the description of the goods in the contract of hiring (*Astley Industrial Trust Ltd.* v. *Grimley*).[159] (The view was also expressed in Grimley's case that it is not possible to contract out of this fundamental obligation, but this must, provided the exemption clause is clear and explicit, be regarded as doubtful in consequence of opinions expressed in *Suisse Atlantique Société d'Armement Maritime S.A.* v. *N.V. Rotterdamsche Kolen Centrale.*[160])

No implied conditions or warranties concerning the quality or fitness for any particular purpose of goods let on hire-purchase can arise except under an Act of Parliament or by usage (such as the usage of a particular trade).[161]

The hirer is under an implied obligation to take reasonable care of the goods let on hire, and the burden is on the hirer to show that the loss or damage occurred without failure on his part to use reasonable care.[162]

Hirer's right to terminate the agreement

The Hire-Purchase Act, 1965, entitles the hirer under a hire-purchase agreement which comes within the Act to terminate the agreement at any time before the final payment becomes due, by giving notice in writing to any person authorised to receive the sums payable under the agreement. [163] This right cannot be excluded by agreement to the contrary. [164] If he exercises this right, the hirer becomes liable to pay all instalments which have accrued due before he terminates, and also such sum (if any) as is required to bring his total payments up to one half of the hire-purchase price. This requirement that at least one half of the hire-purchase price be paid is doubtless intended as a rough and ready compensation to the owner for the depreciation in the value of the goods during their use by the hirer. But the hirer might terminate the agreement soon after its inception, and in such a case payment of half the hire-purchase price seems an excessive compensation, thus the Act provides that the court may award a lesser sum than one half if satisfied that this covers the owner's loss. If the hirer failed to take reasonable care of the goods he must also pay damages for such failure, and he must permit the owner to retake the goods. [165]

It should be observed that hire-purchase agreements frequently contain a clause, usually referred to as a minimum payments clause, that where the hirer fails to complete the purchase of the goods the hirer shall pay a specific sum to the owner as a minimum. Such a clause is frequently designed to recoup the owner for loss of profit as well as compensate him for depreciation of the goods. Sometimes these clauses are of an extortionate nature as, for example, by requiring a payment of three-quarters of the hire-purchase price, regardless of how soon the hirer terminates the agreement; in one case the actual damage was assessed at £30, whereas £206 was claimed under the minimum payment provision.

Section 29 of the Act makes void any clause in the agreement whereby the hirer after its termination in any manner whatever (e.g. by the owner for breach of agreement by the hirer) is made liable to pay a sum which exceeds whichever is the less of half the hire-purchase price or an amount equal to the loss sustained by the owner. This provision limits the amount which the owner, when he terminates the agreement, can claim under a clause in the agreement stipulating that the hirer shall pay a specified sum as a minimum. If the hirer commits a breach of his obligations under the contract, the owner is entitled to claim damages for this breach. Sometimes it may not be clear whether the hirer is renouncing his obligations under the contract or exercising his right to terminate it under section 27 of the 1965 Act; the financial consequences to the hirer are likely to be different, since the damages recoverable by the owner in the former case are governed by the ordinary law of contract (*ante,* pages 274–6).

As regards hire-purchase agreements which fall outside the 1965 Act, either because the hire-purchase price exceeds £2,000 or because the hirer is a company, the hire-purchase agreement will frequently contain a clause stating what is to happen if the hirer defaults in payment and the minimum sum which the hirer must pay in such a case. If the amount so specified appears to be a penal sum, bearing no relation to the actual loss likely to be suffered by the owner, then if the hirer breaks his part of the bargain the court may grant him relief against this penal clause and award the owner reasonable compensation only. But it is said that this relief can only be granted where the hirer breaks his side of the contract and not when he terminates it under a clause permitting him to do so.[166]

Termination of the hire-purchase agreement by the owner

In practice a hire-purchase agreement will always contain a clause giving the owner the right to terminate the agreement if the hirer breaks the terms. The hirer remains liable to pay the arrears of instalments of hire due at the time when the agreement comes to an end,[167] or to pay compensation to the owner under a valid (see *ante*) minimum payment clause which is operative on termination. But termination ends the hirer's obligation to pay future instalments.

Owner's right to retake the goods

Should the hiring of the goods terminate before the hirer completes the purchase, the hirer is, apart from any protection conferred on him by statute, under a duty to permit the owner to retake the goods, and the owner may recover possession either by retaking them or by bringing an action for possession. If the hirer refuses to allow the owner to retake the goods, it is doubtful whether the owner is justified in retaking them by reasonable force, and the owner is thus best advised to bring a lawsuit. One of the main objects of the Hire-Purchase Act, 1965, is to limit the power of the owner to recover possession of the goods, because hire-purchase agreements normally confer on him the right to end the hiring and repossess the goods upon any breach of its terms by the hirer, or may provide for automatic termination of the agreement upon breach by the hirer. Thus a trifling default by the hirer in the payment of instalments, perhaps due to illness or temporary unemployment, may *prima facie* give the owner an opportunity hastily to recover possession of the goods even though a substantial proportion of the hire-purchase price has already been paid. But as regards a hire-purchase agreement which falls within the Act, such rights cannot be exercised until a default notice has been delivered or addressed to the hirer, stating the amount in arrears and requiring it to be paid within a specified period which must not be less than seven days after service of the notice; if the hirer pays the arrears within the specified period the owner cannot then exercise the above rights. [168]

Any provision in any hire-purchase agreement coming within the Act which permits the owner or his agent to enter upon private premises in order to retake possession of the goods is void, [169] but this does not prevent the hirer consenting, if he sees fit, to their repossession.

Any clause in a hire-purchase agreement coming within the Act which provides that on the death of the hirer the hiring shall end or any sums payable by the hirer shall be increased or accelerated is a void clause. [170]

Once one-third of the hire-purchase price due under a hire-purchase agreement coming within the Act has been paid or tendered, the goods thereupon become protected goods and, unless the hirer himself elects to put an end to the agreement, the owner cannot retake the goods from the hirer without the hirer's consent unless the owner obtains an order of the County Court permitting this. If the owner retakes the goods in disregard of this provision, the agreement forthwith terminates if not already terminated and the hirer and any guarantor may recover all sums which have been paid by them under the agreement. [171] This is a pretty stringent sanction against an owner who disregards this statutory provision, since the hirer ultimately pays nothing in respect of his previous use of the goods, but the hirer only retrieves his money and the court has no power to award him damages or to order return of the goods to him, because the agreement has terminated since the Act says so. [172] If upon demand made by the owner the hirer freely and voluntarily delivers up protected goods to him, there is no breach of the provision in the Act which restricts the retaking of the goods. [173]

If the owner brings an action in the County Court to recover the protected goods the court may (a) order return of all the goods to the owner; or (b) make such an order but suspend its coming into effect on condition that the hirer pays the unpaid balance of the hire-purchase price at such times and in such amounts as the court, having regard to the means of the hirer, thinks just, and subject to fulfilment by the hirer of such other conditions as the court thinks just. Under a postponed order the hirer holds the goods on the terms of the old agreement except insofar as these are varied by the court; the variation will quite probably allow him more time to pay; or (c) order return of some of the goods to the owner and vest the title to the remainder in the hirer, but the maximum value of the goods which can be vested in the hirer is fixed by deducting from the sum paid by him one-third of the sum unpaid;[174] this third order is of course only possible if the goods are divisible in their nature. If the hirer defaults in making payment under the terms of a postponed order made under (b) above, the owner may immediately repossess the goods without any further application to the court, but if the hirer fails to comply with some other provision of the postponed order then the owner cannot re-possess the goods without further application to the court.[175]

Hire-purchase agreements outside the Hire-Purchase Act, 1965

If the agreement falls outside the Hire-Purchase Act, 1965, because the hire-purchase price exceeds £2,000 or because the hirer is a body corpo-rate, the rights and obligations of the parties are governed by the express terms of the contract which they have made, and by such further terms as are implied by law irrespective of any enactment (*ante*, page 295), so far as the express terms do not exclude the implied ones; their rights and obligations are also governed by the Supply of Goods (Implied Terms) Act, 1973 (*ante*, page 295), and the rights and obligations arising under that Act can only be excluded by contrary agreement insofar as is per-mitted by the Act (*ante*, page 295). The impact of the Supply of Goods (Implied Terms) Act, 1973, on hire-purchase agreements is however re-stricted to hire-purchase agreements made on or after 18 May 1973; hire-purchase agreements made prior to that date and which also fall outside the Hire-Purchase Act, 1965, are governed by the express terms of the contract, and by such further terms as are implied by law (*ante*, page 295) insofar as the express terms do not exclude the implied ones.

Purported sale by the hirer of the goods he holds on hire-purchase

Since the hirer has only possession of the goods the general rule is that he cannot pass the title in them to a third party. Hire-Purchase Information Ltd. is a company which keeps a central register of agricultural equip-ment, motor vehicles, caravans and similar chattels let under hire-purchase agreements. These records can be made available to the general public through the Citizens Advice Bureau, thus a prospective purchaser can and should first ascertain whether there is in existence a hire-purchase agree-ment relating to the chattel which he desires to purchase.

A statutory exception to the hire-purchaser's general inability to pass title to the goods on hire-purchase arises under Part III of the Hire-Purchase Act, 1964; this exception applies only to motor vehicles, but applies to all those held under hire-purchase agreements, even if they fall outside the financial limits of the 1965 Act and even if the hirer is a body corporate. Part III applies where a motor vehicle has been let under a hire-purchase agreement and before the property in the vehicle has become vested in the hirer he disposes of the car to another person; this provision also applies to all conditional sale agreements (*post*) whether or not within the statutory limits.[176] 'Disposition' by the hirer to a purchaser is defined to include any sale or contract of sale or letting under a hire-purchase agreement.[177] A private purchaser who takes in good faith and without notice of the hire-purchase agreement or conditional sale agreement obtains a good title.[178] But a 'trade or finance purchaser' does not get a good title; a trade or finance purchaser is defined as a purchaser who at the time of the disposition to him carries on a business which consists wholly or partly of purchasing motor vehicles for the purpose of offering or exposing them for sale, or providing finance by purchasing motor vehicles for the purpose of offering or exposing them for sale, or providing finance by purchasing motor vehicles for the purpose of letting them under hire-purchase agreements or agreeing to sell them under conditional sale agreements.[179] But a private purchaser can obtain a good title from a trade or finance purchaser,[180] and if a private purchaser has obtained a good title he can pass on a good title to a trade or finance purchaser.

The letting of animals on hire-purchase

Where animals are let on hire-purchase, their offspring belong to the hirer and not to the person who let the animals on hire. In *Tucker* v. *Farm and General Investment Trust Ltd.*[181] a farmer acquired some ewes on hire-purchase from a finance company who were the owner of the ewes; under the agreement the farmer was entitled, after paying the final instalment of hire due in August, 1964, to exercise an option to purchase the ewes for an extra £1. The farmer had the ewes served in September, 1963, and lambs were produced in February, 1964. In April, 1964, the farmer sold the lambs to the plaintiff, and the legal question was whether the lambs belonged at that time to the farmer or to the finance company. The Court of Appeal held that the lambs belonged to the farmer immediately before he sold them, since a hire-purchase agreement is merely a letting with an option to purchase at the end of the lease, and under a lease the lessee is entitled to take the produce and progeny arising during the period of the letting from the subject matter of the lease.

300

Credit-sale agreements

The Hire-Purchase Act, 1965, defines a credit-sale agreement as 'an agreement for the sale of goods under which the purchase price is payable by five or more instalments, not being a conditional sale agreement'.[182] Credit-sale agreements so defined are governed by the Act provided the total purchase price does not exceed £2,000, unless the buyer is a body corporate. A credit-sale is a contract of sale of goods within the meaning of the Sale of Goods Act, 1893. The conditions and warranties implied into contracts for the sale of goods and the extent to which these may be excluded under the Supply of Goods (Implied Terms) Act, 1973 (*ante*, pages 278–84) apply to credit-sale agreements made on or after 18 May 1973. The conditions and warranties implied into credit-sale agreements made prior to that date continue to be governed by the Sale of Goods Act, 1893 as it stood being amended by the Supply of Goods (Implied Terms) Act, 1973; details of the law concerning this topic which was in force prior to its amendment by the 1973 Act are not included in this book. Since ownership passes to the buyer under the agreement, he can pass on a good title to a third party.

The statutory right to have second thoughts and serve notice of cancellation of an agreement made away from 'appropriate trade premises' (see *ante*, page 294) applies to credit-sale agreements under which the total purchase price exceeds £30.

The requirements of the 1965 Act regarding hire-purchase agreements and relating to the need to state the cash price in advance, the form in which the agreement must be made (save that the agreement need not contain a notice of matters akin to the hirer's right to terminate the agreement or of restriction upon the owner's right to recover the goods, since these are inappropriate to credit-sale as there the buyer cannot terminate the agreement nor the seller recover at all what are now the buyer's goods) and the supply of copies apply with minor differences of terminology to credit-sale agreements under which the total purchase price exceeds £30, with similar consequences in the event of failure. The buyer has no statutory right to terminate the agreement, such as exists in relation to hire-purchase agreements (*ante*, pages 296–7) by paying a sum of money and fulfilling other statutory conditions.

Conditional sale agreements

The Hire-Purchase Act, 1965,[183] defines a conditional sale agreement as 'an agreement for the sale of goods under which the purchase price or part of it is payable by instalments, and the property in the goods is to remain in the seller (notwithstanding that the buyer is to be in possession of the goods) until such conditions as to the payment of instalments or otherwise as may be specified in the agreement are fulfilled'. Unlike a hire-purchase agreement, the buyer is bound under the terms of the agreement to buy the goods. A conditional sale agreement differs from a credit-sale agreement in that the price in a conditional sale agreement need not be payable by five or more instalments, and that, unlike credit-sale, the ownership of the goods is to remain in the seller until the conditions of the agreement have been fulfilled. The Hire-Purchase Act, 1965, applies to all conditional sale agreements if the total purchase price does not exceed £2,000, unless the agreement is made by or on behalf of a body corporate as the buyer. The statutory right to have second thoughts and serve notice of cancellation of an agreement made away from 'appropriate trade premises' (see *ante*, page 294) applies to conditional sale agreements which fall within the limits of the 1965 Act. The stipulations of the 1965 Act relating to the formal contents of a conditional sale agreement which falls within the statute are roughly similar to those required for hire-purchase agreements. The conditions and warranties to be implied into conditional sale agreements made on or after 18 May 1973 and the extent to which these may be excluded are those applicable to sales of goods under the Sale of Goods Act, 1893, and the Supply of Goods (Implied Terms) Act, 1973 (*ante*, pages 278–84); the law concerning implied conditions and warranties and their exclusion applicable to conditional sale agreements made prior to 18 May 1973 is not included in this book. If the conditional sale agreement falls within the limits of the Hire-Purchase Act, 1965, the buyer has a right to terminate the agreement on similar terms to those in hire-purchase (i.e. paying a maximum of half the price, unless more was already due, etc.; *ante*, pages 296–7).[184] Once the buyer has paid one-third of the total purchase price, the seller's right to recover possession of the goods is restricted in manner and with consequences roughly similar to those which apply in the case of hire-purchase. A person who buys under a conditional sale agreement within the limits of the 1965 Act is deemed not to be a person who has bought or agreed to buy the goods for the purposes of section 25(2) of the Sale of Goods Act, 1893 (see *ante*, page 285) and hence cannot in general pass the ownership of the goods to an innocent third party to whom the purports to sell them (but see Part III of the Hire-Purchase Act, 1964; *ante*, pages 299–300), but where the conditional sale agreement falls outside the limits of the 1965 Act then section 25(2) of the Sale of Goods Act, 1893, applies.

Notes

1   *Pharmaceutical Society of Great Britain* v. *Boots Cash Chemists (Southern), Ltd.* [1952] 2 Q.B. 795.

2   *Hyde* v. *Wrench* (1840) 3 Beav. 334.

3   *Felthouse* v. *Bindley* (1826) 11 C.B. (N.S.) 869.

4   *Adams* v. *Lindsell* (1818) 1B. and Ald. 681.

5   *Byrne* v. *Van Tienhoven* (1880) 5 C.B.D. 344.

6   *Re Casey's Patents, Stewart* v. *Casey* [1892] 1 Ch. 104.

7   *Stilk* v. *Myrick* (1809) 2 Camp. 317.

8   *Foakes* v. *Beer* 1884) 9 App. Cas. 605.

9   Pinnel's Case (1602) 5 Co. Rep. 117a.

10 *Emmanuel Ajayi* v. *R.T. Briscoe (Nigeria) Ltd.* [1964] 3 All E.R. 556.

11 [1938] 2 All E.R. 626.

12 *Balfour* v. *Balfour* [1919] 2 K.B. 571.

13 Family Law Reform Act, 1969, section 1.

14 Infants Relief Act, 1874.

15 *Clements* v. *London and North-Western Railway Co.* [1894] 2 Q.B. 482.

16 Sale of Goods Act, 1893, section 2.

17 *Steinberg* v. *Scala (Leeds) Ltd.* [1923] 2 Ch. 452.

18 Sale of Goods Act, 1893, section 2.

19 Statute of Frauds, 1677, section 4.

20 Law of Property Act, 1925, section 40.

21 *Marshall* v. *Green* (1875) 1 C.P.D. 35; *Saunders* v. *Pilcher* [1949] 2 All E.R. 1097.

22 *Hawkins* v. *Price* [1947] Ch. 645.

23 *Timmins* v. *Moreland Street Property Co. Ltd.* [1958] Ch. 110.

24 *Kingswood Estate Co., Ltd.* v. *Anderson* [1963] 2 Q.B. 169.

25 *Derry* v. *Peek* (1889) 14 App. Cas. 337.

26 Misrepresentation Act, 1967, section 2(1).

27 Misrepresentation Act, 1967, section 2(2).

28 *Leaf* v. *International Galleries* [1950] 2 K.B. 86.

29 *Phillips* v. *Brooks, Ltd.* [1919] 2 K.B. 243.

30 Misrepresentation Act, 1967, section 3.

31 *Jacobs* v. *Batavia and General Plantations Trust* [1924] 1 Ch. 287.

32 *Walker Property Investments (Brighton), Ltd.* v. *Walker* (1947) 177 L.T. 204.

33 The Moorcock (1889) 14 P.D. 64.

34 *Per* Denning, M.R. in *Thornton* v. *Shoe Lane Parking Ltd.* [1971] 1 All E.R. 686.

³⁵ *Chapelton* v. *Barry U.D.C.* [1940] 1 K.B. 532.

³⁶ *L'Estrange* v. *Graucob* [1943] 2 K.B. 394.

³⁷ *Curtis* v. *Chemical Cleaning and Dyeing Co.* [1951] 1 K.B. 805.

³⁸ *Parker* v. *South-Eastern Railway* (1877) 2 C.P.D. 416.

³⁹ *Olley* v. *Marlborough Court, Ltd.* [1949] 1 K.B. 532.

⁴⁰ *Harling* v. *Eddy* [1951] 2 K.B. 739.

⁴¹ *Hollier* v. *Rambler Motors (A.M.C.) Ltd.* [1972] 1 All E.R. 399.

⁴² *Lilley* v. *Doubleday* (1881) 7 Q.B.D. 510.

⁴³ *Joseph Thorley, Ltd.* v. *Orchis Steamship Co.* [1907] 1 K.B. 660.

⁴⁴ *Per* Lord Diplock in *Hill (Christopher) Ltd.* v. *Ashington Piggeries Ltd.* [1972] A.C. 441.

⁴⁵ *Webster* v. *Cecil* (1861) 30 Beav. 62.

⁴⁶ *Saunders* v. *Anglia Building Society* [1971] A.C. 1004.

⁴⁷ *Napier* v. *National Business Agency Ltd.* [1951] 2 All E.R. 264.

⁴⁸ *Bigos* v. *Bousted* [1951] 1 All E.R. 92.

⁴⁹ *Sumpter* v. *Hedges* [1898] 1 Q.B. 673.

⁵⁰ *H. Dakin & Co. Ltd.* v. *Lee* [1916] 1 K.B. 566.

⁵¹ *Charles Rickards, Ltd.* v. *Oppenheim* [1950] 1 K.B. 616; *ante,* page 263.

⁵² *Taylor* v. *Caldwell* (1863) 3 B. and S. 826.

⁵³ Law Reform (Frustrated Contracts) Act, 1943.

⁵⁴ *Hadley* v. *Baxendale* (1854) 9 Exch. 341; *The Heron II, Koufos* v. *C. Czarnikow, Ltd.* [1969] 1 A.C. 350.

⁵⁵ [1953] Ch. 770.

⁵⁶ *Beach* v. *Reed Corrugated Cases, Ltd.* [1956] 2 All E.R. 652.

⁵⁷ *Parsons* v. *B.N.M. Laboratories, Ltd.* [1964] 1 Q.B. 95.

⁵⁸ *Brace* v. *Calder* [1895] 2 Q.B. 253.

⁵⁹ *Dunlop Pneumatic Tyre Company, Ltd.* v. *New Garage and Motor Co. Ltd.* [1915] A.C. 79.

⁶⁰ [1962] A.C. 600.

⁶¹ Limitation Act, 1939, section 2.

⁶² Law Reform (Limitation of Actions, etc.) Act, 1954, section 2(1).

⁶³ Limitation Act, 1963, as amended by Law Reform (Miscellaneous Provisions) Act, 1971.

⁶⁴ Limitation Act, 1939, section 26.

⁶⁵ Sections 22 and 31(2).

⁶⁶ Limitation Act, 1939, sections 23 and 24.

⁶⁷ Sale of Goods Act, 1893, section 1(1).

⁶⁸ Section 1(3).

⁶⁹ *Aldridge* v. *Johnson* (1857) 7 E. and B. 885.

⁷⁰ Supply of Goods (Implied Terms) Act, 1973, section 18.

[71] Sale of Goods Act, 1893, sections 16–19.

[72] Sale of Goods Act, 1893, section 55 as substituted by the Supply of Goods (Implied Terms) Act, 1973, section 4; *post*, pages 283–4. The substituted section and all other provisions relating to sales of goods introduced by the 1973 Act apply only to contracts of sale of goods made on or after 18 May 1973. Contracts of sale of goods made before that date will continue to be governed by the law in force prior to the 1973 Act; details of the earlier law are not included in this book.

[73] *Per* Lord Diplock in *Hill (Christopher) Ltd.* v. *Ashington Piggeries Ltd.* [1972] A.C. 441.

[74] Section 61(2).

[75] Sale of Goods Act, 1893, section 13(1).

[76] [1900] 1 Q.B. 513.

[77] *Nicholson and Venn* v. *Smith-Marriott* (1947) 177 L.T. 189.

[78] [1967] 1 W.L.R. 1193.

[79] *Grant* v. *Australian Knitting Mills* [1936] A.C. 85.

[80] Section 13(2) as inserted by the Supply of Goods (Implied Terms) Act, 1973, section 2.

[81] *Re Moore & Co. and Landauer & Co.* [1921] 2 K.B. 519.

[82] *Manbre Saccharine Co. Ltd.* v. *Corn Products Co. Ltd.* [1919] 1 K.B. 198.

[83] *E. & S. Ruben Ltd.* v. *Faire Bros. & Co., Ltd.* [1949] 1 K.B. 254.

[84] Section 14(5) as inserted by the Supply of Goods (Implied Terms) Act, 1973, section 3.

[85] Section 14(2) as substituted.

[86] Section 62(1A) as substituted by the Supply of Goods (Implied Terms) Act, 1973, section 7(2).

[87] Section 14(2) as substituted by the Supply of Goods (Implied Terms) Act, 1973, section 3(2).

[88] (1877) 46 L.J.Q.B. 677.

[89] Section 14(3) as substituted by the Supply of Goods (Implied Terms) Act, 1973, section 3.

[90] *Priest* v. *Last* [1903] 2 K.B. 148.

[91] [1969] 2 A.C. 31.

[92] [1972] A.C. 441.

[93] Agriculture Act, 1970, section 72.

[94] *Gardiner* v. *Gray* (1815) 4 Camp. 46.

[95] Sale of Goods Act, 1893, section 15.

[96] Sale of Goods Act, 1893, section 12(1), as substituted by the Supply of Goods (Implied Terms) Act, 1973, section 1.

[97] Sale of Goods Act, 1893, section 12(2), as substituted by the Supply

of Goods (Implied Terms) Act, 1973, section 1.

⁹⁸ Sale of Goods Act, 1893, sections 55(3), as substituted by the Supply of Goods (Implied Terms) Act, 1973, section 4.

⁹⁹ *Rowland* v. *Divall* [1923] 2 K.B. 500.

¹⁰⁰ [1949] 2 K.B. 545.

¹⁰¹ Section 55(7) and (8) as substituted by the Supply of Goods (Implied Terms) Act, 1973, section 4.

¹⁰² Section 55 as substituted by the Supply of Goods (Implied Terms) Act, 1973, section 4. It must be noted that the entirety of the above passage concerning exclusion only applies to contracts for the sale of goods made on or after 18 May 1973; exemption clauses in contracts of sale made prior to that date are in general governed by the ordinary law of contract (*ante*, pages 268–70).

¹⁰³ Section 62.

¹⁰⁴ Sections 34 and 35 of the Sale of Goods Act, 1893, as amended by the Misrepresentation Act, 1967, section 4(2).

¹⁰⁵ Section 25(2).

¹⁰⁶ Factors Act, 1889, section 1(1).

¹⁰⁷ *Folkes* v. *King* [1923] 1 K.B. 282.

¹⁰⁸ Factors Act, 1889, section 2(1).

¹⁰⁹ *Budberg* v. *Jerwood and Ward* (1934) 51 T.L.R. 99.

¹¹⁰ *Oppenheimer* v. *Attenborough and Son* [1908] 1 K.B. 221.

¹¹¹ *Pearson* v. *Rose and Young, Ltd.* [1951] 1 K.B. 275.

¹¹² Sale of Goods Act, 1893, section 62.

¹¹³ Section 18, Rule 1.

¹¹⁴ Section 62.

¹¹⁵ Section 18, Rule 2.

¹¹⁶ Section 18, Rule 3.

¹¹⁷ Section 18, Rule 5.

¹¹⁸ (1857) 7 E. and B. 885.

¹¹⁹ Section 18, Rule 4.

¹²⁰ Section 20.

¹²¹ *Demby Hamilton & Co. Ltd.* v. *Barden* [1949] 1 All E.R. 435.

¹²² Section 10.

¹²³ *Hartley* v. *Hymans* [1920] 3 K.B. 475.

¹²⁴ Section 29.

¹²⁵ Section 28.

¹²⁶ Section 38.

¹²⁷ Section 41.

¹²⁸ Section 62.

¹²⁹ Section 43.

130   Section 44.
131   Section 48.
132   *Ward* v. *Bignall* [1967] 1 Q.B. 534.
133   Section 48.
134   Section 49.
135   Section 50.
136   [1955] Ch. 177.
137   [1957] 2 Q.B. 117.
138   *Cohen* v. *Roche* [1929] 1 K.B. 169.
139   *Williams Brothers* v. *Agius Ltd.* [1914] A.C. 510.
140   *Re R. and H. Hall Ltd, and W.H. Pim (Junior) & Co's Arbitration* [1928] All E.R. Rep. 763.
141   [1962] 2 Q.B. 508.
142   *Drury* v. *Victor Buckland, Ltd.* [1941] 1 All E.R. 269.
143   [1957] 1 Q.B. 229.
144   Hire-Purchase Act, 1965, section 16.
145   Section 29.
146   Section 2.
147   Section 4.
148   Section 58.
149   Section 6.
150   Section 5.
151   Section 7.
152   Section 5.
153   Section 10.
154   Section 11.
155   Section 9.
156   *Ante*, pages 278–84; Supply of Goods (Implied Terms) Act, 1973, sections 8 and 12.
157   *Warman* v. *Southern Counties Car Finance Corporation Ltd.* [1949] 2 K.B. 576. Compare page 283, *ante*, concerning sale of goods in such circumstances.
158   *Mercantile Union Guarantee Corporation Ltd.* v. *Wheatley* [1938] 1 K.B. 490.
159   [1963] 1 W.L.R. 584.
160   [1967] 1 A.C. 361.
161   Supply of Goods (Implied Terms) Act, 1973, sections 10(1) and (4).
162   *Travers (Joseph) and Sons Ltd.* v. *Cooper* [1915] 1 K.B. 73.
163   Hire Purchase Act, 1965, section 27.
164   Section 29.
165   Section 28.

[166] *Associated Distributors* v. *Hall* [1938] 2 K.B. 83; also *per* Lords Simonds and Morton (*contra* Lord Denning) in *Bridge* v. *Campbell Discount Co. Ltd.* [1962] A.C. 600; see *ante*, pages 275–6.

[167] *Financings Ltd.* v. *Baldock* [1963] 2 Q.B. 104.

[168] Section 25.

[169] Section 29.

[170] Section 30.

[171] Sections 33 and 34.

[172] *Carr* v. *James Broderick and Co. Ltd.* [1942] 2 K.B. 275.

[173] *Mercantile Credit Co. Ltd.* v. *Cross* [1965] 2 Q.B. 205.

[174] Section 35.

[175] Section 38.

[176] Hire Purchase Act, 1964, section 27.

[177] Section 29.

[178] Section 27.

[179] Section 29.

[180] Section 27.

[181] [1966] 2 Q.B. 421.

[182] Hire-Purchase Act, 1965, section 1(1).

[183] Section 1(1).

[184] Hire-Purchase Act, 1965, section 27.

8 General Purpose of the Law of Tort

General purpose of the law of tort

The principal purpose of the law of contact (*ante*, pages 261–76) is to prescribe the circumstances in which a legally enforceable bargain may be made and to provide a remedy or remedies for breach of the obligations which result from that bargain. The purpose of the law of tort is to lay down rules, for the most part judge-made, which in the absence of any bargain between the parties regulate their mutual obligations towards one another, and to provide a remedy, which usually consists of the awarding of damages by way of compensation, for breach of such obligation. Thus the law of tort for the most part consists of a series of generalised prohibitions. 'Thou shalt not punch another person on the nose' – thereby committing the tort of battery; 'thou shalt not (with narrow exceptions) lock up another person' – the tort of false imprisonment; 'thou shalt not unjustifiably attack the reputation of another person' – the tort of defamation; and so on. Of course the tort law may lay down a positive code of conduct which must be observed by a person who has brought himself into a given fact-situation, thus a person driving his car along a busy street must drive with the degree of care which is normally shown by drivers, though even this could be generalised as being merely a particular instance of a blanket prohibition against exhibiting carelessness with consequent injury to another in circumstances in which the law imposes a duty to be careful.

Where the tortious act and the consequent injury to the plaintiff seem likely to be of a continuing nature, an injunction will often be granted by the court to restrain the continuance of the wrong, in addition to the award of damages.

Having thus briefly sketched the background, it is the purpose of this and the following chapter to give an outline account of such torts as seem most likely to affect the farmer in the course of his farming operations; to give some account of every tort would necessitate a whole book. Further branches of the law of tort are discussed in the later chapters concerning the position of occupiers of property (*post*, pages 323–34) and the master's obligations towards his servants (*post*, pages 337–43).

Negligence

Negligence as a tort consists of three ingredients: (a) a duty, imposed by the general law, upon the defendant to act with care towards the plaintiff in the particular fact-situation which gave rise to the plaintiff's injury; (b) breach of that duty by the defendant in that he in fact failed to exhibit sufficient care for the plaintiff's safety; (c) foreseeable damage inflicted upon the plaintiff as a result. As to the first of these ingredients, it is the decisions of the judges which determine whether or not a duty of care exists, although occasionally the existence of such a duty is laid down by Act of Parliament (see for example the Occupiers' Liability Act, 1957, *post,* pages 323–7). An endeavour to formulate a general test for determining whether or not a duty of care exists was made by an eminent judge in the passage now quoted. 'The rule that you are to love your neighbour becomes, in law, you must not injure your neighbour; and the lawyer's question, Who is my neighbour? receives a restricted reply. You must take reasonable care to avoid acts or omissions which you can reasonably foresee would be likely to injure your neighbour. Who, then, in law is my neighbour? The answer seems to be — persons who are so closely and directly affected by my act that I ought reasonably to have them in contemplation as being so affected when I am directing my mind to the acts or omissions which are called in question' (*per* Lord Atkin in *Donoghue* v. *Stevenson*).[1] Although this attempted formulation of the circumstances in which a duty to take care will arise must not be treated as if it were Holy Writ and as providing a universal solution to this problem in any given fact-situation which is litigated, yet it seems that in practice when some fact-situation is litigated which differs materially from any which has been litigated previously the existence or non-existence of a duty of care is likely to be determined in accordance with the above formula, with the proviso that the existence of a duty of care in a situation which appears to fall within the formula may be denied by the judiciary if they think there are sufficiently cogent reasons of general public convenience and social policy for denying the duty. In *Donoghue* v. *Stevenson* the fact-situation under litigation was that the defendant made ginger beer in dark bottles; one of these dark bottles found its way through various intermediaries into the hands of the plaintiff, who allegedly became seriously ill in consequence of discovering, after having drunk most of the bottle's contents, that these included the remains of a decomposed snail. It was held that the maker of the ginger beer owed a duty in tort to the plaintiff, as a consumer, to take reasonable care to see that harmful material did not get into his bottles of beer; investigation would be required into what steps he had taken to prevent this and thus to ascertain whether reasonable care had in fact been taken.

The importance of all this is that the duty of care is nowadays held to exist in a very wide and increasing range of circumstances; persons are increasingly required to regulate their conduct with due regard to its consequences upon the safety of others, in the sense that if others suffer injury, and especially physical injury, which could have been reasonably foreseen as the result of lack of due care, then the person whose misconduct caused the harm is quite likely to find himself visited with the burden of paying full compensation to the injured plaintiff.

In *Weller* v. *Foot and Mouth Disease Research Institute* [2] the defendants were occupiers of land on which they carried out experiments concerning foot and mouth disease. Cattle in the neighbourhood became infected with the disease, and the Minister made an order closing two markets in the area in consequence. During the closure period the plaintiffs, who were auctioneers, were unable to auction cattle at those markets; they sued the defendants claiming damages for loss of business. The lawsuit was brought to decide whether, if it was assumed as a fact that the defendants had imported a virus on to their land which had escaped and which had caused the spread of disease, the defendants as a matter of law owed a duty of care to the plaintiffs to take reasonable care to prevent this. It was held that the defendants owed such a duty as regards neighbouring cattle owners, but not as regards the plaintiff auctioneers because the duty is owed only to those whose persons or whose property may foreseeably be endangered by a failure to take care; the plaintiffs were not endangered as regards either the safety of their persons or the safety of their property since, even if they owned the premises on which the markets were conducted, the premises themselves were not in jeopardy from the disease but only the use made of those premises.

As regards (b) above (page 310), breach of duty, this consists in failing to behave as the law thinks a reasonable man ought to behave in the given circumstances. A professional man or tradesman will be expected to make a reasonable display of the specialised knowledge or skill associated with his profession or trade,[3] and any man handling a particularly dangerous article, such as explosives or a dangerous type of pesticide, or any article where severe injury is likely to result from lack of care, comes under a legal obligation to use a greater degree of care than would be required to discharge his duty as regards a less dangerous article.

Liability for the fall of a tree adjoining a highway upon some user of the highway may arise either in negligence or nuisance (*post*, pages 312–4). In *Caminer* v. *Northern and London Investment Trust Ltd.* [4] an elm three fell upon the plaintiff's car while the car was being driven along the highway, its fall being due to a disease of the roots called elm butt rot: it was held that the occupiers of the land from which the tree fell were not legally liable because they neither knew nor ought to have known that the tree was diseased; the lay occupier is not required to have the knowledge of trees possessed only by an expert, but it was said in the case that his knowledge is expected to be somewhat above that of the townsman. But the occupier has been held liable where the tree was in an obvious state of decay.[5] In *Quinn* v. *Scott*[6] the plaintiff was injured by the fall of a beech tree while driving along the highway. The tree was one of a number of such trees which were nearing the end of their normal life span, and this particular tree exhibited signs that it was unhealthy. It was held that in the particular circumstances the hypothetical reasonable landowner should have, as had been done by the defendant in this case, provided himself with skilled advice about the safety of the trees; moreover he should have realised that it would be dangerous to postpone the felling of this particular tree, and the liability thus incurred by the defendant to pay damages was not diminished by the fact that felling of the trees had been postponed beyond the period at which it would have been commercially advantageous to cut them in order to preserve the amenities of the countryside and for the general benefit of the public. The spread of Dutch elm disease seems likely to give a wide scope for the practical application of these principles.

Nuisance

The tort of nuisance consists of an unlawful interference with some other person's use or enjoyment of his land; this includes wrongful interference with the enjoyment of an easement (*ante,* pages 19–24), such as improperly preventing the use of a private right of way. In actions of nuisance the remedy which frequently the plaintiff most desires is an injunction against the continuance of the defendant's conduct, and this if granted may be coupled with the award of damages. The different fact-situations which may amount to a legal nuisance are infinitely variable, but a frequent form is interference with the plaintiff's enjoyment of his land by the infliction of an unreasonable amount of noise, smell and other analogous discomforts upon him. In this class of case everything turns on what is reasonable; the law expects a person to endure a certain amount of discomfort of this type and gives no remedy in respect of it, but it is otherwise if a legally excessive amount is inflicted. Thus in an early case where the defendant complained, among other things, about the stench emanating from the defendant's pigs which enveloped his dwelling, the defendant's counsel argued that 'the building of the house for hogs was necessary for the sustenance of man: and one ought not to have so delicate a nose, that he cannot bear the smell of hogs', but a remedy was given for, as Chief Justice Wray put it, 'infecting and corrupting the air' by the building and use of the hogsty near to the plaintiff's house.[7] In another case the defendant kept 750 cockerels in an orchard not far from the plaintiff's house; the cockerels were wont to crow daily almost continuously between the hours of 2 a.m. and 7 a.m. One witness compared the noise to that of a football crowd cheering at a cup-tie, and another to the playing of three cornets, two of which were out of tune. There was some evidence that the defendant could without much difficulty have rearranged his farming activities so as to place the cockerels further away from the plaintiff's house. The defendant's conduct was held to be an actionable nuisance.[8] A person who[9], or whose property[10] is abnormally sensitive to interference gains no extra legal protection on account of this abnormality. Generally speaking, all persons must be prepared to put up with a normal amount of discomfort, having regard to what is usual in that locality in which they have chosen to live. But if a person maliciously interferes with his neighbour's enjoyment of his land, such interference will be unreasonable and therefore actionable notwithstanding that without the malice the discomfort inflicted would not have been in excess of the legally permissible norm. Thus where the defendant, having quarrelled with the plaintiff, caused guns to be fired near the boundary of the plaintiff's land with the sole purpose of upsetting the plaintiff's silver foxes which he kept on a commercial scale and which are nervous while breeding, the defendant's intention was held to convert this otherwise relatively trivial conduct into an actionable nuisance.[11]

Another type of nuisance is the encroachment of the roots and branches of trees on to neighbouring land. Thus in one case the plaintiff owned a number of trees, some of whose branches had for more than twenty years overhung the land of his neighbour; without prior notification of his intention, the neighbour cut off a number of branches back to the boundary fence. The Court of Appeal held that the neighbour was entitled to do this, so long as he did so without entry upon the plaintiff's land, because the overhanging branches were a nuisance.[12] The cut branches and any fruit on them belong to the owner of the tree.

It has been held that there is no tortious liability for failing to prevent the escape of the seed of weeds which have grown naturally on the land. In one case the defendant's property had been woodland, but when cultivated an immense crop of thistles sprang up all over it. The thistles were not cut to prevent their seeding, and the seeds were blown by the wind on to the plaintiff's land. The action was dismissed with much brevity by the Court of Appeal, Lord Coleridge C.J. stating 'I never heard of such an action as this. There can be no duty as between adjoining occupiers to cut the thistles, which are the natural growth of the soil';[13] however in *Davey* v. *Harrow Corporation*[14] the court said that Giles' case, if litigated today, might well be decided differently. Moreover by the Weeds Act, 1959, where the Minister of Agriculture, Fisheries and Food is satisfied that injurious weeds as defined by the Act, including certain types of thistle, dock and ragwort, are growing upon land, he may serve written notice on the occupier of the land requiring him to take such action as may be necessary to prevent the weeds from spreading.[15] Unreasonable failure to comply with the notice is a fineable offence,[16] and the Minister may take any necessary steps to remedy the default and may recover the reasonable cost from the occupier.[17] The Minister may delegate these powers to the council of any county or borough.[18]

Animals

A person can commit a tort through the instrumentality of his animals just as he can commit the tort personally, thus, for example, if Smith deliberately and successfully incites his dog to bite Jones that is as much a tort by Smith as if Smith himself had bitten Jones. Again, excessive noise or smell created by the animals one owns may be the tort of nuisance (*ante,* pages 312–4), and animals may congregate on the highway to such an extent and for such a duration as to amount to an unreasonable obstruction and therefore a tortious nuisance.[19]

If wild animals such as rats or pheasants come on to a person's land of their own accord and there multiply in the ordinary course of nature, that person is in general not liable if they subsequently escape onto a neighbour's land and there do damage to the crops, even if the pheasants multiply in exceptional numbers due to unusually favourable weather conditions and their number is augmented by the defendant employing keepers to prevent vermin attacking the pheasants,[20] but if he actively and deliberately collects such animals on his land to an unreasonable extent he would be liable for such damage;[21] there the defendant had reared 450 pheasants in a wood adjoining a field belonging to the plaintiff in which as many as a hundred pheasants were later seen running while the grain crop was ripening. The statutory right to compensation, within certain limits,

314

conferred by the Agricultural Holdings Act, 1948,[22] is also relevant.

Although at common law the occupier of land owed no duty to prevent his tame animals from straying onto the highway, and hence could not be liable in negligence (*ante*, pages 310–2) (though he might be liable in some other tort; *ante,* page 314) if he did so, this immunity from liability for negligence has now been abolished,[23] hence the question of his liability will depend on the facts of each case, including in particular the degree of care taken by him; it would seem also relevant to consider how much traffic is likely to be on the road and how far the injured person could be reasonably expected to anticipate and guard against the presence of animals. But if animals stray from unfenced land to the highway, a person who placed them on that land and had a right to do so shall not be regarded as being in breach of the duty to take care by reason only of having placed them there, provided the land is common land or land situated in an area in which fencing is not customary.[24]

In general each occupier of land is liable if damage results from his failure to fence to keep his cattle in, and he is not obliged to fence so as to keep his neighbour's cattle out. Exceptionally, however, he may come under a contractual obligation to fence his land for the benefit of his neighbour, or a right in the nature of an easement (see *ante,* pages 19–24) may have arisen for the benefit of his neighbour's land to have the fencing thus maintained.[25]

The Animals Act, 1971, provides that where livestock strays on to land which is owned or occupied by another and does damage to that other's land or to any property which he owns or possesses, then the person to whom the livestock belongs shall in general be liable for the damage;[26] liability is not however incurred by reason only of such straying if the livestock strayed from a highway and its presence there was a lawful use of the highway.[27] The person who incurs liability is the person in whose possession the livestock was at the material time.[28] The liability includes any expenses reasonably incurred by the other person in keeping the livestock until it can be restored to the person in whose possession it previously was or while exercising his legal right to detain the livestock (*post,* page 316). In a case decided prior to the Act, the plaintiff recovered damages in respect of his sheep having been infected with scab by the trespassing sheep of the defendant;[29] it would seem that nowadays the case would be decided in the same way under the Act, unless perhaps the disease in question was a very unusual one and the owner did not know that his animals were infected with it, and hence could not reasonably be expected to have anticipated the possible spread of the disease. 'Livestock' includes cattle, horses, sheep, pigs, goats and poultry.[30]

The occupier of land may detain any livestock which has strayed on to his land and which was then not under the control of any person. The occupier exercising this right of detention must within forty-eight hours thereafter give notice to the police and, if known, to the person to whom the livestock belongs. He is liable for any damage caused to the livestock by failing to treat it with reasonable care and to supply it with adequate food and water while so detained. The right to detain ceases if notice has not been given as above, or on tender of sufficient money to satisfy the damage and expenses claimed in respect of the livestock, or if there is no valid claim and return of the livestock is demanded, or a court order is made for return of the livestock. Having rightfully detained the livestock for not less than fourteen days, the person detaining it may sell it at a market or by public auction, unless proceedings are already pending for return of the livestock or for any claim for damage done by or expenses incurred in respect of it; if the proceeds of sale exceed the claim of the person detaining, the excess must be paid over to the person who would have been entitled to possession of the livestock but for the sale.[31]

Additional liability may be incurred with regard to animals which belong to a dangerous species. The Act defines a dangerous species as 'a species (a) which is not commonly domesticated in the British Islands; and (b) whose fully grown animals normally have such characteristics that any damage they may cause is likely to be severe'.[32] A strict liability attaches to the owner or possessor of such an animal, e.g. a tiger, for damage done by it. The keeping of such animals is of course very rare save in zoos and wildlife parks; of far greater practical importance is that a similar liability attaches for damage done by an animal which does not belong to a dangerous species if that particular animal has dangerous characteristics known to its owner or possessor which make it likely that damage due to those characteristics would occur or that any injury or damage of the kind which might occur would be severe; however, this strict liability only arises in respect of characteristics which are abnormal in animals of the same species, or are abnormal in that species save at particular times or in particular circumstances.[33] Liability attaches whether or not the animal has escaped from control. Hence this liability would arise, for example, in respect of a dog known to be savage, and this would be so even if all dogs could be proven to be savage when they have young since that would be a characteristic which is not normally found except at that particular time or in those particular circumstances. If a person employed to look after the animal knows that it is dangerous, his knowledge will be attributed to the owner or possessor. The head of the household in which a member under the age of sixteen owns or possesses an animal known to be dangerous is legally liable for damage done by it, and proof of knowledge by the head of the household is established by proving knowledge on the part of the member who owns or possesses the animal.[34] The Act provides that it shall be a good defence against liability for animals known to be dangerous if the plaintiff was trespassing on the premises where the animal was kept and it is proved that either the animal was not kept there for the purpose of protecting persons or property, or that it was reasonable to keep it for such a purpose.[35]

There are special rules regarding the killing or injuring of livestock, which here includes pheasants, partridges and grouse while in captivity, by dogs. Here the owner or possessor of the dog is liable[36] unless the livestock was injured while straying on someone else's land and the dog either belonged to the occupier of that land or was there by the occupier's authority.[37]

Conversely a person may wish to kill a dog in protection of his own livestock. The Act states that it shall be a defence to any action brought to recover damages in respect of the injuring or killing of a dog if the defendant proves that the dog was, or was reasonably believed to be, worrying or about to worry livestock, and there were, or were reasonably thought to be, no other reasonable means of preventing the worrying or bringing it to an end. Further, either the livestock must have been in the ownership or possession of the defendant or some other person whose express or implied authority he had to protect it, or must have been on land occupied by the defendant or by some other person whose authority the defendant had to protect the livestock. The dog, if it had been or was reasonably thought to have been worrying livestock, must not have left the vicinity or been under the control of any person and the defendant must either have had no practical means of ascertaining to whom the dog belonged or have reasonably supposed this to be so. The defendant must have notified the incident to the police within forty-eight hours after he killed or injured the dog.[38] It is here convenient to note that criminal liability may sometimes be incurred by the shooting of a dog: it has been said in a criminal context that 'a person may be justified in shooting a dog if he honestly believes that it is necessary as being the only way in which he can protect his property. Therefore if a farmer finds a dog driving his ewe flock, as sometimes happens, chasing sheep, and so forth, which may cause incalculable damage to a farmer, it may be that the only way in which he can protect his flock is by shooting the dog, and he can do it'.[39] In that case the prosecutor owned a labrador dog which frequently trespassed over land on which the defendant had the shooting rights; the accused saw the dog tearing a hen pheasant to pieces and soon afterwards

317

chasing a hare, and thereupon shot the dog dead. When prosecuted for unlawfully and maliciously killing the dog, the accused pleaded that he was entitled to do so in order to protect the game, but the court directed that he be convicted on the grounds that he had no ownership in the wild game to protect, not yet having reduced the game into possession.

It should finally be mentioned that, as regards the various ways in which tortious liability may be incurred for damage done by one's animals, it is a good defence to show that the damage was due wholly to the fault of the person suffering it, if such be the fact, or that he voluntarily accepted the risk; moreover if the damage was caused partly by his fault, the amount awarded him will be proportionately reduced.[40]

The master's liability for his servant's torts

The master is legally liable to pay damages for all torts committed by his servants during the course of their employment; conversely, a person is only liable in particular circumstances for torts committed by his independent contractors. The tests for deciding who is a servant and what is the scope of his employment are somewhat vague, and judicial attempts to define these are not always harmonious with one another. Factors tending to indicate the existence of a contract of service include an extensive right to control the way in which the work is done, payment of remuneration with frequency, whether the work is done as an integral part of the business, and the right of dismissal. A chauffeur, for example, is a servant, whereas a taxi-man is an independent contractor in relation to the person hiring the taxi.[41] Despite the theoretical difficulty of definition, there is in most instances little doubt as to whether or not a person is a servant.

The employer is liable in tort, along with his servant, for torts committed by his servant during the course of his employment. The tort falls within the scope of employment if its commission was expressly or impliedly authorised by the master, or if it was an unauthorised mode of doing an authorised act, or it was necessarily incidental to something which the servant was employed to do.

Litigation has often taken place concerning whether a particular fact-situation falls inside or outside the scope of employment, and many borderline situations have arisen. Thus if, for example, a servant employed to drive a vehicle deviates from his authorised route, it is a question of fact whether the extent and purpose of the deviation is such as to take the driver on an entirely new journey.[42] Again, a servant has implied authority to endeavour to protect and preserve his master's property, and once again it is a question of degree whether the master can be made liable for a mistaken exercise of this authority by his servant.[43]

If a master, without curtailing the type of work which the servant is employed to do, forbids him to carry out this work in a wrongful manner, that prohibition will not protect the master from liability if the servant performs the work in a tortious manner.[44] It is otherwise if the prohibition is construed as reducing the scope of what the servant is employed to do, thus making an act done in breach of the prohibition an act outside the scope of employment; where the employer had forbidden his servant and van-driver to give any lifts to strangers, and the driver did give a lift to such a person and killed him because of the driver's negligent driving, the giving of a lift was held to be outside the scope of the driver's employment (although it might have been otherwise had there been no prohibition), and hence the employer was not liable for it.[45]

The fact that the servant was performing his task in a wrongful manner with a view to his own benefit rather than to the benefit of his master,[46] or that the act of the servant was criminal as well as tortious,[47] does not necessarily take his act out of the course of employment, although often it will have this effect.

If the master has to pay damages to the injured third party in respect of a tort committed by the master's servant within the course of his employment, and if the servant was morally alone to blame for the tort, the master is entitled to recover an indemnity from his servant in respect of the damages and thus recoup himself. The claim to indemnity could be based either on breach of an implied term in the servant's contract of service that he will perform his duties with reasonable care, or upon statute.[48] Thus where a servant employed to drive a lorry injured a third party by his negligent driving, the employer, having paid damages to the third party, was held entitled to recover that sum from the driver for breach of an implied undertaking in his service contract that he would drive with reasonable care.[49] But if the employer, or another servant of the same employer, is also partly to blame, the employer has no right to complete reimbursement although the court may award him some degree of recoupment proportionate to the relative extent of fault of the parties involved.[50]

If a person hires or lends the benefit of his servant's services to a third party, the question may arise as to whether the permanent or the temporary employer is liable in tort for wrongs committed by the servant during that time. Legally speaking it is for the permanent employer to try and prove that the burden of liability has shifted to the temporary employer; this burden is a heavy one and very difficult to discharge, but it is somewhat lighter when the labour alone is lent rather than when the servant is lent along with the use of complicated machinery belonging to the general employer. The principal test to apply is to ask which employer had authority, at the material time, to tell the servant not only what work he was to do, but also how he was to do it.[51]

Notes

[1]   [1932] A.C. 562.

[2]   [1966] 1 Q.B. 569.

[3]   *Bolam* v. *Friern Hospital Management Committee* [1957] 1 W.L.R. 582.

[4]   [1951] A.C. 88.

[5]   *Brown* v. *Harrison* (1947) 177 L.T. 281.

[6]   [1965] 1 W.L.R. 1004.

[7]   Aldred's Case (1610) 9 Co. Rep. 57b.

[8]   *Leeman* v. *Montagu* [1936] 2 All E.R. 1677.

[9]   *Heath* v. *Brighton (Mayor of)* (1908) 98 L.T. 718.

[10]   *Robinson* v. *Kilvert* (1889) 41 Ch. D. 88.

[11]   *Hollywood Silver Fox Farm, Ltd.* v. *Emmett* [1936] 2 K.B. 468.

[12]   *Lemmon* v. *Webb* [1894] 3 Ch. 1.

[13]   *Giles* v. *Walker* (1890) 24 Q.B. 656.

[14]   [1958] 1 Q.B. 60.

[15]   Weeds Act, 1959, section 1(1).

[16]   Section 2.

[17]   Section 3.

[18]   Section 3.

[19]   *Cunningham* v. *Whelan* [1917] 52 Ir. L.T. 67.

[20]   *Seligman* v. *Docker* [1949] 1 Ch. 53.

[21]   *Farrer* v. *Nelson* (1885) 15 Q.B.D. 258.

[22]   Agricultural Holdings Act, 1948, section 14 (*ante*, pages 53–4).

[23]   Animals Act, 1971, section 8(1).

[24]   Section 8(2).

[25]   *Crow* v. *Wood* [1971] 1 Q.B. 77.

[26]   Section 4(1).

[27]   Section 5(5).

[28]   Section 4(2).

[29]   *Theyer* v. *Purnell* [1918] 2 K.B. 333.

[30]   Section 11.

[31]   Section 7.

[32] Section 6(2).
[33] Section 2(2).
[34] Sections 2(2) and 6(3).
[35] Section 5(3).
[36] Section 3.
[37] Section 5(4).
[38] Section 9.
[39] *Gott* v. *Measures* [1948] 1 K.B. 234.
[40] Law Reform (Contributory Negligence) Act, 1945, section 1(1).
[41] *Stevenson, Jordan and Harrison, Ltd.* v. *Macdonald* [1952] 1 T.L.R. 101.
[42] *Storey* v. *Ashton* (1869) L.R. 4 Q.B. 476.
[43] *Poland* v. *Parr & Sons* [1927] 1 K.B. 236.
[44] *Limpus* v. *London General Omnibus Co.* (1862) 1 H. and C. 526.
[45] *Twine* v. *Bean's Express, Ltd.* (1946) 62 T.L.R. 155, affirmed 62 T.L.R. 458.
[46] *Lloyd* v. *Grace, Smith & Co.* [1912] A.C. 716.
[47] *Morris* v. *C.W. Martin & Sons, Ltd.* [1966] 1 Q.B. 716.
[48] Law Reform (Married Women and Tortfeasors) Act, 1935, section 6.
[49] *Lister* v. *Romford Ice & Cold Storage Co.* [1957] A.C. 555.
[50] *Jones* v. *Manchester Corporation* [1952] 2 Q.B. 852.
[51] *Mersey Docks and Harbour Board* v. *Coggins & Griffiths (Liverpool), Ltd.* [1947] 1 A.C. 1.

9　The Legal Position of the Occupier of the Premises

Occupier's liability

The topic about to be discussed is the liability of the occupier of land, including buildings, for injury inflicted on third parties in consequence of the dangerous condition of such property. As regards those whom the occupier has either invited or permitted to be on the premises, his duty in respect of the premises themselves is in general regulated by the Occupiers' Liability Act, 1957; whether the Act also regulates the occupier's liability towards such persons in respect of injury inflicted upon them by the active conduct of the occupier, such as his driving a tractor, is a matter of doubt and controversy (as indeed is the dividing line between the static condition of the premises and active operations conducted there; 'does a bull grazing in a field belong to static condition or to current operations?' (*per* Pearson L.J. in *Videan* v. *British Transport Commission*)),[1] but the precise source of his duty of care with regard to this is a matter of little practical significance since if it does not flow from the Act a similar duty of care will be imposed upon him by the tort law of the realm as declared by the judges; the relevant tort is that of negligence (*ante*, pages 310–2). The Act regulates the occupier's liability towards his 'visitors' (see *post*, pages 324–5) in respect of his land, buildings and other structures whether moveable or not. As regards persons who enter without the express or implied permission of the occupier and are therefore classed as trespassers, the occupier's duty towards them is wholly regulated by the common law (*post*, pages 327–9).

To find out who is the occupier of premises it is necessary to establish who has control over them. The control which a master has through his servants is the control of the master. Different persons may be in occupation of different parts of a single building, and since control may be shared it is feasible that there should sometimes be two or more occupiers of the identical premises. In *Wheat* v. *E. Lacon and Co. Ltd.*[2] a company owned an inn occupied by their manager; the agreement between the company and the manager provided that the manager should occupy the inn without having a tenancy of it, the company retaining the right to enter the premises in order to view the state of repair. It was held that on the facts the company was in occupation of the inn although the manager might also be in occupation. 'There is no difficulty in having more than one occupier at one and the same time, each of whom is under a duty of care to visitors' (per Lord Denning). 'The safety of premises may depend on the acts or omissions of more than one person, each of whom may have a different right to cause or continue the state of affairs which creates the danger, and on each a duty of care may lie; but where seperate persons are each under a duty of care the acts or omissions which would constitute a breach of that duty may vary very greatly. That which would be negligent in one may well be free from blame in the other' (per Lord Pearce).

The occupier's 'visitors' comprise all persons whom the occupier has expressly or impliedly invited or permitted to enter the premises,[3] and also persons who enter premises in pursuance of a right of entry conferred on them by the general law,[4] such as the police or employees of an Electricity Board in certain circumstances. However, it is expressly provided that an entrant to premises in exercise of a right conferred on him by virtue of an access agreement or order under the National Parks and Access to the Countryside Act, 1949, is not to be regarded as a 'visitor' for the purpose of the Occupiers' Liability Act;[5] although such an entrant is not a trespasser, it seems that the occupier's duty concerning his safety is that which would be appropriate to a trespasser (post, pages 327–9). A person using a public or a private right of way seems not to be a 'visitor' within the meaning of the Act. As regards implied permission to enter, it has been judicially stated that 'a canvasser who comes without your consent is a trespasser'. Once he has your consent he becomes what is now termed a 'visitor' (per Denning L.J. in Dunster v. Abbott).[6] Despite this, the law might infer permission to have been given in favour of a canvasser who, albeit previously unknown to the occupier, enters in the hope of securing an order for goods or a charitable subscription, unless he has been told to clear off and given a reasonable time to do so or the entry of such persons is expressly prohibited by a conspicuous notice. Permission may also be inferred from the occupier's failure to make an effective protest against a longstanding practice of intrusion by the public upon that part of his land, thus where the public had for thirty-five years used a short cut across a farmer's field, and he had never taken any legal proceedings against them although he sometimes protested, the farmer was held liable to a person taking the short cut who was injured by a savage horse whom the farmer had without warning suddenly placed in the field.[7]

However the entrant ceases to be a 'visitor' and turns for the time being into a trespasser if he goes to a part of the premises where the occupier has forbidden or could not reasonably expect him to be, or makes a use of the premises which could not have reasonably been anticipated; 'when you invite a person into your house to use the staircase you do not invite him to slide down the bannister'.[8] An accidental deviation of slight extent, such as in darkness, from the permitted area will not necessarily turn him into a trespasser; it is a question of degree in each case.

The duty of care owed by an occupier towards his 'visitors' is stated in the Occupiers' Liability Act as 'a duty to take such care as in all the circumstances of the case is reasonable to see that the visitor will be reasonably safe in using the premises for the purposes for which he is invited or permitted to be there';[9] this duty extends to the safety of property which the 'visitor' brings with him, whether or not he owns it,[10] as well as to his personal safety. The Act further states that, when applying the duty, it is relevant to have regard to the degree of care or lack of care that the occupier might reasonably anticipate from his particular visitor, thus in proper cases the occupier must be prepared for a child to be less careful than an adult, and conversely he can expect that a person who enters in pursuance of his calling 'will appreciate and guard against any special risks ordinarily incident to it, so far as the occupier leaves him free to do so'.[11] 'When a householder calls in a specialist to deal with a defective installation on his premises, he can reasonably expect the specialist to appreciate and guard against the dangers arising from the defect' (*per* Lord Denning M. R. in *Roles* v. *Nathan*).[12]

The Act further provides that to warn his 'visitor' of a danger does not absolve the occupier from liability unless the warning enables the visitor to be reasonably safe.[13]

If the occupier has employed an independent contractor to do work on the premises, and a 'visitor' is damaged by a danger due to its faulty execution, the occupier shall not without more be liable for this if in all the circumstances he acted reasonably in entrusting the work to an independent contractor and had taken such steps (if any) as he reasonably ought in order to satisfy himself that the contractor was competent and that the work had been properly done.[14] Thus generally speaking the occupier is not liable for defects in the contractor's work if he has taken reasonable care to select a competent contractor and to see, so far as can reasonably be expected of him, that the work has been well done; where large and complex schemes of building are involved the discharge of this latter function might well necessitate the occupier employing an architect to see that the work was indeed properly done. If the

325

'visitor' fails to take reasonable care for his own safety, his damages will be reduced 'to such extent as the court thinks just and equitable having regard to the claimant's share in the responsibility for the damage.[15]

Since the occupier of land is in general entitled to state the terms and conditions on which he either is or is not willing to permit persons to enter upon his land, it follows that the occupier can in general exclude the duty of care which he would otherwise owe to the 'visitor' by making known to him in clear and unambiguous fashion that entry is to be on this basis only[16]. 'It is not in dispute that it is competent to an occupier of land to restrict or exclude any liability he might otherwise be under to any licence of his, including liability for his own or his servants negligence by conditions aptly framed and adequately made known to the licensee'[17] (the word 'licensee' is nowadays to be included in the term 'visitor'). It seems that the occupier will have 'adequately made known' the conditions to the visitor if he has taken all reasonable steps to bring the conditions to his attention. Where, however, the right of entry is conferred by the law, such as is for example enjoyed by the police in certain circumstances, the occupier could not attach conditions since the right to enter does not derive from him. Furthermore, in *Burnett* v. *British Waterways Board*[18] it was held that the mere display of a notice, apt in its wording to exclude liability for the accident in question, is insufficient to exclude liability to a person who has no choice but to enter on the land and hence cannot be said to have agreed, either expressly or impliedly, to be bound by the terms of the notice. Apart from this, to plaster one's entrances with conspicuous notices saying 'all persons who enter these premises do so entirely at their own risk and with no claim against the occupier for any unintended injury whatsoever' would, while doubtless tending to diminish the supply of 'visitors', probably do much to confer a legal immunity on the occupier in respect of their safety.

Entry on the land in pursuance of a contract

Such entrants are 'visitors', but there are additional provisions relating to the occupier's duty towards them.

If the occupier makes a contract whereby the other contracting party enters the occupier's land or brings goods there, the duty of care owed to him by the occupier is the common duty of care unless some other standard is expressly agreed in the contract[19]

Where the occupier is bound by contract to permit persons who are strangers to the contract[20] to enter or use his premises, the common duty of care imposed on the occupier by the Act as regards those persons as his

326

visitors cannot be restricted or excluded by the contract, though if the terms of the contract impose some higher duty of care this is to be owed to the non-contracting parties also unless the contract otherwise provides.[21] Thus if a farmer engaged a contractor to do work on the farm, and the contractor sent his servants to carry out the work, the farmer would owe the common duty of care, as a minimum, to the contractor's servants and could not exclude this duty by agreement with the contractor; conversely if the contract required the farmer to take some extra precaution beyond the common duty of care, the contractor's servants would, unless the contract expressly provided to the contrary, take the benefit of this additional obligation. However an occupier who has taken all reasonable care is not, unless the contract expressly so provides, to be answerable to strangers to the contract for dangers due to the faulty execution of works of construction, maintenance, repair and the like carried out by independent contractors[22].

Trespassers

As has already been stated, the occupier's liability towards trespassers is regulated entirely by the common law as declared by the judges, and is at present in a state of some upheaval and uncertainty; the only certain thing, and one calculated to depress all occupiers, is that their legal liability for the safety of trespassers has been very substantially increased. It may appear strange to many that a person who choses, without any authority, to enter upon another person's premises should be able to present the occupier of those premises with the bill should he chance to injure himself while there, but the judiciary have in their wisdom recently decided to pitch the occupier's duty at a level which seems likely to ensure that such will be the fact in many instances. Until recently it had been laid down that an occupier owed no duty to protect a trespasser, but need merely abstain from deliberately harming the trespasser or acting with reckless disregard of his precence.[23] But in recent years conflicting judicial opinions were expressed as to whether the duty should be thus restricted, and in *Herrington* v. *British Railways Board*[24] all the judges of the House of Lords, the highest Appeal Court in the realm, agreed that in effect the occupier's duty as previously laid down should now be extended. Beyond this, however, there was no unanimity concerning how the occupier's duty should now be precisely defined; various forms of wording were suggested for this but the most favoured formula was that the occupier should be required to treat the trespasser 'with common humanity'. It does, however, seem from the judgements that this duty owed to a trespasser is less onerous than the duty owed to a 'visitor' (*ante*, pages 324–5), and that the occupier's resources are a relevant factor in determining what can be expected of him, so that an occupier with large wealth and resources is likely to find that correspondingly more is required of him in performance of the duty. In deciding what can reasonably be expected of the occupier, account will be taken of the fact that usually he has much less reason to foresee the presence of a trespasser than that of a 'visitor'. 'There is considerably more need that there used to be for occupiers to take reasonable steps with a view to deterring persons, especially children, from trespassing in places that are dangerous for them . . .' (*per* Lord Pearson in Herrington's case). 'The relevant likelihood to be considered is of the trespasser's presence at the actual time and place of danger to him. The degree of likelihood needed to give rise to the duty cannot, I think, be more closely defined than as being such as would impel a man of ordinary humane feelings to take some steps to mitigate the risks of injury to the trespasser to which the particular danger exposes him. It will thus depend on all the circumstances of the case: the permanent or intermittent character of the danger; the severity of the injuries which it is likely to cause; in the case of children, the attractiveness to them of that which constitutes the dangerous object or condition of the land; the expense involved in giving effective warning of it to the kind of trespasser likely to be injured, in relation to the occupier's resources in money or in labour' (*per* Lord Diplock in *Herrington's* case).

That the duty upon occupiers generally is no light one is shown by the decision in *Pannett* v. *P. McGuinness & Co. Ltd.*,[25] although there it was said 'Each of these cases . . . depends eventually on the special circumstances'. In Pannett's case the defendants were contractors who had been engaged to demolish a warehouse on a small site thirty yards square adjoining a public park in a densely populated area where many children played. Their workmen made a bonfire of the rubbish from the warehouse, and three workmen were on duty to feed and control the fire and to look out for trespassing children who often came on the site and were as often chased off. The five year old plaintiff had trespassed on the site before when there had been no fire, and had on a number of occasions been chased off by the workmen and had understood their warnings; he came on the site again when the bonfire was lit and was severely burned. The Court of Appeal held that the contractors were, by reason of their workmen's failure to keep a proper lookout, in breach of the duty of care which they owed to the trespassing child, having regard to his age, the nature and situation of the site, the creation of the allurement of the fire,

328

and the knowledge that children trespassed and were likely to trespass on the site. Nothing in the recent formulation of the duty owed to a trespasser supported the view that previous warnings to the trespassing child or chasing him off the site were sufficient to absolve the contractors from liability.

It should be noted that the law has long been somewhat leniently applied in favour of children when considering the occupier's liability towards them. Thus in the past occupiers have often been held, on somewhat slender evidence, to have given an implied permission to the child to enter the land, particularly where the occupier kept some alluring and conspicuous object upon his land which he must have known was bound to attract children to it. But it was said in Herrington's case (*ante*) that in view of the extension of the duty owed to a trespasser therein laid down, it will no longer be necessary or desirable to resort to the fiction of implied permission in favour of the child, although it may be noted that if the duty owed to a trespasser is indeed appreciably less than that owed to a 'visitor' the child would in strict logic be worse off in consequence of this new approach. However, irrespective of the legal category of entrant into which the child falls, the occupier should bear in mind when seeking to discharge his duty that what would be an obvious source of danger to an adult entrant, and which therefore the adult entrant would usually himself be blameworthy if he failed to avoid, may be a hidden danger to a child and the full legal responsibility may thus be thrown upon the occupier. 'What may amount to an effective warning to an adult may be no warning at all to an infant. What may amount to an invitation or a licence to a child may be neither the one nor the other to an adult' (*per* Bankes L.J. in *Hardy* v. *Central London Railway Company*).[26]

Landlord's duty of care arising from his obligation or right to repair the premises leased

The Defective Premises Act, 1972, has imposed an extensive duty of care upon landlords (whether or not in occupation) as regards persons injured by the defective state of premises which the landlord has either an obligation or a right to repair (see *ante,* pages 16–17). The Act comes into effect on 1 January 1974.

Where premises are let under a tenancy which places on the landlord an obligation towards the tenant as regards the maintenance or repair of premises (this will include obligations of this type which are imposed by Act of Parliament as implied terms of the tenancy; *ante,* pages 16–17), the

329

landlord owes to all persons who might reasonably be expected to be affected by defects in the state of the premises a duty to take such care as is reasonable in all the circumstances to see that they are reasonably safe from personal injury or damage to their property caused by a 'relevant defect'. The duty is owed if the landlord knows or ought in all the circumstances to have known of the 'relevant defect'. 'Relevant defect' means a defect in the state of the premises existing at or after the 'material time' and arising or continuing because of the landlord's failure to carry out his obligation to the tenant for the maintenance or repair of the premises; 'material time' means 1 January 1974, if the tenancy commenced before that date, and, if the tenancy commenced after that date, the earliest of either the time when the tenancy began, or the time when the tenancy agreement was entered into, or the time when possession was taken of the premises in contemplation of their being let. Moreover if premises are let under a tenancy which expressly or impliedly gives the landlord the right (though under no duty) to enter the premises to carry out any kind of maintenance or repair of the premises, then for as long as he could exercise that right he is to be treated for the purpose of the above rules as if he was under an obligation to the tenant as regards that kind of maintenance and repair; this does not however impose any duty on the landlord with regard to injury to the tenant himself caused by the defective state of the premises arising from the tenant's failure to carry out an obligation expressly imposed on the tenant by the terms of the tenancy.[27]

Any clause in an agreement which seeks to exclude or restrict the operation of any of the above provisions shall be void.[28]

Rights against trespassers

Trespass may be committed either to land, goods or to the person.

The criminal aspect

Contrary to fairly widespread supposition, it is not in general a criminal offence to trespass upon the land of another person; occasionally however the bare fact of trespass is criminal, as when trespassing upon a railway line, and of course the trespass may be criminal if coupled with some further and criminal intention on the part of the entrant, such as trespassing in pursuit of game (*post*, page 332). But in *R*. v. *Kamara*[29] the Court of Criminal Appeal held that an agreement of two or more persons to commit a civil trespass constitutes the criminal offence of conspiracy to trespass, although the accused cannot be convicted unless they knew that they were trespassers and decided to enter, or were reckless as to whether they were entering the premises without consent; the Court also said that 'perhaps as a matter of practice prosecutions should not be brought unless a combination of persons to trespass is likely to cause a breach of the peace or to affect the public interest in some other way or to be an outrageous interference with the rights of others'. On further appeal, the House of Lords held that a conspiracy to trespass on private property is only criminal if its execution necessarily involved, and was known and intended to involve, the infliction on its victim of something more than purely nominal damage; this requirement must necessarily be satisfied where the intention was to occupy the premises to the exclusion of the owner's right, either by expelling him altogether or otherwise effectively precluding him from enjoying his property (*The Times*, 4 July 1973).

Theft by a trespasser

A person is guilty of theft if he dishonestly appropriates property belonging to another person with the intention of permanently depriving the other person of it.[30] Theft is punishable with a maximum of ten years imprisonment.[31]

In general a person cannot steal land or things forming part of the land and severed from it by him or by his directions; he may however steal land when he is not in possession of the land and he appropriates anything forming part of the land by severing it or causing it to be severed or after it has been severed, or when, being in possession of the land under a tenancy, he appropriates the whole or part of any fixture or structure let to be used with the land.[32]

A person who picks mushrooms growing wild on any land, or who picks flowers, fruit or foliage from a plant growing wild on any land does not (although not in possession of the land) steal what he picks, unless he does it for reward or for sale or other commercial purposes; 'plant' includes any shrub or tree.[33]

Wild creatures, tamed or untamed, are regarded as property, but a person cannot steal a wild creature not tamed nor ordinarily kept in captivity, or the carcass of any such creature, unless either it has been reduced into possession by or on behalf of another person and possession of it has not since been lost or abandoned, or another person is in course of reducing it into possession.[34] Thus a person cannot generally be convicted of stealing a wild creature which prior to his act was still at large, though he may commit other crimes relating to poaching (*post*, page 332).

Armed trespassers

A person commits an offence if, while he has a firearm with him, he enters or is in any building or on any land as a trespasser and without reasonable excuse.[35] Trespassing with a firearm in a building carries a maximum punishment of five years imprisonment or a fine, or both; trespassing with a firearm on other land carries a maximum punishment of three months imprisonment or a fine of £100, or both.[36]

Trespass in pursuit of game and related offences

It is a criminal offence for a trespasser to enter or be on any land in the daytime in search or pursuit of game or rabbits.[37] There must be an actual entry by a person on to the land, thus to discharge a gun into or over the land is not of itself sufficient.[38]

The occupier, his servant or a police constable can require such a trespasser forthwith to quit the land and also to state his christian name, surname and place of abode, and if the trespasser either does not quit or does not give his real name and address the occupier, his servant or a police constable have power to arrest him and to convey him or cause him to be conveyed before a Justice of the Peace as soon as conveniently may be; he must be released if he cannot be brought before a Justice within twelve hours from the time of the arrest.[39] Such an arrest cannot be made unless the trespasser has first been asked to state his name and address.[40]

It is a criminal offence to take or destroy any game or rabbits unlawfully by night upon any land, whether open or enclosed, or upon any public road, highway or path.[41] It is also a crime unlawfully to enter or be upon any land, whether open or enclosed, by night with a gun, net, engine or other instrument for the purpose of taking or destroying game.[42] The owner or occupier of the land or his servant have power to arrest persons found committing these offences.[43] 'Night' covers the period from one hour after sunset to one hour before sunrise.[44]

Intentional or reckless damage to property

By the Criminal Damage Act, 1971, a person who, without lawful excuse, destroys or damages any property belonging to another, intending to destroy or damage any such property or being reckless as to whether any such property would be destroyed or damaged, is guilty of a criminal offence.[45] Also a person who, without lawful excuse, makes a threat to another person to destroy or damage any property belonging to that other

332

person or to a third person, intending the other person to fear the threat will be carried out, is guilty of a criminal offence.[46] The above offences are punishable with a maximum of ten years imprisonment.[47] Moreover where a person is convicted of destroying or damaging property belonging to another as above the court may, on being satisfied as to the approximate cost of making good the loss or damage, order the convicted person to pay to the person to whom the property belongs or belonged immediately before its destruction or damage such sum by way of compensation in respect of this (not exceeding £400 in the case of a magistrate's court) as the court thinks just.[48]

For the purpose of the above offences 'property' means property of a tangible nature including money and including wild creatures which have been tamed or are ordinarily kept in captivity, and any other wild creatures or their carcasses if, but only if, they have been reduced into possession which has not been lost or abandoned or are in the course of being reduced into possession, but not including mushrooms growing wild on any land or flowers, fruit or foliage of a plant, shrub or tree growing wild on any land.[49]

Civil liability for trespass

Only the possessor of goods or land can maintain a civil action of trespass in respect of these; an owner who has let his land or made a binding contract to hire out his goods for an unexpired period and has thus lost the possession cannot do so, though some other remedy in tort may be available to him.

An action of trespass will only lie if the injury to the plaintiff is direct. 'The distinction in law is, where the immediate act itself occasions a prejudice, or is an injury to the plaintiff's person, house, land, etc., and where the act itself is not an injury, but a consequence from that act is prejudicial to the plaintiff's person, house, land, etc. In the first case trespass . . . will lie; in the last it will not . . . '[50] though some other remedy, such as nuisance, may in the latter case be available to the plaintiff (*ante,* pages 312–4).

So long as the physical act of entering the land was a voluntary act, it is no defence that the trespass was committed under a mistake of either fact or law. Thus where the defendant mowed the plaintiff's grass in mistake for his own this constituted a trespass.[51]

In *Paul* v. *Summerhayes*[52] it was held that there is no principle of law which justifies trespassing over the lands of others for the purpose of fox hunting.

A trespass is a tort against the possessor of the land or goods; there is no necessity to prove damage since this tort is actionable without proof of actual loss, although if no damage is proved it would rarely be worthwhile to bring the action since the award would be small and the plaintiff might well find himself out of pocket over the costs of litigation. But if the trespasser's conduct is threatening or insulting the damages awarded by the court may be substantially increased to take account of this and the consequent discomfort to the plaintiff; in one case £500 damages were awarded against the defendant because he had deliberately knocked off the plaintiff's hat (*per* Heath J. in *Merest* v. *Harvey*).[53] 'It must be remembered that in many cases of tort damages are at large, that is to say, the award is not limited to the pecuniary loss that can be specifically proved . . . . Moreover, it is very well established that in cases where the damages are at large the jury (or the judge if the award is left to him) can take into account the motives and conduct of the defendant where they aggravate the injury done to the plaintiff. There may be malevolence or spite or the manner of committing the wrong may be such as to injure the plaintiff's proper feelings of dignity and pride. These are matters which the jury can take into account in assessing the appropriate compensation' (*per* Lord Devlin in *Rookes* v. *Barnard*).[54]

Whether or not he claims damages, the possessor of land or any person authorised by the possessor may exercise his right of self help by evicting the trespasser with no greater force than is reasonably necessary. If the trespasser has behaved peaceably, it is necessary to request him to go and give him a reasonable opportunity to do so before exercising this remedy; this preliminary step is however unnecessary if the trespasser has behaved violently or broken down the fence or gate.[55] In *Harrison* v. *Duke of Rutland*[56] the plaintiff was a trespasser who deliberately interfered with the Duke's shooting party by letting off bombs and rockets. He was seized and held down for a time by the orders of the Duke, which one judge not surprisingly described as 'a strong proceeding'; the Duke was held to be justified in this exercise of his right of self help, but the manner and duration of its exercise must have gone very close to the legal verge in that case, and anyone wishing to exercise this right should be careful not to overstep the bounds.

Notes

1   [1963] 2 Q.B. 650.
2   [1966] 1 All E.R. 582.
3   Occupiers' Liability Act, 1957, section 1(2).
4   Section 2(6).
5   Section 1(4).
6   [1954] 1 W.L.R. 58.
7   *Lowery* v. *Walker* [1911] A.C. 10.
8   *Per* Scrutton L.J. in *The Carlgarth* [1927] P. 93.
9   Section 2(2).
10 Section 1(3)(b).
11 Section 2(3).
12 [1963] 1 W.L.R. 1117.
13 Section 2(4)(a).
14 Section 2(4)(b).
15 Law Reform (Contributory Negligence) Act, 1945, section 1(1).
16 Occupiers Liability Act, section 2(1) of the Act, and *Ashdown* v. *Samuel. Williams & Sons* [1957] 1 Q.B. 409.
17 *Per* Jenkins L.J. in Ashdown's case.
18 [1973] 1 W.L.R. 700.
19 Section 5(1).
20 As defined in section 3(3).
21 Section 3(1).
22 Section 3(2).
23 *Robert Addie and Sons (Colleries), Ltd.* v. *Dumbreck* [1929] A.C. 358.
24 [1972] A.C. 877.
25 [1972] 2 Q.B. 599.
26 [1920] 3 K.B. 459.
27 Defective Premises Act, 1972, section 4.
28 Section 6(3).
29 [1973] 2 W.L.R. 126.
30 Theft Act, 1968, section 1.
31 Section 7.
32 Section 4(2).
33 Section 4(3).
34 Section 4(4).
35 Firearms Act, 1968, section 20.
36 Schedule 6, Part I.
37 Game Act, 1831, section 30.
38 *R.* v. *Pratt* (1855) 4 E. and B. 860.

[39] Game Act, 1831, section 31, as amended by the Game Laws (Amendment) Act, 1960, section 1(2).

[40] *R.* v. *Wilson* [1955] 1 All E.R. 744.

[41] Night Poaching Act, 1828, section 1; Night Poaching Act, 1844, section 1.

[42] Night Poaching Act, 1828, section 1.

[43] Night Poaching Act, 1828, sections 1 and 2, as amended by Night Poaching Act, 1844, section 1.

[44] Night Poaching Act, 1828, section 12.

[45] Criminal Damage Act, 1971, section 1.

[46] Section 2.

[47] Section 4.

[48] Section 8.

[49] Section 10.

[50] *Reynolds* v. *Clarke* (1725) 2 Lord Raym. 1399, but see *Letang* v. *Cooper* [1965] 1 Q.B. 232.

[51] *Basely* v. *Clarkson* (1682) 3 Lev. 37, but see *Letang* v. *Cooper* [1965] 1 Q.B. 232.

[52] (1878) 4 Q.B.D. 9.

[53] (1814) 5 Taunt. 442.

[54] [1964] A.C. 1129.

[55] *Green* v. *Goddard* (1704) 2 Salk. 641.

[56] [1893] 1 Q.B. 142.

10 Some Obligations of the Employer Towards his Employees

Claims by an injured employee against the State

Under the National Insurance (Industrial Injuries) Act, 1965, there is in force a national insurance system under which benefits are payable to employees injured by industrial accidents or by certain prescribed industrial diseases. Employers and employees must make contributions to the Industrial Injuries Fund. Benefits related to the size of the injured person's family and to his earnings prior to the injury or, if disabled for more than six months, to the extent of his disability are payable in respect of personal injury caused to an employee by an accident arising out of and in the course of insurable employment. An accident arising in the course of the employment is deemed to have arisen out of the employment unless the contrary is proved. The employee is covered against injury sustained while travelling to and from work in a vehicle provided by the employer. Claims under the Act are made against the State and not against the employer, and can be made irrespective of whether or not the employer was at fault.

Claims by an injured employee against his employer

The above scheme in no way detracts from the possibility that the employee may be entitled to sue his employer for damages if the employer breaks his duty regarding the safety of the injured employee (save that the damages recoverable by the employee for loss of his earnings are subject to a deduction of half the value of the national insurance benefits)[1] ; such actions are in fact of frequent occurrence, and may be based on any one or more of the three grounds which are set out below.

Breach of the employer's general duty of care

The employer is under a duty 'not to subject the employee to any risk which the employer can reasonably foresee and which he can guard against by any measure, the convenience and expense of which are not entirely disproportionate to the risk involved' (*per* Slade J. in *Harris* v. *Brights Asphalt Contractors Ltd.*)[2]; the fulfilment of such a duty includes 'the provision of a competent staff of men, adequate material and a proper system and effective supervision' (*per* Lord Wright in *Wilsons and Clyde Coal Co.* v. *English*).[3] The employer's duty is a duty of care, and does not amount to a guarantee that the employee shall be safe irrespective of whether the employer has been at fault. But there is a special obligation relating to defective equipment; an exception to the need for proof of fault on the part of the employer arises if an employee is injured in the course of his employment in consequence of a defect in equipment provided by his employer and the defect is due to the fault of a third party, whether the third party is identified or not; if so the injury is deemed to be also attributable to negligence on the part of the employer and the employer is not permitted to rebut his presumed negligence.[4] The employer cannot contract out of the liability which the Act places upon him,[5] but he may seek to recover indemnity or contribution from the person to whose fault the defect is attributable. The effect of the Act is thus to place on the employer the burden of compensating the employee for an injury sustained by reason of the negligent manufacture, repair and the like by a third party of equipment provided by the employer, leaving the employer to seek redress against the third party; to succeed under the Act the employee must however prove that the defect in the equipment was due to fault, although he need not show whose fault it was. 'Equipment' includes any plant and machinery, vehicle and clothing.[6]

The employer's duty of care extends to the employee's place of work,[7] and also to premises occupied by a third party if the employer sends the employee to do work there, although the steps required in order to discharge the duty may well be less in the latter case.[8] 'Whether the servant is working on the premises of the master or those of a stranger, that duty is still, as it seems to me, the same; but as a matter of commonsense its performance and discharge will probably be vastly different in the two cases' (*per* Pearce L.J. in *Wilson* v. *Tyneside Window Cleaning Co., ante*).

It is a question of fact whether a system of work should be prescribed, and in deciding this regard must be had to the nature of the operation, and whether it is one which requires proper organisation and supervision in the interests of safety or one which a reasonably prudent employer would properly think could safely be left to the man on the spot.[9] Not only must the employer take reasonable care to devise a safe system of working where the nature of the task to be performed requires this, but he must also take reasonable care to see that the system of working, together with any reasonable safety precautions, is in fact put into effect.[10] Where an employer uses a dangerous process he must supply the necessary protective clothing or appliances and must take reasonable steps to see that they are used.[11] In *Beer* v. *Wheeler*[12] the employer was held liable for failure to instruct his servant in a safe method in handling a herd of cattle which included a dangerous bull. Some degree of supervision may well also be required, although this does not mean 'that an employer is bound, through his foreman, to stand over workmen of age and experience every moment they are working and every time that they cease work, in order to see that they do what they are supposed to do' (*per* Singleton L.J. in *Woods* v. *Durable Suites Ltd.*).[13] Less instruction and admonition to use safety precautions may be required on the part of the employer if he is dealing with an experienced man who fully appreciates the risks of the work.[14]

The employer's duty is owed to each of his employees individually and not merely to his employees collectively, thus where a one-eyed man was employed to hammer bolts and a splinter entered his eye, it was held that on the facts the employer should have provided goggles for this particular workman because of the risk of his total blindness, even though the risk of injury involved in the work would have been insufficient to require the provision of goggles for a two-eyed man engaged on such a task.[15]

In considering the employer's liability for breach of his duty to take reasonable care for the safety of his employees during the course of their work, the liability appears to extend to the situation where he entrusts the fulfilment of some aspect of the duty to an independent contractor who in fact performs this task negligently.[16]

In *Matthews* v. *Kuwait Bechtel Corporation*[17] the court held that where an employer breaks his duty to take all reasonable care for the safety of his employees, an employee thus injured can claim damages either in tort or for breach of an implied term of the contract of employment.

Vicarious liability

In addition to liability for breach by the employer of his own duty of care, the employer also incurs a vicarious liability if his employee is injured by the negligence of another employee acting within the course of his employment by the same employer (*ante,* pages 318–20).

Breach of statutory duty by the employer

A third way in which the employer may incur tortious liability to his employee arises where the employee is injured by reason of the employer's breach of some obligation imposed by statute on the employer in order to promote the safety of the employee; in such a case the standard of precaution required depends solely on the words of the statute, so that liability without fault might or might not be imposed by the words.

The Agriculture (Safety, Health and Welfare Provisions) Act, 1956, for example, enables regulations to be made for protecting workers employed in agriculture against risks of bodily injury or injury to health arising out of the use of any machinery, plant, equipment or appliance, the carrying out of any operation, the use of any process or the management of animals; for securing to such workers safe places to work in and safe means of access thereto and for protecting them against risks of bodily injury arising out of their falling through apertures in floors or walls, or from their work places, or while ascending or descending staircases or ladders.[18] Without prejudice to the above, regulations may provide for regulating or prohibiting the use of any machinery, plant, equipment or appliance, the carrying on of any operation or the use of any process; imposing requirements with respect to the construction, installation, examination, repair, maintenance, alteration, adjustment and testing of machinery, plant, equipment or appliances and the safeguarding of dangerous parts thereof, and prohibiting the sale or letting on hire of any machinery, plant, equipment or appliance which does not comply with the requirements of the regulations; requiring the observance of precautions in connection with the management of animals and imposing requirements with respect to the construction of enclosures in which animals are kept; requiring the giving of instructions with respect to the proper manner of using any machinery, plant, equipment or appliance, carrying on any operation, using any process or managing animals; imposing requirements with respect to the fencing of apertures in floors or walls, the construction and maintenance of staircases and the provision in connection therewith of handrails and other safeguards and the construction and maintenance of ladders; certain other matters; requiring the taking of such steps as may be prescribed by the regulations for the purpose of bringing the provisions of the regulations to the notice of workers employed in agriculture.[19]

A young person must not be employed as a worker in agriculture to lift, carry or move a load so heavy as to be likely to cause injury to him;[20] 'young person' means a person who is over compulsory school age but has not reached the age of eighteen.[21] Regulations may be made prescribing the maximum weights which may be lifted, carried or moved by workers employed in agriculture;[22] in pursuance of this power the Agriculture (Lifting of Heavy Weights) Regulations[23] have been made.

The provision of sufficient and suitable sanitary conveniences for agricultural workers employed on an agricultural unit which appears to lack such conveniences can be required by a notice served by the county district council for the area;[24] the Minister of Agriculture, Fisheries and Food has a similar power to require washing facilities.[25] An appeal against the reasonableness of this can be made to the magistrates.[26]

A worker employed in agriculture must not be employed to work on land occupied for agricultural purposes unless there is provided on the land a first-aid box or cupboard containing such first-aid requisites and in such quantities as may be prescribed by regulations, containing no other articles, conspicuously marked on the outside with the words 'First Aid', and accessible to the worker.[27]

More detailed provisions concerning the matters set out in the 1956 Act may be found in the Agriculture (Power Take-off) Regulations 1957,[28] the Agriculture (Circular Saws) Regulations 1959,[29] the Agriculture (Stationery Machinery) Regulations 1959,[30] the Agriculture (Field Machinery) Regulations 1962,[31] the Agriculture (Threshers and Balers) Regulations 1960,[32] the Agriculture (Tractor Cabs) Regulations 1967,[33] the Agriculture (Safeguarding of Workplaces) Regulations 1959,[34] the Agriculture (Ladders) Regulations 1957,[35] and the Agriculture (First Aid) Regulations 1957.[36]

It is a defence to a person charged with contravening the Act or regulations made thereunder to prove that he used all due diligence to secure compliance with their requirements.[37]

In order to execute the Act or any regulations made under it a Ministry inspector may, having produced some duly authenticated document showing his appointment if required to do so, enter at any reasonable hour upon land which is being used for agriculture; twenty-four hours' notice of intended entry must be given in the case of entry to a dwelling house.[38]

Moreover the Agriculture (Poisonous Substances) Act, 1952, empowers the making of regulations for the purpose of protecting workers against risks of poisoning by substances to which the Act applies, arising from their working in connection with the use in agriculture of such substances, or on land on which such substances are being or have been used in agriculture.[39] The matters for which the regulations may provide include imposing restrictions or conditions as to the purposes for which or circumstances in which a substance may be used (including involving a general prevention of the use of a particular substance in agriculture); requiring the provision and keeping available of protective clothing and equipment and of other things necessary for protecting persons and their clothing from contamination or removing sources of contamination; requiring the observance of precautions against poisoning; securing intervals between the periods of exposure to risk of poisoning; requiring the provision of and submission to instruction and training in the use of things provided in pursuance of the regulations and the observance of precautions.[40] The Agriculture (Poisonous Substances)(Extension) Orders 1960 to 1966[41] have been made applying the Act to the substances specified in the Orders and other regulations. The precautions to be taken are detailed in the Agriculture (Poisonous Substances) Regulations 1966 to 1969.[42] Ministry inspectors have certain powers of entry to ensure observance of the regulations[43].

Breach of the regulations made under either of the above Acts is in general a criminal offence punishable by a fine, and may give rise to tortious liability towards an employee who is injured in consequence of the breach.

Effect of employee also being at fault

If the employee suffers damage as a result partly of his own fault and partly of the fault of another, the damages recoverable by him shall be reduced to such extent as the court thinks just and equitable having regard to the employee's share in the responsibility for the damage;[44] this applies whether the employee's claim is based on the employer's breach of statutory duty, or his duty of care for the servant's safety irrespective of statute, or his vicarious liability. Moreover the employee's claim can in some circumstances be altogether defeated if he voluntarily and with full knowledge of the risk consents to incur it.

Employer's obligation to insure against liability

Every employer, with certain specified exceptions, carrying on any business in Great Britain must take out and maintain insurance with an authorised insurer against liability for bodily injury or disease sustained by

342

his employees and arising out of and in the course of their employment in Great Britain in that business.[45] Regulations may provide the amount for which an employer is required to insure;[46] this amount has been fixed at £2 million as regards claims by employees arising out of any one occurrence.[47] 'Employee' means a person who has entered into or works under a contract, whether express or implied, of service or apprenticeship.[48] Thus independent contractors and their employees are excluded. An employer is not required to insure an employee who is either the spouse or a specified relative of the employer.[49] Failure to insure where required to do so is a criminal offence punishable by a fine.[50]

Some further obligations of the employer

Agricultural wages

The Agricultural Wages Act, 1948, establishes an Agricultural Wages Board with autonomous powers. The members of the Board consists of five independent or 'appointed' members appointed by the Minister of Agriculture — one of these is designated chairman; — eight representatives of the employers nominated by the National Farmers' Union, and eight representatives of the workers of whom five are nominated by the National Union of Agricultural Workers and three by the agricultural section of the Transport and General Workers' Union.[51]

Under the Act the Board have the duty of fixing minimum rates of wages for workers employed in agriculture on time work. The Board are also empowered, at their discretion, to fix minimum wage rates for workers employed on piece work, such rates to be fixed both by reference to the piece and so as to secure to these workers a minimum wage rate on a time basis. The Board are also empowered to define the employment which is to be treated as overtime employment, to fix differential rates of wages for overtime employment, to make directions regarding holidays and to fix holiday remuneration, and to define and put a value upon the benefits or advantages which may be regarded as payment of wages in kind in lieu of payment in cash.[52]

The Agricultural Wages Board has power to fix minimum rates of wages for periods when a worker is absent through sickness or injury, whether remuneration is payable under the contract of employment in respect of such a period or not.[53]

The exercise of power to make an order increasing wages or improving the terms of agricultural employment is temporarily restricted by a Pay Code and prohibited unless the approval of the Pay Board has been obtained.[54]

The minimum wage rates, once fixed, have the force of law; such rates apply to all agricultural workers in England and Wales, and those rates at least must be paid by their employers. An agreement for the payment of wages which contravenes the Act, or to abstain from exercising a right of enforcing the payment of wages in accordance with the Act, is void.[55]

An employer who fails to pay a worker employed in agriculture wages (including holiday wages) at a rate not less than the minimum fixed by the order of the Agricultural Wages Board is liable on conviction to a fine; whether there is a conviction or not, the court must order the employer to pay such sum as is found to represent the difference between the amount which ought to have been paid to the worker during the six month period immediately preceding the date on which the proceedings were commenced and the amount actually so paid to him.[56] Further, an officer authorised by the Minister may institute civil proceedings on behalf of the worker to recover any deficiency in the payment of wages below the minimum rates fixed,[57] or the worker may himself take proceedings within six years of the date of the underpayment;[58] the worker's claim is contractual, being based on his contract as altered in accordance with the Act.

Length of notice to terminate a contract of employment

Under the Contracts of Employment Act, 1972, as amended by the Redundancy Payments Act, 1965, and the Industrial Relations Act, 1971, both employers and employees have the right to certain specified minimum periods of notice in order to terminate the contract of employment. An employer must give an employee at least one week's notice of termination of the employment if the employee has been with that employer continuously for thirteen weeks or more; at least two weeks' notice if continuously employed for two years or more; at least four weeks' notice if continuously employed for five years or more; at least six weeks' notice if continuously employed for ten years or more; and at least eight weeks' notice if continuously employed for fifteen years or more.[59] Conversely an employee must give his employer at least one week's notice if he has been with him continuously for thirteen weeks or more,[60] and this period of notice does not increase with longer service.

The above periods are minimum periods of notice, and if the contract of employment gives a right to longer notice than that specified by the Act then the contract of employment governs and not the Act.

The provisions relating to minimum notice do not apply to certain employees, and in particular exclude employees who work, or are normal-

344

ly expected to work, less than twenty-one hours a week for the employer, and also employees who are engaged for a fixed period exceeding four weeks.

Continuity of employment is not regarded as broken where a business is transferred from one person to another, and if so the whole of the employee's service in the business is regarded as service to the transferee; the same principle applies where the employee is taken into the service of the personal representatives (*ante,* page 120) or trustees of his previous employer, or there is a change in the partners, personal representatives or trustees who employ the employee.[61]

The right of either party to terminate the contract without notice if the behaviour of the other justifies such a course is not affected by the legislation, nor are either the employer or employee prevented from waiving the right to notice or from accepting a payment in lieu of notice.[62]

Unless the employee is working throughout his normal working hours during the period of notice, an employee (other than an employee with a right to a period of notice which exceeds the statutory minimum by a week or more) is guaranteed minimum pay during the period of notice if he does not work some or all of his normal working hours because the employer provides no work for him although he is ready and willing to work, or he is incapable of work because of sickness or injury, or he is on holiday; there are detailed rules as to how the guaranteed minimum pay during this period is to be calculated.[63]

Employee's right to written particulars of the terms of employment

Section 4 of the Act imposes a duty upon employers to give their employees written information about the main terms of the contract of employment, and the purpose is to give employees a clear understanding of their rights and obligations under the contract. The contract of employment itself need not be made in writing, but the employee must be given a written record of its important terms. This written statement must be furnished within thirteen weeks after the employment commences; certain employees, such as those who are normally employed for less than twenty-one hours a week or who are the parent, spouse or child of the employer, need not be furnished with a written statement. Moreover an employer who re-engages on the same terms an employee whose period of employment ended within the six months prior to re-engagement need not give the employee another written statement.

The written statement must give the names of employer and employee, the date when the employment began, and certain particulars of the terms of employment as they stood at a date (which must be specified) not more than a week before the statement is given to the employee. In the particulars there must be stated the scale or rate of remuneration or the method of calculating remuneration; the intervals at which remuneration is paid; any terms of the contract relating to hours of work (including any terms relating to normal working hours); any terms relating to entitlement to holidays, including public holidays, and holiday pay (with sufficient information to enable the employee's entitlement, including any entitlement to accrued holiday pay on the termination of employment, to be exactly calculated); terms relating to incapacity for work due to sickness or injury (including any provision for sick pay), pensions and pension schemes (with certain exceptions), and the length of notice of termination of the employment which the employee is obliged to give and is entitled to receive or, if the contract is for a fixed period, then the date on which the contract expires. If the contract of employment did not contain any terms concerning one or more of these matters, then the written statement must say that this is so.

The written statement must also contain a note setting out the employee's statutory rights regarding trade union membership and activities. These comprise his right to belong to a registered trade union of his choice or to choose not to belong to such a union or to an unregistered organisation of workers or to any particular union, and to take part at any appropriate time in the activities, including seeking and holding office, of a registered trade union. The note must also explain the effect on the above rights of any agency shop agreement (meaning an agreement between employer(s) and trade union(s) that employees shall be engaged on the terms that they must become members of a union or pay the union dues)[64] or approved closed shop agreement which applies to him;[65] an 'approved close shop agreement' means an agreement made between employer(s) and trade union(s) that workers of the description(s) specified in the agreement shall be employed on terms including that every such worker must (unless specially exempted) be a member of that union or one of those unions, such agreement being made in accordance with proposals approved by an order of the Industrial Court.[66] It must specify the person, either by his name or his position, to whom the employee can apply if he has a grievance about his employment and how the application should be made, and must explain the subsequent steps in any grievance procedure which may be available to the employee.[67]

Instead of itself setting out all or any of the particulars and information mentioned above, the written statement may instead merely refer the employee to a document or documents containing such particulars as are omitted from the written statement; the document or documents must be such as the employee has reasonable opportunities of reading in the course of his employment, or must be made reasonably accessible to him in some other way.[68]

If there is a written contract of employment covering each of the particulars set out above (other than those relating to trade union membership and activity and redress of the employee's grievances) the employer need not issue a written statement of particulars provided that the employee concerned has a copy of the written contract or has reasonable access to a copy. Nevertheless the employer must still issue a note stating the position as regards trade union membership and activity and redress of grievances, unless he refers the employee to a reasonably accessible document containing the same information.[69]

The written information must be kept up to date. If there is a change in the terms of the contract of employment the employer must inform the employee about it by means of a further written statement issued within one month after the change, or, if the employee has been referred to reasonably accessible documents containing some or all of the terms, those documents must be brought up to date within a month of the change.[70]

An employee who is aggrieved because no written particulars have been given to him may require the matter to be referred to an industrial tribunal; the tribunal has power to determine what particulars the written statement should have included in order to comply with the legislation, and may either confirm or amend the particulars or substitute other particulars; the particulars decided upon by the tribunal then take effect as if they had been included in a written statement issued by the employer.[71] Industrial tribunals were established under the Industrial Training Act, 1964. Each tribunal consists of a legally qualified chairman, and two other members selected from panels appointed after consulting organisations of employers and employees respectively.[72] The tribunals sit in different parts of the country as required. These tribunals have no power to grant redress for a breach of the terms of the contract of employment; redress for such a breach must be sought in the ordinary courts of law, usually by means of an action for damages. The tribunals do however have power to grant redress in respect of 'unfair dismissal' (*post*).

Unfair dismissal

Certain employees have the right not to be unfairly dismissed by the employer; their unfair dismissal constitutes an unfair industrial practice.[73] Employees excluded from this protection include those employed by the spouse or a close relative of the employee, or those employed in a business in which, immediately before the employment ceased, there were in the aggregate less than four employees who had been continuously employed for a period of not less than thirteen weeks.[74] Moreover the Act does not confer any protection against unfair dismissal upon an employee who was not continuously employed for a period of at least two years ending with the date when the employment ceased, or if when his employment ceased he had reached the age upon which it was normal in that business for a person occupying his position to retire, or reached the age of sixty-five if male or sixty if female;[75] this exclusion does not however apply if the principal reason for his dismissal was the employee's exercise of, or intention to exercise his right to be a member of a trade union of his choice, or in general to refuse to be a member, or his right to take part at any appropriate time in the activities of the union of which he was a member.[76] In deciding whether the dismissal of an employee was unfair, it is for the employer to show the principal reason for the dismissal and that the reason was one either specified in the Act or some other substantial reason sufficient to justify the dismissal of an employee holding that position;[77] the reasons specified in the Act are those relating either to the employee's capability or qualifications for performing work of the kind he was employed to do or related to the conduct of the employee, or because the employee was redundant or could not continue to work in the post he held without contravening some enactment.[78] The dismissal is regarded as unfair if the principal reason for it was that the employee had exercised or shown an intention to exercise his right to join a trade union of his choice, or in general to choose not to do so, or to take part at any appropriate time in activities of a trade union of which he was a member;[79] if he was made redundant in circumstances where the person selected for redundancy might equally well have been another employee or one of several employees of similar rank in the business, and if the person actually dismissed for redundancy was selected primarily because of his exercise or intended exercise of any of his rights set out above relating to trade unions, or if he was selected for dismissal in contravention of a customary arrangement or agreed procedure relating to redundancy and with no special reason for departing from it, then the dismissal is to be regarded as unfair.[80]

As mentioned above, unfair dismissal of an employee who is protected by the provisions of the Act is an 'unfair industrial practice'; a complaint against this may be presented to an industrial tribunal by the person

348

dismissed.[81] If the tribunal finds the complaint to be well founded it may recommend re-engagement of the complainant if this appears to be both practicable and equitable, stating the terms on which it thinks it would be reasonable for the complainant to be thus re-engaged;[82] if the tribunal does not recommend re-engagement, or if the recommendation is not complied with, the tribunal must award compensation to be paid to the complainant by the employer.[83]

Redundancy payments

Under the Redundancy Payments Acts, 1965 and 1969, as amended by the Industrial Relations Act, 1971, and regulations made thereunder, employers are required to make lump sum payments, known as 'redundancy payments', by way of compensation to employees who have been dismissed because of redundancy. Such payments must also be made in certain circumstances to employees who have been merely laid off or kept on short-time for a substantial period.

In general the Redundancy Payments Act, 1965, extends to all employees, but there are certain specified groups who are excepted; the excepted groups include employees with less than two years continuous service with their employer,[84] employees who work, or are normally expected to work, less than twenty-one hours a week,[85] or who are the spouse, or domestic servants who are close relatives, of their employer,[86] or whose reckonable service ends on or after their sixty-fifth birthday if male and sixtieth birthday if female.[87] In deciding whether an employee has given continuous service, if he has received a redundancy payment his continuity of employment is regarded as broken for the purpose of assessing any subsequent redundancy payment, even if the employee is re-engaged immediately after the termination of his original contract of employment.[88] As to what is continuous service, the provisions of the Contract of Employment Act, 1972, Schedule 1 (*ante,* page 345) apply.[89]

In order to be eligible for a redundancy payment, an employee who is otherwise qualified for one must as a rule have been dismissed because of his redundancy, and this will be so if the whole or the main reason for his dismissal is that the employer's needs for employees to do work of a particular kind have diminished or ceased;[90] the reason why the employer needs fewer employees to do work of that particular kind is irrelevant. If the reason of the dismissal is disputed, the employer has the burden of proving that the employee was not redundant. The employee is only 'dismissed' if it is the employer who terminates the contract expressly or by conduct, or if a fixed period of employment expires without being renewed under the contract, or the employee becomes entitled to end the contract without notice by reason of his employer's conduct and does so.[91] If the employee's dismissal was wholly or mainly due to some cause other than redundancy, such as inefficiency, unsuitability or for reasons of health, then the employee is not entitled to a redundancy payment. An employee who is dismissed on account of misconduct by him justifying summary dismissal is disentitled to a redundancy payment.[92]

Moreover an employee who is either laid off or kept on short-time (as defined by section 5) for the period or periods set out in the Act is entitled, subject to compliance with certain other conditions, to give the employer a week's notice terminating the employment and to claim redundancy payment even though he has not been dismissed.[93]

If a redundant employee is given an offer in writing of other work by his employer, then if the employee accepts the alternative work he is in general not entitled to redundancy payment, but his new and his old work will count as a continuous period of service.[94] If the employee refuses the alternative work he is in general disentitled to redundancy payment if the terms (including the place of work and his rank) of the new work offered are similar to those in force immediately before his dismissal and he unreasonably refuses the offer;[95] he is also debarred from receiving such a payment if, although the new terms offered are different from the previous terms, the new terms are nevertheless suitable to the employee in question and he unreasonably refuses them.[96]

If an employee of a company is taken into the employment of another company at a time when one of the companies is a subsidiary (as defined in the Companies Act, 1948, section 154) of another company, or both companies are subsidiaries of a third company, this is not in general regarded as breaking the continuity of his employment. If an employee with one such company becomes redundant there but is offered alternative work with the second such company, this is treated as if it was an offer of work with the same employer.[97]

If there is a change in the ownership of a business but the employee continues to work for the new owner on the same terms (ignoring the change of employer) as before with no break in employment, or accepts re-engagement on different terms and without a break in employment exceeding four weeks, the employee is not entitled to any redundancy payment. In such circumstances the change of ownership is not regarded as breaking the employee's continuity of employment, thus if at some later date he is dismissed by the new owner so as to qualify for a redundancy payment, that payment (which will all be payable by the new

350

owner) will be based on the whole of the employee's continuous service with the business and including service with both owners. An employee who refuses a suitable offer of re-engagement from the new owner is in general not entitled to a redundancy payment unless his refusal was reasonable. The rules regarding change of ownership also apply if the person who owned the business immediately before the change is one of the persons who own it immediately after the change, or if the persons who owned it immediately before the change include the person or persons who own it immediately after the change. [98]

Effect of the employer's death

If the business ceases as a result of the employer's death, then the employer's executors or administrators (*ante,* page 120) must treat any redundancy payments to the deceased's employees as a debt to be met out of the deceased's estate. If the executors or administrators carry on the business and the employees accept re-engagement with them within eight weeks of the employer's death, the employees are not entitled to redundancy payments; moreover if a written offer is made to re-engage the employee on the same (ignoring the change of employer) or on suitable terms under a new contract to take effect within eight weeks after the employer's death, then if the employee refuses the offer he is not entitled to redundancy payment if his refusal was unreasonable. [99]

Contracts for a fixed period

Employees engaged under a contract for a fixed period of two years or more are, provided the contract was made on or after 6 December 1965, as much entitled to redundancy payments as any other employees unless they have made a written agreement with their employer to waive any right to a redundancy payment if they are not re-engaged at the end of the contractual period, [100] although if they are dismissed because of redundancy before the end of the contractual period they are entitled to redundancy payment to the normal extent.

The time within which an employee's claim must be made

If the employee thinks he has not received a sufficient redundancy payment, he must in general make his claim in writing to reach the employer within six months after the date of his dismissal. [101]

The amount of the redundancy payment

The amount of the payment is related to the number of complete years (each year being reckoned as a period of fifty-two weeks and not as a calendar year) of continuous employment with the present employer, subject to a maximum period of twenty years and reckoned backwards from the date on which the employee is dismissed because of redundancy; service rendered before the employee reached the age of eighteen is not counted.

For each completed year of service payment must be made as follows:

(a)   for each year of employment rendered at the age of forty-one or over but under the age of sixty-five (or sixty if a woman) – one and a half week's pay;

(b)   for each year of employment rendered at the age of twenty-one or more but under the age of forty-one – one week's pay;

(c)   for each year of employment rendered at the age of eighteen and over, but under the age of twenty-two – half a week's pay.

No payment is made for a fraction of a year, and there are detailed rules for calculating what is 'a week's pay'; the weekly earnings as defined are subject to an upward limit of £40 per week.

As already seen (*ante,* page 349), an employee is not entitled to a redundancy payment if he has reached the age of sixty-five if male and sixty if female before his contract terminates; moreover if the employee's contract ends after the employee has reached the age of sixty-four if male and fifty-nine if female, the redundancy payment to which the employee would otherwise have been entitled is reduced by one-twelfth for every complete month of service after that age.

The rules above are set out in the Redundancy Payments Act, 1965. [102]

Effect of pension or lump sum superannuation payment

If the employer pays a pension or a lump sum superannuation payment, or a combination of these, to a redundant employee, the employer may if he wishes reduce or avoid making the redundancy payment to an extent depending on the size of the pension or the lump superannuation payment. [103]

Written explanation to employee

The employer must at or before the time of making a redundancy payment furnish the employee with a written statement indicating how the amount of the payment has been calculated. Neglect to do so without reasonable excuse is a criminal offence punishable by a fine. [104]

The tax aspect

An employee who receives a redundancy payment calculated in accordance with the Act does not have to pay income tax upon it under Schedule E[105] (*ante*, pages 139–43). Conversely, contributions to the Redundancy Fund made by an employer and his share of a redundancy payment (*post*) are deductible business expenses for tax purposes (*ante*, pages 130–2).

The redundancy fund

Employers make weekly contributions to the Redundancy Fund;[106] the contributions are collected with the National Insurance contributions and are thus payable even in respect of employees who are not entitled to redundancy payments.

An employer who is liable to make a redundancy payment which is required by the Act may claim a rebate from the Fund of half the cost of the redundancy payment. [107] Advance notice of intention to dismiss an employee because of redundancy should in general be given in writing by the employer to the employment exchange not less than fourteen days before the employment is to terminate; failure to give this notice without reasonable excuse may result in a reduction of rebate by up to 10 per cent. [108] The advance notice must contain certain specified particulars about each employee who is to be dismissed.

A rebate on a redundancy payment must be claimed within six months of the date on which the payment was made to the employee. [109]

Reference of disputes to a tribunal

Disputes concerning the right to or the amount of redundancy payments or about rebates from the Fund are referred to an industrial tribunal (*ante*, page 347) for decision.[110] In general application to a tribunal must be made within six months after the date on which the employment was terminated.[111]

Notes

[1] Law Reform (Personal Injuries) Act, 1948, section 2.

[2] [1953] 1 Q.B. 617.

[3] [1938] A.C. 57.

[4] Employer's Liability (Defective Equipment) Act, 1969, section 1(1).

[5] Section 1(2).

[6] Section 1(3).

[7] *Davidson* v. *Handley Page* [1945] 1 All E.R. 235.

[8] *Wilson* v. *Tyneside Window Cleaning Co.* [1958] 2 Q.B. 110.

[9] *Jenner* v. *Allen West and Co. Ltd.* [1959] 1 W.L.R. 554.

[10] *Clifford* v. *Charles H. Challen & Son* [1951] 1 K.B. 495.

[11] *Finch* v. *Telegraph Construction and Maintenance Co.* [1949] 1 All E.R. 452.

[12] (1965) 109 S.J. 133.

[13] [1953] 1 W.L.R. 857.

[14] *Qualcast (Wolverhampton) Ltd.* v. *Haynes* [1959] A.C. 743.

[15] *Paris* v. *Stepney Borough Council* [1951] A.C. 367.

[16] *Wilsons & Clyde Coal Co.* v. *English* [1938] A.C. 57; *Paine* v. *Colne Valley Electricity Supply Co.* [1938] 4 All E.R. 803.

[17] [1959] 2 Q.B. 57.

[18] Agriculture (Safety, Health and Welfare Provisions) Act, 1956, section 1(1).

[19] Section 1(3).

[20] Section 2(1).

[21] Section 24(1).

[22] Section 2(2).

[23] 1959 S.I. 1959 No. 2120.

[24] Section 3(1).

[25] Sections 3(2) and 24(1).

[26] Section 3(7).

[27] Section 6(1).

[28] S.I. 1957 No. 1386.

[29] S.I. 1959 No. 427.

[30] S.I. 1959 No. 1216.

[31] S.I. 1962 No. 1472.

[32] S.I. 1960 No. 1199.

[33] S.I. 1967 No. 1072.

[34] S.I. 1959 No. 428.

[35] S.I. 1957 No. 1385.

[36] S.I. 1957 No. 940.

[37] Section 16.

[38] Section 10.

[39] Agriculture (Poisonous Substances) Act, 1952, section 1(1).

[40] Section 1(3).

[41] S.I. 1960 No. 398, S.I. 1965 No. 1395, S.I. 1966 No. 645.

[42] S.I. 1966 No. 1063, S.I. 1967 No. 1860, and S.I. 1969 No. 84.

[43] Section 3.

[44] Law Reform (Contributory Negligence) Act, 1945, Section 1(1).

[45] Employers' Liability (Compulsory Insurance) Act, 1969, Section 1(1).

[46] Section 1(2).

[47] Employers' Liability (Compulsory Insurance) General Regulations 1971 (S.I. 1971 No. 1117).

[48] Section 2(1).

[49] Section 2(2).

[50] Section 5.

[51] Agricultural Wages Act, 1948, section 1 and First Schedule.

[52] Section 3.

[53] Agriculture Act, 1967, section 67(1).

[54] Counter-Inflation Act, 1973, section 2; The Counter-Inflation (Price and Pay Code) Order (No. 2) 1973, S.I. 1973 No. 1785.

[55] Agricultural Wages Act, 1948, section 11(1).

[56] Agricultural Wages Act, 1948, section 4(1).

[57] Section 12.

[58] *Gutsell* v. *Reeve* [1936] 1 K.B. 272.

[59] Contracts of Employment Act, 1972, section 1(1).

[60] Contracts of Employment Act, 1972, section 1(2).

[61] Schedule 1.

[62] Section 1(3) and (6).

[63] Section 2 and Schedule 2.

[64] Industrial Relations Act, 1971, section 11(1).

[65] Contracts of Employment Act, 1972, section 4(2); Industrial Relations Act, 1971, section 5.

[66] Industrial Relations Act, 1971, section 17(1).

[67] Contracts of Employment Act, 1972, section 4.

[68] Contracts of Employment Act, 1972, section 4(5).

[69] Contract of Employment Act, 1972, section 6.

[70] Contracts of Employment Act, 1972, section 5.

[71] Contracts of Employment Act, 1972, section 8.

[72] Industrial Tribunals (England and Wales) Regulations 1965, S.I. 1965 No. 1101; 1967 No. 301; 1968 No. 729; 1970 No. 941).

[73] Industrial Relations Act, 1971, section 22(1).

[74] Section 27(1).

[75] Section 28.

[76] Section 29(1).

[77] Section 24(1).

[78] Section 24(2).

[79] Section 24(4).

[80] Section 24(5).

[81] Section 106(1).

[82] Section 106(4).

[83] Section 106(5).

[84] Redundancy Payments Act, 1965, section 8.

[85] Redundancy Payments Act, 1965, section 8, incorporating Contracts of Employment Act, 1963, Schedule 1.

[86] Redundancy Payments Act, 1965, sections 16(3) and 19(2).

[87] Section 2(1).

[88] Section 24.

[89] Redundancy Payments Act, 1965, section 8(2); Contracts of Employment Act, 1972, section 13(6).

[90] Redundancy Payments Act, 1965, section 1(2).

[91] Section 3.

[92] Section 2(2).

[93] Sections 6 and 7.

[94] Section 3.

[95] Section 2(3).

[96] Section 2(4).

[97] Section 48.

[98] Section 13.

[99] Section 23 and Schedule 4.

[100] Section 15(2).

[101] Section 21; Industrial Relations Act, 1971, section 150.

[102] Sections 8 and 24 and Schedule 1.

[103] Section 14 and the Redundancy Payments (Pensions) Regulations 1965, S.I. 1965 No. 1932.

[104] Section 18.

[105] *Ante*, pages 139–43; Income and Corporation Taxes Act, 1972, section 412(1).

[106] Section 27.

[107] Schedule 5; Redundancy Rebates Act, 1969, section 1(1).

[108] Section 30(6).

[109] Section 30 and the Redundancy Payments Rebates Regulations 1965, S.I. 1965 No. 1893, amended as by the Redundancy Payments Rebates (Amendment) Regulations, 1965, S.I. 1965 No. 2067.

[110] Sections 9(1) and 56(1).

[111] Section 21; Industrial Relations Act, 1971, section 150.

11 Insurance

General principles

A contract of insurance is one whereby the insurer, in return for a money payment called the premium, or a series of such payments, agrees to pay a sum of money to the insured on the happening of a specified event. Most contracts of insurance are contracts of indemnity, which means that the insurer's liability is limited to the actual loss which is sustained and proved by the insured; the sum recoverable is also limited to the amount for which he has insured, so that recovery by the insured is limited to the lesser of either the actual loss sustained by him by reason of a risk against which he has insured or the sum for which he is stated to be covered in the policy. If the insured wishes to avoid a possible subsequent dispute with his insurance company concerning value in the event of loss or damage to the thing insured, he should seek to obtain the insurer's agreement about the value of the article and get this agreement recorded in the policy when it is taken out, thus making it a valued policy; the insurer then cannot dispute the value unless fraud or something analogous is proved.

Exceptionally, policies of life insurance and insurances against personal accident or illness of the insured himself are not indemnity policies, thus in general the amount stipulated in the policy is recoverable regardless of what the actual loss may be.

The insurer's rights of subrogation and contribution (*post*, pages 361–2), apply in connection with policies of indemnity, but not otherwise.

In all policies of insurance the utmost good faith must by law be shown on both sides, and if this principle is broken the other party may avoid the contract. Thus there must be no misrepresentation, however innocent, of a material fact, nor must a party neglect to make full and positive disclosure, whether or not asked, of all material facts known to him. This duty in practice falls most heavily upon the insured, in that it is he who is in possession of most of the facts relating to the subject matter which he wishes to insure. The test of what is material is whether disclosure would affect the mind of a prudent insurer in deciding whether to take the risk at all or what premium to fix.

It would for example, be material for the insurer to know, in relation to a proposal for fire insurance on a building, that a previous proposal for motor insurance by the would-be insured had been declined by another company.[1] The test of materiality is objective and does not depend on what the insured thinks to be material; in borderline cases the court usually tends to regard facts as material. There is no duty to disclose facts which are a matter of common knowledge, or which have no bearing upon the risk, or which are known to the insurer, nor can the insured be expected to disclose facts of which he did not know, unless perhaps he ought reasonably to have been aware of them. The duty to disclose persists right up to the moment that the contract of insurance comes into existence, and frequently the contract stipulates that the insurance will not commence until the first premium has been paid. In the case of what are in fact new policies such as the annual renewal of most fire insurance and motor insurance policies, a duty to make disclosure of all material facts which have arisen since the inception of the last policy arises each time the new policy is taken out; contrast the usual type of life insurance policy which is usually made once and for all throughout the period of the insurance upon its inception, despite the premiums being payable annually. Sometimes, however, the questionnaire which is usually issued by the insurance company to be filled in by the insured before a contract of insurance is effected will be found to contain the stringent clause 'the insured's answers shall be the basis of the contract' or analogous words; the effect of such a clause is to raise the status of each of his replies, whether important or not, to that of a vital term, breach of which would entitle the insurer to avoid the policy, and also to entitle the insurer to repudiate if there has been any inaccuracy in the answers, whether or not the insured knew or indeed could have known his reply to be inaccurate! The policy or the negotiations leading up to it may contain other and perhaps severe terms concerning disclosure, which will according to their construction either supersede or supplement what would otherwise be the position implied by law, as previously discussed.

The fact that the risk insured against does not materialise does not, of course, mean that the consideration for the payment of the premiums has failed, because the insurer has been potentially liable to pay out under the policy should the risk have materialised. But if the insurer elects to avoid the policy for misrepresentation or non-disclosure of material fact, his election to do this nullifies the contract of insurance with retrospective effect from its inception, thus any premium paid must be refunded.[2] An exception to this principle exists if the insured has been guilty of **fraud**; he will not be allowed to make his own fraud the basis of a claim for the return of his premium.[3]

The general law does not make any provision that a proportionate part of the premium shall be returned if the policy terminates before the end of the full period of insurance which was contemplated, but the policy itself will often be found to contain a clause permitting this.

Any ambiguity in the insurance policy itself is resolved against the insurer in so far as he chose the words, as he usually does; it is his task to ensure that words chosen by him are clear. But, somewhat perplexingly, the word 'warranty' in relation to insurance law is equivalent to the word 'condition' throughout the rest of the law of contract (*ante,* page 266), so that a breach of it entitles the insurer to repudiate the contract altogether. The insurer may expressly or impliedly waive a breach by the insured of his obligations; waiver would for example be constituted by subsequent acceptance of a premium by the insurer with full knowledge of the insured's breach.

The policy itself may contain terms concerning the period within which notice of loss or a claim must be given and the evidence which must be furnished; although the effect of failure to do so will depend on the precise words of the policy, the result of such failure will usually be to prevent any claim by the insured.

The making of a fraudulent claim by the insured, as distinct from an honest but erroneous assessment of his loss, causes him to forfeit all his rights under the policy.

The right of subrogation, which applies to all contracts of insurance which are contracts of indemnity (*ante,* page 359) enables an insurer, having compensated his insured under the policy for a loss incurred, to take over all rights of the insured against a third party who is responsible for causing the loss or otherwise legally liable to make it good.[4] Thus if a neighbour by his negligence burns down X's house, X's insurer, having compensated X, takes over X's right to sue the neighbour for damages for negligence. The action against the third party must be brought in the name of the insured, and it is the insured's duty, on receipt of a satisfactory indemnity against costs, to permit the insurer to use his name for this;[5] if the insurer recovers more damages than he paid·out to the insured, he must hand over the excess to the insured. The insured must not do anything which may prejudice the exercise by the insurer of this right of subrogation, otherwise he releases his own insurer by so doing.[6]

Subject to contrary agreement, the insured may insure against the same risk with as many different insurers as he wishes, and he can recover from any of them. If the policy is one of indemnity, he will not be able to recover in total more than his actual loss,[7] and an insurer who has paid more than his share will be able to claim rateable contribution from the other insurers where the same interest was insured against the same risk.

Life insurance

In life insurance the insurer undertakes, usually in return for premiums which are paid periodically, to pay a specified sum on the death of the person insured, who may or may not be the person paying the premiums. There are various kinds of life insurance policy. An endowment policy provides for payment of the sum assured in the event of survival to an agreed age or at the end of an agreed term of years, with the proviso that the sum assured will be paid in any event if death occurs before the full age is reached or the full length of time expires. A whole life policy provides that the sum assured shall be paid on death whenever the death may occur, and not before then. A policy may either be a with-profits policy or a without-profits policy, and depending on which of these it is the policy holder either will or will not share in the benefit of the profits earned by his insurance company; if the policy is with profits the company will declare bonuses from time to time and the value of the bonuses will be added to the amount payable under the policy, the total sum being actually paid out by the company when the policy matures. There are also policies where the contract between the insurance company and the insured is that the great bulk of the premiums paid by the insured shall be invested in the shares of selected public companies which are quoted on the Stock Exchange, and that the sum ultimately payable to the policy holder when his policy matures shall depend upon the upward or downward fluctuation of the stock market quotation for the shares.

Investing in a life policy confers the following tax advantages. Firstly, some relief against income tax is normally claimable in respect of life insurance premiums paid by the taxpayer (see *ante,* pages 150–1). Moreover the income obtained by the life insurance company from investing the premiums paid by the policy holders is taxed at a special rate of tax which is lower than that which would be payable by the tax payer were he in receipt of the income unless he has a very low income.

A life policy can often be used as security for the obtaining of a loan, either from one's banker by means of an overdraft or in most cases from the insurance company who issued the policy, the rate of interest charged usually being more favourable to the borrower in the latter case; such loans are often sought in conjunction with house purchase. A life policy may be assigned either by endorsement on the policy or by a separate document in the form set out in the Schedule to the Act.[8] Written notice to the insurer is necessary to preserve the priority of the transferee.[9]

A policy can be taken out on the insured's own life with a view to the proceeds becoming available to meet the liability for estate duty which may arise on the insured's death. In such a case it is important to see that the policy monies do not themselves become part of the estate of the deceased, thus increasing the liability to estate duty; this lamentable result can be avoided by taking out the policy in trust for the person who will inherit the property and who, had this procedure not been followed, might well have had to bear the duty (see *ante*, page 181).

Prima facie it is an implied condition of the policy that the insured will not intentionally terminate his own life.

A policy of insurance in which the insured has no insurable interest is at least void as a wager under the Gaming Act, 1845. Moreover the Life Assurance Act, 1774, prohibits the making of any insurance on the life or lives of any person, or persons, or on any other event or events whatsoever, wherein the person for whose benefit the policy is made has no interest;[10] such policies are therefore not merely void but also illegal, the great practical difference being that under a void policy the premiums paid are in general recoverable if the insurer has never been potentially liable to make a payment in the event of the risk materialising and there is thus a total failure of consideration (*ante,* pages 262–3), whereas premiums paid under an illegal contract are in general irrecoverable (*ante*, page 271). The 1774 Act prohibits recovery of any greater sum than the amount of the insurable interest, and requires the name of the person for whose benefit the policy is taken out to be inserted in the policy. Despite its title the Life Assurance Act is not limited to life insurance, but section 4 of the Act exempts policies of insurance on ships, goods and merchandise from its other provisions; these latter policies are therefore void but not illegal.

A person has an insurable interest in the property or life insured if he is likely to benefit from its continued existence or be prejudiced by its destruction. [11] A shareholder in a company, for example, has no insurable interest in the assets of the company, since the assets are not his property but are the property of the company, thus any policy taken out by him purporting to insure those assets is ineffective. [12]

Everyone is deemed to have an unlimited insurable interest in his or her own or spouse's life. Other relatives are not presumed to have an insurable interest in each other's lives, and the existence of such an interest must therefore be proved if the insurance is to be valid; a creditor may insure the life of his debtor up to the amount of the debt, and a master and his servant have insurable interests in each other's lives. In life insurance, it is sufficient that the insurable interest exists when the policy is taken out, and it need not continue until the date of death and is not affected by the subsequent divorce of the spouse.

A policy taken out by a man on his life and expressed to be for the benefit of his wife and/or children, or by a woman on her life and expressed for the benefit of her husband and/or children, will create a trust in favour of the named persons, thus the money payable under the policy will not form part of the estate of the deceased person. [13] The policy usually names trustees to receive the policy monies on behalf of the beneficiaries.

Fire insurance

The insured must have an insurable interest (*ante,* page 363) in the property insured, otherwise he can suffer no loss through its destruction against which to be indemnified; in general the insurable interest must exist both at the time when the policy is taken out and at the time of the loss. With regard to a contract for the purchase of land, it should be noted that the beneficial interest passes to the buyer as soon as an enforceable contract has been made, thus he can and should insure the property from that time. If several persons are interested in the same property, each may insure his own interest therein, or one of them may insure for himself and as agent for the other interested parties. A policy of fire insurance is personal to the insured and, subject to statute, the benefit of the policy will not pass to a third party merely because the property which was insured was transferred to him. But by section 47 of the Law of Property Act, 1925, where money becomes payable under the vendor's insurance policy in respect of harm to the property contracted to be sold, the vendor holds the money on trust for the purchaser on completion, provided (a) the contract for the sale of the land does not stipulate to the contrary; (b) payment of a proportionate part of the premium is made by the purchaser; (c) the consent of the insurer, if requisite (and *prima facie* his consent is requisite) is obtained.

There cannot be a fire without ignition, but it is immaterial whether the fire is caused by negligence, including negligence of the insured himself. [14]

In the event of total destruction of the property, the amount recoverable is the value of the property, up to the amount for which it is insured (*ante,* page 359). Value is assessed on the basis of the market value at the time and place of the fire, but if the property had no market value, or the insured needs and needed it to carry on his business, the value is based on the cost of reinstating the property. [15] In the case of a partial loss, the amount recoverable is the cost of repair, up to the sum insured. The insured cannot recover more than the value of his own interest in the property since that is the loss to him, unless the policy was expressed to be for the benefit of all parties interested in the property. A further possible consequence of under-insurance is dealt with later (*post*).

The obligation of the insurer is to pay out in money, and therefore, unless an Act of Parliament or the terms of the policy so provide, the insurer cannot insist upon a right of reinstatement by replacing the property as it was before the fire. But by the Fires Prevention (Metropolis) Act, 1774, the insurer of any building in England and Wales against loss by fire, against whom a valid claim is made, must expend the insurance money, as far as it will go, upon reinstating the property at the request of any person interested in it or entitled to it; such persons include the legal owner, landlord and tenant, tenant for life and remainderman (*ante,* pages 4–6) and mortgagor and mortgagee. But it is doubtful whether a purchaser under a contract to buy the property is 'a person interested' within the meaning of the Act, so until this point is settled it is better that he should not risk it but should take out his own policy or make other similar arrangements. The policy itself may confer an option on the insurer to reinstate if the insurer wishes; this option is solely for the insurer's benefit, thus the insured cannot call upon him to reinstate. But if the insurer elects to reinstate, he comes under a contractual obligation to do so notwithstanding that the work may subsequently turn out to be much more expensive than he supposed, and if he fails to do so damages may be awarded against him for a sum which is not necessarily limited to the amount which would have been payable under the policy had the insurer paid in money.

Many fire insurance policies will be found to contain an 'average' clause; its effect is that if the property covered by the policy is insured for less than its actual value, the insurer will only pay a similar proportion of the loss suffered. Thus if property worth £2,000 is insured for £1,000 and is later totally destroyed by fire, the insurer is only liable to pay £500. The clause thus increases the penalty for being under-insured.

In order that the insurer may minimise his loss, he may enter and remain on the premises damaged by fire and take possession of any salvage there; when the insurer has paid the insured the full amount of the loss, title to the salvage thereupon passes to the insurer.

Consequental loss insurance

This type of insurance may be sought against, for example, loss of profits due to the disruption of a business from the destruction of the business premises by fire; insurance of the building against fire would of itself cover no more than the value of the building and confer no protection against loss of profit during a period when the building could not be used.[16]

Liability insurance

An insurance of property by its owner does not usually protect the insured against a liability which is connected with the property, thus, for example, if a house owner has insured his house against fire, and by the owner's negligence a fire begins which burns down both his own house and his neighbour's house, his policy will not cover him against his liability for his negligence to his neighbour. Special policies may be taken out to secure indemnity against this and against other risks, such as liability for straying animals and liability for breach of a master's obligation for the safety of his servants (*ante,* pages 337–43).

As in all forms of insurance, great care should be taken in scrutinising the policy in order to see precisely which risks are covered by it and which risks are not; as regards the latter, it may if desired be possible to take out a further policy regarding these.

If an employer's liability policy is taken out, it usually provides the employer with cover against any liability to a person who has a contract of service or apprenticeship with him and is injured by accident or disease arising out of and in the course of the employment; the cover therefore excludes liability (which it is possible to incur, although the likelihood is less) to a person who is not the servant of the insured, such as employees of an independent contractor engaged in doing work on the insured's premises. The policy may contain conditions, often of a somewhat vague nature, designed to restrict the insurer's liability by requiring the employer to have taken safety precautions, and these should be carefully studied.

Livestock insurance

Most farm animals can be insured by taking out a policy upon the life of the animal insured; the policy will usually be expressed to cover death by disease, and may cover death by accident, but death from old age is usually not covered. Where the policy covers death by accident, this will include the reasonable slaughter of the animal from humane motives in consequence of it having been seriously injured in an accident. Alternatively a policy may be taken out in respect of death from a particular disease, such as foot and mouth disease, or from particular diseases only.

A policy insuring farm animals against the risk of death from accident or disease may limit the amount which the insurers will pay in respect of each animal, although the value of the animal may in fact be in excess of this limit.

Motor vehicle insurance

In general it is not lawful for a person to use, or to cause or permit any other person to use, a motor vehicle on a road unless there is in force in relation to such user a policy of insurance, issued by an authorised insurer, which complies with the requirements of the Road Traffic Act, 1972, section 143, as regards third party risks; a cover note is a sufficient policy of insurance for this purpose. The policy must provide insurance cover against any liability incurred in respect of death or bodily injury to any person, including passengers, which is caused by or arises out of the use of the insured vehicle on a road; the policy must also cover, up to the amounts laid down by sections 154–155 of the Act, the cost of providing emergency medical treatment to injured third parties. [17] But the policy need not cover liability for death or bodily injury sustained by a person in the employment of a person insured under the policy if the death or injury arises out of and in the course of the employment. [18] If the insured causes or permits his car to be driven by another person, and neither have an insurance policy covering use of the vehicle when driven by this person in respect of the compulsory risks, the insured becomes liable to criminal penalties and is also liable in tort for breach of statutory duty to compensate a third party injured in respect of such a risk. [19]

The Act confers further benefits on a third party who is injured in respect of the compulsory risks. This is achieved, firstly, by making certain limiting clauses in the policy void to exclude his claim. Thus any clause in the policy excluding the insurer's liability by reason of anything done or omitted after the accident, such as the insured's failure to give notice of the claim within seven days, will not prevent a third party claiming in respect of the compulsory risks, though the policy may contain a clause that in such an event the insured must indemnify his in-

367

surer. [20] Moreover clauses in the policy restricting cover by reference to the age or physical or mental condition of the driver, the condition of the vehicle, the number of persons carried or area within which the vehicle may be driven and analogous clauses, are made void against a third party as regards the compulsory risks, though if the insurer has to pay despite a breach of the clause he has a right to recover an indemnity from his insured. [21] Secondly, although the third party is a stranger to the contract between the insurer and the insured, if he obtains judgement in court against the insured in respect of a compulsory risk he may enforce the judgement and costs directly against the insurer. [22] But the use of the vehicle must have been a use covered by the policy, and there are also certain procedural requirements. The insurer may however avoid liability if before or within three months after the start of proceedings by the injured third party against the insured, the insurer obtains a declaration that he is entitled to avoid the policy on the ground of fraud or non-disclosure by the insured; the injured person must be notified of and may if he wishes contest such proceedings. [23]

Notwithstanding all this, it is still possible for an injured third party to have no enforceable claim against an insurer in respect of a compulsory risk; the insurer might for example be able to avoid the policy for non-disclosure, or the motorist may have been driving for a purpose not covered by his policy. The policy will usually contain a statement of the purpose or purposes for which the vehicle may be used, and the insurer is only at risk while the vehicle is in fact being so used, thus if the vehicle is being used for another purpose the policy affords no cover until the permitted use is resumed. [24] Thus if the permitted user is 'domestic and pleasure purposes', as is the case concerning many private cars, the insurance will not attach while the vehicle is being used for a journey the purpose of which is to negotiate a business transaction. [25] Similarly, if the permitted use is for agricultural purposes, this will not cover moving household furniture for a farm servant. [26]

By an agreement between the Minister of Transport and the Motor Insurers Bureau the Bureau have agreed to pay the injured third party, where no insurance exists, in respect of damage inflicted on him from a risk against which it is compulsory to insure.

With regard to risks against which it is *not* compulsory to insure, the policy may also, for example, provide cover, in return for an enhanced premium, against damage to the property of third parties, and also against loss or damage to the insured's vehicle itself either arising only from specified risks or 'however caused'. Where the vehicle itself is insured against damage, insurers have usually found it desirable to seek to exclude a multitude of small claims. This is normally achieved either by inserting a clause in the policy that the insured shall himself bear the cost of the damage up to a certain figure, or by contracting to allow the insured a sizeable rebate of premium provided he makes no claim upon the insurer, thus deterring him from making a claim unless a substantial sum is involved.

Notes

[1] *Locker & Woolf, Ltd.* v. *Western Australian Insurance Co. Ltd.* [1936] 1 K.B. 408.

[2] *Hemmings* v. *Sceptre Life Association* [1905] 1 Ch. 365.

[3] *Anderson* v. *Thornton* (1853), 3 Ex. Ch. 425.

[4] *Castellain* v. *Preston* (1883) 11 Q.B.D. 380.

[5] *Dane* v. *Mortgage Insurance Corporation* [1894] I Q.B. 54.

[6] *West of England Fire Insurance Co.* v. *Isaacs* [1897] 1 Q.B. 226.

[7] *North British and Mercantile Insurance Co.* v. *London, Liverpool and Globe Insurance Co.* (1877) 5 Ch. D. 569.

[8] Policies of Assurance Act, 1867, section 5.

[9] Section 3.

[10] Life Assurance Act, 1774, section 1.

[11] *Lucena* v. *Crauford* (1806) 2 Bos. and Pul. (N.R.) 269 H.L.

[12] *Macaura* v. *Northern Assurance Co. Ltd.* [1925] A.C. 619.

[13] Married Women's Property Act, 1882, section 11.

[14] *Harris* v. *Poland* [1941] 1 K.B. 462.

[15] *Westminster Fire Office* v. *Glasgow Provident Investment Society* (1888) 13 App. Cas. 999.

[16] *Re Wright and Pole* (1834) 1 Ad. and El. 621.

[17] Road Traffic Act, 1972, section 145(3).

[18] Section 145(4).

[19] *Monk* v. *Warbey* [1935] 1 K.B. 75.

[20] Section 148(2).

[21] Section 148(1).

[22] Section 149(1).

[23] Section 149(3).

[24] *Farr* v. *Motor Traders Mutual Insurance Society* [1920] 3 K.B. 669.

[25] *Wood* v. *General Accident Fire & Life Assurance Corporation* (1948) 65 T.L.R. 53.

[26] *Agnew* v.*Robertson* [1956] S.L.T. (Sh. Ct.) 90.

12 The Institutions of the European Economic Community

The Treaty establishing the European Economic Community (the Rome Treaty) is the constitution of the Community; the Community itself is designed to pave the way to political unity among the member states and the creation of a federal system of government. The Treaty lays down a number of basic principles, and creates a number of institutions through whose working the Community is to function. The principal institutions thus created are

1 *The Commission.* Each of the thirteen Commissioners is in theory nominated by the representatives of all member states acting collectively, but in practice is a national nominee. A person nominated to be a Commissioner is not intended to behave as a national representative but is responsible to the Community as a whole. Each Commissioner is appointed for four years at a time. The Commission initiates legislation, and to that extent may be likened to one of our own government departments preparing a Bill. The Commission may either be required or empowered to carry out this function under the Treaty; before doing so it will probably have consulted experts from the national governments of the member states and their staffs. Consultation may also have taken place with the Economic and Social Committee, which consists of representatives of producers, farmers, carriers, workers, craftsmen, professional occupations and the like; members are appointed by the Council of Ministers (*post*) for a period of four years, such appointments being renewable. The Committee, which has an agricultural section, must be consulted by the Commission where the Treaty so provides, and may be consulted on such other occasions as the Commission think appropriate.

'As to the function to be performed by the Economic and Social Committee' with reference to agriculture 'its agricultural section shall hold itself at the disposal of the Commission to prepare . . . the deliberations of the Committee'.[1]

371

'After consulting the Economic and Social Committee ... the Commission shall submit proposals for working out and implementing the common agricultural policy ... [and] the Council [of Ministers] shall, on a proposal from the Commission and after consulting the Assembly ... make regulations, issue directives, or take decisions ...'.[2] Thus in finding out how the Community has dealt with agricultural problems, the normal solution is to see what the Commission has recommended and what the Council of Ministers (*post*) has agreed should in fact be done.

The Commission frequently also undertakes the administrative function of seeing that the laws which have been made are in fact being carried out; sometimes it undertakes this task because the Treaty itself so requires, and sometimes because the laws produced by the Community institutions so require.

The European Commission also have power to adjudicate on national legislation passed by a member state. It is provided in the Treaty that 'if ... the Commission find that aid granted by a State or through State resources is not compatible with the common market ... it shall decide that the State concerned shall abolish or alter that aid ...'.[3] But aid granted by a member state within the Community in order to promote the economic development of areas where the standard of living is abnormally low or to facilitate the development of certain economic activities or of certain economic areas may be considered an aid compatible with the common market.[4] Thus the Commission either may or may not permit such aids to be granted, as the Commission thinks fit.

The Commission may bring the governments of member states within the Community before the European Court of Justice (*post*) if they fail to obey the Treaty or to abide by the laws which have been made by the institutions of the Community.

2 *The Council of Ministers.* These are a body of national Ministers appointed by the member states of the Community; each Minister is there to represent the state which appointed him. The Council of Ministers represent the member states individually, whereas the Commission represent the Community and take decisions or make proposals from the standpoint of the overall effect on all member states and not just from the national standpoint of individual member states. Legislative proposals drafted by the Commission must be sent to the Council of Ministers to be approved before the proposals can come into effect; when the Council of Ministers meet for this purpose, a delegation from the Commission is also present. The delegation from the Commission does not vote there but may influence the manner in which the votes are cast, and may modify the Commis-

sion's proposals, as a result of what is being said in the Council of Ministers, in order to facilitate agreement. The Council of Ministers can only modify the proposals of the Commission if the Council is unanimous, otherwise the Council must either accept or reject the proposals.

The Council of Ministers must, in accordance with the provisions of the Treaty, ensure co-ordination of the general economic policies of the member states.

3   *The European Assembly.* The Assembly is the nearest approach to a Parliament within the Community institutions. The Assembly is not directly elected, but is appointed by and from the members of the legislative bodies of the member states of the Community. The Assembly is empowered by the Treaty to dismiss the Commission by a two-thirds majority of the votes cast by the Assembly; the built-in safeguard against dismissal by requiring this specially high majority is noteworthy, and in any event the Assembly has no power to appoint a new Commission and indeed the governments of the member states might simply re-appoint the Commissioners who have just been dismissed. Apart from this (in practice somewhat theoretical) power, the Assembly has very little power. Draft legislative proposals must usually be sent to the Assembly for discussion, and amendments can there be suggested but cannot be enforced. The Assembly can put questions, usually in writing, to the Commission or to the Council of Ministers.

4   *The European Court of Justice.* The judges of this Court are appointed by agreement of the governments of the member states of the Community to hold office for a period of six years. The Court must ensure that in the interpretation and application of the Treaty the law is observed. Either the Commission or a member state of the Community which considers that another member state has failed to fulfil an obligation under the Treaty may ultimately bring the matter before the European Court, and if the Court agrees that there has been a failure the member state is required to take the necessary measures to comply with the judgement of the Court.

In *Commission of the European Communities* v. *the Italian Republic* the Council had in 1969 issued Regulation No. 2517/69 in an attempt to rationalise fruit production within the Community; under the regulation fruit producers within the Community were to receive upon request a premium for the destruction of apple trees, pear trees and peach trees. The rates and conditions governing the payment of premiums were laid down by regulation No. 2637/69 made by the Commission in 1969. Some two years later the Commission brought to the attention of the Italian government the fact that these regulations had not yet been implemented in Italy, and invited the Italian government to do so, otherwise the Commission would take legal proceedings in accordance with the machinery of the Treaty to ensure the observance of Community law. As the Italian government made no reply, the Commission took legal proceedings against the Italian government before the European Court of Justice. The Court held that member states within the Community are not entitled to invoke rules of domestic law or domestic practice to justify failure to give effect to Community regulations; judgement was therefore given against Italy, and Italy was ordered to pay the costs of the proceedings.

The Court can review the legality of most acts of the Council or the Commission and where necessary declare the act to be void, and may also review an alleged failure, in infringement of the Treaty, to act by the Council or Commission. Also the opinion of the European Court concerning the interpretation of Community legislation may, and sometimes must, be sought by the court or tribunal of a member state before whom the issue is first raised.[5] Moreover in all questions concerning Community law the United Kingdom courts are to give effect to any relevant decisions of the European Court, whether or not the United Kingdom court has actually referred the issue to the European Court for its opinion.[6]

European Economic Community legislation

In order to carry out their tasks the Council of Ministers and the Commission are required, in accordance with the provisions of the Treaty, to make regulations, issue directives, take decisions, make recommendations or deliver opinions. Moreover if action by the Community should prove necessary, in the course of the functioning of the Common Market, to attain one of the objectives of the Community and the Treaty has not provided the necessary powers, the Council, acting by a unanimous vote on a proposal from the Commission and after consulting the Assembly, are to enact the appropriate measures.

A Regulation is a Community law; the great majority of the Regulations are made by the Commission but the most important are made by the Council of Ministers. In recent years there have been several thousand Regulations made each year. A Regulation once made is immediately binding upon all member states of the Community and on all the citizens of those states, as is provided by the Treaty. All such Regulations become the law of the United Kingdom as soon as they are made by virtue of the provision that 'all such rights, powers, liabilities, obligations and restrictions from time to time created or arising by or under the Treaties . . . as in accordance with the Treaties are without further enactment to be given legal effect . . . in the United Kingdom shall be recognized and available in law, and be enforced, allowed and followed accordingly . . . '.[7] Such laws are passed through the machinery of Brussels and not the machinery of Whitehall and Westminster. There are, for example, numerous agricultural regulations (*post,* pages 379–81); these have been made on topics including animal feeding stuffs, animal health, beef and veal, cereals, eggs, fruit and vegetables, milk and milk products, and pig and poultry meat. The present British statutory grading system (applying to apples, pears, cucumbers, tomatoes and cauliflowers) is being replaced by Community grading standards which cover a much wider range of fresh horticultural produce; these Community standards will come into operation over a two-year period for British produce sold on the domestic market.

Regulation (E.E.C.) No. 1105/68 is printed as Appendix V as an example of Community legislation affecting agriculture.

Secondly, the relevant organs of the Community may issue a Directive. A directive is binding, as regards the result to be achieved, upon each member state of the Community to whom the Directive is addressed, but leaves to the governing bodies of the member states concerned the choice of the form and methods which are to be used in achieving the result specified in the Directive; Directives are relatively scant in number compared with Regulations.

In *Commission of the European Communities* v. *Italy* the Council of the Communities had enacted Directive No. 66/404 (as amended by Directive No. 69/64) obliging the member states of the Community to establish national registers for seeds and seedlings for forestry purposes, and ordering the member states to enact by 1 July 1969 the requisite national legislation within their states in order to give effect to the Directive. As Italy had not done so by 1 July 1969, the European Commission sued Italy in the European Court of Justice under Article 169 of the Treaty. The Court held that a Directive is compulsory in the obligations which it imposes, including the time limits laid down by the Directive for passing national legislation bringing the Directive into effect; judgement was therefore given against the Republic of Italy which had defaulted in the performance of a Treaty obligation binding upon it, and Italy was ordered to pay the cost of the proceedings.

Thirdly, a decision taken by the relevant organs of the Community is binding in its entirety upon those to whom the decision is addressed.

Recommendations and opinions of the Community organs have no binding force.

The provisions of the Treaty of Rome concerning agriculture

It is laid down in the Treaty of Rome that 'the operation and development of the Common Market for agricultural products must be accompanied by the establishment of a common agricultural policy among the Member States'.[8]

The objectives of the common agricultural policy are stated to be:

(a) to increase agricultural productivity by promoting technical progress and by ensuring the rational development of agricultural production and the optimum utilisation of the factors of production, in particular labour;

(b) thus to ensure a fair standard of living for the agricultural community, in particular by increasing the individual earnings of persons engaged in agriculture;

(c) to stabilise markets;

(d) to assure the availability of supplies;

(e) to ensure that supplies reach consumers at reasonable prices.[9]

The Treaty further states that 'In order to attain the objectives set out in Article 39 (above) a common organisation of agricultural markets shall be established'.

This organisation shall take one of the following forms, depending on the product concerned:

(a) common rules on competition;

(b) compulsory co-ordination of the various national market organisations;

(c) a European market organisation.

'The common organisation established in accordance with the above may include all measures required to attain the objectives set out in Article 39, in particular regulation of prices, aids for the production and marketing of the various products, storage and carry-over arrangements and common machinery for stabilising imports or exports.

In order to enable the common organisation referred to above to attain its objectives, one or more agricultural guidance and guarantee funds may be set up.[10]

The Agricultural Guidance and Guarantee Fund of the European Economic Community

Article 40 of the Treaty of Rome, dealing with the establishment of a common organisation for agricultural markets, states that in order to achieve such an organisation one or more guarantee funds may be set up. The Treaty only provided for the possibility of ensuring the financing of agriculture by the Community, and did not impose any obligations to do so. The Treaty left it to the Council of Ministers to settle the principles for operating such a fund or funds on the basis of proposals by the Commission. Resolutions were passed in 1960 setting out the basic principles of a common agricultural policy, including retention of the system of levies. In 1962 a European Agricultural Guidance and Guarantee Fund was instituted so as to enable the common organisation of agricultural markets to attain its objective; this fund is a financial instrument of the common agricultural policy. Since the common policy is a Community one, the consequent financial repercussions fall upon all member states. The Agricultural Fund forms part of the Budget of the Community. The Commission, assisted by a number of committees consisting of delegates from the member states and from the Commission, is responsible for managing the Fund.

Under the Community agricultural support system, the income support to agricultural producers is guaranteed by manipulating the market so as to bring a high price which will in itself provide an adequate remuneration to farmers, and by creating a number of protective devices operating at the Community frontiers to prevent imports from the world market at lower prices from reducing the internal price levels. The Community apply a system of variable levies to agricultural supplies emanating from countries outside the Community. Moreover provision is made for official support buying within the Community itself so as to remove from the market, at any rate temporarily, the excess of supply over demand at the support-price levels which have already been fixed. The common prices are agreed yearly by the Commission; there are approximately three hundred products for which the Commission has a pricing policy.

This approach is contrary to that hitherto adopted in the United Kingdom, where in general the policy has been to import food at low world prices and to grant deficiency payments financed by the taxpayer where this has been necessary to increase the price received by the farmer to a desired level fixed at an annual price review. The terms of entry of the United Kingdom into the Community oblige this country to introduce the Community system of support for agriculture. Threshold and intervention prices are to be fixed, which at first are to be lower than those which prevail in the Community but are to be gradually increased to the higher Community levels over a period of five years following entry.

The common agricultural policy has four key prices. First there is the market price. Then there is the intervention price, meaning the price at which state agencies will enter into the market and start buying up surpluses if the market price falls below it, hence acting as a floor price for domestic output.[11] Next comes the threshold price; this is normally slightly above the intervention price, and is a minimum import price, from which import levies are calculated so as to stop imports from coming in if Community market prices fall to that level and to raise money from imports if market prices are above it.[12] Finally, there is the target price which is fixed in relation to a particular place and represents the price at the wholesale marketing stage, on the assumption that the product concerned is delivered to the warehouse and not unloaded. The target price is published before the winter in order to permit producers to make their plans for cropping, and indicates the price level which is intended to prevail during the coming year and upon which the intervention price is therefore based, although the intervention price is somewhat lower than the target price.[13]

One objective of the common agricultural policy was to introduce a single price level for farmers throughout the Community, permitting food to flow freely across the frontiers of member states within the Community.

Under the policy the price of agricultural products is expressed in terms of the Community's unit of account. A devaluation carried out by a member state within the Community causes its farm prices to rise as expressed in terms of its national currency, unless further measures of adjustment are taken within the Community and the member state which has devalued. A change in currency exchange rates thus immediately upsets the operation of the common pricing policy, at the very least as regards the member state which has just revalued its currency; indeed for one reason or another most of the member states within the Community do not at the present time apply the officially agreed common price to all products.

The common organisation of the market imposes on the member states the obligation of intervening on the market either by way of purchasing or stock-piling goods or in the form of aid to producers. This is done in order to provide farmers with such incomes as are considered desirable and to ensure that there is a regular cash return during periods of fluctuating prices. Such activities involve expenditure which is chargeable to the Fund.

378

The Guidance Section of the Fund allows the financing of actions concerned with the adaptation and improvement of conditions in agricultural holdings, the improvement of rural roads, investment in vocational training for agriculture and publicity for agricultural produce. The Guidance Section also is concerned with the adaptation and direction of production and sales outlets, such as the desirable relationship between beef and dairy production. It can also finance the adaptation and improvement of the marketing of agricultural products, as by improving facilities such as slaughterhouses, dairies and premises used for preparing produce such as fruit and vegetables for the market. It can also be used to develop sales outlets for agricultural products.

The Commission has submitted to the Council nine programmes concerning the restructuring of landed estates, irrigation, land drainage, afforestation, improvements in the marketing of fruit and vegetables, structural improvements in the milk industry, the beef and veal sector, the vine growing and wine industries and the olive oil industry. In the event of these programmes being adopted, and in order to concentrate the resources of the Fund on a limited number of objectives in order to increase effectiveness, any sectors not mentioned above—such as cereals—would, unless included in a further programme, be excluded from Community financing in the event of the former programmes being adopted.

Article 18 of Regulation (E.E.C.) No. 17/64 requires the financial participation of the beneficiary in the improvement and also of the member state on whose territory the project is carried out. The contribution of the beneficiary at present stands at 38 per cent as regards marketing projects and 20 per cent as regards production projects. The contribution of the beneficiary may take the form of borrowed money. The Fund participates in financing the project at the general level of 25 per cent although the rate could be less or could rise to as much as 45 per cent. Although the member state must also participate financially, the extent of such participation varies from state to state. The beneficiary is defined by this Regulation as 'persons or groups who are ultimately liable, directly or indirectly, to bear the financial burden incurred by the realisation of the project'.

Aid from the Fund must be preceded by a claim on it, the claimant usually being the same person as the beneficiary. The claim must be accompanied by sufficient statistical data to enable the Commission to verify the conditions for granting financial aid for the project and to assess whether it is advisable to give such aid. Claims must be made through the medium of the member state on whose territory the project is to be carried out, and the project in respect of which the claim is made must have been approved by that member state. The minimum size of application which our own government is prepared to consider is a project costing at least £100,000. The claim is then examined to see that it satisfies the formal conditions for making a claim, that the financial benefit to be obtained from the project merits the expenditure upon it and that the beneficiary is financially stable and able to carry the project through to fruition, and that the project is economically sound in relation to the overall commercial and regional environment. Priority is given to projects forming part of a group of measures intended to promote the harmonious development of the overall economy of the region in which the projects are to be carried out. One general principle is that projects should be selected with a view to ensuring that contributions from the Fund are shared equally and harmoniously throughout the Community, thus the distribution of aid takes some regard of national factors as well as the economic or financial worth of the projects viewed from the European angle.

Work on a project can commence as soon as the application has been acknowledged from Brussels, but it may be a year or more afterwards before a decision is given concerning the application, and even longer before any grant is actually paid.

Proof that the project to be aided by the Fund has been properly carried out must be furnished to the Commission by the authority or agency appointed by the member state concerned. Subsidies are not paid direct to beneficiaries but are made through the intermediary of the agencies appointed for that purpose by the member state concerned; the agency must transfer the subsidy to the beneficiary without delay.[14]

An alternative system, which is at present of very limited scope, is one whereby the member state instead of the Commission considers the applicant's case and contributes towards the cost of the project undertaken in accordance with the appropriate Regulation, and the state itself recovers a part of this cost from the Fund. This mitigates the delay and uncertainty of the principal system contained in Regulation (E.E.C.) No. 17/64.

Expenditure on projects has in practice been divided roughly equally between projects concerned with structural aspects of production and projects concerned with structural aspects of marketing, although this overall Community breakdown varies internally within the different member states concerned according to their individual needs. The improvement of water resources has been the head of project which has hitherto attracted most aid from the Fund.

Article 12 of Regulation (E.E.C.) No. 159/66 provides for reimbursement, subject to certain conditions, to member states of half the amount of aid granted by those states to producer groups, co-operatives and the like in the fruit and vegetable sector. Article 2 of the Regulation encourages the formation of such groups in order to improve the organisation of the market.

Regulation (E.E.C.) No. 1035/72 is designed to set up 'producer organisations' to organise a system of market intervention and to govern the system of exports outside the Community. A 'producer organisation' is defined as 'any organisation of . . . producers which is formed on the initiative of producers themselves' with certain defined aims and obligations relating to production, marketing and the like. It is for the member state to decide what organisations it will recognise within this definition; the Fund will reimburse 50 per cent of the expenditure of member states in granting aid for the setting up of these producer organisations.

Expenditure from the Fund may be financed either through contributions from the member states, or contributions based on an agricultural element such as the charging of levies, or through compulsory contributions from producers or other fiscal imposts, or by direct Community financing at Community level.

The common agricultural policy has been the cornerstone of European integration, since a common policy on agriculture has been taken further than any other common policy, and the agricultural policy cost four-fifths of the Community's budget in 1972. Both price and structural policies have now been formulated. The Council of Ministers decides target prices, intervention prices and threshold prices (*ante,* page 378). Structural policy is to be directed to the improvement of the economic and social conditions of farmers. Although the policy for this is to be a Community policy the policy is to be administered by member states and allow for regional differences. There is to be a financial contribution from the Community towards the cost of implementation of the policy. The Mansholt Plan tried to shift the emphasis in Community policy from market and price support to that of structural improvement; it was sought to achieve the latter by giving financial encouragement to the creation of farms of larger size and to a reduction of the total work force engaged in agriculture. Legislation is to be introduced to encourage persons to leave agriculture, and to use such land as is released in consequence either to help with improvement of the structure of the remaining farms or for non-agricultural purposes such as growing timber or recreation. Financial inducements will be given to older farmers, and sometimes their workers, to leave the land, but the member states have considerable discretion as to the details of such schemes. The land thereby released must be either sold or leased to a potentially economically viable farm or to an existing viable farm or to a landbank, or transferred to use for recreation, forestry or some other use in the public interest. There are extremely complicated provisions for improving the structure of farming; these are related primarily to the level of income currently enjoyed by the farmer and likely to be enjoyed by him in the near future; various subsidies and loans at low rates of interest may be made available to the lower-income groups. Again, member states are permitted to apply these provisions flexibly with regard to their own needs and conditions. As a result of these policies, the number of smallholdings is likely to diminish, and a trend towards greater specialisation is likely to become established, with farms reaching a sufficient scale and volume of production to justify the high capital cost of modern technology and to spread the resulting overheads.

Legislative provisions giving effect to the Community Directive 72/159 concerning the modernisation of farms must be introduced within the United Kingdom not later than 31 January 1974.

Notes

[1] Article 47 of the Treaty of Rome.
[2] Article 43 of the Treaty of Rome.
[3] Article 93.
[4] Article 92.
[5] Article 177.
[6] European Communities Act, 1972, section 3(1).
[7] European Communities Act, 1972, section 2(1).
[8] Article 38 of the Treaty of Rome.
[9] Article 39.
[10] Article 40.
[11] E.E.C. Council Regulation 120/67.
[12] Regulation 120/67.
[13] Regulation 120/67.
[14] Article 8 of Regulation (E.E.C.) No. 99/64.

Appendix I

Agricultural Holdings Act, 1948 (as amended)
First Schedule: Matters for which provision is to be made in written tenancy agreements

1   The names of the parties.
2   Particulars of the holding with sufficient description, by reference to a map or plan, of the fields and other parcels of land comprised therein to identify the extent of the holding.
3   The term or terms for which the holding or different parts thereof is or are agreed to be let.
4   The rent reserved and the dates on which it is payable.
5   The incidence of the liability for land tax and rates (including drainage rates).
6   In respect of all work of maintenance and repair of fixed equipment comprised in the holding, a covenant by one or other of the parties to carry out the work.
7   A covenant by the landlord in the event of damage by fire to any building comprised in the holding to reinstate or replace the building if its reinstatement or replacement is required for the fulfilment of his responsibilities to manage the holding in accordance with the rules of good estate management, and (except where the interest of the landlord is held for the purposes of a Government department, or a person representing His Majesty or the Duke of Cornwall under subsection (I) of section eighty-seven of this Act is deemed to be the landlord, or where the landlord has made provision approved by the Minister for defraying the cost of any such reinstatement or replacement as aforesaid), a covenant by the landlord to insure all such buildings against damage by fire.
8   A covenant by the tenant in the event of the destruction by fire of harvested crops grown on the holding for consumption thereon, to return to the holding the full equivalent manurial value of the crops destroyed, in so far as the return thereof is required for the fulfilment of his responsibilities to farm in accordance with the rules of good husbandry, and (except where the interest of the tenant is held for the purposes of a Government Department or where the tenant has made provision approved by the Minister in lieu of such insurance) a covenant by the tenant to insure all

dead stock on the holding, and all such harvested crops as aforesaid, against damage by fire.

9   A power for the landlord to re-enter on the holding in the event of the tenant not performing his obligations under the agreement.

Appendix II

The Agriculture (Maintenance, Repair and Insurance of Fixed Equipment) Regulations, 1948: S.I. 1948 No. 184

1 The provisions set forth in the Schedule hereto relating to the maintenance, repair and insurance of fixed equipment, shall be deemed to be incorporated in every contract of tenancy of a holding, whether made before of after the commencement of Part III of the said Act, except in so far as they would impose on one of the parties to an agreement in writing a liability which under the agreement is imposed on the other:

> Provided that where the interest of the landlord is held for the purposes of a Government department, or a person representing His Majesty or the Duke of Cornwall under sections forty-three to forty-five of the Agricultural Holdings Act, 1923, is deemed to be the landlord, or where the landlord has made provision approved by the Minister for defraying the cost of any such works of repair or replacement as are referred to in paragraph 2 of the Schedule hereto, the provisions of the said paragraph 2 requiring the landlord to insure against loss or damage by fire shall not apply.

2 The Interpretation Act, 1889, shall apply to the interpretation of these regulations as it applies to the interpretation of an Act of Parliament.

3 (1) These regulations may be cited as the Agriculture (Maintenance, Repair and Insurance of Fixed Equipment) Regulations, 1948, and apply to England and Wales.

(2) These regulations shall come into operation on the first day of March, 1948.

SCHEDULE: MAINTENANCE, REPAIR AND INSURANCE OF THE FIXED EQUIPMENT OF A HOLDING

Part I: Rights and liabilities of the landlord

1 (1) To execute all repairs and replacements to the undermentioned parts of the farmhouse, cottages and farm buildings, namely: − main walls

and exterior walls, including walls of open and covered yards and garden walls (whether constructed of brick, stone, timber or other material) but excluding the interior covering of exterior walls save where such interior covering is affected by structural defect of the wall; roofs, including eaves-guttering and downpipes (tenant supplying straw and reed for thatching); and floors, doors and windows (excepting glass, locks and fastenings); provided that in the case of repairs and replacements to floor-boards, doors, windows, eaves-guttering and downpipes, the landlord may recover one half of the reasonable cost thereof from the tenant.

(2) To execute all repairs and replacements to the water mains, the sewage disposal systems (excepting the cleaning thereof and excepting the drains) and to the structure of reservoirs or pump houses of a water supply system.

2 To keep the farmhouse, cottages and farm buildings insured to their full value against loss or damage by fire and to execute all works of repair or replacement to the farmhouse, cottages and farm buildings necessary to make good damage by fire, being damage not due to the wilful act or negligence of the tenant.

3 As often as may be necessary in order to prevent deterioration, and in any case at intervals of not more than five years, properly to paint with at least two coats of a suitable quality or properly and adequately to gas-tar or creosote all outside wood and ironwork (including the inside of all external doors and windows which open outward) of the farmhouse, cottages and farm buildings which have been previously painted, gas-tarred or creosoted, or which it is necessary so to paint, gas-tar or creosote: provided that in respect of doors, windows, eaves-guttering and downpipes the landlord may recover one half of the reasonable cost of such work from the tenant, subject nevertheless to the provisions of sub-paragraph (2) of paragraph 12 hereof.

4 (1) The landlord shall be under no liability to execute repairs or replacements or to insure buildings or fixtures which are the property of the tenant, or to execute repairs or replacements rendered necessary by the wilful act or negligence of the tenant, or any members of his household or his employees.

(2) If the tenant fails to execute repairs for which he is liable under paragraphs 5, 6 and 7 hereof within one month of receiving from the landlord a written request specifying the necessary repairs and calling on him to execute them, the landlord may enter and execute such repairs and recover the reasonable cost from the tenant forthwith.

Part II: Rights and liabilities of the tenant

Except in so far as such liabilities fall to be undertaken by the landlord under Part I hereof:

5   To repair and to keep and leave clean and in good tenantable repair, order and condition, the farmhouse, cottages and farm building, together with all fixtures and fittings, drains, sewers, water supplies, pumps, fences, live and dead hedges, gates, field walls, posts, stiles, bridges, culverts, ponds, water courses, ditches, roads and yards in and upon the holding, or which during the tenancy may be erected or provided thereon, and to keep clean and in good working order all roof valleys, eaves-guttering and downpipes, gulleys and grease-traps; and also to use carefully so as to protect from wilful, reckless or negligent damage all items for the repair of which the landlord is responsible under paragraph 1 hereof, and also to report in writing immediately to the landlord any damage, however caused, to items for the repair of which the landlord is responsible.

6   To replace or repair and, upon replacement or repair, adequately to paint, gas-tar or creosote as may be proper, all i tems of fixed equipment, and to do any work, where such replacement, repair or work is rendered necessary by the wilful act or negligence of the tenant or any members of his household or his employees.

7   As often as may be necessary, and in any case at intervals of not more than seven years, properly to clean, colour, whiten, paper and paint with materials of suitable quality the inside of the farmhouse, cottages, and buildings which have been previously so treated, and in each year of the tenancy to limewash the inside of all farm buildings which previously have been limewashed.

8   Notwithstanding the general liability of the landlord for repairs and replacements, to renew all broken or cracked tiles or slates and replace all slipped tiles or slates from time to time as the damage occurs, but so that the cost shall not exceed five pounds in any one year of the tenancy.

9   To cut out and lay a proper proportion of the hedges in each year of the tenancy so as to maintain them in good and sound condition.

10   To dig out, scour and cleanse all ponds, water courses, ditches and grips, as may be necessary to maintain them at sufficient width and depth, and to keep clear from obstruction all field drains and their outlets.

11   To provide free of charge suitable straw or reed for the repair or renewal of thatch.

12   (1) If the last year of the tenancy is not a year in which such cleaning, colouring, whitening, papering and painting as is mentioned in paragraph 7 hereof is due to be carried out, the tenant shall then pay to

the landlord at the end of such last year one-seventh part of the estimated reasonable cost thereof in respect of each year that has elapsed since last cleaning, colouring, whitening, papering and painting as aforesaid; and in such a case, the landlord shall pay to the tenant at the time of the next subsequent occasion that such work is carried out, the reasonable cost thereof less one-seventh part in respect of each year that has elapsed since the commencement of the tenancy.

(2) If the last year of the tenancy is not a year in which the landlord is liable, under paragraph 3 hereof, to paint, gas-tar or creosote the doors, windows, eaves-guttering and downpipes of buildings, the tenant shall then pay to the landlord at the end of such last year one-tenth part of the estimated reasonable cost thereof in respect of each year that has elapsed since such last painting, gas-tarring or creosoting as aforesaid; and in such a case, the landlord shall be entitled to recover from the tenant at the time of the next subsequent occasion that such work is carried out, one-tenth part only of the reasonable cost thereof in respect of each year that has elapsed since the commencement of the tenancy.

(3) In the assessment of any compensation payable by an outgoing tenant in respect of dilapidations, any accrued liability under the two preceding sub-paragraphs shall be taken into account.

13   If the landlord fails to execute repairs which are his liability within three months of receiving from the tenant a written request specifying the necessary repairs and calling on him to execute them, the tenant may execute such repairs and, except to the extent to which under the terms of Part I hereof the tenant is liable to bear the cost, recover the reasonable cost from the landlord forthwith.

Part III: General proviso

14   Nothing contained in Part I or Part II hereof shall create any liability, on the part of either landlord or tenant:

(1) to maintain, repair or insure any item of fixed equipment which is obsolete, and which the landlord and the tenant agree in writing that neither party shall be liable to maintain, repair or insure;

(2) to execute any work if and so far as the execution of such work is rendered impossible (except at prohibitive or unreasonable expense) by reason of subsidence of any land or by the blocking of outfalls which are not under the control of either the landlord or the tenant.

Appendix III

Agricultural Holdings Act, 1948 (as amended)
Second, third, fourth and fifth Schedules: Improvements

SECOND SCHEDULE: IMPROVEMENTS BEGUN BEFORE IST MARCH, 1948, FOR WHICH COMPENSATION IS PAYABLE

Part I: Improvements for which compensation is payable if consent of landlord was obtained to their execution

1   Erection, alteration or enlargement of buildings.
2   Formation of silos.
3   Laying down of permanent pasture.
4   Making and planting of osier beds.
5   Making of water meadows or works of irrigation.
6   Making of gardens.
7   Making or improvement of roads or bridges.
8   Making or improvement of watercourses, ponds, wells or reservoirs or of works for the application of water power or for supply of water for agricultural or domestic purposes.
9   Making or removal of permanent fences.
10   Planting of hops.
11   Planting of orchards or fruit bushes.
12   Protecting young fruit trees.
13   Reclaiming of waste land.
14   Warping or weiring of land.
15   Embankments and sluices against floods.
16   Erection of wirework in hop gardens.
17   Provision of permanent sheep-dipping accommodation.
18   In the case of arable land, the removal of bracken, gorse, tree roots, boulders or other like obstructions to cultivation.

Part II: ,,,Improvement for which compensation is payable if notice was given to landlord before execution thereof

19   Drainage.

Part III: Improvements for which compensation is payable without either consent of or notice to landlord of their execution

20   Chalking of land.
21   Clay-burning.
22   Claying of land or spreading blaes upon land.
23   Liming of land.
24   Marling of land.
25   Application to land of purchased artificial or other purchased manure.
26   Consumption on the holding by cattle, sheep or pigs, or by horses other than those regularly employed on the holding, of corn, cake or other feeding stuff not produced on the holding.
27   Consumption on the holding by cattle, sheep, or pigs, or by horses other than those regularly employed on the holding, of corn proved by satisfactory evidence to have been produced and consumed on the holding.
28   Laying down temporary pasture with clover, grass, lucerne, sainfoin, or other seeds, sown more than two years prior to the termination of the tenancy, in so far as the value of the temporary pasture on the holding at the time of quitting exceeds the value of the temporary pasture on the holding at the commencement of the tenancy for which the tenant did not pay compensation.
29   Repairs to buildings, being buildings necessary for the proper cultivation or working of the holding, other than repairs which the tenant is himself under an obligation to execute.

THIRD SCHEDULE: IMPROVEMENTS BEGUN ON OR AFTER 1ST MARCH, 1948, FOR WHICH COMPENSATION IS PAYABLE IF CONSENT OF LANDLORD OR APPROVAL OF THE AGRICULTURAL LAND TRIBUNAL IS OBTAINED TO THEIR EXECUTION

Part I: Improvements to which consent of landlord required

1   Making or planting of osier beds.
2   Making of water meadows or works of irrigation.
3   Making of watercress beds.
4   Planting of hops.
5   Planting of orchards or fruit bushes.
6   Warping or weiring of land.
7   Making of gardens.

Part II: Improvements to which consent of landlord or approval of the agricultural land tribunal required

8 Erection, alteration or enlargement of buildings, and making or improvement of permanent yards.
9 Construction of silos.
10 Claying of land.
11 Marling of land.
12 Making or improvement of roads or bridges.
13 Making or improvement of water courses, culverts, ponds, wells or reservoirs, or of works for the application of water power for agricultural or domestic purposes or for the supply of water for such purposes.
14 Making or removal of permanent fences.
15 Reclaiming of waste land.
16 Making or improvement of embankments or sluices.
17 Erection of wirework for hop gardens.
18 Provision of permanent sheep-dipping accommodation.
19 Removal of bracken, gorse, tree roots, boulders or other like obstructions to cultivation.
20 Land drainage (other than mole drainage and works carried out to secure the efficient functioning thereof).
21 Provision or laying-on of electric light or power.
22 Provision of means of sewage disposal.
23 Repairs to fixed equipment, being equipment reasonably required for the proper farming of the holding, other than repairs which the tenant is under an obligation to carry out.
24 The growing of herbage crops for commercial seed production.

FOURTH SCHEDULE: IMPROVEMENTS BEGUN ON OR AFTER 1ST MARCH, 1948, FOR WHICH COMPENSATION IS PAYABLE WITHOUT CONSENT OF LANDLORD TO THEIR EXECUTION, AND OTHER MATTERS FOR WHICH COMPENSATION IS PAYABLE

Part I: Improvements

1 Mole drainage and works carried out to secure the efficient functioning thereof.
2 Protection of fruit trees against animals.
3 Chalking of land.
4 Clay burning.
5 Liming of land.

6 Application to land of purchased manure (including artificial manure).
7 Consumption on the holding of corn (whether produced on the holding or not) or of cake or other feeding stuff not produced on the holding, by—

(*a*) horses, cattle, sheep or pigs,

(*b*) poultry folded on the land as part of a system of farming practised on the holding.

Part II: Other matters

8 Growing crops and severed or harvested crops and produce, being in either case crops or produce grown on the holding in the last year of the tenancy, but not including crops or produce which the tenant has a right to sell or remove from the holding.

9 Seeds sown and cultivations, fallows and acts of husbandry performed on the holding at the expense of the tenant.

10 Pasture laid down with clover, grass, lucerne, sainfoin or other seeds, being either—

(*a*) pasture laid down at the expenses of the tenant otherwise than in compliance with an obligation imposed on him by an agreement in writing to lay it down to replace temporary pasture comprised in the holding when the tenant entered thereon which was not paid for by him; or

(*b*) pasture paid for by the tenant on entering on the holding.

11 Acclimatisation, hefting or settlement of hill sheep on hill land.

FIFTH SCHEDULE: MARKET GARDEN IMPROVEMENTS FOR WHICH COMPENSATION MAY BE PAYABLE

1 Planting of standard or other fruit trees permanently set out.
2 Planting of fruit bushes permanently set out.
3 Planting of strawberry plants.
4 Planting of asparagus, rhubarb and other vegetable crops which continue productive for two or more years.
5 Erection, alteration or enlargement of buildings for the purpose of the trade or business of a market gardener.

Appendix IV

Rates of estate duty applicable to deaths on or after 31 March 1971

(1) Slice		(2) Width of Slice	(3) Rate on Slice	(4) Duty on Whole Slice	(5) Cumula- tive Duty	(6) Effective Rate (approx.)
£	£	£	%	£	£	%
0 to	12,500	12,500	Nil	Nil	Nil	—
12,500 to	17,500	5,000	25	1,250	1,250	7·14
17,500 to	30,000	12,500	30	3,750	5,000	16·67
30,000 to	40,000	10,000	45	4,500	9,500	23·75
40,000 to	80,000	40,000	60	24,000	33,500	41·88
80,000 to	150,000	70,000	65	45,500	79,000	52·67
150,000 to	300,000	150,000	70	105,000	184,000	61·33
300,000 to	500,000	200,000	75	150,000	334,000	66·80
500,000 to	750,000	250,000	80	200,000	534,000	71·20
750,000 to 2,070,000		1,320,000	85	1,122,000	1,656,000	80·00

The rates set out above do not take into account any reliefs (such as the reduced rate of duty charged on the agricultural value of agricultural property) or exemptions which may be applicable.

Appendix V

European Communities Regulation (EEC) No. 1105/68 of the Commission of 27 July 1968 on the procedure for granting aids for skimmed milk for animal feeding stuffs

THE COMMISSION OF THE EUROPEAN COMMUNITIES

Having Regard to the Treaty setting up the European Economic Community;

Having Regard to Council Regulation (EEC) No. 804/68 of 27 June 1968, on the common organisation of the market in milk and dairy products, and in particular Article 10(3) and Article 35 thereof;

Whereas Council Regulation (EEC) No. 986/68 of 15 July 1968, laying down general rules on granting aid for skimmed milk and powdered skimmed milk for animal feeding stuffs requires the adoption of a specific procedure with respect to the payment of aids granted for skimmed milk;

Whereas so as to ensure that skimmed milk whose price is reduced will be used exclusively for animal feeding stuffs, it should be provided that it must be denatured before delivery and also that the farmers be compelled to use that skimmed milk in their own farms;

Whereas it is essential to leave to the user a choice of several denaturing processes affording a clear differentiation of the denatured milk;

Whereas for breeders who use skimmed milk manufactured in their own farm for cattle feeding, it is possible, when they deliver cream to dairies or when they make butter, to make a standard assessment of the quantity of skimmed milk for which an aid may be granted on the basis of the quantity of cream delivered to the dairies or of butter sold;

Whereas to ensure that the amount of milk used by a breeder for cattle feeding and manufactured by himself is proportionate to the importance of his livestock consuming skimmed milk, adequate maximum quantities should be fixed;

Whereas taking into account, on the one hand, the value of skimmed milk resulting from the intervention price of powdered skimmed milk, and on the other, the aid granted for skimmed milk and the prices of other animal feeding stuffs, the maximum price of milk for animal feeding stuffs must be fixed at 1.6 u.a. per 100 kg.;

394

Whereas to make an efficient control possible dairies should be required to keep records in accordance with the special requirements of the grant of aids and breeders making their own skimmed milk should be compelled to supply certain data;

Whereas since it may happen that the denaturing agents specified in the provisions of this Regulation are not immediately available in sufficient quantity, the grant of aid for non-denatured skimmed milk or skimmed milk denatured acording to other processes must be authorised for a short transitional period;

Whereas the measures laid down in this Regulation are in accordance with the opinion of the Management Committee for milk and dairy products;

HAS ADOPTED THIS REGULATION:

Article 1

1   Skimmed milk produced and processed in a dairy shall only be granted aid if it has been denatured in accordance with one of the two methods referred to in Article 2 and if its specific gravity prior to denaturation was at least 1.03.

Denatured skimmed milk is hereinafter called "animal milk".

2   Aids shall only be granted for quantities of skimmed milk mixed with animal milk.

Article 2

Skimmed milk shall be denatured:—

1   when it is soured;

Skimmed milk can be soured when the degree of acidity in it is:

(*a*)   20° SH measured according to the Soxhlet-Henkel process,

(*b*)   45° SH measured according to the Dornic process,

(*c*)   50° N measured according to the Kruisher process.

2   by adding not less than 30 kilograms of concentrated whey per 100 kilograms;

Whey whose specific gavity is not less than that of the skimmed milk shall be taken as concentrated whey.

3   by adding at least 0.5 kilograms starch paste or puffed starch flour per 100 kilograms;

4   by adding at least 1 gram carmoisine (azorubin E 122) or 1 gram eosin, per 100 kilograms.

Article 3

1   The maximum price referred to in Article 2(1)(*a*) of Regulation (EEC) 986/63 shall be fixed at 1.60 u.a. per 100 kilograms of animal milk.

2   The maximum price shall be applicable ex dairy.

Article 4

1   A dairy which delivers animal milk to breeders shall only be granted aid for those quantities of skimmed milk mixed with the animal milk which the breeder has stated in writing that he needs on his own farm.

2   The dairy shall keep this statement for at least two years.

Article 5

1   A dairy which delivers animal milk to breeders shall only be granted aid providing monthly records of quantities delivered, manufactured, used and sold, of milk, dairy products, including animal milk and compound animal feeding stuffs are kept.

2   The records of quantities shall include at least the following particulars:—

(*a*)   intake of raw milk and cream from producers,

(*b*)   intake of milk, skimmed milk and cream from dairies,

(*c*)   date of processing and quantities of skimmed milk made,

(*d*)   quantities of other dairy products made,

(*e*)   quantities of skimmed milk sold, date of sale and name and address of consignee,

(*f*)   losses, samples, quantities of skimmed milk returned and replaced,

(*g*)   price invoiced for animal milk.

3   The particulars referred to in paragraph 2 shall be supported by delivery vouchers and invoices.

Article 6

1   Breeders who use skimmed milk processed on their own farm for animal feeding stuffs shall only be granted aid if they state in writing that they use on their own farm and for their animals the skimmed milk which they have.

2   If they are breeders who:—

(*a*)   deliver cream to a dairy, the statement shall be forwarded to the dairy in question which shall keep it for at least two years;

(*b*)   sell butter made on their own farm, the statement shall be forwarded to the competent authority.

Article 7

Breeders who use skimmed milk made on their own farm for feeding their animals and who deliver cream to a diary shall be granted for each kilogram of fat delivered to the dairy the aid granted for 23 kilograms of skimmed milk.

Article 8

1   Without prejudice to the provisions in paragraph 3, breeders who use skimmed milk made on their own farm for feeding stuffs for their own animals and who sell butter made on their own farm, shall be granted for each kilogram of butter sold the aid granted for 20 kilograms of skimmed milk.

2   Aid shall only be granted to breeders registered as butter makers.

They shall register in each Member State with the agency empowered to grant aid. That agency shall issue a registration card which shall show the number of cows whose milk may be used for butter making.

3   Aid shall only be granted for a quantity of skimmed milk not exceeding a maximum yearly quantity for each cow shown in the registration card.

The maximum yearly quantity shall be 3,000 kilograms of milk per cow. The quantity of milk delivered by the breeder to a dairy shall however be deducted from that figure.

4   Breeders shall only be granted aid if they support with adequate documents statements as to the quantity of butter made and sold as well as the growth of their livestock.

Article 9

Groups of producers recognised by a Member State shall also be considered as breeders for the purpose of this Regulation.

Article 10

Member States shall take all necessary measures of control to ensure that the conditions relative to the grant of aid are observed.

Article 11

1   In derogation from the provisions of **Article** 1(1), aid shall be granted until 1 September 1968, for skimmed milk processed and made in dairies which has not been denatured or which has been denatured according to a method applicable in the Member State in question prior to 28 July 1968.
2   Member States shall take all necessary measures to guarantee the effective control of the use of such skimmed milk.

Article 12

This Regulation shall come into force on 29 July 1968.

This Regulation shall be binding in its entirely and directly applicable in all Member States.

Done at Brussels, 27 July 1968

By the Commission
The President
JEAN REY

Table of Statutes

Indexer's note: References are given as follows: 16[51] (35), where 16 is the page of the text, 51 is the note number thereon, and (35) is the page on which the note itself appears. The latter is omitted unless additional information is to be found in the note.

1267   Statute of Marlbridge,
       17[64] (36)
1677   Statute of Frauds
       s.4, 264[19]
1774   Fires Prevention
       (Metropolis) Act, 365
       Life Assurance Act
       s.4, 363
       s.10, 363[10]
1815   Stamp Act, 117[40] (124)
1828   Night Poaching Act
       s.1, 332[41] (335)
       s.2, 332[43] (335)
       s.12, 332[44]
1831   Game Act
       s.30, 332[37]
       s.31, 332[39] (335)
1832   Prescription Act
       ss. 1, 2, 22[83, 84]
       s.3, 23[90]
       s.4, 22[86]
       s.7, 23[87]
       s.8, 23[89]
1833   Fines and Recoveries Act,
       3[8] (34)
1837   Wills Act
       s.7, 111[1]
       s.9, 112[12], 113[13]
       s.15, 113[16]
       s.18, 115[27]

       s.20, 114[18,22]
       s.21, 115[31]
       s.22, 115[33]
       s.28, 2[4] (34)
       s.34, 2[4] (34)
1844   Night Poaching Act
       s.1, 332[41] (335), 332[42],
       332[43] (335)
1845   Land Clauses Consolidation
       Act
       s.68, 222[166] (256),
       241[254] (259)
       s.85, 248[285] (260)
1852   Wills Act Amendment Act,
       112
1856   Mercantile Law Amendment Act
       s.3, 265
1867   Policies of Assurance Act
       s.3, 363[9]
       s.5, 363[8]
1874   Infants Relief Act,
       264[14]
1881   Customs and Inland Revenue Act 117[40] (124)
1882   Married Women's Property Act, 169
       s.11, 364[13]
1889   Factors Act
       s.1(1), 286[106]

s.2(1), 286 [108]
1890 Partnership Act, 81
  s.1, 80[3]
  s.5, 81[6]
  s.8, 81[7]
  s.10, 81[8]
  s.24, 82 [12-15]
  s.25, 82 [16]
  s.26, 82 [17] (108)
  s.28, 82[9]
  s.29, 81 [11]
  s.30, 82 [10]
  s.32, 82 [17] (108), 83 [21]
  s.33, 82 [18]
  s.35, 83[20]
  s.39, 88 [22]
  s.44, 83 [23]
1893 Sale of Goods Act, 265, 277, 278, 280, 281
  s.1(1), 277 [67]
  s.1(3), 277 [68]
  s.2, 264 [16,18]
  s.10, 288[122]
  s.11(1)(c), 285
  s.12(1), 283 [96] (305)
  s.12(2), 283 [97] (305)
  s.13(1), 278 [75]
  s.13(2), 279 [80] (305)
  s.14(2), 285[85,87] (305)
  s.14(3), 280 [89] (305).
  s.14(5), 280 [84] (305)
  s.55, 284 [102] (306)
  s.55(7), (8), 284[101] (306)
  s.62 1A, 280 [86] (305)
  s.15, 282[95]
  s.16, 277 [71]
  s.18, 277[71], 287[15-17], 288 [119] (306)
  s.19, 277 [71]
  s.20, 288 [120]
  s.25(1), 285

s.25(2), 285 [104], 302
s.29, 289, 289 [124]
ss. 34, 35, 285 [104] (306)
s.38, 289 [126]
s.41, 289 [127]
s.43, 289 [129]
s.44, 290 [130]
s.48, 290 [131], 290 [133]
s.49 290 [134]
s.50, 290 [135]
s.55, 278 [72] (305)
s.55(3), 283 [98] (306)
s.62, 284[103], 287 [112],[114], 289 [128]
1894 Finance Act
  s.1, 163 [182]
  s.2, 172[220]
  s.2(1)(a), 175 [224]
  s.2(1)(b), 170 [212] (196)
  s.2(1)(c), 166 [195]
  s.5, 171 [216] (196)
  s.6, 180 [252,253]
  s.7, 172[219], 178[243], 179 [248]
  s.8, 180[249] (197), 180[250]
  s.10, 182 [260]
  s.15, 172 [218]
  s.15(2), 165 [191]
  s.22, 172
1896 Friendly Societies Act, 15
1907 Limited Partnership Act
  s.4, 84 [24]
  s.6, 84 [27]
  s.8, 84 [25]
  s.11, 84 [26]
1909 Finance Act
(1910) s.59, 169[209]
  s.60, 178 [245]
1911 Finance Act
  s.18, 179 [247]

1916 Registration of Business Names Act
    s.1, 82 [19]

1925 Administration of Estates Act, 12
    s.7(1), 116 [36]
    s.33(1), 117 [41]
    s.37, 122 [56]
    s.41, 119 [46] (124)
    s.46, 117 [42] (124)
    s.49, 120 [48]
    s.49(1), 120 [49] (125)
    s.55(1), 119 [43]
    Sch. 1 (Part II), 181 [256]

Finance Act
    s.23(2), 164 [186]
    s.23(3), 164 [189]
    s.23(4), 163 [184]

Judicature Act
    s.160, 121 [53]
    s.160(1), 116 [37]

Law of Property Act, 3 [8] (34), 12
    s.16, 181 [257]
    s.25(1), 12 [45]
    s.26(1), 12 [42]
    s.26(3), 13 [47]
    s.28(1), 12 [40] (35)
    s.29(1), 13 [49]
    s.30, 12 [43], 13 [50]
    s.36(2), 14 [51]
    s.40, 264 [20], 265
    s.47, 364
    s.53, 167 [196,197]
    s.54(2), 15 [56]
    s.60(1), 2 [4] (34)
    s.60(4), 3 [6] (34)
    s.62, 20
    s.79, 30 [118]
    s.84, 31 [126] (37)
    s.84(2), 31 [122]
    s.101(1), 27 [107]
    s.103, 27 [108]
    s.109, 28 [112]
    s.109(8), 29 [113]
    s.121, 19 [72]
    s.130(1), 3 [6,7]
    s.137, 29 [114] (37)
    s.137(4), 29 [115]
    s.138, 29 [114] (37)
    s.176, 3 [9]
    s.177, 115
    s.191, 19 [73]
    s.205(1), 7 [18], 12 [39]

Settled Land Act, 3, 4, 8, 12, 22, 164
    s.24(1), 12 [37]
    s.38, 8 [19,20]
    ss.45-47, 5 [17]
    s.65, 10 [23]
    s.66, 5 [16]
    s.68, 11 [28]
    s.84(2), 9 [21]
    s.97, 11 [29]
    s.101(4), 11 [30]
    s.101(5), 11 [31]
    s.105(1), 11 [36]
    s.106(1), 11 [33]
    s.107(1), 10 [24]
    s.108(2), 11 [32]

Trustee Act
    s.34, 14 [52]
    s.36(1), 15 [53] (35)
    s.39(1), 15 [55]
    s.41, 15 [53] (35)

1926 Law of Property (Amendment) Act, 2 [5]

1933 Administration of Justice (Miscellaneous Provisions) Act
    s.3, 182 [259]

1935 Law Reform (Married Wo-

men and Tortfeasors) Act
s.6, 319 [48]

1938 Inheritance (Family Provision) Act 123[58] (125)
    s.1(1), 122 [57] (125)
    s.1(4), 123 [59]
    s.3, 123 [62] (125)

1939 Limitation Act
    s.2, 276 [61]
    s.4(3), 33 [131]
    s.6(2), 33[132,133]
    s.18, 33 [135]
    s.22, 34 [137], 276 [65] (304)
    s.23, 34 [140] (37), 276 [66] (304)
    s.24, 34 [140] (37), 277 [66] (304)
    s.26, 276 [64]
    s.31(2), 276 [65] (304)

1940 Finance Act
    s.44, 168 [203]
    s.46, 90 [42] (109), 178 [239]
    s.47, 178 [240]
    s.54, 180 [251]
    s.55, 176 [227, 228]
    s.58, 176 [229]

1943 Law Reform (Frustrated Contracts) Act 273[53]

1945 Law Reform (Contributory Negligence) Act
    s.1(1), 318 [40], 326 [15], 342 [44]

1946 Acquisition of Land (Authorisation) Procedure Act
    s.1, 219[153] (256), 221[158] (256),
    Sch. 1, 219[153],[154] (256), 221[158]
    Hill Farming Act
    s.21(1), 47 [31] (73)

1947 Agriculture Act

    s.10, 49 [36]
    s.11(1), 49 [37]
    s.11(2), (3), 49 [38, 39]
    s.73(2), 48 [34] (74)
    Sch.9, 48 [34] (74)

1948 Agricultural Holdings Act, 9, 19 [69] (36), 39, 69
    s.1(1), 39 [3], 41 [9] (73)
    s.1(2), 39 [1]
    s.2(1), 41, 42 [13], 240
    s.3, 42 [14]
    s.4, 42, 47
    s.5, 44 [18]
    s.6, 45
    s.6(2), 46 [20]
    s.7(1), (2), (3), (5), 46 [21 − 24]
    s.8, 50 [40]
    s.8(1), 50 [42] (74)
    s.8(2), (3), (4), 50[43 − 46]
    s.9, 48 [32] (74)
    s.9(1), 52 [49] (74)
    s.10, 52 [51] (74)
    s.11(1), 46 [26]
    s.11, (2), (3), (4), (5), 46 [27 − 28], 47 [29 − 30]
    s.12(1), 60 [89]
    s.14, 53 [57], 54 [59] 315 [22]
    s.14(3), 54 [60]
    s.15, 44 [17]
    s.16, 53[54], 66, 68
    s.17, 53 [55]
    s.18, 33 [135]
    s.23(1), 54 [61]
    s.24(1), 39, 55 [65] (75), 224
    s.24(2), 56 [66] (75), 64
    s.24(2)(b), 224, 230
    s.25(1), 59 [82] (75)
    s.25(1)(e), 224, 230
    s.26, 57 [75] (75)

s.27, 56 [69] (75)
s.30, 59 [85]
s.31, 60 [86] 64
s.32, 60 [87, 88] 64
s.33, 51 [48], 60 [87]
s.34(1), 64 [109]
s.34(2), 62 [93] (75), 64[110]
s.34(4), 65 [111]
s.35, 52 [52] (74), 62 [95] (75)
s.36, 52 [52] (74), 62 [95] (75)
s.37, 52 [52] (74), 62 [94], 62 [95] (75)
ss. 38-40, 62 [95] (75)
ss. 41-45, 52 [52] (74), 62 [95] (75)
ss. 46-47, 52 [52] (74)
s.48, 63 [101]
s.49, 63 [102]
s.50, 63 [103]
s.51, 52 [52] (74)
s.51(1), 63 [105]
s.51(2), 63 [106]
s.52, 52 [52] (74)
s.53, 52 [52] (74), 63 [100]
s.54, 52 [52] (74), 62 [97]
s.55, 52 [52] (74)
s.55(1), 62 [98]
s.55(2), 62 [99]
s.56, 62 [93] (75)
s.56(1), (2), (3), 66[115-117]
s.57, 68
s.57(1), (2), 67 [119, 120]
s.57(3), 67, 68
s.58, 67,68
s.59, 68 [123]
s.65(1), 61 [91]
ss.67-69, 64 [108] (76)
s.70(1), 68 [124]
s.70(2), 68 [125] (76)

s.70(3), 69 [126] (76)
s.70(4), 69 [126] (76)
s.70(5), 68 [125] (76)
s.71, 69 [131]
s.72, 69 [132]
s.77, 57
s.77(1), 69 [127]
s.91, 53 [56]
s.92(1), 54 [62]
s.92(2), 54 [63]
s.92(4), 55 [64]
s.94, 63, 64
s.94(1), 39 [2], 67 [118]
Sch.1, 44, 383-4
Sch.2, 52 [52] (74), 62, 62 [95] (75), 66, App III
Sch.3, 62, 63, 66, App III
Sch.4, 52 [52] (74), 62, 63, 66, App III
Sch.5, 62, 64 [108] (76), App III
Sch.6, 57, 69 [128 - 130] (76)
Agricultural Wages Act
  s.1, 343 [51] (355)
  s.3, 343 [52]
  s.4(1), 344 [56]
  s.11(1), 344 [55]
  s.12, 344 [57]
  Sch.1, 343 [51] (355)
Companies Act
  s.1., 87 [31] (108), 92 [46]
  s.2, 87 [31] (108)
  s.10, 90 [44]
  s.28, 92 [47 - 49]
  s.38, 93 [50] (109)
  s.43, 93 [51]
  s.44, 93 [51], 107 [109] (110)
  s.44(1), 97 [75]
  s.47, 93[53]

s.53, 94[54]
s.61, 88[36], 96[67] (109)
s.66, 87[33]
s.104, 350
s.109, 94[55]
s.124, 84[28] (108)
s.127, 84[28] (108)
s.130, 94[56]
s.131, 89[38]
s.136, 89[40]
s.137, 89[39]
s.137(2), 89[41]
s.176, 89[37]
s.184, 90[45]
s.434, 80[4]
Sch.4, 93[50] (109)
Law Reform (Personal Injuries) Act
s.2, 337[1]
1949 Finance Act
s.33, 169[208] (196)
Land Tribunals Act, 182[258]
s.2, 229[193]
National Parks and Access to the Countryside Act, 324
1952 Agriculture (Poisonous Substances) Act, 341
s.1(3), 342[40]
s.3, 342[43]
s.10(1)(1), 342[39]
Intestates' Estates Act, 117[42] (124), 120[50] (125), 123[62] (125)
ss.3, 4, 120[49] (125)
s.5, 119[45] (124)
Part II, 122[57] (125)
Sch.1, 120[49] (125)
Sch.2, 119[45] (124), 119[46] (124)
Sch.3 and 4, 122[57] (125)

1953 Historic Buildings and Ancient Monuments Act
s.4, 210[70]
1954 . Agriculture Act
s.4, 48[32] (74)
Agriculture (Miscellaneous Provisions) Act
s.7, 57[78]
Finance Act
s.28, 164[190], 177[238]
s.29, 176[231 – 234]
s.30, 177[236, 237]
s.31, 176[230]
Landlord and Tenant Act
s.37, 223[171] (256), 223[173] (257)
ss.39, 43, 223[171] (256)
s.52, 31[126] (37)
Law Reform (Limitation of Actions etc.) Act
s.2(1), 276[62]
1956 Agriculture (Safety, Health and Welfare) Provisions Act, 51, 340
s.1(1), 340[18]
s.1(3), 340[19]
s.2(1), 341[20]
s.2(2), 341[22]
s.3(1), 341[24]
s.3(2), 341[25] (354)
s.3(7), 341[26]
s.6(1), 341[27]
s.16, 341[37]
s.24(1), 341[21,25] (354)
Restrictive Trade Practices Act, 106
1957 Finance Act
s.38, 168
Housing Act
s.6, 16[58]

s.6(2), 16 [62]
Occupiers' Liability Act, 323
  s.1(2), 324[3]
  s.1(3), 325 [10]
  s.1(4), 324 [5]
  s.1(6), 325 [10]
  s.2(1), 326 [16]
  s.2(2), 325 [9]
  s.2(3), 325 [11]
  s.2(4)(a) and (b), 325[13,14]
  s.2(6), 324 [4]
  s.3(1), 327[21]
  s.3(2), 327 [22]
  s.3(3), 326 [20]
  s.5(1), 326 [19]

1958 Agriculture Act
  s.2, 50 [42] (74)
  s.3(2), 59 [82] (75)
  s.4, 51, 52 [49] (74)
  s.8, 47[31] (73), 63 [103] (76)
  s.8(1), 47 [30] (73), 48 [34] (74), 53 [53] (74), 55 [65] (75), 55 [66] (75), 56 [69] (75), 57 [75] (75)
  s.10, 63 [103] (76)
  Sch.1, 47 [30] (73), 47 [31] (73), 48 [34] (74)
  Sch.52 [51] (74), 53 [53] (74), 55 [65] (75)
  Sch.56 [69] (75), 57 [75] (75), 63 [103] (76)
  Sch.2, 63 [103] (76)
Finance Act
  s.30, 166 [194] (195)
  s.34, 175 [225, 226]
  s.35(2), 167 [200]

1959 Highways Act, 25
  ss. 28, 31, 32, 25 [102]
  s.34, 25 [104]

s.34(1), 25 [103]
Rights of Light Act
  s.2(1), 23 [92]
  s.3, 23 [93]
Weeds Act
  s.1(1), 314 [15]
  s.2, 314 [16]
  s.3, 314 [17, 18]

1960 Caravan Sites and Control of Development Act
  s.1(1), 217 [128]
  s.1(2), 217 [129]
  s.1(4), 217 [130]
  s.2, 219 [150] (256)
  s.3, 217[126,134]
  s.3(1), 217 [131]
  s.3(2), 217 [132]
  s.3(6), 219 [147]
  s.4(1), 218 [138]
  s.5(1), 218 [139] 219 [141]
  s.5(3), 219 [142]
  s.5(4), 219[143]
  s.5(6), 218 [140] (256)
  s.7(1), 219 [145]
  s.8(1), 219 [148]
  s.8(2), 219 [149]
  s.9, 219 [144, 146]
  s.10(1), 218 [137]
  s.25(1), 218 [136]
  s.26, 219 [151]
  s.29, 217 [127]
  Sch.1, 219 [150] (256)
Finance Act
  s.66, 177 [235]
Forestry Act
  s.12(1), 212 [83]
Game Laws (Amendment) Act
  s.1(2), 332[39] (335)

1961 Housing Act
  s.32, 17 [63] (36)

405

s.33, 17 [63] (36)
Land Compensation Act
  s.1, 219 [155], 229 [192]
  s.2, 229 [193]
  s.4, 230[195]
  s.5, 231 [201, 203]
  s.6, 233 [224] (258)
  s.6(1), 231 [205] (257)
  s.7, 231 [206]
  s.9, 231 [207]
  s.9(1), (2), (3), (4), 226 [180 – 182]
  s.14, 231 [208]
  s.14(2), 231 [209]
  s.15(1), 232 [212]
  s.15(3), 231 [210] (258)
  s.15(4), 231[210,211]
  s.16(1), 232 [213] (258)
  s.16(2), 232 [214] (258)
  s.16(3), 232 [214] (258)
  s.16(4), 232 [215] (258)
  s.16(5), 232 [215] (258)
  s.16(6), 232 [216]
  s.16(7), 232 [217]
  s.17(1), 233 [218]
  s.17(2), (3), (4), (5), 233 [219 – 222]
  s.17(7), 233 [223]
  s.23, 226 [179]
  s.31(1), 225
  s.31(2), 225 [177]
  s.31(3), 225 [178]
  s.32, 239 [244] (259), 242 [255] (259), 245 [271] (259)
Sch.1, 231 [205] (257), 233 [224] (258)
Trustee Investments Act, 10
1962 Agricultural and Forestry Associations Act, 106
  s.1, 107 [106]

Buildings Society Act
  s.36, 28 [110]
Finance Act
  s.28, 180 [249] (197)
1963 Agriculture (Miscellaneous Provisions) Act
  s.19, 56 [71]
  s.20, 69 [128] (76)
Contracts of Employment Act
  Sch.1, 349 [85] (356)
Finance Act
  s.53(1), 169 [206]
Limitation Act, 276 [63] (304)
Water Resources Act
  ss. 23, 24, 135, 2 [2, 3] (34)
1964 Hire-Purchase Act
  s.27, 300 [176, 180]
Industrial Training Act, 347
Perpetuities and Accumulations Act
  s.13, 103 [101]
1965 Administrations of Estates (Small Payments) Act, 98
  s.2, 98 [81]
Compulsory Purchase Act, 241, 245
  s.1(1), 221 [161], 234 [226]
  s.3, 221 [162]
  s.4, 222 [163]
  s.5(1), 222 [164]
  s.5(2), 222 [165]
  s.6, 225 [176]
  s.7, 234 [227]
  s.8, 221 [156] (256)
  s.8(1), 226 [183], 226 [185]
  s.8(2), 227 [186]
  s.8(3), 229 [191]

s.10, 222[166] (256), 241[254] (259)
s.11(1), 224, 225, 246[277]
s.11(2), 246[278] (260)
s.11(3), 245[275]
s.11(4), 246[280]
s.12, 247[281]
s.20, 223[170, 224, 225, 236]
s.20(1), 222[167]
s.20(2), 222[168]
s.20(5), 223[169]
s.20(6), 223[171] (256)
s.22, 247[282]
s.32, 246[276]
Sch.3, 246[278] (260), 248[285] (260)
Finance Act
s.19, 152[107], 152[112]
s.20, 152[111,112]
s.20(4), 156[140, 141]
s.21, 152[108, 110]
s.21(2)(c), 152[109]
s.22, 152[113] (193)
s.22(5), 154[126] (194)
s.22(6), 152[117]
s.23(4), 152[115]
s.23(5), 152[116]
s.24(1), 153[124] (194)
s.24(7), 153[125]
s.25(1), 154[128]
s.25(2), 154[127]
s.25(3), 154[129]
s.25(4), 154[130] (194)
s.27, 156[142, 143]
s.28, 156[144]
s.29, 156[146, 147]
s.30, 157[148, 149]
s.31, 157[150]
s.33, 157[151, 152] (194)
s.33(2), 158[154]

s.33(3), 158[153]
s.33(5), 158[156]
s.33(6), 158[155] (194)
s.34, 159[158]
s.45, 152[113] (193)
s.45(1), 154[126] (194)
s.57, 156[145] (194)
s.70, 107[109]
Sch.6, 151, 152[114], 155[133, 135], 156[137-139]
Sch.7, 153[118,119,121-123]
Sch.8, 156[136]
Sch.11, 156[145] (194)
Hire-Purchase Act, 293–4
s.1, 292
s.1(1), 301[182, 183]
s.2, 293[146]
s.4, 293[147]
s,5, 294[150, 152]
s.6, 294[149]
s.7, 294[151]
s.9, 294[155]
s.10, 294[153]
s.11, 294[154]
s.16, 293[144]
s.25, 298[168]
s.27, 294, 296[163], 267, 302[184]
s.28, 296[165]
s.29, 293[145], 296[164], 298[169], 300[177, 179]
s.30, 298[170]
ss.33, 34, 298[171] (308)
s.35, 299[174]
s.38, 299[175]
s.58, 294[148]
Industrial and Provident Societies Act, 88, 95, 97
s.1, 95[58]
s.1(1), 95[59], 96[66,67],

97[72,74] (110), 98[77,82,84] (110), 99[85] (110)
s.1(3), 95 [60]
s.2(1), 95 [61]
s.2(2), 95 [62], 96 [64]
s.3, 95 [57], 96 [65]
s.5, 96 [63]
s.6(1), 97 [70]
s.14(1), 96 [68]
s.14(2), 96 [69]
s.16(1), 101 [97]
s.23, 98 [78]
s.24(1), (2), 98 [79,80]
s.49, 98 [83]
s.50, 101 [95]
s.52, 100 [94]
s.53, 101 [96]
s.55, 101 [98]
s.57, 98 [76]
s.58, 101 [99]
s.60, 100 [93]
Sch.1, 96[67] (109), 97[72,74] (110), 98,[77] [82,84] (110), 99[85] (110)

National Insurance (Industrial Injuries) Act, 337

Redundancy Payments Act
s.1(2), 349 [90]
s.2(1), 349 [87]
s.2(2), 350 [92]
s.2(3), (4), 350 [95–96]
s.3, 350[91,94]
ss.6-7, 350 [93]
s.8, 349 [84,85] (356), 352 [102] (356)
s.8(2), 349 [89] (356)
s.9(1), 353
s.13, 351[98]
s.15(2), 351 [100]
s.16(3), 349 [87] (356)
s.18, 353 [104]
s.19(2), 349 [87] (356)
s.21, 351 [101], 353 [110] (357)
s.23, 351[99] (356)
s.24, 349 [88], 352 [102] (356)
s.27, 353 [106]
s.30, 353 [109] (357)
s.30(6), 353 [108]
s.48, 350 [97]
s.56(1), 353
Sch.1, 352 [102] (356)
Sch.4, 351 [99] (356)
Sch.5, 353 [104]

Rent Act
s.33, 71 [140], 71 [141] (77)
s.33(2), 71 [142]

1966   Family Provision Act
117 [42] (124)
s.1, 120 [50] (125)
s.1(2), 120 [49] (125)
s.2, 122 [57] (125)
Sch.3, 123 [61]

1967   Agriculture Act, 65
s.67(1), 343 [53]

Companies Act
s.47, 86 [30]

Forestry Act, 211
s.1, 212 [79]
s.10, 212 [80,81] (254)
s.11, 212 [81] (254)
s.11(3), 212 [82]
s.12(1), 212 [83]
s.13, 212 [84]
s.15, 212 [85] (254)
s.17, 212 [86]
s.18, 212 [87]
s.21, 213 [89]
s.22, 213 [90]
s.24, 213 [91]
s.26, 213 [91]

Misrepresentation Act
   s.2(1), 267 [26]
   s.2(2), 267 [27]
   s.3, 267 [30]
   s.4(2), 285 [104] (306)

1968 Agriculture (Miscellaneous Provisions) Act
   s.9, 65 [112] (76), 224, 239
   s.10, 65 [112,113] (76)
   s.12, 224, 225, 230, 238 [240], 240 [245] (259)
   s.12(2), 240 [248]
   s.13 and 13(1), 240 [245-247]
   s.15(2), 66 [114], 224
   s.44, 107
Capital Allowance Act
   s.68, 139 [44]
   s.68(3), 139 [45]
   s.69, 139 [44]
Finance Act
   s.36, 169 [204]
   s.37(1), 169 [207]
Firearms Act
   s.20, 332 [35]
   Sch.6, 332 [36]
Friendly and Industrial and Provident Societies Act
   s.1, 99 [88]
   s.3, 100 [89]
   s.4, 100 [90]
   s.7, 100 [91]
   s.8, 100 [92]
Rent Act, 69
   s.1, 70 [138]
   s.2(1), 70 [133]
   s.7(2), 72 [143]
   s.10, 70 [139] (77), 72 [144] (77)
   s.10(2), 73 [145] (77)
   Sch.3, 70 [139] (77), 72 [144] (77), 73 [145] (77)

Theft Act
   s.1, 331 [30]
   s.4(2), (3), (4), 331 [32-34]
   s.7, 331 [81]
Town and Country Planning Act
   s.30, 246 [279] (260)
Wills Act
   s.1, 113 [17]

1969 Administration of Justice Act
   s.17, 112 [7]
Employers' Liability (Compulsory Insurance) Act
   s.1(1), 343 [45]
   s.1(2), 343 [46]
   s.2(1), (2), 343 [48,49]
   s.5, 343 [50]
Employers' Liability (Defective Equipment) Act
   s.1(1), 338 [4]
   s.1(2), (3), 338 [5,6]
Family Law Reform Act, 117 [42] (124), 123 [58] (125)
   s. 111 [2], 264 [13]
   s.3(1), 111 [2]
Finance Act, 104, 170 [212] (196)
   s.35, 163 [183]
   s.37, 170 [213], 171 [214]
   s.38, 171 [215]
   s.42, 158 [157] (194)
   Sch.17, 163
   Sch.19, 153 [120], 158 [157] (194)
Redundancy Rebates Act
   s.1(1), 353 [107] (356)

1970 Agriculture Act
   s.37, 46 [25] (73)
   s.64, 46 [25] (73)

409

s.72, 282 [93]
s.99, 71 [141] (77)
s.100, 73 [145] (77)
Sch.4, 46 [25] (73)
Finance Act
  s.21, 142 [59]
  s.23, 142 [60]
  s.24, 142 [61]
Income and Corporation
Taxes Act
  s.21, 150 [102]
  s.42, 149 [97]
  s.54, 151 [104] (193)
  s.54(2), 151 [106]
  s.54(3), 151 [105]
  s.67(1), 143 [69], 144 [70, 71]
  s.69, 144 [73]
  s.71, 146 [82] (193), 147 [86]
  s.72, 146 [82, 83, 85]
  ss.73-77, 146 [82] (193)
  s.80, 145 [76, 78]
  s.80(2), 144 [74]
  s.81, 145 [77]
  s.82, 146 [80]
  s.87, 144 [72]
  s.90, 144 [75]
  ss.91-92, 147 [89] (193)
  s.108, 127 [1] (190)
  s.109, 127 [1] (190)
  s.111, 147 [90]
  ss.115-117, 134
  s.118, 135 [27]
  s.130 [12], 131 [14, 17], 132 [26]
  s.137, 130 [10]
  s.139, 129 [7] (191)
  s.154, 135 [28], 136 [33, 34] (191)
  s.168, 137 [37]
  s.170, 137 [38]
  s.171, 137 [35]
  s.172, 137 [36]
  s.174, 138 [40]
  s.177, 160 [166]
  s.180, 138 [39]
  s.185, 141 [53, 55]
  s.187, 141 [57]
  s.188, 141 [57, 58]
  s.189, 142 [62]
  ss.195-203, 143 [67] (192)
  s.202(2), 143 [66]
  s.243(3), 160 [161]
  s.248(1), 160 [162]
  s.250(1), 160 [163]
  s.250(2), 160 [164]
  s.252(1), 161 [167]
  s.253, 161 [168]
  ss. 258-264, 161 [169]
  s.265(2), 160 [165]
  282(1), 161 [172]
  s.283, 162 [176]
  s.284, 162 [177]
  s.285, 162 [178]
  s.286(1), 162 [179]
  s.286(5), 162 [180]
  ss.296-297, 162 [181] (195)
  s.302, 162 [173]
  s.303, 162 [174, 175]
  s.304, 147 [88]
  s.411, 132 [23]
  s.454(3), 150 [101]
  s.528, 148 [92]
  s.531, 141 [54]
  s.533, 146 [79]
  Sch.1 Part I, 151 [103]
  Sch.3, 146 [81]
  Sch.6, 129 [7] (191)
  Sch.A, 143-7
  Sch.B, 148
  Sch.D, 139, 143, 144, 145
  Sch.E, 139, 142, 143
Matrimonial Proceedings

and Property Act
  s.40, 120 [47]
Taxes Management Act
  s.9, 135 [31]
1971 Animals Act
  s.2(2), 316 [33], 317 [34]
  s.3, 317 [36]
  s.4(1), 315 [26]
  s.4(2), 315 [28]
  s.5(3), 317 [35]
  s.5(4), 317 [37]
  s.5(5), 315 [27]
  s.6(2), 316 [32]
  s.6(3), 317 [34]
  s.7, 316 [31]
  s.8(1), 315 [23]
  s.8(2), 315 [24]
  s.9, 317 [38]
  s.11, 315 [30]
Criminal Damage Act
  s.1, 332 [45]
  s.2, 332 [46]
  s.4, 332 [47]
  s.8, 333 [48]
  s.10, 333 [49]
Finance Act
  s.16, 150 [100]
  s.17, 136 [34] (191)
  s.23, 150 [98,99] (193)
  s.34, 149 [93]
  s.40(1), 138 [41] (192)
  s.41(3), 138 [42]
  s.43, 138 [43]
  s.59, 153 [124] (194)
  s.60, 157 [152] (194)
  s.62, 181 [254]
  Sch.4, 150 [98,99] (193),
  Sch.12, 153 [124] (194),
  154 [130] (194), 154 [131,132]
Industrial Relations Act
  s.5, 346 [65] (355)

  s.11(1), 346 [64]
  s.22(1), 348 [73]
  s.24(1), (2), (4), (5),
  348 [77–80]
  s.27(1), 348 [74]
  s.28, 348 [75]
  s.29(1), 348 [76]
  s.106(1), (4), (5), 349 [81-3]
  s.150, 351 [101], 353 [110]
Law Reform (Miscellaneous
Provisions) Act,
  276 [63] (304)
Town and Country Planning
Act
  s.1(1), 199 [1]
  s.6, 199 [4]
  s.7, 200 [5]
  s.8, 200 [6]
  s.9, 200 [6]
  s.11, 200 [7]
  s.12, 200 [8]
  s.14, 200 [9]
  s.20, 231 [205] (257),
  232 [213] (258), 233 [218],
  [223] (258)
  s.22, 201 [12]
  s.22(2), 201 [16,18], 202 [20]
  s.22(3), 201 [14]
  s.22(4), 201 [15]
  s.24, 202 [22]
  s.27, 203 [25]
  s.29, 203 [26], 218 [135]
  s.29(1), 201 [10], 204 [30]
  s.30, 204 [31]
  s.32, 203 [27]
  s.33, 206 [39]
  s.36, 206 [40]
  s.36(8), 206 [41] (253)
  s.37, 206 [40]
  s.41, 205 [37]
  s.42, 204 [28]

s.44, 206 [38]
s.45, 208 [55]
s.51, 209 [57]
s.53, 202 [21 a]
s.54, 209 [60]
s.54(2), 209 [61]
s.55(1), 209 [62]
s.58, 209 [63]
s.59, 210 [71] (254)
s.60, 210 [71, 72] (254), 211 [74] (254)
s.61, 211 [74] (254)
s.62, 211 [75]
s.63, 215 [102]
s.64, 215 [103]
s.65, 214 [97]
s.87, 207 [46]
s.88, 207 [47]
s.89, 208 [53]
s.90, 208 [54]
s.91, 208 [48]
s.91(2), 208 [49]
s.93(1), 208 [50]
s.93(2), 208 [51]
s.93(3), 208 [52]
ss.96-99, 209 [64]
s.102, 211 [76]
s.103, 211 [77]
s.104, 214 [99]
s.105, 214 [98]
s.107, 214 [100]
s.108, 209 [59]
s.109, 215 [106]
s.109(3), 215 [107]
s.112, 219 [152]
s.114, 210 [65, 67]
s.115, 210 [66]
s.116, 210 [68]
s.117, 210 [69]
s.164, 208 [56]
s.169, 207 [45]

s.170, 209 [58]
s.174, 211 [73]
s.176, 217 [124] (255)
s.180, 213 [92]
s.181, 213 [93]
s.183, 213 [94]
s.192, 249 [287]
s.193, 250 [292] (260)
s.194, 251 [300]
s.194(2), 251 [301]
s.195. 251 [304]
s.195(5), 251 [302]
s.196, 251 [305] (260)
s.198, 252 [306]
s.201, 250 [296]
s.203, 250 [295]
s.205, 250 [294]
s.207, 250 [298]
ss.242 and 245, 206 [43] (253)
s.277, 217 [125]
s.290, 201 [13], 202 [21]
s.291, 231 [205] (257), 232 [213, 215] (258) 233 [218] (258)
Sch.8, 207 [44], 231 [210]
Sch.9, 206 [41] (253)
Sch.23, 231 [205] (257), 232 [213, 215] (258) 233 [218] (258)
Unsolicited Goods and Services Act, 262
1972 Agriculture (Miscellaneous Provisions) Act
s.24, 73 [145] (77)
Contracts of Employment Act
s.1(1), 344 [59]
s.1(2), 344 [60]
s.1(3), (6), 345 [62]
s.2, 345 [63] (355)

s.4, 346 [67]
s.4(2), 346 [65]
s.4(5), 347 [68]
ss.5, 6, 8, 347 [69-71]
s.13(6), 349 [89] (356)
Sch.1, 345 [61], 349
Sch.2, 345 [63] (355)
Defective Premises Act
  s.4, 330 [27]
  s.6(3), 330 [28]
European Communities Act
  s.9, 87 [32]
Finance Act, 159, 170 [210,211] (196)
  s.2(2), 184 [264]
  s.3, 184 [266]
  s.4, 184 [263]
  s.7, 186 [268]
  s.9, 182 [261]
  s.10, 185 [267]
  s.12, 186 [270], 187 [272]
  s.21, 190 [273]
  s.31, 190 [275]
  s.32(2), 190 [276]
  s.37, 190 [274]
  s.45, 184 [265]
  s.66, 148
  s.67, 138 [41] (192)
  s.75, 149 [94-96] (193)
  s.85, 161, [170,171]
  s.93, 160 [160]
  s.95, 159 [159]
  s.121, 165 [192], 166 [193]
  Sch.1, 183 [262]
  Sch.4, 186 [271]
  Sch.5, 186 [269]
  Sch.9, 149 [96] (193)
Income and Corporation Taxes Act
  s.412(1), 353 [105] (356)
Local Government Act
  s.1(1), (10), 199 [3] (252)
  s.2, 199 [3] (252)
  s.20(1), (6), 199 [3] (252)
  s.21, 199 [3] (252)
  s.182(1), (2), (5), 199 [3] (252)
  Sch.16, 199 [3] (252)
Road Traffic Act
  s.143 [367]
  s.145(3), (4), 367 [17-18]
  s.148(1), (2), 368 [20-21]
  s.149(1)(b), 368 [22,23]
  ss.154-155, 367
Town and Country Planning (Amendment) Act
  s.1, 201 [11]
Counter-Inflation Act, The
  s.2, 343 [54]
  s.11, 51 [47] (74)
  s.23(2), 51 [47] (74)
  Sch.3, 51 [47] (74)
1973 Land Compensation Act
  s.1, 243 [258]
  s.2, 243 [259]
  s.3, 243 [260]
  s.3(2), 245 [272]
  s.4, 244 [261]
  s.5, 244 [262]
  s.6, 244 [263]
  s.7, 244 [264]
  s.8, 244 [265]
  s.9, 244 [266]
  s.11, 244 [267]
  s.14, 244 [268]
  s.16, 245 [269]
  s.17, 243 [257]
  s.18, 245 [271] (259)
  s.19, 245 [270] (259)
  s.20, 245 [273]
  s.28, 245 [274]
  s.29, 237 [236]

s.30, 237 [237]
s.32, 237 [238]
s.34, 238 [241]
s.35, 239 [243]
s.36, 239 [144] (259)
s.36(4), 238 [242]
s.37, 223 [171] (256), 223 [172]
s.37(4), 223 [173] (257)
s.38, 223 [173] (256-7), 240 [249] (259)
s.44, 234 [229]
s.46, 236 [234]
s.47, 223 [171] (256)
s.48, 230 [198]
s.48(5), 230 [199] (257)
s.50, 240 [250]
s.52, 241 [252]
s.53, 220 [157] (256), 227 [187]
s.54, 228 [188]
s.54(6), 228 [189, 190]
s.55, 247 [283]
s.56, 248 [284]
s.57, 249 [286]
s.58, 226 [184]
s.59, 224 [174]
s.61, 220 [157] (256), 225 [175]

s.63, 242 [255] (259)
s.68, 249 [288]
s.69, 249 [289]
s.71, 249 [290]
s.72, 249 [291]
s.77, 250 [292] (260)
s.77(3), 250 [293]
s.78, 250 [297]
s.79, 251 [299]
s.80, 251 [303] 251 [305] (260)
s.81, 251 [305] (260)
s.84, 243 [256]
s.89, 230 [200], 235 [230], 236 [235], 240 [251], 245 [270] (259)

Sale of Goods (Implied Terms) Act, 277, 278, 281
s.1, 283 [96, 97] (305)
s.2, 279 [80]
s.3, 280 [84, 89]
s.3(2), 305 [87]
s.4, 278 [72] (305), 283 [98] (306), 284 [101, 102] (306)
s.7(2), 280 [86] (305)
s.8, 295 [156] (307)
s.10(1), (4), 295 [161]
s.12, 295 [156] (307)
s.18, 277 [70]

414

European Community Legislation

Treaty of Rome:
    Article 38 376[8]
    Article 39 376[9]
    Article 40 376[10], 377
    Article 43 372[2]
    Article 47 371[1]
    Article 92 372[4]
    Article 93 372[3]
    Article 169 375
    Article 177 374[5]

European Economic Community Council:
    Directive 66/404 375
    Directive 69/64   375
    Directive 72/159 382

European Economic Community Council:
    Regulation 17/64   379, 380
    Regulation 99/64   380[14]
    Regulation 159/66   380
    Regulation 120/67   378[11,12,13]
    Regulation 804/68   App. V
    Regulation 986/68   App. V.
    Regulation 1105/68 375, App. V
    Regulation 2517/69 373
    Regulation 2637/69 373
    Regulation 1035/72 381

Table of Statutory Instruments

Indexer's note: References are given as follows: 16[57] (35), where 16 is the page of the text, [57] is the note number thereon, and (35) is the page on which the note itself appears. The latter is omitted unless additional information is to be found in the note.

1948   Agriculture (Maintenance, Repair and Insurance of Fixed Equipment) Regulations, S.I. No. 184 45[19]

1950   Town and Country Planning General Development Order, S.I. No. 729 202[24]

Town and Country Planning (Landscape Areas Special Development) Order, S.I. No. 729 203[24]

1957   Agriculture (First Aid) Regulations, S.I. No. 940 341[36]

Agriculture (Ladders) Regulations, S.I. No. 1385 341[35]

Agriculture (Power Take-off) Regulations, S.I. No. 1386 341[28]

Agricultural Land Tribunals and Notices to Quit Order, S.I. No. 81 48[35], 56[70], 59[83]

1959   Agriculture (Areas and Agricultural Land Tribunals) Order, S.I. No. 83 48[33]

Agriculture (Circular Saws) Regulations, S.I. No. 427 341[29]

Agriculture (Forms of Notices to Remedy) Regulations, S.I. No. 707 56[72]

Agriculture (Lifting of Heavy Weights) Regulations, S.I. No. 2120 341[23]

Agriculture (Safeguarding of Work Places) Regulations, S.I. No. 428 341[34]

Agriculture (Stationary Machinery) Regulations, S.I. No. 1216 341[30]

1960   Agriculture (Poisonous Substances) (Extension Orders) Regulations, S.I. No. 398 342[41] (355)

Agriculture (Threshers and Balers) Regulations, S.I. No. 1199 341[32]

Caravan Sites (Licence Applications) Order S.I. No. 1474 217[133]

1962   Agricultural and Forestry Associations (Exceptions) Order, S.I. No. 1892 107[107]

Agriculture (Field Machinery) Regulations, S.I. No. 1472 341[31]

1964   Agricultural and Forestry Associations (Exceptions) Order, S.I.
       No. 14 107[108]

       Agriculture (Forms of Notices to Remedy) Regulations, S.I. No.
       707 56[72]

       Agriculture (Notices to Remedy and Notices to Quit) Order, S.I.
       No. 706 57[74,77] (75)

1965   Agriculture (Poisonous Substances) (Extension Orders), S.I. No.
       1395 342[41] (355)

       Industrial Tribunals (England and Wales) Regulations, S.I. No.
       1101 347[72]

       Redundancy Payments (Pensions) Regulations, S.I. No. 1932
       352[103]

       Redundancy Payments Rebates Regulations, S.I. No. 1893
       353[109] (357)

       Redundancy Payments Rebates (Amendment) Regulations, S.I.
       No. 2067 353[109] (357)

1966   Agriculture (Poisonous Substances) (Extension Orders) S.I. No.
       645 342[41] (355)

       Agriculture (Poisonous Substances) Regulations, S.I. No. 1063
       342[42] (355)

1967   Agriculture (Poisonous Substances) Regulations, S.I. No. 1860
       342[42] (355)

       Agriculture (Tractor Cabs) Regulations, S.I. No. 1072 341[33]

       Industrial Tribunals (England and Wales) Regulations, S.I. No.
       301 347[72]

1968   Industrial Tribunals (England and Wales) Regulations, S.I. No.
       729 347[72]

1969   Agriculture (Calculation of Value for Compensation) Regulations,
       S.I. No. 1704 63[104]

       Agriculture (Poisonous Substances) Regulations, S.I. No. 84
       342[42] (355)

       Town and Country Planning (Control of Advertisements) Regula-
       tions, S.I. No. 1532 215[104]

1970   Secretary of State for Environment Order, S.I. No. 1681 199[1]

       Industrial Tribunals (England and Wales) Regulations, S.I. No.
       941 347[72]

       Town and Country Planning (Determination of Appeals) (Prescrib-
       ed Classes) Regulations, S.I. No. 1454 206[42]

1971   Employers' Liability (Compulsory Insurance) General Regulations,
       S.I. No. 1117 343[47]

1972   Agriculture (Calculation of Value for Compensation) Regulations, S.I. No. 864 63[104]

Agriculture (Notices to Remedy and Notices to Quit) Order, S.I. No. 1207 57[74,77] (75)

Family Provision (Intestate Succession) Order, S.I. No. 916 117[42]

Town and Country Planning (Control of Advertisements) (Amendment) Regulations, S.I. No. 904 215[105], 215[108,109], 216[110-123], 217[124]

Town and Country Planning (Use Classes) Order, S.I. No. 1385 201[19]

1972   Town and Country Planning (Use Classes) Order, S.I. No. 31 202[23]

1973   Counter-Inflation (Agricultural Rents) (No. 2) Order, S.I. No. 1717 51[47] (74)

Counter-Inflation (Price and Pay Code) Order, S.I. No. 646 344[54] (355)

418

Table of Cases

Indexer's note:
1 For Acts of Parliament, etc., see separate Table of Statutes and Table of Statutory Instruments.
2 References are given as follows: 16[57](35) where 16 is the page of the text, [57] is the note number thereon and (35) is the page for the note itself. The latter is omitted unless additional information is to be found in the note.

Adams v. *Lindsell* (1818) 1 B. & Ald. 681 262[4]
Agnew v. *Robertson* [1956] S.L.T. (Sh. Ct.) 90 368[26]
Ajayi, Emmanuel v. *Briscoe, RT (Nigeria) Ltd* [1964] 3 All E.R. 556 263[10]
Aldin v. *Latimer Clark, Muirhead and Co.* [1894] 2 Ch. 437 16[57], 32[127]
Aldred's case (1610) 9 Co.Rep.57b 313[7]
Aldridge v. *Johnson* (1857) 7 E. & B. 885 277[69], 288[118]
Alexander v. *Duddy* (1856) S.C. 24 97[73]
Anderson v. *Thornton* (1853) 3 Ex.Ch. 425 361[3]
Andrews v. *Hopkinson* [1957] 1 Q.B. 229 293[143]
Anisminic v. *Foreign Compensation Commission* [1969] 2 A.C. 147 221[160]
Ashdown v. *Samuel Williams and Sons* [1957] 1 Q.B. 409 326[17]
Associated Distributors v. *Hall* [1938] 2 K.B. 83 297[166] (307)
Astley Industrial Trust Ltd v. *Grimley* [1963] 1 W.L.R. 584 295[159]
Attorney-General v. *Boden* [1912] 1 K.B. 539 173[221]
Attorney-General v. *Johnson* [1903] 1 K.B. 617 168[202]
Attorney-General v. *Melville Construction Co. Ltd* (1968) L.G.R. 309 211[78]
Attorney-General v. *Seccombe* [1911] 2 K.B. 688 167[201]

Balfour v. *Balfour* [1919] 2 K.B. 571 263[12]
Ballard's Conveyance, re. [1937] Ch. 473 30[120]
Banks v. *Goodfellow* (1870) L.R. 5 Q.B. 549 111[3,5]
Basely v. *Clarkson* (1682) 3 Led 37 333[51] (336)
Beach v. *Reed Corrugated Cases Ltd* [1956] 2 All E.R. 652 274[56]
Beal v. *Taylor* [1967] 1 W.L.R. 1193 279[78]
Beale's Settlement Trusts, re. [1932] 2 Ch. 15 12[44]

Beer v. *Walker* (1877) 46 L.J.Q.B. 677 280 [88]

Beer v. *Wheeler* [1965] 109 S.J. 133 339 [12]

Bentleys Stokes and Lowless v. *Beeson* (1952) 33 T.C. 491 131 [15]

Biggs v. *Hoddinott* [1898] 2 Ch. 307 27 [106]

Bigos v. *Bousted* [1951] 1 All E.R. 92 271 [48]

Birmingham City Corporation v. *West Midland Baptist (Trust) Association Inc.* [1969] 3 All E.R. 172 230 [196]

Blackmore v. *Butler* [1954] 2 Q.B. 171 39 [4]

Blackwell v. *Mills*, (1945) 26 T.C. 468 142 [63]

Blewitt, in b. (1880) 5 P.D. 116 115 [32] (32)

Bolam v. *Friern Hospital Management Committee* [1957] 1 W.L.R. 582 311 [3]

Booth, re, [1926] 114 118 [25]

Boyd v. *Wilton* [1957] 2 Q.B. 277 67 [122]

Boyse v. *Rossborough* (1857) 6 H.L.C. 248 112 [9]

Brace v. *Calder* [1895] 2 Q.B. 253 275 [58]

Bridge v. *Campbell Discount Co. Ltd* [1962] A.C. 600 275 [60], 297 [166] (307)

British Insulated and Helsby Cables Ltd v. *Atherton* [1926] A.C. 205 131 [13]

Brown v. *Harrison* (1947) 177 L.T. 281 312 [5]

Budberg v. *Jerwood and Ward* (1934) 51 T.L.R. 99 286 [109]

Budd v. *Silver* (1813) 2 Phill. 115 121 [52]

Burnett v. *British Waterways Board* [1973] 1 W.L.R. 700 326 [18]

Byrne v. *Van Tienhoven* (1880) 5 C.B.D. 344 262 [5]

Cable v. *Bryant* [1908] 1 Ch. 259 20 [74]

Caminer v. *Northern and London Investment Trust Ltd* [1951] A.C. 88 311 [4]

Camrose, Viscount v. *Basingstoke Corporation* [1966] 1 W.L.R. 1100 233 [225]

Carlisle and Silloth Golf Club v. *Smith* [1913] 3 K.B. 75 105 [104]

Carr v. *Broderick, James and Co. Ltd* [1942] 2 K.B. 275 298 [172]

Cartwright, re, (1889) 41 Ch. D. 532 4 [11]

Casey's Patents, re Stewart v. *Casey* [1892] 1 Ch. 104 262 [6]

Castellain v. *Preston* (1883) 11 Q.B.D. 380 361 [4]

Chapelton v. *Barry UDC* [1940] 1 K.B. 532 269 [35]

Charter v. *Sullivan* [1957] 2 Q.B. 117 290 [137]

Chatsworth Estates Co. v. *Fewell* [1931] 1 Ch. 224 31 [124]

Chick v. *Commission of Stamp Duties* [1958] A.C. 435 167 [199]

Clark, re, (1906) 40 Ir. L.T. 117 173 [222]

Clarke v. *Hall* [1961] 2 Q.B. 331 57 [79]

Clements v. *London and North Western Railway* Co. [1894] 2 Q.B. 482 264 [15]

Clifford v. *Challen, Charles and Son* [1951] 1 K.B. 495 339 [10]

Clifton v. *Bury, Viscount* (1887) 4 T.L.R. 8 1 [1] (35)

Clore v. *Theatrical Properties, Ltd* [1936] 3 All E.R. 483 32 [130] (37)

Coates v. *Diment* [1951] 1 All E. R. 890 61 [92]

Cohen v. *Roche* [1929] 1 K.B. 169 291 [138]

Collins v. *Fraser* (1969) 46 T.C. 143 148 [91]

Colls v. *Home and Colonial Stores, Ltd* [1904] A.C. 179 24 [99]

Corporation of London v. *Riggs* (1880) 13 Ch.D. 798 24 [97]

Costagliola v. *Bunting* [1958] 1 All E.R. 846 57 [80]

Cowan v. *Wrayford* [1953] 1 W.L.R. 1340 56 [67]

Craig v. *Lamoureux* [1920] A.C. 349 112 [11]

Crow v. *Wood* [1971] 1 Q.B. 77 315 [25]

Cunningham v. *Whelan* [1917] 521 IP.L.T. 67 314 [19]

Curtis v. *Chemical Cleaning and Dyeing Co.* [1951] 1 K.B. 805 269 [37]

Dakin, H. and Co. Ltd v. *Lee* [1916] 1 K.B. 566 271 [50]

Dale v. *De Soissons* (1950) 32 T.C. 118 141 [56]

Dalton v. *Angus and Co.* (1881) 6 App. Cas. 740 22 [81]

Dane v. *Mortgage Insurance Corporation* [1894] 1 Q.B. 54 361 [5]

Daniel v. *North* (1809) 11 East 372 23 [88]

Dashwood v. *Magniac* (1891) 3 Ch. 306 4 [12]

Davey v. *Durrant* (1857) 1 De G. & J. 535 28 [109]

Davey v. *Harrow Corporation* [1958] 1 Q.B. 60 314 [14]

Davidson v. *Handley Page* [1945] 1 All E.R. 235 338[7]

Davies v. *Price* [1958] 1 W.L.R. 434 59 [84]

Davis, in b. [1952] P.279 115 [34]

Demby Hamilton and Co. Ltd v. *Barden* [1949] 1 All E.R. 435 288 [121]

Derry v. *Peek* (1889) 14 App.Cas. 337 267 [25]

D'Eyncourt v. *Gregory* (1866) L.R. 3 Eq. 382 18 [68]

Doe v. *Manifold* (1813) 1 M. & S. 294 113 [14]

Doherty v. *Allman* (1878) 3 App.Cas. 709 4 [10]

Donoghue v. *Stevenson* [1932] A.C. 562 310 [1]

Drury v. *Buckland, Victor, Ltd* [1941] 1 All E.R. 269 293 [142]

Ducksbury, re, [1966] 1 W.L.R. 1226 123 [60]

Duke of Norfolk v. *Arbuthnot* (1880) 5 C.P.D. 390 22[80]

Dunlop Pneumatic Tyre Co. Ltd v. *New Garage and Motor Co. Ltd* [1915] A.C. 79 275 [59]

Dunn v. *Fidoe* [1950] 2 All E.R. 685 40[6]

Dunster v. *Abbott* [1954] 1 W.L.R. 58 324 [6]
Dynevor, Lord, v. *Tennant* (1888) 13 App.Cas. 279 24[96]

Edwards v. *Bairstow and Harrison* [1956] A.C. 14 128 [5]
Elliston v. *Reacher* [1908] 2 Ch. 374 30 [119]
Elwes v. *Maw* (1802) 3 East 38 18 [66], 60 [90]

Farr v. *Motor Traders Mutual Insurance Society* [1920] 3 K.B. 669 368 [24]
Farrer v. *Nelson* (1885) 15 Q.B.D. 258 314 [21]
Fawcett Properties Ltd v. *Buckingham County Council* [1958] 1 W.L.R. 1161 205 [34] (253)
Fawcett Properties Ltd v. *Buckingham County Council* [1961] A.C. 636 205 [36]
Felthouse v. *Bindley* (1826) 11 C.B. (N.S.) 869 262 [3]
Financings Ltd v. *Baldock* [1963] 2 Q.B. 104 297 [167]
Finch v. *Telegraph Construction and Maintenance Co.* [1949] 1 All E.R. 452 339 [11]
Fletcher v. *Income Tax Commissioner* [1972] A.C. 414 105 [105]
Foakes v. *Beer* (1884) 9 App.Cas. 605 263 [8]
Folkes v. *King* [1923] 1 K.B. 282 286 [107]
Ford v. *Langford* [1949] L.J.R. 586 70 [137]
Fowkes v. *Pascoe* (1875) L.R. 10 Ch. 343 174 [223]

Gardiner v. *Grey* (1815) 4 Camp. 46 282 [94]
Gaskin v. *Balls* (1879) 13 Ch.D. 324 31 [123]
Gibson, in the estate of, [1949] P. 434 113 [15]
Giles v. *Walker* (1890) 24 Q.B. 656 314 [13]
Gladstone v. *Bower* [1960] 2 Q.B. 384 42 [15]
Goldsack v. *Shore* [1950] 1 K.B. 708 42 [12]
Gott v. *Measures* [1948] 1 K.B. 234 317 [39]
Grant v. *Australian Knitting Mills* [1936] A.C. 85 279 [79]
Grey v. *Inland Revenue Commissioners* [1960] A.C. 1 167 [197]
Green v. *Goddard* (1704) 2 Salk. 641 334 [55]
Gutsell v. *Reeve* [1936] 1 K.B. 272 344 [58]

Hadley v. *Baxendale* (1854) 9 Exch. 341 274 [54] (305)
Hall R. and H., Ltd, re, and Pim W.H. (Junior) and Co's Arbitration [1928] All E.R. Rep. 763 291 [140]
Hall and Co. Ltd v. *Shoreham-by-Sea UDC* [1964] 1 All E.R. 1 205 [34] (253)
Hardy v. *Central London Railway Co.* [1920] 3 K.B. 459 329 [26]

Harling v. *Eddy* [1951] 2 K.B. 739 269[40]

Harris v. *Bright's Asphalt Contractors Ltd* [1953] 1 Q.B. 617 338[2]

Harris v. *Poland* [1941] 1 K.B. 462 364[14]

Harrison v. *Duke of Rutland* [1893] 1 Q.B. 142 334[56]

Harrison-Broadley v. *Smith* [1964] 1 All E.R. 687 41[10]

Hartley v. *Hymans* [1920] 3 K.B. 475 289[123]

Harvey v. *Crawley Development Corporation* [1957] 1 Q.B. 485 235[231]

Hawkins v. *Price* [1947] Ch. 645 265[22]

Hawksley's Settlement, re, [1934] Ch. 384 114[19]

Haynes, re, (1887) 37 Ch.D. 306 11[35]

Hayward v. *Challoner* [1968] 1 Q.B. 107 33[134] (37)

Heasman v. *Jordan* [1954] Ch. 744 140[49]

Heath v. *Brighton, Mayor of,* [1908] 98 L.T. 718 313[9]

Hemmings v. *Sceptre Life Association* [1905] 1 Ch. 365 360[2]

Heron II, Koufos v. *Czarnikow C. Ltd* [1969] 1 A.C. 350 274[54] (304)

Herrington v. *British Railways Board* [1972] A.C. 877 327[24], 329[24]

Hidderley v. *Warwickshire County Council* (1963) 14 P 201[17]

Higgs v. *Brown* [1946] L.J.N.C.C.R. 149 70[135]

Hill, Christopher Ltd v. *Ashington Piggeries Ltd* [1972] A.C. 441 270[44], 278[73], 281[92]

Hirst v. *Sargent* (1966) 65 L.G.R. 127 70[136]

Hochstrasser v. *Mayes* [1960] A.C. 376 140[48]

Hollier v. *Rambler Motors (A.M.C.) Ltd* [1972] 1 All E.R. 399 269[41]

Hollywood Silver Fox Farm Ltd v. *Emmett* [1936] 2 K.B. 468 313[11]

Honywood v. *Honywood* (1874) L.R. 18 Eq. 306 5[13]

Hope-Brown, in b. [1942] P. 136 114[21]

Horn v. *Sunderland Corporation* [1941] 2 K.B. 26 235[233]

Horton v. *Young* (1971) 47 T.C. 60 132[25]

Howkins v. *Jardine* [1951] 1 K.B. 614 40[5]

Hunt's Settled Estates, re, [1906] 2 Ch. 11 10[26]

Hurst v. *Picture Theatres, Ltd* [1915] 1 K.B.1 32[129]

Hyde v. *Wrench* (1840) 3 Beav. 334 261[2]

Hyman v. *Van den Bergh* [1908] 1 Ch. 167 22[85]

Imperial Gas Light and Coke Co. v. *Broadbent* (1859) 7 H.L.Cas. 600 234[228], 241[253]

Income Tax Commissioners for the City of London v. *Gibbs* [1942] A.C. 402 135[32]

International Tea Stores Co. v. *Hobbs* [1903] 2 Ch. 165 21[78]

I.R.C. v. *Alexander Von Glehn and Co. Ltd* [1920] 2 K.B. 553 132[21]

I.R.C. v. *Cock, Russell and Co. Ltd* (1949) 29 T.C. 387 128[6]

I.R.C. v. *Crossman* [1937] A.C. 26 179 [246]
I.R.C. v. *Graham's Trustees* (1970) 49 A.T.C. 365 178 [244]
I.R.C. v. *Nelson* (1938) 22 T.C. 716 130 [9]

Jacobs v. *Batavia and General Plantations Trust* [1924] 1 Ch. 287 268 [31]
James Jones and Sons, Ltd v. *Tankerville, Earl of,* [1909] 2 Ch. 440 32 [128]
Jenkin R. Lewis and Son Ltd v. *Kerman* [1971] 1 C.L. 477 58 [81]
Jenner v. *Allen West and Co. Ltd* [1959] 1 W.L.R. 554 339 [9]
Jones v. *Manchester Corporation* [1952] 2 Q.B. 852 319 [50]
Jones v. *Vernon's Pools Ltd* [1938] 2 All E.R. 626 263 [11]

Kendall, Henry and Sons v. *Lillico, William and Sons, Ltd* [1969] 2 A.C. 31 281 [91]
Kent v. *Conniff* [1953] 1 All E.R. 155 67 [121]
Kent County Council v. *Kingsway Investments (Kent) Ltd* [1971] A.C. 72 205 [33,34] (253)
Kilgour v. *Gaddes* [1904] 1 K.B. 457 21 [79]
Kingswood Estate Co. Ltd v. *Anderson* [1963] 2 Q.B. 169 266 [24]

Langston, in the estate of, [1953] p. 100 115 [29]
Law Shipping Co. Limited v. *I.R.C.* (1924) 12 T.C. 621 131 [18]
Leaf v. *International Galleries* [1950] 2 K.B. 86 267 [28]
Leeman v. *Montagu* [1936] 2 All E.R. 1677 313 [8]
Leigh v. *Taylor* [1902] A.C. 157 18 [67]
Lemmon v. *Webb* [1894] 3 Ch. 1 313 [12]
L'Estrange v. *Graucob* [1943] 2 K.B. 394 269 [36]
Letang v. *Cooper* [1965] 1 Q.B. 232 333 [50,51] (336)
Letterstedt v. *Broers* (1884) 9 App.Cas. 371 15 [54]
Lewis Bowles' Case (1615) 11 Co.Rep. 79b 5 [15]
Lilley v. *Doubleday* (1881) 7 Q.B.D. 510 269 [42]
Limpus v. *London General Omnibus Co.* (1862) 1 H. & C. 526 319 [44]
Lister v. *Romford Ice and Cold Storage Co.* [1957] A.C. 555 319 [49]
Lloyd v. *Grace, Smith and Co.* [1912] A.C. 716 319 [46]
Locker and Woolf Ltd v. *Western Australian Insurance Co. Ltd* [1936] 1 K.B. 408 360 [1]
Lomax v. *Newton* [1953] 2 All E.R. 801 142 [64]
London County Council v. *Tobin* [1959] 1 All E.R. 649 235 [232]
Lory v. *London Borough of Brent* [1971] 1 All E.R. 1042 41 [8]
Lowery v. *Walker* [1911] A.C. 10 324 [7]
Lucena v. *Crauford* (1806) 2 Bos. and Pul. (N.R.) 269 H.L. 363 [11] (369)

Lurcott v. *Wakely and Wheeler* [1911] 1 K.B. 905 132 [20]

Macaura v. *Northern Assurance Co. Ltd* [1925] A.C. 619 363 [12]
McCarrick v. *Liverpool Corporation* [1947] A.C. 219 16 [60]
McMillan v. *Guest* [1942] A.C. 561 139 [46]
Major v. *Williams* (1843) 3 Curt. 432 115 [35]
Manbre Saccharine Co. Ltd v. *Corn Products Co. Ltd* [1919] 1 K.B. 198 279 [82]
Marshall v. *Green* (1875) 1 C.P.D. 35 265 [21] (303)
Martin v. *Lowry* [1927] A.C. 312 127 [2]
Mason v. *Burningham* [1949] 2 K.B. 545 283 [100]
Matthews v. *Kuwait Bechtel Corporation* [1959] 2 Q.B. 57 339 [17]
Mayo, re, [1943] Ch. 302 13 [46]
Mercantile Credit Co. Ltd v. *Cross* [1965] 2 Q.B. 205 298 [173]
Mercantile Union Guarantee Corporation Ltd v. *Wheatley* [1938] 1 K.B. 490 295 [158]
Merest v. *Harvey* (1814) 5 Taunt. 442 334 [53]
Mersey Docks and Harbour Board v. *Coggins and Griffiths (Liverpool) Ltd* [1947] 1 A.C. 1 320 [51]
Midleton, Earl, v. *Cottesloe, Baron,* [1949] A.C. 418 164 [187]
Mills v. *Edwards* [1971] 2 W.L.R. 418 56 [67, 68]
Mitchell and Edon v. *Ross* [1962] A.C. 814 139 [47]
Monk v. *Warbey* [1935] 1 K.B. 75 367 [19]
Moorcock, The, (1889) 14 P.D. 64 268 [33]
Moore and Co., and Landauer and Co., re [1921] 2 K.B. 519 279 [81]
Moore v. *Rawson* (1824) 3 B. & C. 32 24 [95]
Morgan v. *Fear* [1907] A.C. 425 23 [91]
Morris v. *Martin and Sons Ltd* [1966] 1 Q.B. 716 319 [47]
Municipal Mutual Insurance Ltd v. *Hills* (1932) 48 T.L.R. 301 105 [103]
Munro v. *Commissioner of Stamp Duties* [1934] A.C. 61 167 [198]
Murray, re, [1956] 1 W.L.R. 605 114 [20]

Napier v. *National Business Agency Ltd* [1951] 2 All E.R. 264 271 [47]
Nash v. *Lynde* [1929] A.C. 158 93 [52] (109)
National Provincial Bank, Ltd v. *Ainsworth* [1965] A.C. 1175 32 [130] (37)
Newsom v. *Robertson* [1953] Ch. 7 132 [24]
New York Life Insurance Co. v. *Styles* (1889) 14 App.Cas. 381 104 [102]
Nicholson and Venn v. *Smith-Marriott* (1947) 177 L.T. 189 279 [77]
Nicoll v. *Austin* (1935) 19 T.C. 531 140 [50]
Norman v. *Golder* (1944) 26 T.C. 293 131 [16]

North British and Mercantile Insurance Co. v. *London Liverpool and Globe Insurance Co.* (1877) 5 Ch.D. 569 362 [7]
Nunn, re, (1936) 52 T.L.R. 322 114 [24]

Odeon Associated Theatres Ltd v. *Jones* [1972] 2 W.L.R. 331 131 [19]
Ogilvy, re, [1942] Ch. 288 119 [44]
Olley v. *Marlborough Court, Ltd* [1949] 1 K.B. 532 269 [39]
Oppenheimer v. *Attenborough and Son* [1908] 1 K.B. 221 286 [110]
Orlebar, re, [1936] Ch. 147 11 [34]

Paine v. *Colne Valley Electricity Supply Co.* [1938] 4 All E.R. 803 339 [16] (354)
Pannett v. *McGuinness and Co. Ltd* [1972] 2 Q.B. 599 328 [25]
Parfitt v. *Lawless* (1872) L.R.2 P. & D. 462 112 [10]
Paris v. *Stepney Borough Council* [1951] A.C. 367 339 [15]
Park, deceased (No.2), re, [1972] 2 W.L.R. 276 169 [205]
Parker v. *South-Eastern Railway* (1877) 2 C.P.D. 416 269 [38]
Parsons v. *B.N.B. Laboratories Ltd* [1964] 1 Q.B. 95 274 [57]
Paterson's Will Trusts, re [1963] 1 W.L.R. 623 181 [255]
Paul v. *Summerhayes* (1878) 4 Q.B.D. 9 333 [52]
Pearson v. *Rose and Young Ltd* [1951] 1 K.B. 275 286 [111]
Pelly's Will Trusts, re, [1957] 1 Ch. 1 9 [22]
Penrose, re, [1933] Ch. 793 172 [217]
Pharmaceutical Society of Great Britain v. *Boots Cash Chemists (Southern), Ltd* [1952] 2 Q.B. 795 261 [1]
Philipson-Stow's Special Representatives v. *IRC* [1959] T.R. 23 164 [188]
Phillips v. *Brooks Ltd* [1919] 2 K.B. 243 267 [29]
Phillips v. *Lamdin* [1949] 2 K.B. 33 19 [70]
Phillips v. *Low* [1892] 1 Ch. 47 20 [76]
Pickford v. *Quirke* (1927) 13 T.C. 251 127 [4]
Pilkington v. *Wood* [1953] Ch. 770 274 [55]
Pinnel's Case (1602) 5 Co. Rep. 117A 263 [9]
Poland v. *Parr and Sons* [1927] 1 K.B. 236 319 [43]
Pook v. *Owen* [1970] A.C. 244 142 [65]
Priest v. *Last* [1903] 2 K.B. 148 281 [90]
Price v. *Romilly* [1960] 3 All E.R. 429 57 [76]
Pyne v. *Stallard-Benoyre* (1964) 42 T.C. 183 146 [84]
Pyx Granite Co. Ltd v. *Ministry of Housing and Local Government* [1960] A.C. 260 205 [34] (253)

Qualcast (Wolverhampton) Ltd v. *Haynes* [1959] A.C. 743 339 [14]

Quinn v. *Scott* [1965] 1 W.L.R. 1004 312[6]

R. v. *Kamara* [1973] 2 W.L.R. 126 330[29]
R. v. *Minister of Housing and Local Government, ex parte Chichester R.D.C.* [1960] 2 All E.R. 407 214[96]
R. v. *Pratt* (1855) 4 E. & B. 860 332[38]
R. v. *Wilson* [1955] 1 All E.R. 744 332[40]
Reid v. *Dawson* [1955] 1 Q.B. 214 41[7]
Reynolds, Sons and Co. Ltd v. *Ogston* (1930) 15 T.C. 501 135[29]
Reynolds v. *Clarke* (1925) 2 Lord Raym. 1399 333[50] (336)
Rickards, Charles, Ltd v. *Oppenheim* [1950] 1 K.B. 616 272[51]
Robert Addie and Sons (Colleries) Ltd v. *Dumbreck* [1929] A.C. 358 327[23]
Roberts v. *James* (1903) 89 L.T. 282 22[82]
Robinson v. *Kilvert* (1889) 41 Ch.D. 88 313[10]
Roles v. *Nathan* [1963] 1 W.L.R. 1117 325[12]
Rookes v. *Barnard* [1964] A.C. 1129 334[54]
Ross v. *Watson* [1943] S.C. 406 53[58]
Rousou v. *Photi* [1940] 2 K.B. 379 16[59]
Rowland v. *Divall* [1923] 2 K.B. 500 283[99]
Ruben, E. and S. Ltd v. *Faire Bros. and Co. Ltd* [1949] 1 K.B. 254 279[83]
Rugby Joint Water Board v. *Shaw-Fox* [1972] 2 W.L.R. 757 230[197]
Rutledge v. *IRC* [1929] 14 T.C. 490 127[3]
Ryall v. *Kidwell* [1914] 3 K.B. 135 16[61]

Sallis v. *Jones* [1936] P.43 115[28]
Salomon v. *Salomon and Co. Ltd* [1897] A.C. 22 85[29]
Samuel v. *Jarrah Timber Wood Paying Corporation, Ltd* [1904] A.C. 323 27[105]
Saunders v. *Anglia Building Society* [1971] A.C. 1104 271[46]
Saunders v. *Pilcher* [1949] 2 All E.R, 1097 265[21] (303)
Saunders v. *Vautier* (1841) 4 Beav. 115 (affirmed) Cr. and Ph. 240 13[48]
Sclater v. *Horton* [1954] 2 Q.B. 1 50[41]
Secretan v. *Hart* (1969) 45 T.C. 701 155[134]
Seligman v. *Docker* [1949] 1 Ch. 53 314[20]
Sharkey v. *Wernher* [1956] A.C. 58 130[11]
Shaw, John and Sons (Salford), Ltd v. *Shaw* [1935] 2 K.B. 113 90[43]
Simmons v. *Norton* (1831) 7 Bing. 640 52[50]
Smith v. *East Elloe RDC* (1956) A.C. 736 221[159]
Smith's Potato Estates Ltd v. *Bolland* [1948] A.C. 508 132[22]
Somers, Earl of, deceased, re, (1895) 11 T.L.R. 567 10[27]

Southerden, in the estate of, [1925] P. 177 114[26]

South of England Natural Gas and Petroleum Co. Ltd, re, [1911] 93[52] (109)

Steinberg v. *Scala (Leeds) Ltd* [1923] 2 Ch. 452 264[17]

Stephens v. *Cuckfield RDC* [1960] 2 Q.B. 373 214[101]

Stephens v. *Taprell* (1840) 2 Curt. 458 114[23]

Stevenson, Jordan and Harrison Ltd v. *Macdonald* [1952] 1 T.L.R. 101 318[41]

Stilk v. *Myrick* (1809) 2 Camp. 317 263[7]

Stoneman v. *Brown* [1973] 1 W.L.R. 459 56[73]

Storey v. *Ashton* (1869) L.R. 4 Q.B. 476 318[42]

Stroyan v. *Knowles* (1861) 6 H.&N. 454 25[100]

Suisse Atlantique Société d'Armement Maritime S.A. v. *N.V. Rotterdam-sche Kolen Centrale* [1967] 1 A.C. 361 295[160]

Sumpter v. *Hedges* [1898] 1 Q.B. 673 271[49]

Swansborough v. *Coventry* (1832) 2 Moo. and Sc. 362 20[77]

Swindon Waterworks Co. Ltd v. *Wilts and Berks Canal Navigation Co.* (1875) L.R. 7 H.L. 697 25[101]

Sykes, in b. (1873) L.R. 3 P. & D. 26 115[30]

Symes v. *Green* (1859) 1 Sw. and Tr. 401 111[6]

Taylor v. *Caldwell* (1863) 3 B. & S. 826 272[52]

Tennant v. *Smith* [1892] A.C. 150 141[52]

The Carlgarth [1927] P. 93 325[8]

Theyer v. *Purnell* [1918] 2 K.B. 333 315[29]

Thomas v. *Sylvester* (1873) L.R. 8 Q. B. 368 19[71]

Thompson, W. L. Ltd v. *Robinson (Gun-makers) Ltd* [1955] Ch. 177 290[136]

Thorley, Joseph, Ltd v. *Orchis Steamship Co.* [1907] 1 K.B. 660 269[43]

Thornhill's Settlement, re, [1940] 4 All E.R. 83 12[38]

Thornton v. *Shoe Lane Parking Ltd* [1971] 1 All E.R. 686 268[34]

Timmins v. *Moreland Street Property Co. Ltd* [1958] Ch. 110 265[23]

Torbett v. *Faulkner* [1952] 2 T.L.R. 659 70[134]

Travers, Joseph, and Sons Ltd v. *Cooper* [1915] 1 K.B. 73 295[162]

Tucker v. *Farm and General Investment Trust Ltd* [1966] 2 Q.B. 421 300

Tulk v. *Moxhay* (1848) 2 Ph. 774 29[116], 30[117]

Twine v. *Bean's Express Ltd* (1946) 62 T.L.R. 155; 62/T.L.R. 458 319[45]

Vane v. *Lord Barnard* (1716) 2 Vern. 738 5[14]

Varley v. *Whipp* [1900] 1 Q.B. 513 278[76]

Videan v. *British Transport Commission* [1963] 2 Q.B. 650 323[1]

Waddington v. *O'Callaghan* (1931) 16 T.C. 181 80[5], 135[30]

Walker, in the estate of, (1912) 28 T.L.R. 466 111[4]

Walker Property Investments (Brighton) Ltd v. *Walker* [1947] 177 L.T. 204 268[32]

Ward v. *Bignall* [1967] 1 Q.B. 543 290[132]

Ward v. *Ward* (1852) 7 Exch. 838 24[94]

Warman v. *Southern Counties Car Finance Corporation Ltd* [1949] 2 K.B. 576 295[157] (307)

Warren v. *Keen* [1953] 2 All E.R. 1118 17[650]

Warwick v. *Greville* (1809) 1 Phill. 123 121[51]

Watson v. *Secretary of State for Air* [1954] 1 W.L.R. 1477 231[202]

Watters v. *Hunter* (1927) S.C. 310 64[107]

Webster v. *Cecil* (1861) 30 Beav. 62 270[45]

Wedd v. *Porter* [1916] 2 K.B. 91 17[65], 44[16]

Weller v. *Foot and Mouth Disease Research Institute* [1966] 1 Q.B. 569 311[2]

West of England Fire Insurance Co. v. *Isaacs* [1897] 1 Q.B. 226 361[6]

Westcott v. *Bryan* [1969] 45 T.C. 476 143[68]

Westminster Fire Office v. *Glasgow Provident Investment Society* (1888) 13 App. Cas. 999 365[15]

Westripp v. *Baldock* [1939] 1 All E.R. 279 31[125]

Wheat v. *E. Lacon and Co. Ltd* [1966] 1 All E.R. 582 323[2]

Wheeldon v. *Burrows* (1879) 12 Ch.D. 31 20[75], 21

Wheelwright v. *Walker* (No.1) (1883) 23 Ch.D. 752 at p. 762 10[25]

White v. *City of London Brewery Co.* (1889) 42 Ch.D. 237 28[111]

Wilkins v. *Rogerson* [1961] Ch. 133 140[51]

Williams Bros v. *Agius Ltd* [1914] A.C. 510 291[139]

Williams v. *James* (1867) L.R. 2 C.P. 577 24[98]

Williams and Sons [1957] 1 Q.B. 409 326[17]

Wilsons & Clyde Coal Co. v. *English* [1938] A.C. 57 338[3], 339[16] (354)

Wilson v. *West Sussex County Council* [1963] 2 Q.B. 764 205[35]

Wilson v. *Tyneside Window Cleaning Co.* [1958] 2 Q.B. 110 338[8]

Wood v. *General Accident Fire and Life Assurance Corporation* (1948) 65 T.L.R. 53 368[25]

Woods v. *Durable Suites Ltd* [1953] 1 W.L.R. 857 339[13]

Woolley v. *Clark* (1822) 5 B. & Ald. 744 117[38]

Wright and Pole, re, (1834) 1 Ad. and El. 621 366[16]

Yeoman Credit Ltd v. *Apps* [1962] 2 Q.B. 508 293[141]

Zetland, Marquess of, v. *Driver* [1939] Ch. 1 31[121]

General Index

Acts of Parliament, *see* separate Table of Statutes
Administration:
    grant of administration required to deal with the estate if no executor obtains probate 120–2;
    procedure for obtaining grant of administration 121–2;
    revocation of grant of administration 122;
    to whom grant will be made 120–1
Adverse possession:
    rights conferred by 32;
    time for suing in respect of 32–4
Agency,
    partners 81;
    see also Partnership
Agricultural Guidance and Guarantee Fund, European, *see* European Community
Agricultural land:
    compulsory purchase, notice by certain occupiers to take whole when acquiring authority seek only part 247–9;
    compulsory purchase, notice by owner to take whole when acquiring authority seek only part 227–8;
    service of blight notice in respect of 250–1;
    see also Compulsory purchase and compensation
Agricultural Land Tribunal 31, 47–8, 51, 55–9, 63, 65, 224–9, 233–4, 239, 243, 245, 248, 251
Agricultural Land Tribunals:
    composition of and procedure before 48;
    consent to notice to quit agricultural holding 55, 58–9
Agricultural leases:
    agricultural holding, definition of 39–40;
    agricultural land, definition of 39–40;
    agricultural tenancies,

between one and two years 42,
    for less than a year 41–2,
    formalities for creation of 40,
    for two years or more 42,
    matters to be borne in mind when granting 43,
    terms of 43–4;
alteration of rent, right of landlord or tenant to require 49–52;
breach of terms of the tenancy, restriction of landlord's claim 44;
compensation,
    for adoption of especially beneficial system of farming 66,
    for disturbance 64–5,
    for improvements 62–3,
    for tenant of market garden 63–4,
    on disturbance for reorganisation of the tenant's affairs 65–6,
    tenant's right to, on departure 61–7;
condition of holding, right to require record to be made 53;
crops damaged by game 53–4;
entry on agricultural holding, landlord's power of 53;
fixed equipment, provision of by landlord 47–8;
fixtures, tenant's right to remove 60–1;
landlord's responsibilities concerning good estate management 48–9;
maintenance; repair and insurance of fixed equipment 45–6;
notice to quit,
    consent of Agricultural Land Tribunal 55, 58–9,
    contents of 56,
    effect of landlord contracting to sell during currency of 59,
    on ground of death of tenant 56–8,
    part of holding 59–60,
    period of 54,
    prohibition of removal of manure and certain crops after 60,
    service of 54–5,

tenant's right to contest in certain
cases 56–7,
tenant's right to serve counter-
notice 55–6;
plough grassland, tenant's right to
52–3;
procedure for settling terms of the
tenancy when written agreement lack-
ing 44–5;
tenant's responsibility concerning
good husbandry 49;
tenant's right to burn heather or grass
47;
tenant's right to dispose of produce
and to vary system of cropping 46–7;
tenant's security of tenure 54–9
Agricultural Wages Board,
composition and powers of 343–4
Animals:
insurance of 366–7;
see also Insurance;
liability in tort for 314–18;
see also Tort
Art,
works of art exempt from estate duty
164;
see also Estate duty
Auctions,
oral undertakings given at 269;
see also Contract

Base fee,
nature of 4
Blight notices 249–52
Business organisations, see Companies;
Co-operative societies; Mutual orga-
nisations; Partnerships; Trusts

Capital allowances, see Income tax
Capital gains tax:
business, conversion of, into company
153;
companies, liability to 159;
computation of gain or loss 155–6;
death, effect of 153;
destruction of asset, tax provisions
concerning 152;
dwelling houses may be exempt from
156–7;
exemption, assets which may carry
156–7;
general principles of 151–3;
losses, calculation and treatment of

155–6;
rate of tax 152;
replacement of business assets, postponement of tax 157–8;
retirement, exemption from tax on
disposal of business 158–9;
rollover relief 157–8;
settled property 155,
see also Estate duty;
shares bonus or rights issues of 152–3;
shares, sales of to another company
153;
spouses, disposal of assets by one
spouse to the other 153;
wasting assets 155–6
Caravan sites 217–19;
see also Town and country planning
Close companies 161–2;
see also Corporation tax
Common Agricultural Policy, European
Communities, see European Community
Companies:
articles of association of 88;
borrowing by 90–1;
classification of 85–6;
Corporation Tax on profits of
159–62,
see also Corporation tax;
decisions of 88–90;
differences between private and public
92–4;
directors of 88–90;
dissolution of 91;
division of powers between the organs
of 90;
estate duty on shares in 175–9, 181,
where deceased derived certain
benefits from 177,
see also Estate duty;
formation of 86;
liability to capital gains tax 159;
limitation of liability of members of
85–6;
liquidation of 91;
meetings of 88–90;
memorandum of association of 88;
minimum membership of 92;
payment for shares in 87–8;
prospectus 93;
repayment of share capital in 87–8;
restriction of right to transfer shares in
92, 94;

separate identity of 84–5;
underwriting of shares in 93–4;
voting at meetings of 89–90
Compensation:
for compulsory acquisition of land, *see* Compulsory purchase and compensation;
landlord's right to claim from departing tenant for deterioration of agricultural holding 67–8;
of landlord for deterioration of holding 67–8;
procedure for settlement of claims 68–9;
tenant's right to claim on quitting agricultural holding 61–7
Compulsory purchase and compensation 219–52:
acquisition of land by general vesting declaration 246;
advance payment of compensation 240–1;
agricultural holdings tenanted for a year or from year to year, occupier's right to treat notice of entry as notice relating to the entire holding 247–9;
agricultural property, compulsory purchase of only part of 227–8;
agricultural tenants for a year or from year to year, right to elect where interest compulsorily acquired 223–5;
application for certificate of alternative development 232–3;
assumptions regarding planning permission 231–4;
authorisation of public authority to acquire compulsorily 220–1;
blight notices 249–52;
certificate of appropriate alternative development 232–3;
compensation, assessment of 'hope' value 233–4,
costs of preparing claims for 235,
farm loss payments to certain agricultural occupiers 238–9,
for compulsory purchase, general heads of claim for 230,
for disturbance 234–40,
for injurious affection 234–5, 241–5,
for severance 234,
liability to pay costs of dispute concerning 229–30,

notice of claim for 225, 229–30,
reorganisation compensation for agricultural tenants 239–40 (*see also* Agricultural leases),
right to advance payment of 240–1;
compulsory purchase, of only part of property 226–8,
orders 220–1,
procedure for authorising 220–1;
costs of preparing claim for compensation 235;
disturbance, compensation for 234–40,
of certain agricultural occupiers, farm loss payments 238–9,
of occupiers of certain dwellings 237,
of trader aged 60 years or more 236;
easements, position concerning 222;
entry on land, powers of acquiring authority 245–7;
farm loss payments 238–9;
general vesting declaration, acquisition of land by 246;
how value of land assessed 230–4;
injurious affection, compensation for 234–5,
from use of public works 242–5,
where no land taken from claimant 241–2;
land affected by planning blight 249–52;
land owners buying out interests of 221–49;
Lands Tribunal, composition of 229;
notice of claim, for advance payment of compensation 240–1,
for compensation for compulsory purchase 225, 229–30,
for farm loss payment 238–9;
notice of election by agricultural tenant for a year, or from year to year 223–5;
notice to purchase served by owner of a property affected by planning blight 249–52;
notice to treat 222, 225–6,
right of acquiring authority to withdraw 225;
powers conferred by Acts to buy land compulsorily 219–20;

433

public works, injurious affection from use of 242−5;
refusal to convey by owner 226;
reorganisation compensation 239−40;
severance, compensation for 234;
tenancies for a year, or from year to year, acquisition of 222−5;
see also Hire-purchase agreement; Sale of goods
Conditional sale of goods 301−2;
see also Contract; Sale of goods; Hire purchase; Credit-sale agreements
Contract:
acceptance of offer 261−2;
auctions, undertakings given at 269;
capacity to make 264;
conditional sale, see Conditional sale agreements;
conditions in contracts 266−8,
see also Hire-purchase agreements; Sale of goods;
consideration, generally essential to formation of 262−3;
contract under seal 262;
contracts,
conditions in 266−8,
see also Hire-purchase agreements; Sale of goods,
consideration necessary to support 262−3,
discharge of 271−3,
effect of mistake on 270−1,
formalities for making 264−5,
illegality of 271,
intention, necessity for 263,
remedies for breach of 273−6,
representations inducing 266−8,
terms of 266−8,
see also Hire-purchase; Sale of goods,
terms implied into 268,
warranties in 266−8;
credit sale contracts, see Credit-sale agreements;
damages for breach of 274−5,
pre-estimated, distinguished from penalty 275−6,
mitigation of 274−5;
deed, contract by 262;
definition of 261;
discharge of 271−3;
drunken persons, by 264;
frustration of 272−3;

guarantee of 264−5;
hire-purchase, see Hire-purchase;
illegality, effect upon contract 271;
implied terms of 268;
infants, by 264;
injunction restraining breach of 273−4;
intention to contract 263;
land, contracts for the sale of or other disposition of 264−6;
mentally disordered persons, by 264;
misrepresentation, exemption clause excluding liability for 267;
mistake, effect of 270−1;
offer and acceptance 261−2,
communication by post 262;
offers to contract 261−2;
part performance, effect of, on contracts for sale of land 265−6;
remedies for breach of 273−6;
specific performance 273;
terms of 266−8;
time limits for suing for breach of 276;
unsolicited goods, offer of 262;
warranties in 266−8;
written evidence of, when essential 264−6;
see also Hire-purchase; Sale of goods; Employment
Contract farming,
Committee of Enquiry on 79−80, 99, 103
Co-operative societies 94−103;
conversion of society into company 100−1;
disputes between the society and its members 100;
liability of members of 97−8;
management of 97;
members, withdrawal and death of 98;
registration and entitlement to register 95−6;
registration of society, cancellation by registrar 101;
societies,
accounts and audit of 99−100,
dissolution of 101,
investment of funds and distribution of profits 99,
meetings of 98,
probable effect of European Community legislation on 102−3,
rules and their binding effect 96,

tax factors affecting investment in 102,
voting at meetings of 98

Co-ownership:
estate duty on property held in 173–4, 179;
see also Estate duty; Land

Corporation tax:
close companies, definition of 161–2, special provisions concerning 161–2;
company profits liable to 159–60;
interest paid by company usually deductible from profits 160;
losses, group relief concerning 161, tax relief on 160;
see also Income tax

Counter-notice:
agricultural holding, tenant's right to serve, on receiving notice to quit 55–9;
tenant's right to serve on receipt of notice to quit part of the holding 59–60;
see also Agricultural leases

Covenants:
affecting the fee simple 29–32;
restrictive, discharge or modification of 31–2, registration of 30;
whether benefit and burden pass with the land 29–31

Credit-sale agreements 301;
see also Contract; Hire-purchase; Sale of goods

Crown,
rights over land 1

Damages,
for breach of contract 274–6

Defective premises:
liability for 323–30;
see also Leases; Tort

Discretionary trusts:
estate duty on property held on 171;
see also Estate duty

Dogs:
liability for harm done by 316–17;
right to kill in protection of livestock 317–318;
see also Tort

Dwellings:
let to agricultural employees, recovery of possession by landlord 70–3;
occupied by agricultural employees recovery of possession of by landlord 70–3

Easements:
analogous claims by fluctuating groups 26;
compulsory powers concerning 222, 241–2;
creation of,
by express grant 20,
by implied grant 20–1,
by prescription 21–3;
extent of easement of way 24;
extent of right to light 24;
extinguishment of 24;
natural rights distinguished from 25;
nature and characteristics of 19–20;
remedies for inference with 23–4;
see also Compulsory purchase and compensation

Employment:
Agricultural Wages Board, composition and powers of 343–4;
compulsory insurance against injury to employees 342–3;
contracts of employment,
employee's right to written particulars of 345–7,
length of notice to terminate 344–5,
written particulars of 345–7;
employee,
claim against employer if injured 337–43,
claim against State if injured 337,
safety regulations concerning 340–2,
some obligations of employer towards 337–53,
'unfair dismissal' of 347–9;
employer,
duty to insure his employees,
vicarious liability of 339–40;
Industrial Tribunals 347–9, 353;
notice to terminate contract of 344–5;
redundancy payments,
alternative work offered, 350,
amount of 352,
continuity of employment 349–51,
disputes as to payment 353,

employee's eligibility for 349—50,
employee's right to 349—53,
groups excluded from 349,
redundancy fund 353,
tax aspects concerning 353;
regulations dealing with safety of employees 340—2;
safety regulations concerning employees 340—2;
statutory duty, breach by employer of 340—2;
taxation of employees 139—43,
see also Income tax;
torts committed by servant, employer's liability for 318—20,
employer's right to indemnity 319,
see also Tort;
trade union membership 346;
'unfair dismissal' of employees 347—9;
wages, minimum rates of 343—4
Entail:
barring 3—4;
must be created through a trust 3;
nature and duration of 3—4
Estate duty:
aggregation, exemptions from 164—5,
of property 164—5;
agricultural property, reduced rates of estate duty on 163—4;
art, works of art exempt from estate duty 165;
business assets, reduced rate of estate duty on 163—4;
charities, gifts to 166;
clause in deceased's will stating who is to bear duty 181;
companies, duties on shares in controlled 175—7;
controlled companies, estate duty if deceased derived certain benefits from 177—8;
co-ownership, estate duty on property held in 173—4;
debts and expenses deductible for estate duty 179—80;
dispositions for partial consideration 168;
disputes concerning 182;
general principles of 163;
gifts, estate duty on 165—70,
identification of the dutiable property 168;
inland revenue, affidavit concerning 180;
life insurance policies, estate duty on 174—5;
marriage, gifts made in consideration of 168—9;
partnerships, estate duty on goodwill 163, 173;
payment, date when estate duty must be paid 181,
persons liable to pay estate duty to the revenue 180;
quick succession, relief from 166;
small gifts 169;
spouses, exemption from estate duty on death of survivor 171—2,
gift to surviving spouse 166, 171—2,
postponement of estate duty until death of survivor 172—3;
timber, estate duty on 164—5;
trustees, estate duty on property charged with paying remuneration to 173;
valuation,
effect of 'special purchaser' 178—9,
of farm leased to partnership ceasing on death 178,
of farm workers' cottages 179,
of land held by co-owners 179,
of property for estate duty, general principles of 178—9,
of shares in private companies 175—7, 179,
of shares quoted on the stock exchange 178,
on the assets basis of certain shares in controlled companies 175—7;
see also Insurance
Estates in land:
entails 2—4;
fee simple, absolute in possession 1—2;
life interest 4—6;
remainders 6;
reversions 6
European community 371—82;
Agricultural Guidance and Guarantee Fund 377—82;
agriculture, provisions of the Treaty of Rome concerning 376;
Assembly, The 373;
Commission, The 371—2;
Council of Ministers, The 372—3;
Court of Justice, The 373—4;

legislation by, and different types of 374—5;
principal institutions of 371—4;
regulations issued by 374—5;
Treaty of Rome 371, 377;
see also Companies; Co-operative societies; Mutual organisations; Partnerships; Trusts
Executors 116—17, 121;
see also Wills
Exemption clauses, *see* Contract; Sale of goods

Fee simple,
absolute in possession, nature and duration of 1—2
Fire insurance, *see* Insurance
Fishing,
right to fish in a stream 2
Fixtures 18—19, 60—1;
right of tenant of agricultural holding to remove 60—1
Forestry,
licence to fell trees 211—13

Game:
crimes relating to 332;
damage of crops by 53—4;
liability in tort for damage done by 314—15;
see also Tort

Hired servants:
employer's liability in tort for 319—20;
see also Independent contractors; Tort
Hire-purchase:
animals, hire-purchase of 300;
cancellation of agreement by hirer 294;
dealers, representations made by 293;
death of hirer, effect on agreement 298;
entry on premises to retake goods 298;
general principles concerning 292—3;
goods on hire-purchase, restrictions on, owner's right to retake 297—9;
Hire—Purchase Act, 1965, agreements falling outside 299,
agreements governed by 293—4;
Hire-Purchase agreements 292,
conditions and warranties in 295,
see also Contract; Sale of goods,

formalities when making 294,
hirer's duty to take care of goods on 295,
right to cancel by hirer 294,
right to terminate, by hirer 296—7,
termination of by owner 297;
Hire-Purchase Information, Limited 299;
motor vehicles on hire-purchase 299—300;
protected goods 298—9;
retaking of goods on hire-purchase, restrictions on owner's right to 297—9;
sale of motor vehicle by hirer 299—300;
termination of agreement by owner 297;
'trade or finance purchasers' of motor vehicles 300

Income tax:
assignment of lease granted at an under value, taxation on premium 145;
basic rate of tax 148;
basis of assessment 132—4;
benefits in kind paid to employee, taxation of 140—1;
buildings used for agriculture or forestry, capital allowances on 138—9;
calculation of tax on taxable premiums 146;
capital allowances 138—9;
computation of profits of trader 128—32, 138—9;
deductible expenses of employee 142—3;
discontinuance of business, assessment of, 134—5;
employees, taxation of 139—43;
employer's duty to deduct tax 143;
expenses, deductible 130—2,
deductible from rent receipts 146—7,
deductible when landlord is a company 147;
furnished letting 143—4;
general liability to 148—51;
hardship waiver of rent by landlord 144;
higher rate of tax 148—9;
husband and wife, assessment of tax 149—50;
income assessable under Schedule A

143–6;

income profits distinguished from capital profits 128;

income taxable under Schedule E 139–42;

improvements by tenant carried out under obligation, taxation of landlord on 144–5;

infant children, taxation of income of 150;

interest paid by tax-payer, when deductible from income 149;

land, taxation of income arising from 143–8;

life insurance premiums, taxation relief on 150–1;

livestock, valuation of, by farmers 128–30;

losses on discontinuance of business, tax relief on 138;

losses, tax relief on 137–8;

machinery and plant, capital allowances on 138–9;

partnerships, taxation of 135–6;

payment of interest, deduction of tax by payer 151;

persons taxed under Schedule E 139;

premiums, taxation of 144, 146;

sale of land, subject to right of reconveyance, taxation of 145–6;

taxation of self-employed persons carrying on a trade, profession or vocation 127–39;

termination of employment, sums paid to employee on 141–2;

valuation of farming livestock 128–30;

whether a person is trading 127–8;

woodlands, taxation of 147–8

Independent contractors 318;

see also Tort;

distinguished from servants 318;

liability to visitors for work done by 325–6;

see also Occupiers of premises

Industrial tribunals 347–9, 353;

see also Employment

Injunctions,

to restrain breach of contract 273–4, 276

Insurance:

against injuries to employees 342–3;

compulsory, against injuries to employees 342–3;

compulsory, when using motor vehicles 367–9;

consequential loss 366;

contribution, insurer's right of 359, 361–2;

fire, replacement by insurer of property destroyed 365;

fire insurance 364–5,

policies, average clauses in 365;

general principles 359–62;

good faith, insured's duty of 359–60;

insurable interest, need for 363–4;

liability insurance 366,

see also Employment;

life insurance 362–4,

borrowing on security of 362–3,

estate duty on 165, 174–5,

tax advantages 362,

see also Estate duty; Income tax;

livestock insurance 366–7;

Motor Insurer's Bureau 368–9;

motor vehicle insurance 367–9;

spouse, insurance policy on life of 364;

subrogation, insurer's right of 359, 361;

vehicles, insurance of 367, 369

Intestacy:

partial 117, 120;

persons entitled to the intestate's property 117–20;

total 117–20

Land:

adverse possession of 32–4;

see also Adverse possession;

contracts for sale of 264–6;

see also Contract;

co-ownership of 7, 13–14, 173–4;

covenants affecting the fee simple 29–32;

see also Covenants;

Crown rights over 1;

easements 19–24;

leaseholds, nature and duration of 6–7, 15–18;

licences affecting 32;

life interest in 4–6;

mortgages of 26–9;

profits 19–24;

remainders, nature and duration of 6;
rentcharge on 19;
reversions, duration and nature of 6;
settlements of 7–12;
taxation of 143–8;
see also Income tax;
trust for sale of 12–13;
see also Agricultural leases
Leasehold:
assignment of, distinguished from sub-letting 16;
covenants in 16–18;
creation of 15–16;
nature of 6–7;
tenant's right to assign or sub-let 18;
tenant's right to remove fixtures 18–19
Leases:
landlord's duty arising from obligation or right to repair 329–30;
see also Agricultural leases; Occupiers of premises
Liability:
co-operative societies, liability of members of 97–8;
liabilities of members of unlimited companies 86;
limited liability of members of certain companies 85–6;
limited partnerships, liability of partners 83;
ordinary partnerships, liability of partners 81–3
Licences,
conferring rights over land 32
Life insurance 362–4;
see also Income tax; Estate duty
Life interest:
must be created by means of a trust 4;
nature and duration of 4–6;
owner's liability,
for committing waste 4–6,
in dealing with the land 4, 7–12,
regarding timber and minerals 4–5,
right to take crops after expiration 6
Limited partnerships, *see* Partnerships

Mortgages:
contractual date for repayment of 26–7;
mortgagee's remedies to enforce repayment 27–9;
nature and creation of 26–7;

priority of 29;
unfair terms in 27
Motor vehicles,
insurance of 367–9
Mutual organisations 104–6
Natural rights 25
Negligence, *see* Tort
Notice to quit:
agricultural holding 54–9;
part of agricultural holding 59–60;
see also Agricultural leases
Nuisance, *see* Tort

Occupiers of premises 323–4;
see also Leases;
contracts, entrants in pursuance of 326–7;
entrants pursuant to contract 326–7;
independent contractors, liability to 'visitors' for work done by 325–6;
landlord's duty arising from obligation or right to repair 329–30;
liability to 'visitors' 324–7;
occupier's liability for defective premises 323–30;
trespassers, occupier's duty of care towards 327–9;
'visitors' liability to 324–7;
'visitors', notices excluding duty of care towards 326
Output tax, *see* Value added tax

Partnership agreement,
matters to be dealt with 82–3
Partnerships:
agency of partners 81;
commencement of 80–1;
definition of 80;
dissolution of 82–3;
implied rules governing 81–3;
taxation of 135–6;
see also Income tax
Penalties,
penalty clauses in contracts 275–6
Personal representatives 120;
see also Administration; Executors
Probate:
grant of probate to executor 116–17;
see also Executors;
revocation of grant of 122
Profits:
acquisition by prescription 21–3;
extinguishment of 24;

439

nature of 19;
remedies for interference with 23–4
Public rights of way, *see* Rights of way

Redundancy payments 349–53;
  see also Employment
Remainder,
  nature of 6
Rent,
  alteration of rent of agricultural holding 49–52
Rentcharges,
  on land 19
Restrictive covenants, *see* Covenants
Restrictive trade practices,
  exemption of certain agricultural organisations from the legislation concerning 106–8
Reversion,
  nature of 6
Rights of way:
  private 19–24;
  public 25

Sale of goods:
  see also Contract;
  'consumer sales' 284;
  damages, buyer's right to claim from seller 291,
    mitigation of 291,
    seller's right to claim from buyer 290–1;
  deliverable state, when goods are in a 287;
  delivery, meaning of 289,
    place of 289;
  description, implied condition that goods shall correspond with 278–9;
  exemption clauses in contract for 283–4;
  feeding stuffs, implied warranties relating to 282;
  future goods 287–8;
  general principles concerning 277–8;
  goods,
    definition of 277,
    on approval 288;
  implied conditions and warranties, buyer's remedies for breach of 284–5;
  implied conditions in contracts for sale of goods 278–83;
  lien of unpaid seller 289;
  loss of goods, risk of 286–8;
  mercantile agents 286;
  merchantable quality, implied condition relating to 279–80;
  ownership of goods, transfer of 285–8;
  price, seller's right to sue buyer for 290;
  remedies against seller 291;
  remedies for breach of implied conditions and warranties 284–5,
    see also Contracts;
  resale of goods by seller 285, 290;
  resale of goods, unpaid seller's right to 290;
  samples, sales by, implied conditions relating to 282;
  seller, remedies of, if unpaid 289–91;
  specific goods 287–91;
  specific performance of contract for sale of goods 291;
  stoppage of goods in transit, unpaid seller's right to 289–90;
  time for delivery of goods 289;
  time for payment of the goods 288–9;
  time when ownership passes 286–8;
  title, implied conditions and warranties relating to 282–3,
    to goods, power to transfer 285–6;
  unascertained goods 287–8;
  unpaid seller, definition of 289;
Settled land:
  compared with trust for sale 13;
  meaning of 7;
  tenant for life,
    consent required to exercise powers by 9–10,
    loss of powers by 11–12,
    power to dispose of own beneficial interest 8,
    powers cannot be restricted 11,
    safeguards concerning exercise of powers by 10–11,
    to exchange 8,
    to grant options 9,
    to lease 8,
    to make improvements 8–9,
    to mortgage 9,
    to sell 8,
    to take lease of certain other land 9;
  trustees of 7–8;
  who is tenant for life 7
Settled property:
  estate duty on 163, 170–3,

on enlargement of life interest in
171,
on termination of life interest in
170
Specific performance:
of contract of sale of goods 291;
of contracts 273, 276
Spouses:
exemption from estate duty on certain
property 170–2;
right of surviving, to property of
person dying intestate 117–20;
see also Estate duty
Squatter's rights, *see* Adverse possession

Taxation 127–90;
see also Capital gains tax; Corporation
tax; Estate duty; Income tax; Value
added tax
Tenant for life, *see under* Settled land
Timber:
definition of 5;
See also Trees;
estate duty on 164–5;
licence to fell 211–13
Time:
for bringing actions for breach of contract 276;
for bringing actions to recover land
32–4;
for delivery of goods 289;
for payment for goods 288–9;
of payment of estate duty 180–2,
see also Estate duty *under* Payment;
when value added tax is chargeable on
transaction 186;
when value added tax is payable to the
government 189
Tort:
see also Employment; Game; Occupiers;
animals, dangerous, liability for
316–18,
liability for straying 315,
liability in tort for 314–18,
straying to other land, occupier's
right to detain 316;
dogs, liability for harm done by
316–17;
game, liability for damage done by
314–15;
general purpose of law of 309;

hired servants, employer's liability in
tort for 319–20;
indemnity for employer for torts committed by servant 319;
independent contractor, distinguished
from servant 318;
injured employees, claims against employer 337–43;
negligence 310–12;
nuisance 312–14;
servant, master's liability for torts
committed by 318–20;
trees, liability for encroachment of
313,
liability for fall of 311–12;
weeds, liability for escape of seed
313–18
Town and country planning:
action areas 200;
advertisements, control of 215–17;
agricultural development, compensation for refusal of permission in certain cases 206–7;
authorities responsible for administering 199;
building preservation notices 209;
caravan sites, planning permission for
217,
site licence in general required
217–19;
conservation areas 217;
development,
appeals against refusal of permission or conditions 206,
application for planning permission
203–4,
definition of 201–2,
grant of planning permission and
conditions attached 204–6,
orders, general planning permission
granted by 202–3,
outline applications for permission
204,
permission sometimes granted by
General Development Order
202–3,
refusal of permission to develop,
compensation for in certain cases
206–7,
time within which development
must be begun 205–6;
enforcement notices 207–8;
land incapable of reasonably beneficial

use, purchase notice 213–14;
listed buildings 209–10,
    enforcement notices 209;
local plans 200–1;
planning authorities, administration by 199,
    survey of areas by 199;
planning blight, land affected by 249–52;
planning permission, revocation of 208–9;
purchase notice where land incapable of reasonable beneficial use 213–14;
revocation of planning permission 208–9;
site licences for caravan sites 217–19;
structure plans 200–1;
trees, licence to fell 211–13,
    preservation orders 210–11;
unauthorised development, remedies of planning authorities against 207–8;
waste land injurious to amenity 214–15;

Trees:
encroachment on adjoining land by 313;
see also Tort;
liability for fall of 311–12

Trespassers:
civil liability of 333–4;
crimes by 330–3;
in pursuit of game 332;
occupier's duty of care towards 327–9;
occupier's right to evict 334

Trustees:
appointment, removal and retirement of 14–15;
for sale of land 12–13;
of settled land 7–12

Trust for sale:
compared with settled land 13;
creation of 12;
definition of 12;
trustees, powers of 12–13

Trusts 103–4;
to conduct farming 103–4

Value added tax 182–90;
accounts and records 189–90;
bad debts 188;
collection, machinery for 184;
contractor's services 187;
computation of 185–6;
customs and excise, powers of, relating to 190;
example of how the tax operates 182–3;
exemptions 186;
farmers, general effect of tax on 183;
invoices for 188–9;
machinery on hire-purchase or credit sale, tax on 185;
motor vehicles, tax on 187;
particular transactions subject to 187–8;
repairs, tax on 187;
zero rated supplies 186

Wages,
minimum rates of 343–4

Waste:
ameliorating 4;
cutting timber 4–5;
equitable 5;
impeachment for 5;
opening mines 4–5;
permissive 4;
remedies for 4–5;
voluntary 4–6

Water,
right to take, when flowing through land 2

Weeds:
liability for 313–14;
see also Tort

Wild animals,
right to catch and kill 2

Wills:
alterations to 115;
attestation of 113;
capacity to make 111–12;
death of executor before estate completely administered 121,
    see also Intestacy;
executors, definition and appointment of 116,
    obtaining probate 116–17;
formalities when making 113;
grant of administration where no proving executor 120–2;
inadvisability for laymen to make 111;
restriction on testator's freedom to dispose of his property by 122–3;
revocation 113–15;
undue influence 112

Woodlands:
  estate duty on 164–5;
  income tax upon 147;
  see also Income tax
Words of limitation:

to create a fee simple 2;
to create an entail 3;
to create a life interest 4

Zero-rating, *see* Value added tax